THE RUSSIAN ARMY UNDER NICHOLAS I

CENTRAL HISTORICAL MUSEUM, MOSCOW

Recruit Training

THE RUSSIAN ARMY UNDER NICHOLAS I, 1825-1855

John Shelton Curtiss

DUKE UNIVERSITY PRESS   DURHAM, N. C.   1965

© 1965, Duke University Press
Library of Congress Catalogue Card number 65-24927
Printed in the United States of America
by the Seeman Printery, Inc., Durham, N. C.

PREFACE

Because the Russian army, along with the Third Section (the political police) and the Russian Orthodox church, was a pillar of the regime of Nicholas I, it has seemed fitting to make an investigation to discover what sort of army it was on which the might of the Tsar depended. Was its power as awesome as many, perhaps even *most* Europeans of 1850 believed, or was it the giant with feet of clay that Western public opinion—especially its liberal and radical wing—believed after the Crimean War? An inquiry into this problem should also serve to clarify more fully the long reign of the Emperor Nicholas, as well as to add to Western knowledge of this period of Russian military history, on which there is little monographic material.

As yet Soviet scholars have published no study of the Russian army for this entire period, although they have studied the Decembrist movement intensively and have written at length on the Crimean War. They have also written about individual campaigns of the second quarter of the nineteenth century and have discussed certain aspects of the army, but so far no full-length study of the Russian army under Nicholas I has yet appeared.

While it would be possible to deal with the problem under consideration in a purely descriptive fashion, taking up each of several different aspects of the army in turn, or else in a narrative account of the military events of the reign, a simple treatment combining both methods appeared to be the most suitable one. Of necessity this created difficulties of co-ordinating the topical approach to the army with analyses of the various campaigns. Nevertheless, this method permits the presentation of a more complete and rounded view of the army than does any other.

Although this study deals with the period of Nicholas I, it does not end precisely with his death in February, 1855, in the midst of the Crimean War, but continues until the end of active hostilities in late autumn of that year. The justification for this is the fact that, even though Alexander II was then on the throne, it was still the army of

Nicholas that held out in Sevastopol until late August, when it evacuated the city. Similarly, it was the forces trained under Nicholas I that, failing in the assault on Kars, continued the siege and forced its surrender in November.

The primary sources for this book consist entirely of printed material, of which there is a great abundance, in the form of diaries, letters, legislation, and official reports, as well as contemporary books and periodicals. The works of foreign observers who were well informed about the Russian army of Nicholas I and its activities have also supplied much interesting and significant evidence. Because, however, until quite recently it was difficult to gain access to Soviet archives, it has not been possible to use the wealth of manuscript material in the U.S.S.R.

Fortunately, the nineteenth-century historical periodicals *Russkaia Starina* (*Russian Antiquity*) and *Russkii Arkhiv* (*Russian Archive*) published many important historical documents, and *Stoletie Voennago Ministerstva* (*Centennial of the Ministry of War*) contains a good deal of documentary material. The *Svod Voennykh Postanovlenii* (*Code of Military Rulings*) of 1838 supplies the complete basic military legislation and much additional information about the army.

There is a large supply of secondary material available, including memoirs of military men which, especially when written well after the events that they witnessed, must be handled with caution. Some regimental histories, based on careful study of the archives and interpreted objectively, proved helpful. Others had little value. Some histories of individual campaigns are scholarly and based on good documentation. Biographies of famous soldiers of the Nicholaian era did not, however, supply much reliable information, almost all of them lacking objectivity. Military periodicals of these times were disappointing, as they contained little but routine announcements and technical articles, usually from foreign countries. On the other hand, *Voennyi Sbornik* (*Military Magazine*), which began publication in 1858, with N. G. Chernyshevskii as editor, in its first years contained much sober and penetrating criticism of the failings of the army in the preceding reign. Thus, in spite of the absence of full archival documentation, the richness of the available material made it possible to produce a study that supplies much that is new to many Western scholars and, it is hoped, presents an essentially correct picture.

All dates in the text are in the Old Style (according to the Julian calendar, which in the nineteenth century was twelve days behind the Gregorian calendar). The transliteration system is that of the Library of Congress, without the diacritical marks and ligatures.

Thanks to the generous aid of a fellowship from the John Simon Guggenheim Memorial Foundation, it proved possible to complete the major part of the research for this project during a sabbatical year in 1954-55—most of it spent in London and Helsinki. Further study continued at a less intensive pace for several more years. The Research Council of Duke University also assisted the undertaking by providing funds for obtaining microfilms of additional material and for shorter periods of research and, through a substantial grant, has made it possible to meet the cost of publishing this study.

To the staffs of the Columbia University Library, the Library of Congress, the New York Public Library, and the Library of the University of Hawaii, as well as those of the British Museum and of the Slavic Library of the University of Helsinki, my thanks are tendered for their unfailing courtesy and helpfulness, typical of the profession of librarians, without whom few scholarly books could be written. Especial thanks go to Simeon Bolan, who supplied most helpful bibliographical assistance, and to Michael I. Pavlov, for his careful check of the citations and bibliography. And to my valued colleague Theodore Ropp, my sincere appreciation of his penetrating criticism and suggestions regarding the first part of the manuscript. Only the author, however, bears responsibility for the judgments and conclusions presented in the following pages.

JOHN SHELTON CURTISS

Duke University

CONTENTS

MAPS

THE RUSSIAN ARMY UNDER NICHOLAS I

CHAPTER I. INTRODUCTION. THE BEGINNING OF THE REIGN

In the centuries before Nicholas I, Russians had fought in numerous wars—against Byzantines, Turkish nomads, Mongol hordes, Swedes, Germans, Lithuanians, Poles, and many another. While they had occasionally enjoyed the flavor of victory, they also had known the sour taste of defeat. For two centuries the Mongols dominated Russia, and it was only by extreme exertion and through favorable circumstances that Russia had gained independence. For centuries after the Mongols, Russians had to contend with hostile Tatar principalities that raided and burned Russian lands and cities—on one occasion, Moscow itself. Later, Polish forces occupied the Kremlin and tried to bring Russia under Polish sway. Gradually, however, as enemies decayed and Russia grew stronger, Russian military power waxed, until, early in the eighteenth century, a burst of offensive might surprised the world as the armies of Peter the Great dominated northeastern Europe. With Peter, Russia became one of the leading military states.

Over the centuries the Russian armies had changed in nature and become more effective. For long they were composed of the nobles and their retainers, with little or no central organization, so that the armies had to be formed anew for every campaign. In the sixteenth century the appearance of the service nobility, dependent on the tsar and loyal to him, strengthened the monarch's hand, and permanent forces of artillery and *Strel'tsy* (musketeers) formed a rudimentary standing army. Under Tsars Michael and Alexis, bodies of mercenary troops were added and regiments of Russian soldiers under foreign officers made their appearance, although they often proved to be of dubious value. Such were the Russian troops that took the field in imposing numbers in 1700, only to flee from Charles XII's Swedes at Narva. Fortunately for Peter, he could profit from this lesson by building up a new and modern army.

Peter was the founder of the Russian army. In place of the rebellious *Strel'tsy* he put the Preobrazhenskii and Semenovskii regiments—formerly his "play regiments," now raised to the status of Guards. He also formed a number of line regiments, filling them with volunteers and above all with peasant conscripts, while he used young nobles, who had received basic training as privates, to command them. A supply system was created, modern weapons were provided, and, once these forces had gained experience and confidence, Russia had a formidable army. Poltava in 1709 saw the end of Swedish power, although Russian forces had to fight for many years in Poland, Germany, Finland, and even on the Swedish coasts before Sweden admitted defeat. Although Peter himself was humbled by the Turks in 1711, Russia had become the dominant power in eastern Europe. Even a series of incompetent rulers after Peter did not destroy the power that he had created, for Sweden and Poland were far too weak to challenge Russia, and the Turks declined rapidly. Thus Russia in the eighteenth century was a force to be reckoned with. In the Seven Years' War, Russia, allied with Austria and France, almost administered the coup de grâce to Frederick the Great, who escaped ruin only because Russian rule fell from the hands of his enemy Elizabeth into those of the pro-Prussian Peter III.

Under Catherine II, who speedily deposed and murdered Peter III, the Russian armies won new laurels. Her brilliant commanders, P. A. Rumiantsev and A. S. Suvorov, easily defeated huge Turkish forces, and Suvorov crushed Polish insurgents. Like their Western contemporaries, these leaders had evolved a method of attack in columns, preceded by skirmishers, and Suvorov developed a system of operations that influenced Russian military thinking for over a century. He stressed concern for the well-being of the soldiers and even appealed to their intelligence by explaining what would be wanted of them in battle, as he felt that the morale of the troops was highly important. Strict discipline, rapid maneuvers, and quick and decisive attack were his cardinal principles. Although he did not deny the value of effective musketry and artillery fire, he trained his troops to charge rapidly with the bayonet without stopping to fire and to pursue a defeated enemy relentlessly. He embodied these rules in a set of maxims couched in the language of the soldiers, such as: "The bullet is a fool, the bayonet is a hero" and "The head does not wait for the tail." Under the conditions of eighteenth-century warfare these methods proved very effective, against Poles, Turks, and in 1799 against French forces in Italy. In his Italian campaign, in spite of the often incomplete co-operation of the Austrian forces under his command, he won a series of victories over MacDonald, Joubert, and Moreau and drove the French from Italy. An unsuccessful campaign in Switzerland, required of him against his will, ended his career.

The Suvorov period soon ended, although his disciples, like M. I. Kutuzov and P. I. Bagration, continued his tradition. Already the worst aspects of the eighteenth-century military system were reviving in the Russian army, thanks to the reactionary nature of Paul I and his henchman, the brutal A. A. Arakcheev. Paul's efforts stressed harsh discipline and pedantic parade-ground training, to the detriment of the effective methods of Suvorov.

Paul's outrageous conduct led to his death at the hands of assassins and the enthronement of Alexander I. The latter ruler at first eliminated the worst features of Paul's military regime, so that the Russian armies that fought at Austerlitz, Eylau, and Friedland gave an excellent account of themselves and proved stubborn opponents. Unfortunately, Russian leadership proved faulty and the traditional steadfastness of the Russian soldier could not prevent defeat. After Friedland, Alexander had to sign the Treaty of Tilsit in 1807.

During the campaigns of 1805-07 the all too prevalent failings of Russian armies—inefficiency and corruption—had severely hampered the Russian forces. During the few years of peace with France much was done to improve the tactics and eliminate some of the grafting, and Arakcheev, an able artillery officer, reorganized the artillery with great benefit. This evil man was personally honest and devoted to the Tsar, who learned to value his services. It was not until several years later, however, that he reached the height of his career.

Russia had no peace after Tilsit. In 1808-09 the Russian armies easily defeated the Swedes in Finland and annexed that duchy, while Kutuzov was fighting an indecisive war with the Turks that ended only in 1812. These conflicts, however, were soon overshadowed by the approaching major conflict with France.

In order to compel Russian submission, in 1812 Napoleon massed an army of some five hundred thousand men drawn from much of Europe, but with a nucleus of veteran French troops. The numerically inferior Russian troops had no choice but to evade complete destruction by retreating. When Barclay de Tolly, Scottish commander of the main Russian forces, surrendered the barrier position of Smolensk after only limited resistance, Russian opinion, already angered by the endless retreats, forced Alexander to name Kutuzov in place of Barclay. The old veteran, whom Alexander heartily disliked, continued to retreat until he reached a defensive position at Borodino on August 23, 1812. Here on the following day occurred a battle of rare ferocity.

At Borodino the Russians, well entrenched, were fighting to save Moscow and Russia. The French sought to end the war by a single decisive blow. In this combat between almost equal armies the entrenchments repeatedly changed hands, and although the Russians had to retire to their third line, Napoleon did not dare throw in his Guards for a last blow. Each side lost almost half of its men. Kutuzov had planned a counterattack, but the expected reserves had not arrived, so he again retired, passing through Moscow to a safe position beyond it.

The French thus could occupy Moscow, but it proved an empty triumph. The Russians would not consider peace, although Napoleon sent three envoys to urge Alexander to negotiate. Finally, the French position proved untenable and on October 7 the French began their retreat, with the weather still favorable. Kutuzov's army marched parallel to the French, somewhat south of the route of the latter. His plan was to force the French out of Russia without risking a general engagement, as his forces were still small and weak. Thus the French were able to retreat, terribly harassed by Cossack parties and bands of infuriated peasants, who wiped out thousands of demoralized invaders, already suffering from the cold. At the Berezina River, not far from Minsk, Russian troops coming up from the north and the south attempted to cut off the remnants of the French, but failed to do so. The survivors, deprived of cavalry and artillery by the death of most of their horses, continued to flee, but of the original Grande Armée only some thirty thousand reached safety in East Prussia and Poland.

Kutuzov had accomplished his chief purpose of freeing Russia from the invaders, but there remained the task of driving Napoleon from his throne. While Kutuzov was somewhat more cautious in this respect than Alexander, he advocated invasion of East Prussia and the Grand Duchy of Warsaw and was in command of the Russian armies that advanced to Dresden, Breslau, and Berlin in February and March, 1813. By this time he was so ill that he could not even ride in a carriage and his death followed in April.[1]

Under Field Marshal L. A. P. Wittgenstein, the Russian and Prussian armies suffered defeats at the hands of Napoleon at Lützen and Bautzen, in Saxony, but in the summer, reserves came up and Austria finally decided to enter the war against Napoleon. In October, 1813, the allied armies massed for the decisive battle at Leipzig, in which Napoleon lost almost half of his army and had to retire across the Rhine.

In January, 1814, the Russian armies, along with those of Prussia and Austria, invaded France, while the British pushed up from the Pyrenees. Alexander, who went with his troops, entered Paris on March 19, along with the King of Prussia. Like the British, the Russians had been the most determined foes of Napoleon. During the Waterloo campaign, however, Russian forces did not see action, although they were ready to march when Napoleon suffered final defeat. Russian troops formed part of the armies of occupation in France after 1815.

With the war ended, Alexander turned to other problems. While he was greatly interested in matters of foreign policy, he also had to reorganize his army on a peace footing. Here he came more and more under the influence of Arakcheev and others who clung to the worst aspects of the old school. Harsh, pedantic discipline was stressed to tighten up the relatively easy control over the troops, who had become accustomed to relaxed formalities during the war years. Finally, in 1820 it was the turn of the crack Semenovskii regiment, of which Alexander himself was honorary commander, to receive proper orientation. Under Col. Schwartz, personal choice of Alexander's younger brother, the Grand Duke Michael, the life of this regiment became almost unbearable, with endless routine drill—often ending in flogging for many of the soldiers—personal abuse, and abolition of customary privileges reducing the men to despair. Finally, when Schwartz ordered the flogging of decorated soldiers, by regulation

1. S. B. Okun', *Ocherki Istorii SSSR* (Leningrad, 1956), pp. 249-58. The author rejects the widely held belief that Kutuzov opposed pursuing Napoleon's armies beyond the Russian borders and cites a proposal of the prudent commander drafted on December 2, 1812, to push on to the Vistula, although he felt that the Russian forces required rest and reinforcement before making large-scale advances. In a letter to a friend written on March 28, 1813, he approved of the advance to the Elbe, but stated that it would be risky to send anything but light forces across this river until more reserves were available.

exempt from corporal punishment, the first or "Tsar's" company petitioned the commander not to carry out the sentence. He treated this as mutiny and had the first company imprisoned in the fortress. The other companies then declared their solidarity with the first and protested repeatedly to various generals. As a result, merciless flogging of numbers of the enlisted men occurred, and the personnel of the regiment, both officers and men, was sent in disgrace to other regiments of the army. It should be said that this was not the only sign of disaffection in the army that appeared in these years. According to a Soviet dissertation on unrest among the soldiers after 1816, there were fifteen incidents in the postwar decade, most of them protests against cruel commanders or graft by officers at the soldiers' expense. Thirteen of these protests, often in noted regiments, occurred between 1820 and 1825.[2]

Another feature of the period, which also led to disturbances, was the introduction of military colonies. Probably as a result of the success of somewhat similar institutions in Austria and Sweden, Alexander established one such unit in 1810, hoping that it would ease the financial burden on the country. After the Napoleonic Wars the system spread rapidly, with Arakcheev in charge of organizing a cluster of military colonies in the province of Novgorod and another in the southern Ukraine. Here the government removed the private serfs and replaced them with state peasants, who, organized into battalions, received the name of "farmer-colonists." Each of these unfortunates had the obligation to farm his allotment of land and to feed therefrom not only his family but also two "soldier-lodgers." For each battalion of farmer-colonists there were two battalions of soldier-lodgers, who were available for active duty and also did work constructing buildings and clearing or draining land.

Alexander I hoped for great benefits from the military colonies. Through the trusted Arakcheev, the Tsar poured much money into them for the construction of well-designed houses, headquarters, and other structures, all provided with good roads and sidewalks planted with trees. The farming activities of the peasants were raised to a high level. Thus the military colonies became show places that the Tsar loved to show to visitors.[3] The peasants who became military colonists, however, hated them.

2. Cited in *ibid.*, pp. 322-23.
3. P. P. Kartsov, *Iz proshlago. Lichnyia i sluzhebnyia vospominaniia* (St. Petersburg, 1888), p. 7.

Although the colonists received better housing than most peasants and good equipment and livestock, they found their lot unbearable and from the beginning petitioned the authorities to return them to their previous status. Their grievances were many. Their chief complaint was that their lives ran to drumbeats, from waking hours, to their mornings spent at drill, and including their afternoons spent on their farming. It was compulsory to wear uniforms at all times. Even their six-year-old sons had to drill, and at twelve they were taken from their parents and under the name of "cantonists" sent to special military schools. At seventeen they began regular military service.[4]

These facts, plus the severe discipline and at times the peculations of the officers, from which enlisted men suffered, produced a number of disturbances in the military colonies, which included approximately one-third of the army. In 1819 an especially large protest by two cavalry regiments in the Ukraine drew Arakcheev to the scene, where he used other troops to arrest over two thousand men. There were numerous floggings, with forty receiving the most severe punishment. Arakcheev offered to pardon those who would repent and ask mercy, but as he wrote to the Tsar:

> The ferocity of the criminals reached such a degree that out of forty men only three, who repented of their crimes, asked mercy—they were pardoned on the spot, and the other thirty-seven were punished. But this punishment did not have effect upon the other prisoners, who were present at it, although it was strict and exemplary. At the end of the punishment all the prisoners who had been punished were asked if they repented of their crime and would cease their violence. But they unanimously rejected this.

He added that "after the punishment proper to their ranks, several of the criminals died."[5] In spite of the ominous nature of this episode, Alexander and his military advisers regarded it as a minor matter and continued to increase the size of the military colonies. Perhaps the trouble in the Semenovskii and other regiments led them to believe that the army units were even less reliable than the military colonies.

In one additional respect the army was unreliable. While the above disturbances had involved only enlisted men, many Guards and army officers had already joined secret societies dedicated to changing Russian institutions. Many of these young men who had served abroad, often with distinction, probably had observed the reforms in the

4. Okun', pp. 295-97.
5. *Ibid.*, p. 318.

Prussian army introduced by Scharnhorst and Gneisenau. To these returned heroes the realities of Russian life, especially when contrasted with the freer societies that they had observed elsewhere, were shocking. The miserable lot of the peasants, the callousness of the ruling groups, and the sufferings of the soldiers, conquerors of the French, at the hands of men of the Arakcheev school, aroused the indignation of the young idealists, nobles though they were. At first they hoped that Alexander would introduce needed reforms, but these hopes soon waned, especially after his handling of the protest of the Semenovskii regiment. The transfer of many of the officers of this unit to assignments in the Second Army in the Ukraine, far from ending their efforts for fundamental reforms, enabled them to find kindred spirits in this area. In addition, the movement survived in St. Petersburg, among the officers of other Guards regiments, along with some civilians: the poet K. F. Ryleev was one of the foremost figures in the northern grouping.

Thus the secret protest movement, far from collapsing, grew into a widespread conspiracy with two centers: the Northern Society, in St. Petersburg, led by Prince S. P. Trubetskoi, Nikita M. Muraviev, E. P. Obolenskii, and Ryleev; and the Southern Society, in the Second Army, with P. I. Pestel and Sergei Muraviev-Apostol as chief figures. With the exception of Ryleev, all the leaders were military men. There were differences betwen the two groups, for Trubetskoi and Muraviev desired a constitutional monarchy, while Pestel favored a democracy after a temporary dictatorship. But both groups wanted to end serfdom, to reform the military system, to abolish the military colonies, and to institute representative government. The conspirators, realizing that Alexander would never accept these proposals, planned to assassinate him in the summer of 1826, when he should come to the Second Army for the annual maneuvers.[6] The Tsar, however, foiled the conspirators by dying of cholera in Taganrog on the Sea of Azov, on November 19, 1825.

This sudden development, which caught the revolutionaries by surprise, also caused great confusion in government circles. As Alexander had no children, his oldest brother Constantine was next in line for the succession. The latter, however, enjoyed living in Warsaw as viceroy of the kingdom of Poland, had a Polish wife, and had no desire to be tsar. In fact, in 1823 Alexander had signed a manifesto

6. *Ibid.*, pp. 346-69.

naming his second brother Nicholas as his successor, and Constantine had written a letter renouncing his right to the throne. As this had been done in secrecy, even Nicholas did not know of it, and so on November 27, 1825 he had officials and army take the oath of allegiance to Constantine and urged him to come to the capital. Constantine, however, refused to rule and would not leave Warsaw, but told Nicholas to take the throne. The latter continued to urge his brother to come to St. Petersburg to make public renunciation of the crown. Both men proved stubborn. Thus, while the messengers galloped back and forth between Warsaw and St. Petersburg, there was confusion in official circles. During this period of more than two weeks the Northern Society decided to act.

While the conspirators had no fondness for Constantine, who was harsh and autocratic and had a violent temper, they disliked Nicholas even more. After the Napoleonic Wars he had commanded a division of the Guards, only to incur the hostility of a number of the officers, as M. A. Fonvizin of the Northern Society stated, "because of his cruel treatment of officers and soldiers, for constant petty nagging in service." Prince S. P. Trubetskoi gave similar testimony. Col. Alexander Bulatov stated that Nicholas had the reputation of being malicious, vengeful, and stingy and that his subordinates were displeased with his fondness for frequent drills and his unpleasantness in service relations.[7] The leaders of the Northern Society were sure that if Nicholas should become tsar, they could hope for none of the reforms that they felt were essential for Russia. For two weeks they had been considering what course to pursue. Now, on the afternoon of December 13 they learned that Nicholas had finally decided to order a new oath of allegiance to himself.[8]

Although the conspirators did not know that he had received information about their plans, they realized that for them it was now or never. If they failed to eliminate Nicholas and did not push through their program of reforms, he would consolidate his position as tsar, and then their lives would be in danger, while all hope of a better day for Russia would be lost.

This was no petty cabal that was about to raise its hand against the Grand Duke Nicholas, but an impressive movement that included much of the flower of the Guards and the army. The official roster

7. V. I. Semevskii, *Politicheskie i obshchestvennye idei Dekabristov* (St. Petersburg, 1909), p. 82.
8. M. V. Nechkina, *Vosstanie 14-go Dekabria 1825 g.* (Moscow, 1951), pp. 44-45.

of those implicated that was drawn up by the special Investigating Commission after the uprising included 570 names, to which nine more from the Southern Society should be added. In the list were sixteen major generals, and one adjutant general of the Tsar's suite. There were 115 colonels and majors and 315 company officers. Many were commanders of regiments or battalions. Thus forty of the 256 regiments of the Russian army were under the influence of the conspirators, while there probably were sympathizers with the movement in many other units. Most of the plotters were thirty years of age or less, while only 2.9 per cent were forty or older.[9]

The plans of the conspirators were carefully worked out at a long meeting on the night of December 13. Many of the officers promised to lead their regiments to the Senate Square and to the Winter Palace, while two desperate men swore that they would assassinate Nicholas and capture the Palace. The conspirators, who ever since have been known as Decembrists, elected Prince Trubetskoi as their dictator, to command the insurgent troops. The program was to compel the Senate to read a manifesto to the people announcing the end of serfdom, the reduction of the term of military service to ten years, and the granting of civil liberties. They also planned to force the Senate to issue a call for a Constituent Assembly to meet and decide on the future government of Russia, and to name a temporary government of elder statesmen. Until the new government provided by the Constituent Assembly could meet, the insurgents would keep the imperial family under arrest. If, however, the plans should miscarry, the troops should fight their way to the military colonies near Novgorod, south of St. Petersburg, where they expected to find strong support. Most of the Decembrists, however, were confident of success.[10]

In these plans only the soldiers would play a role, with the troops firmly under the control of their officers. Even Ryleev, one of the leading figures of the movement, was to play no part in the action. Above all, the Decembrists strongly opposed any participation by the masses of working people of the capital, who, they hoped, would look on with passive approval. In this way the insurgent officers hoped to avoid the bloodshed that they expected from a popular uprising. They did not want a French Revolution. "Our revolution," said Michael Bestuzhev-

9. E. A. Prokof'ev, *Voennye vzgliady Dekabristov* (Moscow, 1953), pp. 35-37. The data on the ages of the conspirators are based on an incomplete sample of 254 persons.
10. Nechkina, p. 47.

Riumin, "will be like the Spanish revolution [of 1820] . . . . It will not cost a single drop of blood, for it will be made by the army alone, without the participation of the people."[11]

Early on the fateful morning of December 14 these confident hopes of the revolutionaries began to suffer mortal blows. Nicholas, warned by a renegade conspirator, took measures to have the Senate take the oath early in the morning, before the rebels could act. Even worse, the Decembrists found it very difficult to bring their regiments out in defiance of the government. Although many of the enlisted men were ready and even eager to march, most of the regimental commanders were able to confine their men to barracks. Only eight hundred men of the Moscow Guards regiment, led by three officers, marched forth, arriving at the Senate Square at about eleven o'clock. Although they did not have their overcoats, they had muskets and cartridges and formed a hollow square, with a line of pickets in front. Here they were to stand all day in the cold, repulsing cavalry attacks and emissaries who sought to overcome their resistance.[12]

The inability of other units to join the Moscow regiment was the first failure of the carefully laid plan. There were others. Prince Trubetskoi, the veteran soldier who had been elected dictator, could not bring himself to face the horrors of civil war and went into hiding, without telling his fellow-Decembrists of his intention. Likewise the two men pledged to kill Tsar Nicholas lacked the will to carry out their parts, although they had abundant opportunity. One of them did not desert his comrades, however, but joined the Moscow regiment in the Senate Square. At this point several essential parts of the plan had already broken down.[13]

But in official circles there was no feeling of easy optimism. While the Winter Palace was now guarded by numerous regiments, many of the troops showed reluctance to act and the Tsar could not be sure of their loyalty. Moreover, when Count M. A. Miloradovich, the popular governor general of St. Petersburg, attempted to persuade the Moscow regiment to obey his orders, the soldiers fired on him and one of the insurgent officers shot him down. The efforts of Metropolitan Serafim of St. Petersburg to admonish the rebels ended in his discomfiture.[14] Furthermore, when the Horse Guards, by Nicholas'

11. Okun', p. 371; Nechkina, pp. 47-48.
12. Nechkina, pp. 71-80.
13. *Ibid.*, pp. 85-98.
14. *Ibid.*, pp. 80-86 and 118-22.

orders, made a series of charges against the hollow square before the Senate building they were met with shots, and the troopers, who had shown signs of sympathy with their fellow-soldiers, apparently did not try to push home their attacks. Later the government, perhaps to minimize the extent of the disaffection, stated that the charges had failed because the horses had slipped on the icy pavement—although by mid-December they must have been shod for the winter.[15]

In addition, the attitude of the enormous crowd that watched the events caused grave concern to the Tsar and his supporters. Although the Decembrists made no appeals to them, the servants, artisans, peasants, and others of low degree who formed the bulk of the spectators clearly were ardent supporters of the rebels and would have rushed to the attack if the latter had urged them. As it was, they over-powered the police and almost pulled Gen. Voinov, commander of the Guards Corps, from his horse when he tried to calm the rebel troops. They stoned other government officers and threw chunks of firewood at the Horse Guards, and even roughed up Metropolitan Serafim and his attendant clergy and tore their vestments. The in-surgents, however, discouraged these popular manifestations and tried to drive the crowd away.[16]

Thus to the new Tsar the situation seemed very grave. In his memoirs he repeatedly expressed his dismay,[17] even though the troops under his orders vastly outnumbered the eight hundred men of the Moscow regiment. And then, about three o'clock in the afternoon, his position became even worse. Reinforcements came to the Decembrists. The first to arrive was a company of the Grenadier Guards, followed by almost the whole Guards Naval Crew. As they took up positions alongside the rejoicing Moscow regiment, another, larger column of Grenadier Guards marched up. These fresh troops, who with difficulty had broken out of their barracks in spite of the restraining efforts of their commanders, raised the number of the insurgents to over three thousand. Although they were still heavily outnumbered by the gov-ernmental forces, their morale was high and they continued to beat off cavalry attacks.[18] On the other hand, although Prince E. P. Obolenskii assumed command over the whole force, they did not attempt to attack with the help of the ever increasing crowd, but continued to

15. *Ibid.*, pp. 114-17.
16. *Ibid.*, pp. 98-110.
17. *Ibid.*, pp. 117-18.
18. *Ibid.*, pp. 156-58.

stand in the Senate Square. Although they kept shouting for "Constantine," most of the men must have realized that they really were attempting a revolution. But they failed to seize the initiative.[19]

The Tsar, however, could not longer delay. By four o'clock the long winter night had already begun, bringing with it the very real danger that under cover of darkness the governmental troops would go over to the Decembrists. Moreover, the vast crowd might attack, with fatal consequences. Nicholas, who had sent for artillery, decided to open fire on the rebels. But after the guns had been put into position they did not have the necessary grapeshot, which no one had ordered them to bring.[20] One of the Tsar's generals had to gallop to the Artillery Laboratory to procure the proper ammunition. Here the officer on duty, perhaps sympathizing with the insurgents, at first refused to surrender it without a written order, and a threat of force was necessary to obtain it. After the authorities had surmounted these obstacles and the cannon, with their deadly charges, menaced the Decembrists, the latter received a last chance to surrender. When they refused, Nicholas himself gave the order to fire. But the gunner at the first piece refused to fire it, saying to his officer: "But they are *our* men, your honor." The officer seized the linstock from him and touched off the gun.[21]

In all, at least seven rounds of grapeshot tore through the ranks of the insurgents, killing and wounding hundreds. The survivors, after firing back, dispersed, many seeking refuge in nearby buildings. A considerable number reached the ice in the river Neva, where some of the officers attempted to reorganize them for a march on the nearby fortress of Peter and Paul. But as they formed the column, round shot fell among them and the ice broke, threatening to drown them all. Most reached shore, only to fall prisoners to the Tsar's cavalry.[22] A vast manhunt now began, with the authorities seeking to capture, question, and punish all who had been actively involved in the uprising.

While this drama was taking place in the capital, the members of the Southern Society knew little or nothing of what was going on. The government had already learned from informers many of the details of the conspiracy and it arranged for Field Marshal Wittgenstein to arrest Pestel and other known plotters.[23] Some of the others,

19. *Ibid.*, pp. 158-60.
20. *Ibid.*, p. 162.
21. *Ibid.*, pp. 167-68.
22. *Ibid.*, pp. 168-70.

however, with the aid of enlisted men of the Chernigov regiment, on December 29 freed Sergei Muraviev-Apostol from arrest and marched forth under him and M. P. Bestuzhev-Riumin. Several other companies of this regiment, headed by sergeants, joined Muraviev. They had high hopes that other regiments would also rise, and indeed several commanders greatly feared that this would happen.[24] The expected reinforcements never came to the Chernigov regiment, however, and on January 3, 1826, as Muraviev, with no definite objective, led it on, a force of cavalry and horse artillery loyal to the government overtook it. Cannon fire shattered the ranks of the insurgents, after which the cavalry easily captured the rest.[25]

Thus neither the Northern nor the Southern Society achieved a revolutionary overturn. Their outbreaks, however, made a great impression on Nicholas, who investigated the conspiracy with minute thoroughness and personally interrogated many of the prisoners. In all, 579 of the Decembrists were imprisoned and interrogated. Of these, many were released after brief periods of imprisonment, while 131 were given formal trial by the special military court set up by the Tsar.

As the Decembrists were almost all officers and nobles and had no enlisted men as members, the Tsar took pains to declare that the latter were innocent victims of the plotters. In his manifesto of December 19, 1825, he announced:

> Neither by word nor by intention did the erring companies of enlisted men, who were drawn into this abyss, participate in these evil deeds. Having assured myself of this by most strict investigation, I regard it as the first act of justice and my first consolation to declare them innocent.
>
> But the same justice forbids the sparing of the offenders. They, implicated by the investigation and the trial, will receive justified punishment, each according to his acts.[26]

Nicholas did not adhere firmly to this policy, for some of the soldiers were punished severely. The men who voluntarily returned to their barracks after the fray, however, got off lightly. By order of

23. Okun', pp. 402-3.
24. Sergei Hessen, "Soldaty i Matrosy v Vosstanii Dekabristov," *Katorga i Ssylka*, 1930, No. 3, pp. 86-97.
25. Okun', pp. 411-12.
26. Russia, Voennoe Ministerstvo, *Stoletie Voennago Ministerstva* (56 vols.; St. Petersburg, 1902-1908), II, Pt. III, *Imperatorskaia Glavnaia Kvartira. Istoriia Gosudarevoi Svity. Tsarstvovanie Imperatora Nikolaia I-go*, p. 191. Hereafter cited as SVM.

the Tsar of February 17, 1826, some 1,333 enlisted men of the Moscow and Grenadier regiments were assigned to a composite Guards infantry regiment to "expiate their guilt" by service in the army of the Caucasus. Later they were joined by additional participants in the uprising. This regiment retained the privileges of the Guards. It served valiantly in the Turkish War of 1828-29, being in combat in the chief battles and losing 320 men from wounds and disease. After the war it returned to St. Petersburg, where the Moscow and Grenadier battalions rejoined their regiments.[27]

On the other hand, the men who had played a more active part in the uprisings were imprisoned in fortresses, under very severe conditions, until the end of the investigations, when the government sent them to garrison or army duty, chiefly in the Caucasus. Often they found themselves in posts where mortality from fever and other disease was extremely high. About one hundred of the ringleaders—chiefly sergeants and first sergeants (*fel'dvebely*)—were reduced to the ranks and then had to run the gantlet, receiving from one thousand to twelve thousand blows each. Two artillerymen received three thousand, while two sergeants and a private ran the gantlet of one thousand men twelve times, and then went to penal labor for life. Offenders of secondary importance had to serve in the Caucasus, usually after receiving less severe flogging.[28]

In the area of the Southern Society, where there had been more overt activity by enlisted men, the punishments were more severe, although soldiers who had allegedly taken part only out of stupidity received light floggings before going to the Caucasus. Fortunately for the southern insurgents, Maj. Gen. Vrede asked the soldiers who inflicted the punishment to treat the culprits lightly, which they were doubtless glad to do.[29]

Many of the soldiers who had not taken part in the uprisings showed marked sympathy for the convicted men. The Cavalier Guards, who were on duty during the infliction of punishment, were very considerate of them. Some of the men whose regiments had failed to join the Decembrists on the fatal day apologized to the prisoners for not supporting them, saying that they would have done so if the insurgents had acted more energetically. A number of soldiers showed

27. G. S. Gabaev, "Gvardiia v Dekabr'skie dni 1825 goda," in A. E. Presniakov, *14 Dekabria 1825 goda* (Moscow, 1926), pp. 196-97.
28. *Ibid.*; see also Hessen, pp. 102-7.
29. Hessen, pp. 105-6.

hostility toward the Horse Guards because they had charged the rebels on December 14. Others, who had served under Pestel or in the Chernigov regiment, voiced regret at the fate of their former leaders.[30] These incidents suggest that many of the enlisted men fully realized that the Decembrists had risked their lives to improve the lot of the soldiers and to bring a better life to the people of Russia.

While the actions of the Emperor show that he felt concern over the attitude of the rank and file, his main interest centered on the officers and civilians who had joined the secret societies. He went to great lengths to discover why they had conspired, conferring personally with the leading figures and reading their writings. Although he abhorred their actions, he recognized that these men were the flower of his officers and were highly intelligent and patriotic. Perhaps this fact helps to explain why he failed to wreak wholesale vengeance, but contented himself with hanging five: Pestel, Bestuzhev-Riumin, Sergei Muraviev-Apostol, P. G. Kakhovskii, who had killed Gen. Miloradovich, and Ryleev, the fiery poet. Also it may be that Nicholas remembered that an uprising of the Guards had brought his grandmother, Catherine the Great, to the throne. Another conspiracy of Guards officers, in which Nicholas' revered brother Alexander had been involved, had gone unpunished, although it had resulted in the murder of Paul I, father of Alexander and Nicholas. Doubtless Nicholas had no desire to start *his* reign with a great blood bath, but wished to minimize publicly the disaffection that had threatened him. At any rate, he refused to approve the penalty of drawing and quartering and reduced the number of executions from the thirty-six recommended by the court-martial to five. Those who thus escaped death received sentences to penal labor for life. Eighty-seven others were sentenced to compulsory residence in Siberia, where they continued to feel the wrath of the Tsar until his death. On the other hand, about half of the members of the two secret societies escaped all punishment.[31]

In some instances Nicholas went out of his way to overlook the activities of some of the Decembrists. Although A. A. Suvorov, grandson of the great general, had been closely connected with the Northern Society, the Tsar, after questioning him briefly, ordered that he be freed—probably because of the great name he bore. Similarly, Capt.

30. *Ibid.*, pp. 110-14.
31. Anatole Mazour, *The First Russian Revolution, 1825. The Decembrist Movement* (Stanford, California, 1937), pp. 212-17, 222-43, *passim.*

N. D. Seniavin, son of a noted Russian admiral, received freedom after three months in prison. The Emperor also freed the sons of Field Marshal Wittgenstein and two other generals, although they also had been involved in the movement.[32]

Several officers indirectly implicated in the insurrection received assignments to the army in the Caucasus during the wars with Persia in 1826-27 and Turkey in 1828 and 1829. In the latter war two commanded regiments, and another served as quartermaster general. Gen. I. F. Paskevich warmly received the Decembrist D. Iskritskii, whom he assigned to his staff. In one of the chief battles the latter commanded an important detachment, which he led with brilliant success.[33]

Other Decembrists, after demotion, served in the Caucasus Corps as privates. A. A. Fok, formerly of the Izmailovskii Guards regiment, though a private, commanded a force of sharpshooters in a crucial battle on August 9, 1828. The Tsar was so pleased with Fok's conduct that he awarded the latter the silver Cross of St. George.[34] Even more striking was the success of M. I. Pushchin, whose skilful service in the Caucasian Sapper battalion won him the favor of Paskevich. At the attack on Erivan in 1826 Pushchin, still a private, was in charge of much of the siege operations. After the capture of this place Paskevich made him a sergeant, and promoted him to ensign for his success during the winter invasion of Persia. In the Turkish War Pushchin, now in high favor, continued his exploits, winning the Cross of St. Anne, 4th degree, and the rank of lieutenant.[35]

This benevolence toward men who had formerly opposed him was not typical of the Tsar's attitude toward the Decembrists, for he regarded those who had taken up arms against him as his personal foes and encouraged his subordinates to treat them severely. In 1829, Gen. N. N. Raevskii, with Paskevich's army on the Turkish front, drew the wrath of a visiting aide of the Minister of War merely by having one of the Decembrists take breakfast with him. As a result, the general was put under arrest for two weeks.[36] Another, more serious incident, occurred in Tiflis in 1830. Several of the Decembrists in this city usually spent several evenings a week in conversation,

32. Prokof'ev, pp. 41-43.
33. A. S. Ganglebov, "Vospominaniia," *Russkii Arkhiv*, XXIV (1886), Pt. II, 253 and 257.
34. *Ibid.*, p. 257.
35. A. E. Rozen, "Dekabristy na Kavkaze," *Russkaia Starina*, XLI (1884), 305-26.
36. Ganglebov, p. 253.

cards, and other harmless amusements. Unfortunately, one of them incurred the ire of Field Marshal Paskevich by some petty misdemeanor, and at once three of the group were sent off under arrest to exile in remote places.[37] Nicholas was especially relentless toward the more important offenders whom he had sent to Siberia. He pardoned few of them, and most lived out their lives in exile, under hostile surveillance.[38]

The Tsar's continued hostility toward the Decembrists is not surprising, for he had been terribly shocked and frightened by their outbreaks, believing that only by a miracle had he escaped overthrow by his once trusted troops. This belief had lasting consequences, for it reinforced Nicholas' predeliction for strict discipline and the endless formal, routine drilling to which he subjected his army. Having been profoundly disturbed by the disloyalty of well-educated, intelligent officers, apparently he felt that unquestioning obedience and an absence of dangerous initiative on the part of subordinates were essential to the security of his realm. These attitudes became the dominant attributes of his army throughout the reign of Nicholas I.

37. *Ibid.*, pp. 259-62.
38. Mazour, *First Russian Revolution*, pp. 231-39.

CHAPTER II. THE PERSIAN AND TURKISH CAMPAIGNS AND THE RISE OF PASKEVICH

The Decembrist uprising was only one of a series of urgent problems that faced Nicholas I when he began his reign. The list included such perennial difficulties as Poland, peasant unrest, and financial stringency, and relations with Turkey were deteriorating rapidly as a result of the Greek rebellion. His program required peace with Persia, and Count K. R. Nesselrode, his foreign minister, earnestly sought to compromise the differences over the border provinces, some of which Persia still held in violation of the treaty between the two countries, while the Russians held a small portion of Persian territory. As the Shah also favored peace, Nicholas and Nesselrode were confident that they could settle all issues, for which purpose they sent Prince A. S. Menshikov to Teheran. They disregarded the repeated warnings of Gen. A. P. Ermolov, viceroy of the Caucasus, that Prince Abbas-Mirza, ambitious heir to the Persian throne, was massing a large army near the Russian border and that many of the Persians interpreted Nesselrode's conciliatory policy as weakness. The Tsar, angry at Ermolov's insistence on a hard Persian policy, listened readily to Nesselrode's condemnation of the Viceroy, which reinforced his already strong suspicions of the latter.[1]

Alexis Petrovich Ermolov, a hero of the Napoleonic Wars, was a very able and magnetic soldier, who had enjoyed the favor of Alexander I, who named him viceroy of the Caucasus in 1817. With very small forces of troops he greatly strengthened the Russian position in this vast area, building and making safe the Georgia Military Highway through the Caucasus and establishing firm control over the Caspian shore. By using his troops as workers, he was able to accomplish a remarkable amount of building in Tiflis and other towns and con-

1. N. Dubrovin, *Istoriia voiny i vladychestva Russkikh na Kavkaze* (6 vols.; St. Petersburg, 1871-1888), VI, 642-46; A. Grishinskii, ed., *Istoriia Russkoi armii i flota* (15 vols.; Moscow, 1911-1913), VI, 61; P. P. Zubov, *Podvigi Russkikh voinov v stranakh Kavkazskikh, s 1800 po 1834* (2 vols.; St. Petersburg, 1835-1836), II, 9-24.

structed many bridges and roads. As a soldier he paid little attention to formal drill, allowed the troops to wear uniforms more comfortable than elegant, and with some success combatted graft in the army and in civil life. In addition to laying the basis for Russian control over the strife-torn Caucasus, he also inspired his troops almost to the point of idolatry through strict discipline in essentials combined with easy informality. In dealing with the mountaineers he was stern and ruthless in punishing enemies, although to friends he was courteous and trustworthy. In many ways his views on military matters were close to those of the Decembrists, although he apparently had no ties with them and, indeed, was too loyal to his oath to approve their revolt.[2] Ermolov enjoyed wide support in the army and in patriotic circles, especially in Moscow, although official St. Petersburg distrusted him. This did not, however, prevent many of Ermolov's enemies in St. Petersburg from raising a great commotion when no word came that the Caucasus Corps had taken the oath of allegiance to Nicholas. The fact that Ermolov had been in a remote area at the time permitted his foes to circulate rumors that he was in revolt and even that he was leading his armies against St. Petersburg. At length, however, a messenger brought word that all in the Caucasus had taken the oath to Nicholas, for which the latter sent warm thanks to Ermolov. Unfortunately, many curious individuals pestered the messenger as to the reasons for the delay: had there been opposition to swearing allegiance to Nicholas? At this the messenger blurted out: "Alexei Petrovich is so worshipped in Georgia that if he ordered them to swear allegiance to the Shah of Persia they would all immediately do so." His foes used this expression of devotion to reawaken Nicholas' distrust.[3]

In 1826 the Persians proved that Ermolov had been correct in his warnings and his appeals for reinforcements, for the Shah gave in to Abbas-Mirza and the fanatical Moslem element. Shutting off Menshikov's communications with Tiflis, the Persians attacked in force on July 16, 1826. Many Russians, including Berzhe, historian of the Caucasus, hold that Britain encouraged the Persians to attack in order to weaken Russian influence on the approaches to India.[4]

2. M. N. Pokhvisnev, "Aleksei Petrovich Ermolov," *Russkaia Starina*, VI (1872), 479-80. Although the author is partial to Ermolov, the evidence in general supports his views.

3. D. V. Davydov, "Zapiski partizana Denisa Davydova. Vospominaniia o Pol'skoi voine 1831 goda," *Russkaia Starina*, VI (1872), 360-61.

4. Ad. P. Berzhe, "Smert' A. S. Griboedova," *Russkaia Starina*, VI (1872), 189-90.

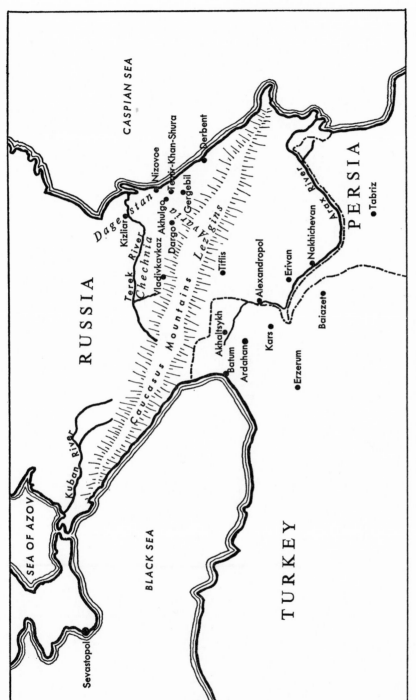

The Caucasus and Transcaucasus area

In addition, much of the Moslem population of the Russian Transcaucasian provinces, aroused by Persian propaganda or hoping for easy loot, joined in the attack.

The tiny Russian forces along the frontier, attacked without warning, were dispersed and unready for combat, and those that could retired before the Persian onslaught. Col. Reut, with a force of about eighteen hundred men, fled under attack to the weak fortress of Shusha, where, with almost no provisions, he held off the enemy. Several Russian detachments were wiped out by the foe, and, except for Georgia, almost all of the Transcaucasus was in enemy hands. Ermolov, with only twelve battalions available for field operations, urged his commanders to retire to Tiflis to hold his capital until the reinforcements which he urgently requested could come.[5]

One fact that facilitated the Persian successes was that most of the local commanders had acquired large estates on which they used their troops as builders and workers, with the result that only a portion of the troops were under arms. In some of the regiments discipline had largely disappeared, so that it was at first impossible to put the troops into fighting trim. Furthermore, in the retreats the officers often were more concerned with evacuating their personal belongings than with saving state property. For a time the situation seemed hopeless.[6]

Fortunately for the Russians, however, the Persian army consisted chiefly of cavalry, much of it irregular troops, and their infantry and artillery were far inferior to the Russians. Moreover, some of the Russian commanders proved to be able men, once they had recovered from their initial dismay. Reut, who had fled in panic at the first attack, held out with great bravery in Shusha, beating off frequent assaults on a very weak position. The slowness of the Persians to attack facilitated his defense, and even when Abbas-Mirza arrived on July 25, with twenty-four cannon and forty thousand infantry, he parleyed with Reut, preferring a negotiated victory to a costly assault. The Russian forces beat off several attempts to storm their position, and finally the Persian agreed on August 17 to an armistice while Reut sent an officer to Tiflis to bring back orders from Ermolov.[7]

5. Dubrovin, *Istoriia*, VI, 617-29.
6. P. O. Bobrovskii, *Istoriia 13-go leib-grenaderskago Erivanskago polka za 250 let* (5 pts.; St. Petersburg, 1892-1898), IV, 70-76.
7. Isidor Grzhegorzhevskii, "General-leitenant Kliuki-fon-Klugenau. Ocherk voennykh sobytii na Kavkaze, 1818-1850 g.," *Russkaia Starina*, XI (1874), 137-49.

Thus Reut held off the Persians for over forty days, during which the Russian forces regrouped and prepared for a counterattack.

Nicholas was furious when he learned of the Persian invasion and the poor performance of the Russian forces, for which he blamed Ermolov, although the latter, in command of a vast and difficult area, probably could not exercise effective supervision over his local commanders. He also felt that the general had fallen victim to panic at the outbreak of the war and greatly exaggerated the danger from the Persians. But before the Tsar could act, the situation changed. By the middle of August, Ermolov's efforts began to produce results. He reorganized and equipped his troops and sent Gen. V. G. Madatov, with perhaps three thousand men and twelve guns, to check the Persian advance guard near Elizabetpol. On September 3, Madatov advanced against a force of ten thousand Persians near Elizabetpol and, thanks to the superiority of his artillery and infantry, routed them with heavy losses and occupied the town. He also captured the Persian camp with great quantities of supplies. This victory had immense consequences, as it shook the morale of the whole Persian army and caused the Moslem population of the area to question the possibility of Persian victory. It also induced Abbas-Mirza to cease his attacks on Shusha and to move his main army to reoccupy Elizabetpol.[8]

In the meantime the Tsar had taken measures regarding the Persian War. The Ministry of War ordered twelve battalions of infantry (Ermolov had requested twenty-four) as well as the six Don Cossack regiments asked. Nicholas himself sent Denis Davydov and Gen. Adj. Paskevich, whom he trusted and admired, to assist Ermolov in the campaign as field commander under the latter's orders. This was clearly a sign of lack of confidence in the redoubtable Viceroy, who, however, accepted the situation without complaint.[9] This inevitably caused friction, for both men had strong, ambitious characters. Paskevich as well as Ermolov was in a difficult situation, as he came to a theater of war that was completely new to him, under difficult strategic conditions. In addition, with rare exceptions all the commanders and the troops were devoted to his rival and did not welcome him. Paskevich, a believer in formal parade-ground training, made matters worse by giving them intensive drill and showed his

8. Dubrovin, *Istoriia*, VI, 662-68; Grzhegorzhevskii, *Russkaia Starina*, XI (1874), 151-52.

9. Dubrovin, *Istoriia*, VI, 646-49; SVM, II, Pt. III, *Tsarstvovanie Imperatora Nikolaia I-go*, 227-28.

low opinion of the hardened veterans. In his first letter to Nicholas he wrote:

> You cannot imagine how badly trained they are. God save me from having to be in action ... with such troops; many of them do not know how to form a square or a column. ... I note that even the commanders themselves regard this as unnecessary. Blind obedience does not please them, they are not used to it; but I shall make them do things my way.[10]

Almost immediately the two leaders clashed. According to Paskevich, when he paid his first call on Ermolov, the latter received him cordially. The next day Ermolov refused to receive anyone, but asked Paskevich to come the following morning. When he arrived, they took him into Ermolov's office—a large room with a long table in the middle.

> On one side of the table sat Gen. Ermolov in his jacket without epaulettes, in a Line Cossack cap. Opposite him were the generals and other persons who usually met with him for talks and discussions. I, the second ranking person, approach. He said: "Ah, how do you do, Ivan Fedorovich,"—and no one gave me his place and there was even no chair for me. Supposing that this was done intentionally, to snub me, I got a chair from a far corner, brought it myself, put it opposite to Ermolov and sat down. I looked at those present: some in jackets, without swords, others without epaulettes and, finally, one young man in a civilian jacket. All those that had just come greeted one another as they did me. "Ah, how do you do, Ivan Kuz'mich, how are you? How do you do, Petr Ivanovich," and so on. All then sit down, and the ensign does not offer his place to a general. Gen. Vel'iaminov, in command of the troops beyond the Caucasus, enters, and there is no chair for him, and no one gives him his place. And he himself brought up a chair and sat down alongside me. I asked him: "Who is this Ivan Kuz'mich?" "That is Lt. So-and-so." "And this one in a civilian jacket?" "That is Ensign So-and-so." To me this seemed very strange.

After this meeting with Ermolov, Paskevich remained in Tiflis for several days without any duties and received assignment, so he wrote, at the very time when Prince Madatov had won the first victory over the Persians.[11] The new commander, while at times he was charming to his subordinates, was extremely suspicious of most of his associates, whom he charged with outright disloyalty and attempts to undermine

10. Bobrovskii, IV, 84.
11. Dubrovin, *Istoriia*, VI, 660-61.

his position. Gen. N. N. Muraviev asserts that in less than twelve months Paskevich had four different chiefs of staff, with all of whom he quarreled bitterly.[12]

On September 12 Paskevich, now in command of the small force at Elizabetpol, faced a vastly larger Persian army. At first he stayed on the defensive, as, according to Dubrovin, who disapproved of Paskevich, he feared to lose his reputation by suffering defeat. His subordinates, however, kept urging him to attack, although he was thinking of retreat. Finally he gave reluctant permission to advance. The Russian attack broke the center of the Persian army and drove them back in rout, taking much booty, as the Persians, thoroughly dismayed, fled to the hills. If Paskevich had had the cavalry and horse artillery that he had asked for, he could have destroyed the whole Persian force.[13]

The successful commander was now delighted with the troops of the Caucasus Corps, which a few days earlier he had disparaged so strongly, and wanted to pursue the beaten Persians into their own territory in order to end the war at once. Ermolov, however, felt that because of the extreme shortage of provisions, the lack of cavalry, and other factors, they should not proceed beyond the Arax until the renowned fortress of Erivan was captured. Instead, he ordered Paskevich to quarter his troops in the frontier provinces and to help subdue them. The absence of pursuit gave Abbas-Mirza a chance to recover, and his forces again approached the Arax, sending raiding parties across to collect provisions and to compel the inhabitants to move into Persian territory. Paskevich now marched to cross the river and destroy the army of Abbas-Mirza. When he penetrated Persian territory he captured large numbers of cattle and brought back many of the people whom the Persians had carried off, but Abbas-Mirza had gone. He had already disbanded his army and had headed back toward Teheran. Paskevich now was more insistent than ever on the need to push on to Tabriz and, if need be, to Teheran. He wrote frequently to St. Petersburg to present his views, which included much criticism of Ermolov for refusing to support him. Baron I. I. Diebitsch, chief of the Tsar's personal staff, who, realizing that Paskevich enjoyed the favor of the Tsar, was not informed as to Ermolov's reasons for re-

---

12. N. N. Murav'ev, "Iz zapisok," *Russkii Arkhiv*, XXXI (1893), Pt. III, 320. The author was very hostile to Paskevich, although he was also critical of Ermolov.
13. Dubrovin, *Istoriia*, VI, 574-80.

fusal, supported Paskevich, and Nicholas naturally became sure that the latter was correct in his views and that Ermolov, perhaps out of spite, was depriving him and Russia of needed victory. The Viceroy, however, was grappling with the realities of the supply situation, which was precarious. In November, after bad weather had set in, Paskevich asked for two thousand measures of flour, but Ermolov, who did not have it on hand, had to refuse and ordered the troops into winter quarters. Madatov with a small detachment took station on the frontier, while Paskevich retired to Tiflis to pen bitter accusations against Ermolov.[14]

Upon Paskevich's return to Tiflis in December, 1826, his relations grew terribly strained, even to the point where he challenged Ermolov to a duel.[15] The latter still retained a sort of moral superiority over his rival, as he was still very popular in Tiflis, while Paskevich antagonized many. Paskevich, however, still had the ear of the Tsar, to whom he poured out his complaints. On December 11, 1826, he forwarded a long report on his experiences in the Caucasus area. On the condition of the troops he was very critical, asserting that many of them were in rags, and that all the uniforms were old. In the second part, on the military events of the past six months, he declared: "The campaign has ended, the campaign has been spoiled." In general, his theme was that Ermolov and Madatov had checked him at every turn, although it would have been possible to inflict a crushing blow on the Persians by capturing Tabriz shortly after the battle of Elizabetpol. As for the coming year, he was warm in praise of the plan that Diebitsch had sent him, but he feared that Ermolov would delay in making preparations so much that the ruinous summer heat would be upon them before they were ready. Perhaps the most remarkable part of his report was his analysis of Ermolov's policies in respect to Persia, which allegedly had compelled the Persians to fight. ". . . all here are agreed that Gen. Ermolov is the cause of the war by his various manipulations." His hostility toward them, and his support for Madatov's depredations against the families of the khans of the border provinces, had brought the Persians to the point where they had to seize the most favorable moment to begin the war that Ermolov had made inevitable. Abbas-Mirza had written him a message to this effect, and two cap-

14. *Ibid.*, pp. 682-96.
15. Murav'ev, *Russkii Arkhiv*, XXXI (1891), Pt. I, 588. Muraviev's testimony on this period, while the most detailed available, is not, however, always reliable.

tured khans also affirmed this.[16] Thus Paskevich accepted the word of the enemy that Ermolov had been responsible for the war.

At first the leading figures at St. Petersburg felt that Paskevich's complaints were exaggerated and that he was picking trouble. He received weighty support, however, from Lt. Gen. Benckendorff, brother of the Chief of Gendarmes. He had asked Ermolov to give him command of a cavalry division, but Ermolov, who was known to be anti-German, was cold to him. He then wrote to his powerful brother, accusing Ermolov of inaction against the Persians. He had built showy public buildings instead of forts and had spent months in the Moslem areas on his own concerns instead of fighting the enemy. Benckendorff accused Ermolov of delay in obtaining provisions and equipment for the troops, so that at the last minute he had to strip the inhabitants bare. He also charged that the Viceroy permitted all manners of intrigues and refused to give others an opportunity to serve, thereby demoralizing all decent men. He also alleged that Ermolov winked at all sorts of administrative abuses, and declared that nothing would go well as long as the latter was there. Paskevich's letter, and one from Baron Alexander Fredericks, accusing Ermolov of delaying the spring campaign, had much effect on the Tsar.

In order to explain the nature of his relations with Ermolov, Paskevich sent the Emperor his journal of the campaign of 1826, in which he constantly complained against Ermolov and Prince Madatov. First he suggested that the former, although he had prophesied a quick victory, had ordered him into great danger. When, after Paskevich's victory, he proposed to go across the Arax into Persia, Ermolov and Madatov failed—apparently wilfully—to supply him with provisions. When he arrived at Shusha ten days later, he found that no shipments had come in and there was food for only two days. ". . . here I learned that there is malevolence or inability to administer. . . ." On October 3 he wrote that he requested Ermolov to send him 1,800 measures of grain, "with which I can drive off the enemy. . . ." On October 5 the journal contained an anguished statement that he had just learned from Lt. Korganov, his Armenian translator, "who with fear declared to me that I am surrounded by spies and intriguers," that Prince Madatov had been publicly cursing Paskevich before his associates. Madatov, according to Korganov, while professing friend-

16. P. I. Vrioni, "Ermolov, Dibich, i Paskevich," *Russkaia Starina*, V (1872), 709-18.

ship for Paskevich, intimated that the latter had no effective authority and that no one should assist him in buying provisions. Paskevich asserted: "*I would at once take measures to stop him* [Madatov], *but I am alone, completely alone....*"[17] Later, Paskevich declared that Madatov had again showed his perfidy by refusing to recommend Korganov for a decoration, although the latter had been twice wounded in action and had had a horse killed under him. Paskevich had learned this from Korganov himself.[18] Paskevich also complained that Ermolov did not send his staff to him, on the pretext that the roads were not safe and there were not enough men to furnish a convoy. Finally, Paskevich was outraged when, on November 2, he learned that Gen. Vel'iaminov, the chief of staff, was sending him a convoy of 248 measures of grain—a mere three days' provisions— instead of eighteen hundred that he had requested. "What pettiness: this was done for ridicule, in order to halt my undertaking completely!" He concluded his journal with the assertion: "In a word, at every step I met no good will toward the common cause."[19]

Perhaps the most remarkable aspect of this tissue of accusations is that they were largely based on the words of Korganov, according to Muraviev "an outcast of the human race," whom Ermolov had removed from his position in the government for his extortion and who now sought to repay old scores.[20] In 1831, Denis Davydov had a chat with Diebitsch about the Caucasus situation in 1826. Diebitsch said: "Korganov embroiled Ermolov with Paskevich, whom he completely controlled...." The Armenian, he asserted, had told the general that Ermolov had even tried to poison him. Diebitsch added: "When I myself became sick, Korganov came to me with a disturbed face and declared to me, in secret, that he knew definitely that Ermolov had poisoned me: but I shouted: 'Get out of here, you scoundrel!'"[21]

Not satisfied with his criticism of Ermolov to the Tsar, on the same day Paskevich wrote to Diebitsch that his position in the Caucasus was impossible, as he was surrounded by spies and foes. "The most lying and deceitful of all is Lt. Gen. Madatov...." The other

17. Dubrovin, *Istoriia*, VI, 724-27.
18. *Ibid.*, pp. 723-36.
19. Vrioni, *Russkaia Starina*, VI (1872), 39-40.
20. Murav'ev, *Russkii Arkhiv*, XXXI (1889), Pt. I, 588; A. L. Zisserman, *Istoriia 80-go pekhotnago Kabardinskago generalfel'dmarshala Kniazia Bariatinskago polka (1726-1880)* (3 vols.; St. Petersburg, 1881), I, 391.
21. Davydov, *Russkaia Starina*, VI (1872), 548n.

generals and officers also were against him. As for the troops, their boots and uniforms were in bad condition, some with four years of patches. He felt it impossible to stay on with Ermolov, as he was sick from the constant friction. He likewise declared that for the good of the service he should leave, since if he remained in command the supplies would be delayed, as in the past campaign, thus bringing all operations to a standstill. "The devices of trickery" were bringing him to a state where he could not act, and hence he begged Diebitsch to recall him. Ermolov, he asserted, could not tolerate anyone who might hurt him, and hence he would wreck everything. The Tsar could find someone else who could get on with Ermolov, but he could not, "for he has completely declared against me; and even in his very communiqués he wishes to darken my name; he does not mention it; I have to deal with the most evil and tricky person." He added that in any circumstances the campaign would be very difficult, because of the lack of provisions in Georgia and the terrible summer. Abbas-Mirza, he declared, wanted peace with him, but not with Ermolov. "But all this has been lost by our inaction."[22]

Ten days later Paskevich sent a note to Diebitsch again declaring that it would be harmful for the cause for him to remain with Ermolov, "for I am sure that all means will be used to bring a halt in all my undertakings." Only one thing, he added, "restrains him from direct unpleasantness, and this is the fact that I have the good fortune to report to the Sovereign Emperor."[23]

Nicholas answered these poorly spelled and somewhat incoherent letters with a cordial note to the effect that he was glad to know the truth and that he shared Paskevich's views in his quarrel with Ermolov. As he had decided to take effective measures, he was secretly sending Diebitsch to the scene to straighten things out. He added that if things had been done as *he* had ordered, they would now be in Tabriz, for Madatov's raid across the Arax showed the possibility of success.[24]

Paskevich continued to send letters. On February 21, 1827 he wrote to Nicholas that he hoped to move in March and by mid-April to push into Persian territory, if provisions were available. Of Ermolov he wrote: "If he now only tries to deceive, this will certainly be very quickly disclosed [in the light of?] the openness of my actions."[25] On

22. Vrioni, *Russkaia Starina*, VI (1872), 41-42.
23. *Ibid.*, p. 43.
24. P. Bartenov, "K biografii fel'dmarshala Kniazia Paskevicha," *Russkii Arkhiv*, XIX (1891), Pt. III, 272-73.
25. Vrioni, *Russkaia Starina*, VI (1872), 43-44.

March 4 he wrote to Diebitsch, about the time of the latter's arrival in Tiflis. Some time before Paskevich had threatened the several regimental commanders that he would report their neglect of their men to the Tsar, although he would ask the latter to pardon them. Ermolov had objected strongly to this threat. Paskevich justified his action by saying that the men had now been clothed, provided for, and somewhat drilled, as a result of his action. If he had threatened to report the colonels to Ermolov, this would have had no result, as the latter was the cause of these failings.[26] On March 16 he again wrote to Nicholas, expressing hopes that the campaign could begin in mid-April, and that by mid-May, if he could obtain considerable provisions in Armenia to supplement those coming from Russia, he could begin his march on Tabriz. He complained of Ermolov's failure to give him information on the civil affairs in the Caucasus, in which, he was sure, there were rather considerable failings. He added, however, that "the charges of evil deeds and crimes, which were based only on rumors, were in no way proved, and very frequently were even improbable, because of the complete absence of cause for ill-intentioned action, do not deserve to be believed."[27] The moderation of Paskevich's charges in this letter, which is in marked contrast to his earlier sweeping and even wild allegations, which probably originated with Korganov, is highly interesting. It may be that this change in attitude reflects the coming of Diebitsch, who was too experienced to be taken in by the former prejudiced assertions.

During this period Ermolov, in addition to his official reports, apparently sent Nicholas only one letter. On March 3, in a missive full of most elaborate expressions of loyalty and devotion, he asserted that the knowledge that he lacked the trust of the Sovereign had made it hard for him to act with confidence and decision. As a result, he found himself unable to perform his service duties properly. As long as the war was in progress he did not think it proper to ask the Tsar to relieve him at this time, but requested that Nicholas should do so when it would benefit the service of the country.[28] Ermolov also sent a brief note to Diebitsch upon his arrival, saying: "I am heartily glad that you are coming here and I know how much easier my activities will become."[29]

26. Ibid., p. 69.
27. Ibid., V (1872), 706-7.
28. Ibid., VI (1872), 64.
29. Ibid., p. 43.

Diebitsch's reports to Nicholas I about the Caucasian situation make fascinating reading because, although he knew that his imperial master strongly favored Paskevich and wanted to get rid of Ermolov, he found the latter much the more appealing and reasonable. In their first interview, Ermolov frankly admitted that he had been mistaken in refusing to push on to Tabriz at once, although he gave weighty reasons for his decision: the shortage of supplies in a devastated country, the need to pacify the rebellious Moslem provinces, and a belief that the Shah would send heavy reinforcements to Abbas-Mirza. He promised that in the future he would do all possible to speed the offensive into Persia. When asked about Paskevich, Ermolov was reluctant to discuss him, but finally he expressed the view that his rival, without a firm character, fell easily under the influence of others. Paskevich, he felt, hoped to succeed him in command. Lately Paskevich had begun to demand all sorts of official documents, including papers on the civil administration, which he, as a military commander, had no right to. Diebitsch assured Ermolov that the Tsar was sure that with tactful treatment Paskevich would be a co-operative assistant. Ermolov said that he would be pleased if Diebitsch would delimit the respective responsibilities of the two generals. When Diebitsch interviewed Paskevich, however, the latter declared that it was impossible for him to serve under Ermolov. He became angry when Diebitsch questioned the soundness of his charges against Ermolov, but soon calmed down, although he insisted that in just one week Diebitsch would certainly share his opinion regarding the falseness of Ermolov and his lack of military capability.[30]

From Paskevich, Diebitsch turned to Gen. Adj. Benckendorff, brother of the Tsar's favorite. As might have been expected, he supported Paskevich and said that Ermolov would have to go. Col. Prince Dolgoruki, aide-de-camp of the Tsar, however, had views of his own. He stated that he believed that it was impossible for Ermolov and Paskevich to live in peace, not because of the hostility of the former, but rather "the extraordinary touchiness of Gen. Paskevich and the tricky activity of an Armenian lieutenant who serves as interpreter with Paskevich, because of the personal hostility of this Armenian toward . . . Prince Madatov." Diebitsch added that young Dolgoruki seemed to be fully aware of the good qualities of Paskevich and appeared to judge things without bias. When questioned about abuses

30. *Ibid.*, pp. 46-48.

in the area, Dolgoruki said that he "believes them to exist, but [the reports about them are] exaggerated." Concerning alleged rash talk on the part of Gen. Ermolov, he said that he had never heard any, but on the contrary had noted "that Gen. Ermolov tries to tell the favorable rumors and anecdotes that come here from St. Petersburg."[31] In his next letter, two days later, Diebitsch considered other charges against Ermolov: stern treatment of Georgians and Armenians; the driving out of Moslem khans and beks from the border provinces; and the fixing of low prices on farm products. Here he could see that Ermolov's conduct might have been beneficial rather than harmful. He did, however, blame Ermolov for letting the economic aspects of the troops deteriorate, although he saw no sign of bad discipline or poor morale.[32]

In these first letters Diebitsch appeared to lean somewhat toward Ermolov, although his knowledge of the Tsar's views pulled him toward Paskevich. Similarly, in his conclusions concerning the situation he gave Ermolov credit for sincerity and capability, in spite of his excess of caution. He believed that the Viceroy would help to reach the Arax by early summer and to take Tabriz in the fall. His comments on Paskevich were far from flattering. After stating that "the intrigues and partisan spirit in this region among the inhabitants, especially the Armenians, exceed my early expectations," he went on to state that Paskevich, "with his noble but extremely sensitive character, combines a passionate suspicion with great trust in those who pose before him as men led by the same noble feelings. . . ." Diebitsch added that, although Paskevich had never commanded large bodies of separate troops, "he will perform according to the will of Your Majesty, if only his prejudice against all who have served more closely to Gen. Ermolov does not have a harmful effect on the military administration." Diebitsch did not attempt to decide between the two rivals, but asked the Tsar to do so.[33]

Diebitsch's second report, dealing with the military aspects of the

31. *Ibid.*, p. 48.
32. *Ibid.*, pp. 49-50. It is interesting to note that in the spring of 1827, when he inspected the advance guard of these same troops, he was delighted. On his return he remarked: "I found these troops inspired by the spirit of Catherine and Suvorov. I . . . can say in truth that I never saw in our troops such zeal and courage as that that inspired the Caucasus soldiers. Our cavalry could never overtake infantry doing fifty *versts* and more a day, especially when, as they told me, Ermolov was leading them. Then neither clouded heights nor wild ravines—nothing could halt the gigantic strides of the infantry." Cited in Shabanov, *Istoriia 13-go leibgrenaderskago Erivanskago Ego Velichestva polka* (3 pts.; Tiflis, 1871), II, 191.
33. Vrioni, *Russkaia Starina*, VI (1872), 50-53.

problem, accompanied his first. He explained Ermolov's failings in the preceding campaign by lack of correct information about the enemy and by fear of revolt among the mountaineers. The troops had deteriorated because of lack of supervision and use of the men on construction projects, but he had "never noted failings in discipline." Ermolov had responded to his questions with frankness and sincerity, had never displayed stubbornness or unwillingness, and even gave Paskevich credit for capability and good intentions, although holding that he was unduly suspicious. Ermolov, Diebitsch stated, was making effective preparations for the spring campaign and would do his duty exactly. Any weakness and lack of zeal on Ermolov's part, he believed, were a result of the loss of the Tsar's confidence in him. As for Paskevich, he gave him "full credit for the frankness and the justice of his views," and although unable to accept his belief that Ermolov was malicious and stubborn, he could see why the former would feel that way.[34]

For about six weeks Diebitsch reported on the situation to the Tsar, with his reports becoming more and more favorable to Ermolov. His inspections of the troops convinced him that their condition was generally good, contrary to report. He exonerated one of Ermolov's generals of charges of mistreatment of a Cossack, declaring that in the Caucasus he found "the greatest proneness to the most vicious fabrications, attacks and slanders." And when he sent Ermolov's rebuttal of Paskevich's charges to the Tsar, he appeared to accept the former's explanations and to sympathize with his complaints that by his hostility and open attacks Paskevich had showed himself to be insubordinate. Ermolov was especially angry at his rival's statement to the regimental commanders that, while they deserved court-martial for neglecting their troops, he would intercede for them. This showed, the Viceroy said, that Paskevich did not regard him as their commander.[35]

Ermolov did admit the justice of the Tsar's rebuke to him for inhuman cruelty toward a Tatar mullah (he had hanged him by the feet for several hours before executing him), but he said that he had been infuriated by the atrocities committed by the victim. During a Moslem raid on a German settlement near Tiflis, the mullah had allegedly tortured pregnant women to death.[36]

34. *Ibid.*, pp. 54-57.
35. *Ibid.*, pp. 254-55, 259-60, 265-67.
36. *Ibid.*, p. 68.

According to Muraviev, who was chief of staff at this time, Ermolov was apparently winning and expected to lead in the coming campaign. Paskevich, who was sure that he had lost, took sick and, blaming Diebitsch for his defeat, was about to return to Russia.[37] Paskevich, however, had sent his own version of the situation to the Tsar,[38] who, indeed, always stood behind him. In his letter of March 8, 1827, to Diebitsch, Nicholas wrote: "I hope that you will not permit yourself to be charmed by this man [Ermolov], for whom a lie is a virtue if he can derive benefit from it. . . . Finally, may God aid you and make you wise, so that you can be just."[39] On March 10 he declared: ". . . it would be extremely essential to try to learn, particularly, who are the leaders of the evil in this nest of intrigues and without fail to remove them. . . ."[40]

By March 12 Nicholas, who had just received Diebitsch's letter of February 28, asking that the Tsar decide the matter, was clearly annoyed. He declared that Diebitsch was shirking responsibility in this case. It would be impossible to leave "this man" in control of things. "Thus, after having weighed everything soundly and while awaiting your second courier, if he does not bring me other data than those that you have already had me look over, I do not see any possibility but to have you use the full power given you to remove Ermolov. It is Paskevich whom I intend to replace him. . . ." He added: "There, dear friend, is my last word: and again I repeat to you that it is in the case your courier, whom I am waiting for, does not bring me other news than the latest received yesterday."[41] Finally, in another letter, written after the arrival of Diebitsch's courier, Nicholas reaffirmed his position, ordering him to remove not only Ermolov, but also Madatov, Vel'iaminov, and any others necessary. "May God bless this important step and give you all the strength and dignity for this important moment."[42] These instructions left Diebitsch (whose equivocal conduct suggests that perhaps *he* had hoped to become commander in chief in the Caucasus) no choice but to dismiss Ermolov and to appoint Paskevich in his place. He carried out the order on March 28. Ermolov "accepted the August decision of Your Majesty with the greatest submissiveness and without the slightest

37. Muraviev, *Russkii Arkhiv*, XXVII (1889), Pt. III, 71-72.
38. Vrioni, *Russkaia Starina*, VI (1872), 58-61.
39. *Ibid.*, XXIX (1880), 619.
40. *Ibid.*
41. *Ibid.*, p. 622.
42. *Ibid.*, p. 625.

complaint or display of displeasure."[43] Muraviev reported that there was, however, much displeasure in the Caucasus Corps, with the enlisted men complaining of the loss of "their favorite commander." Many of the Guards officers in Tiflis showed their sympathy by paying farewell visits to the fallen hero. Muraviev himself wept bitterly when he learned of this event. He went to Diebitsch, who reassured him, but Muraviev wept and moaned in distress. Later he paid a farewell visit to Ermolov, and they parted with tears and a warm embrace.[44]

Thus one of Russia's greatest commanders was swept into the discard. Paskevich soon rose to be the supreme military figure in Russia— a position that he held until the end of the Crimean War. Inasmuch as the failings that he had already displayed remained with him to the end, his hegemony—as will be seen—was a grave misfortune for Russia. In his unwavering support for his "Father-Commander"—as Nicholas addressed Paskevich—the Tsar clearly displayed his inability to choose effective assistants.

As for Prince Madatov, Paskevich forced him out of his command and made him cool his heels in Tiflis before he would permit him to go to St. Petersburg to request a new assignment.[45]

And so in 1827 Paskevich moved forth to war with the Persians as commander in chief of the Russian forces. In spite of his insistence on haste, however, his army did not march until early April, when the grass had grown enough to feed the horses. Count Benckendorff with the advance guard approached Echmiadzin, the seat of the Armenian church not far from Erivan, only to find the Persians had fled, stripping the country of provisions. This at once hampered the Russian operations, and attempts to buy food from the Turks proved useless.[46] In early June, Paskevich concentrated his forces at Echmiadzin for the new campaign. While awaiting his siege-train, he made a difficult march across hot and waterless country to Nakhichevan, which he captured, with the dismayed Persians retiring over the Arax. The inhabitants of the area now gave their support to the Russians as the probable winners. As abundant supplies became available to Paskevich's forces, he could begin the siege of nearby Abbas-Abad. Abbas-

43. *Ibid.*, pp. 266-67.
44. Murav'ev, *Russkii Arkhiv*, XXVII (1889), Pt. III, 76-78, 79-86.
45. Kniagina S. A. Madatova, "Kniaz' V. G. Madatov, general-leitenant," *Russkaia Starina*, VII (1873), 92.
46. A. P. Shcherbatov, *General-fel'dmarshal kniaz' Paskevitch, ego zhizn' i deiatel'-nost'. Po neizdannym istochnikam* (7 vols.; St. Petersburg, 1888-1904), II, 231-32, 245-46. Shcherbatov, Paskevitch's official biographer, is generally sympathetic to him.

Mirza now advanced to the Arax to lure the Russians away from the siege, only to suffer a severe defeat at the hands of the Russian cavalry, which crossed the river and surprised the Persians. They fled, hotly pursued, for twenty-four miles. After this successful encounter Paskevich quickly took Abbas-Abad, and to escape the illness caused by the summer heat, led his forces to a healthy camp in the mountains.[47]

While Paskevich was so employed, Abbas-Mirza, rightly fearing that the Russians would move against Erivan, decided to attack Echmiadzin, thus threatening the rear of Paskevich's army. Gen. Krasovskii, outside Erivan, marching to the rescue with twenty-five hundred men, was surrounded in a defile by over ten times as many Persians. In the ensuing ten-hour battle, Krasovskii managed to fight his way out, but with the loss of over half of his force and all his provisions. Abbas-Mirza also lost very heavily, and retired to Erivan, while Krasovskii lifted the siege of Echmiadzin, and then, with the siege-train, joined Paskevich at the siege of Sardar Abad, which fell on September 19. Paskevich now moved to Erivan.[48]

Erivan, the leading city of Armenia, had the reputation of being an impregnable fortress, although actually its defenses were far from impressive. The Russian forces, with siege artillery, began the attack on September 23. Batteries quickly rose, and the cannonade did great damage to the town. On the night of September 30 there was a terrible bombardment, as a result of which the inhabitants opened the gates on the following day. The garrison then surrendered. This was a great victory, because of the strategic location of the city, and also because the victors took rich supplies.[49]

After this success, Paskevich sent a glowing report to the Tsar of his conquest and of the valor and endurance of his troops.[50] In reality, however, the siege itself was not especially brilliant, as the defenders were not regular troops, they did not put up a strong defense, and the walls were weak.[51] Nevertheless, its capture was a result of good leadership, the bravery and determination of the troops, and of skill in coping with logistical problems. It ensured the success of the Russian army over the Persians.

47. N. K. Schilder, *Imperator Nikolai I. Ego zhizn' i tsarstvovanie* (2 vols.; St. Petersburg, 1903), I, 85; Zubov, *Podvigi*, II, 112-36.
48. A. N. Petrov, ed., *Russkaia voennaia sila. Istoriia razvitiia voennago dela ot nachala Rusi do nashego vremeni* (2 vols.; Moscow, 1897), II, 345-46; Zubov, II, 146-66.
49. Zubov, II, 171-79.
50. Bobrovskii, IV, 110.
51. Davydov, *Russkaia Starina*, VI (1872), 333-34.

In the meantime, the Russian advance forces under Muraviev and Prince Eristov crossed the Arax and easily subdued several weak fortresses. As they approached Tabriz, Abbas-Mirza's forces fled or dispersed, and the inhabitants, eager to avoid a siege, turned against the garrison of the city. As a result, Eristov's forces had no difficulty in occupying it, almost without a shot, on October 13, and Muraviev moved in and established control. Paskevich followed with the main army on the 19th and arranged a formal entry, making a highly favorable impression on a British observer there present.[52] The conquerer, however, was furious with Muraviev for having forestalled him in taking Tabriz, where he had expected to have another personal triumph. "Paskevich could never forgive him for this."[53]

Abbas-Mirza now realized that all was lost and, beginning peace talks on November 10, quickly accepted the Russian terms. The Shah, however, under pressure from the Turks, proved difficult, and the talks broke off, in spite of the eagerness of Abbas-Mirza. Paskevich now pushed ahead toward Teheran, using snowplows to clear the roads, and took several of the cities on the approaches to the capital, to the great terror of the Shah. The Persians quickly agreed to the Russian terms and in February, 1828, paid the indemnity of twenty million rubles, in addition to giving up the border provinces and Erivan and Nakhichevan.[54]

Thus Paskevich won glory in his Persian campaign. If one can believe Muraviev, however, during it he proved to be a far from ideal commander. He insulted many of his subordinates, including Muraviev, whom he tried to catch in wrongdoing. He was inconsiderate of the troops, wearing them out with useless movements. It was especially notable that when crises occurred, he became fearful and indecisive, fearing to suffer defeat and thus lose his reputation. He also believed that his subordinates, allegedly hostile, were seeking to undermine him and ruin his prestige.[55] While Muraviev is not an unprejudiced witness, his statements are corroborated by other sources. Ganglebov declared that after Paskevich's successes in Persia "he became harsh, demanding, and irritable, suspecting intrigues against

52. Murav'ev, *Russkii Arkhiv*, XXIX (1891), Pt. III, 59-81; Zubov, II, 180-96; "Russians and Persia," *Literary Gazette*, Nos. 583-86 (1828), April, pp. 216-17, 233-34.
53. Rozen, *Russkaia Starina*, XLI (1884), 314.
54. P. P. Zubov, *Kartina poslednei voiny s Persieiu 1826-1828* (St. Petersburg, 1834), pp. 74-80; Schilder, I, 87-90.
55. Murav'ev, *Russkii Arkhiv*, XXIX (1891), Pt. III, 6-50; XXVII (1889), Pt. II, 151-52, 543; Pt. III, 314-15.

him, and when he regarded someone as an enemy he did not spare him and blasted him before everyone. . . ." As an example of this, he charged Krasovskii with cowardice, although in relieving Echmiadzin he had performed a great feat.[56] Krasovskii, in fury, refused to serve longer under Paskevich and secured transfer to the army on the Danube, where he did well against the Turks.[57] Probably as a result of this and similar episodes, Nicholas I, in his letter congratulating Paskevich on his victories against the Persians, gave him a friendly scolding for distrusting his subordinates and for too great irritability. He especially mentioned Paskevich's treatment of Gens. Krasovskii and Emanuel.[58] Paskevich, however, continued to display many of the same characteristics in his subsequent campaigns.

His next campaign was not long in coming. The war, for which both Turks and Russians had long been preparing, began on the Danube in the spring of 1828, and of course spread to Asia. Paskevich had had a new and excellent road built to Gumry near the Turkish frontier and here, on June 12 his army of twelve thousand men and seventy guns massed. With a fine supply system established, it could cross the frontier two days later and move toward the great fortress at Kars. The Turks had planned to mass sixty thousand men at Kars, to invade Russia and take Tiflis, while another force invaded from the coastal regions. But because of internal turmoil the Turks were more poorly organized than ever, and the main forces were at Erzerum to the southward. Paskevich had no difficulty in cutting Kars off from the Erzerum force and ringing the city with batteries. On June 23 the Russians, under cover of a heavy bombardment, stormed the Turkish fortified camp before the city and then pushed on into the city from several sides. Finally the defenders surrendered, and Paskevich had captured a fortress with 129 guns and vast supplies, at a trifling price in casualties. The attempt of a relieving army from Erzerum to drive off the besiegers came too late, and they retired in haste.[59]

After the fall of Kars, Paskevich had to remain inactive for three weeks because of administrative matters, the bringing up of supplies, and the plague, which spread from Kars to the Russian troops. By skilful quarantine measures, however, the plague was halted with a minimum of losses, and on July 12 Paskevich could march his small

56. Ganglebov, *Russkii Arkhiv*, XXIV (1886), Pt. II, 258.
57. Murav'ev, *Russkii Arkhiv*, XXXI (1893), Pt. III, 317.
58. Shcherbatov, III, 103.
59. A. K. Ushakov, *Istoriia voennykh deistvii v Aziatskoi Turtsii, v 1828 i 1829 godakh* (2 vols.; St. Petersburg, 1836), II, 181-237.

army toward Akhaltsykh on the upper Kura River. After capturing a small fortress not far from it, he moved his force through very difficult mountains, hoping to reach Akhaltsykh before the main Turkish force could get there. When they made camp on August 5 close to their goal, however, they learned that the Turks had arrived in great strength. Hastily the Russians moved into position near the fortress, where they fortified their defenses with redoubts and welcomed a small party of reinforcements. Their situation, however, was dangerous, as the enemy was far superior and was expecting reinforcements, while the provisions in the Russian camp were running low. Paskevich astounded everyone by rejecting the suggestion of D. E. Osten-Sacken, his chief of staff, to attack, and talked about retiring to Georgia, which would have meant the loss of the siege-train and most of the baggage. Finally Osten-Sacken persuaded him to attack the camp of the Turkish field army. Most of the Russians were joyful at the prospect, but Paskevich became timid and quiet and wanted to cancel the order. His subordinates shamed him into going ahead, which he did with reluctance. The attack, at night, almost failed, as the Turks occupied an almost impregnable position and Paskevich halted his forces, permitting the Turks to make telling attacks on the Russian lines. As a crossfire of the Turkish artillery grew in intensity, Paskevich became enraged, accusing his subordinates of leading him into a trap in order to wreck his reputation. Fortunately for all concerned, without orders from Paskevich, Muraviev led an assault on a hill on the flank of the Turkish position, and by quickly capturing it threw the Turks into a panic. They fled from their camp, abandoning their artillery and baggage, and the Russians had won a great victory.[60]

Paskevich expected the city of Akhaltsykh to surrender when the field army was beaten, but the warlike garrison and defenders, who numbered fifteen thousand men, defied him. The Russians, with eleven thousand, had to begin a siege, and by August 10 they started a bombardment of the town. Several days of heavy fire failed to bring it to surrender and so on the 15th an assault was ordered. At first the attackers met little resistance, but as the defenders recovered from their surprise they fought with ferocity. Even women fought, and each house had to be taken by storm. Fire started in several of the houses, and Paskevich had his men start others with hand grenades and burning hay and straw. The fighting was extremely bitter, with

60. Rozen, *Russkaia Starina*, XLI (1884), 317-22; Murav'ev, *Russkii Arkhiv*, XXXI (1893), Pt. III, 430-31, 445-47.

many Turks dying in the flames. Finally, on August 16 the garrison in the citadel surrendered, and Akhaltsykh, hitherto uncaptured, had fallen. The defenders lost almost five thousand men in the fighting, the Russians about 630.[61]

According to Ganglebov, one of the Decembrist officers with the Caucasian army, the Russian troops looted and otherwise misbehaved, both at Kars and at Akhaltsykh. At Kars, at least, Paskevich gave this tacit approval, for he told one of his subordinates that that was how Suvorov's army had behaved in captured cities, and one should pretend not to see it.[62] Another criticism was that "there were no general orders of Paskevich himself, who in difficult situations not rarely lost his head."[63] On the other hand, in many ways this campaign displayed him at his best. The problem of provisioning the army gave little trouble, in spite of the difficult country, as the arrangements for acquiring and hauling supplies proved adequate. Moreover, Paskevich gave careful attention to the medical problems of the army, with the result that the losses from sickness were not great.[64] Furthermore, under him the Russian movements displayed considerable strategic skill. The fact that they were fighting a poorly organized Turkish army led by poor generals does not detract from the merit of this campaign. While Paskevich by no means deserved all the credit for this result, the Tsar and official circles in St. Petersburg allotted it to him.

After the fall of Akhaltsykh there was no further action of importance, and most of the Russian army went to winter quarters in Georgia, leaving garrisons in Kars, Baiazet, and Akhaltsykh. The Turks, however, encouraged by successes on the Danube, made vast preparations for the campaign of 1829. For his part, Paskevich hoped, with the aid of new formations of Armenian, Georgian, and Kurdish troops, to capture Erzerum and push deep into Asia Minor. But the killing of A. Griboedov, Russian diplomat in Teheran, and the rise of a warlike spirit in Persia, compelled Paskevich to divert part of his troops to guard against this new danger and thus hampered his plans.

In hopes of recovering Akhaltsykh before the Russians were ready, on February 19, 1829, the Turks appeared in strength before this fortress and sought to invade Georgia from other directions. As many of the Moslems of Transcaucasia were ready to turn on the Russians,

61. Ushakov, II, 315-40.
62. Ganglebov, *Russkii Arkhiv*, XXIV (1886), Pt. II, 250-51.
63. Bobrovskii, IV, 134n.
64. *Ibid.*, IV, 160; F. K. Zatler, *Zapiski o prodovol'stvii voisk v voennoe vremia* (4 pts.; St. Petersburg, 1860-1865), I, 127-306.

the situation was dangerous. Muraviev relates that Paskevich, in a fine frenzy of fear that he would lose his conquests and his reputation, dashed around his headquarters dictating orders for regiments to march and then tearing them up to begin again. Fortunately Osten-Sacken intervened to take proper measures, sending Burtsev with the advance guard, followed by Muraviev and other forces.[65] In Akhaltsykh the Russian garrison hung on grimly under heavy attack, until Burtsev's relieving force turned the tide. Another general wiped out a Turkish force on the Black Sea coast. Thus the immediate danger was past, and as the Persians had a change of heart, Paskevich could move the main forces in May to Ardahan, about thirty-five miles from Kars. Here Paskevich did not know what to do. Sometimes, urged by Gens. Sacken and Val'khovskii, he ordered an advance, only to countermand it shortly thereafter. Everyone was upset, and most were eager for an advance, but Paskevich was in despair, fearing that great hordes of Turks would attack. He even ordered the troops to build redoubts at Ardahan, although there was almost no danger at that point. He was frightened and distraught, could give no definite orders, and did not sleep at night. Finally, after much wavering, he gave a hesitant order to advance, and Muraviev, commander of the field troops, gave the detailed orders.[66]

On June 10, near Kars, Paskevich prepared to move, with eighteen thousand men and seventy guns. Opposing him were twenty thousand Turks in a very strong fortified camp, with the Seraskir (generalissimo) with thirty thousand more, on the Russian left flank. Paskevich, after a feint at the Seraskir, secretly moved to the right, through difficult mountains, to attack the Turkish camp. Even from the new position, however, the camp proved impregnable, so that a further risky flank march to the right became necessary. Characteristically, the Turks made no effort to interfere, and the Russians finally could attack strong Turkish forces at Chainla, while the Seraskir with another force was near by. The Russians crushed the first force at Chainla, while the Seraskir fortified his position. Then, by a surprise attack in the early evening, they routed the twelve thousand troops of the Seraskir, capturing all their supplies and artillery.[67]

Although for several days the Russian forces had been extremely

65. Murav'ev, *Russkii Arkhiv*, XXXII (1894), Pt. I, 382-83.
66. *Ibid.*, pp. 515-17.
67. Ushakov, II, 12-114.

active, on the morning after the battle of Chainla, Paskevich ordered them against the fortified camp at Milli-Diuz, eight miles away. The eleven thousand men advanced with enthusiasm and joyful songs. The Turks, dismayed by news of the recent Russian victories, still stood firm until the Russian columns, with drums beating, marched to assault their position. Then they fled in terror, hotly pursued by the Russian horse. This action completed the ruin of the Turkish forces, which in the two battles had lost twenty-eight guns and mortars and over two thousand prisoners.[68]

The Seraskir, most of whose forces had been dispersed, retired to Erzerum, where he tried to rally his reserves and build up a defense. Paskevich, however, gave him no respite, but advanced against him without opposition. Feeble attempts at a stand before the city collapsed, and on June 27 the Russians occupied this vital center.[69]

This was the climax of the campaign. Paskevich was not able to capture either Trebizond or Sivas, while Turkish efforts to recover their losses failed at Baiazet and Baiburt. The war ended in September, 1829, with the Treaty of Adrianople.

In the campaign of 1829, as in 1828, Paskevich, once he had overcome his panic, made the most of his opportunities and accomplished all that anyone could expect. Lt. Gen. William Monteith, a British observer with his army, summed up the campaign of 1829 in the following words:

> This was one of the most fortunate and glorious campaigns in the whole of the Russian annals. It had lasted only four months; and ... it was through one of the strongest countries in the world, defended by an army of at least 80,000 men, with 200 pieces of cannon, who had at least a year to prepare their defence. The Russian army never mustered more than 25,000 men of all arms, and seldom were more than 12,000 in action. Their losses amounted altogether to 4000 men—a small number, considering that the plague had twice broken out. Thanks to the excellent arrangements that had been made, the army was well supplied with provisions, and the strength of the troops had never been taxed by unnecessary haste. ... The numerical strength of the army employed in the conquest of Erzeroum was not half what the service required; yet through the genius of Prince Paskevich, it was brought to a glorious termination.[70]

68. *Ibid.*, II, 115-22.
69. *Ibid.*, pp. 123-63.
70. William Monteith, *Kars and Erzeroum; with the Campaigns of Prince Paskiewitch, in 1828 and 1829* (London, 1856), pp. 300-301.

Thus Paskevich, whom the Tsar had named Count of Erivan in 1827, won new laurels in 1828 and 1829 and was rapidly rising to become the foremost soldier of Nicholas I.

In spite of his successes, however, Paskevich continued to suffer from a gnawing feeling of insecurity, as shown by his treatment of Osten-Sacken during these campaigns. The latter, an admirable soldier and well liked by all, including Paskevich, took over the ineffective staff and made it into a highly efficient organization, which handled the administrative problems to perfection.[71] In 1829, however, Paskevich's liking and trust began to turn into sharp suspicion. One cause of this was the arrival of an issue of the *Journal des Débats* containing an article that asserted that Paskevich was not a very good general and that his successes had resulted from the skill of his chief of staff and several Decembrist exiles in his army. After Osten-Sacken, instead of destroying the paper, had let Paskevich see it, he became suspicious of Osten-Sacken and Pushchin, one of the Decembrists. Not long after, Paskevich, after waiting an hour, sent Osten-Sacken with the cavalry to pursue the Turks fleeing from battle. He followed them for about seven miles, catching a number of stragglers, but as the main force had had an hour's start he could not overtake them and so returned to save the horses from useless exertion. Paskevich, in a rage, at once convened a military court, which ordered a stern rebuke to Osten-Sacken for failure to carry out orders and for an ineffective pursuit. Paskevich put him under house arrest and dismissed him as chief of staff.[72]

Similarly, when Muraviev returned in triumph from a great victory that he and Burtsev had won, Paskevich, instead of giving him warm praise, showered him with criticism for an alleged excessive loss of men.[73]

Gen. Monteith, whose admiration for Paskevich was very keen, observed, however: "In his outward deportment Prince Paskevich was hasty and sometimes violent, which appears to be a fashionable piece of affectation among the Russian officers—perhaps from a desire of immitating the eccentricities of Suvarof—..."[74] Unfortunately, what Gen. Monteith regarded as mere affectations were characteristics

71. Murav'ev, *Russkii Arkhiv*, XXXI (1893), Pt. III, 321-23.
72. Graf Dmitrii Osten-Saken, "Nikolai Nikolaevich Murav'ev v 1828-1856 gg.," *Russkaia Starina*, XI (1874), 536; Rozen, *Russkaia Starina*, XLI (1884), 326-29.
73. Rozen, p. 327.
74. Monteith, pp. 302-3.

that Paskevich repeatedly displayed. He himself realized this, for at the end of the Persian War he wrote to the Grand Duke Michael:

My character has even completely changed. Frequently demanding the impossible from people and circumstances, I cannot maintain myself in my usual frame of mind. The wish to accomplish more than my duty is extraordinary; obstacles irritate me, and involuntarily this shows forth frequently and greatly, and this pleases no one.[75]

75. Shcherbatov, III, 105.

CHAPTER III. NICHOLAS I AS A MILITARY MAN

In spite of his ardent interest in military affairs, during the Persian War Nicholas could not take an active part therein. The arrest, investigation, trial, and punishment of the Decembrist conspirators, grave financial stringency, his coronation in Moscow, and the reorganization of the government, along with other problems, demanded so much of the Tsar's attention that he was unable to concern himself directly with the conflict beyond the Caucasus. To be sure, he did play a part in the Persian War by sending Paskevich, and later Diebitsch, to handle matters to his satisfaction, as well as by sending frequent messages to his envoys. Nevertheless, he relied on Paskevich to win the war and made no effort to take command himself. It was only after these more pressing problems had been solved that he could assume the role that he felt was in keeping with his training and ability as a professional soldier.

The reign of Nicholas I, which began with the booming of cannon on the Senate Square, was to end with cannonfire at the beleaguered city of Sevastopol. There was much that was fitting in this, for the Tsar thought of himself as a military man, and war and army occupied much of his thinking throughout his reign. Although he had not been permitted to take part in the campaigns of the Napoleonic Wars, as a younger son he had been trained for a soldier's life, which he embraced with enthusiasm. He looked the part to perfection. Tall, handsome, and with a fine physique, he had a magnificent posture that gave added dignity to the uniforms that were his regular attire, and his sonorous voice carried to all corners of huge parade grounds. He had a taste for spartan austerity in his personal life, which he carried to the point of regularly sleeping on a hard camp bed.[1] In the eyes of the Tsar, the military profession, marked as it was by unquestioning obedience and willingness to offer one's life for Tsar and fatherland, was the most noble open to man, which naturally led him to surround himself with a numerous suite of aides-de-camp, general adjutants,

1. M. O. Gershenzon, ed., *Epokha Nikolaia I* (Moscow, 1911), pp. 21-22.

and other military functionaries. Indeed, Nicholas' belief in the superiority of soldiers to civilians led him to fill many high government posts with military men. In the 1840's, for example, ten of the thirteen men who held ministerial portfolios were general adjutants, including Count Egor Kankrin, the able minister of finance, Count V. Adlerberg, chief of the Postal Department, and Count N. A. Protasov, Over Procurator of the Holy Synod. The latter, a dashing cavalry officer, was in control of the administration of the Orthodox church. Only the ministries of Foreign Affairs, Education, and Justice remained under civilian control, perhaps because military men suitable for these posts were not available.[2]

During his long reign Nicholas devoted much thought and effort to the army, striving to make it more efficient and to eliminate abuses and failings. He constantly sought to punish commanders who peculated at the expense of the rank and file and reduced the term of service to fifteen years for men with excellent conduct records. He did not, however, introduce any fundamental changes into the army system, and his attention often centered on minor matters. Before he became tsar he kept a diary of his journey about the country, in which, according to Baron Korff, his biographer:

> on military aspects almost all the notes refer to mere unimportant superficialities of military service—clothing, alignment, marching, and the like—and did not touch one essential part of military organization, administration, or the moral spirit and attitude of the troops. Even about so important a side of military affairs as musketry there is no mention whatever, and about hospitals, schools, and the like, there is reference only in passing, extremely briefly.[3]

This rather limited outlook on military affairs continued after he had become tsar. One of his first acts after his accession was to design a new uniform with long trousers instead of breeches and gaiters. The uniform jacket had a single row of nine buttons in place of two rows of six each. The Tsar expected to achieve substantial savings thereby.[4]

Another matter in which the Emperor took great interest was the wearing of mustaches—a privilege possessed only by soldiers. Even the medical personnel of the military administration did not have this right, and the civilian directors of military bands, who directed mus-

2. *Ibid.*; also M. A. Polievtkov, *Nikolai I. Bibliografiia i obzor tsarstvovaniia* (St. Petersburg, 1914), p. 321.
3. N. Epanchin, *Ocherk pokhoda 1829 goda v Evropeiskoi Turtsii* (3 vols.; St. Petersburg, 1905-1907), I, 65, citing Schilder, I, 70.
4. Schiemann, II, 106-7.

tachioed musicians, must perforce be cleanshaven.[5] On occasion Nicholas himself personally enforced this rule. Once, at a review in a provincial town, he happened to notice in the crowd a man with a long hussar-type mustache. The monarch rode up to him and asked where he had done military service. On receiving the answer that he had had no service, the Tsar ordered the commandant of the town to take "this mustachioed beast" to the guardhouse and to shave off his mustaches, which was duly done.[6]

As the above incident indicates, Nicholas at times acted in hasty and capricious fashion. Gen. N. N. Muraviev, who captured Kars in 1855, wrote that in 1837, when he commanded the Fifth Corps, the Sovereign was highly irritable and hostile to him at reviews held at Nikolaevsk and Sevastopol—probably, Muraviev suggests, because his enemies had slandered him to the Tsar. The latter punished commanders of units if their troops were out of alignment or did not maintain a correct posture. At Sevastopol he complained acidly at a review because the drummers were formed in two ranks instead of three, and because two selected sentries were not of the same height. He also was annoyed that the parading troops did not maintain long enough strides, and because the men did not stand perfectly still in ranks. He became furious when, in a severe gust of wind, an ensign held his standard with two hands instead of the prescribed one. And, to cap the climax, some of the men lost their helmets in the high wind. A little later, Nicholas spied a sergeant in the guard of honor who was not standing properly, and at once deprived him of his chevrons and his good conduct badge, which meant that the man lost the right to secure release from service after serving fifteen years. Muraviev received a stiff rebuke from Nicholas for all these failings, and shortly thereafter the latter removed him from command of the 5th Corps.[7]

In 1840 the Emperor vented his wrath on a Gen. B., who, as assistant commandant of St. Petersburg, had the special obligation to supervise the conduct of the officers in the city and to see that they did not gamble. Unfortunately for him, Nicholas learned that the general himself had erred, having won one hundred thousand rubles from a certain Iakovlev. During a review the Tsar called B., who promptly galloped up. "I congratulate you," Nicholas said. B. bowed

5. "Spodvizhniki Nikolaia I," in Gershenzon, p. 21.
6. Neizvestnyi, "Za mnogo let. Vospominaniia," *Russkaia Starina*, LXXXI (1894), 177.
7. Murav'ev, *Russkii Arkhiv*, XXXII (1894), Pt. III, 516-34.

with pleasure, expecting to receive a decoration. "You play *banc* with great skill," the Tsar continued, "and have won one hundred thousand rubles from Iakovlev." B.'s chagrin, which was great, was even greater the next day when he learned that he had been named commandant at Irkutsk, in eastern Siberia.[8]

An even more striking case of the Tsar's punishing hand came in 1837, when he visited the Caucasus. In Tiflis he learned that Col. Dadianov, son-in-law of Baron Rosen, viceroy of the Caucasus, had shamefully abused his enlisted men and had obtained unlawful profit. The angry monarch called Dadianov to him at a review in the center of Tiflis, tore his epaulets from his shoulders, and at once packed him off, in the company of a Gendarme officer, to prison in a fortress in Russia. This example of the Tsar's arbitrary punishment shocked many of the Westerners in St. Petersburg. The French Ambassador wrote: "La conviction qu'il y a une justice rendue après mûr examen et connaissance de cause, ne vient à pensée de personne."[9]

Nicholas also could inflict cruel punishment on commoners. In 1827 a soldier forwarded a secret note written by an imprisoned Moscow student, but was detected and punished by a sentence to run the gantlet through one thousand men, four times. This meant four thousand blows on his back.[10] In 1847 the police swooped down upon the Society of Saints Cyril and Methodius in Kiev and, although it was not especially subversive, the members received severe sentences. The noted painter and poet, Taras Shevchenko, who in the Tsar's eyes seemed to be the most dangerous of the group, received a lengthy sentence to serve as a private in a penal battalion at Orenburg, under strict supervision. Nicholas added: "Under strictest surveillance and with writing and drawing prohibited."[11]

Oddly enough, the Emperor prided himself that the death penalty, which the Empress Elizabeth had abolished in the mid-eighteenth century, did not exist in Russia—although some of the ferocious floggings that he countenanced meant almost certain death. In 1827 Nicholas learned from his governor general in Southern Russia that two Jewish subjects had fled across the frontier into the Turkish Empire, thus violating the strict quarantine against the plague. The complainant added that only the death penalty for such offenses would

8. M. D., "N. O. Sukhozanet—Imperator Nikolai Pavlovich," *Russkaia Starina*, LXV (1890), 228.
9. Schiemann, III, 330.
10. *Ibid.*, II, 209.
11. *Ibid.*, IV, 124-25.

succeed in ending them. On this report the Tsar wrote in his own hand: "Send the guilty ones through one thousand men twelve times [i.e., twelve thousand blows]. God be thanked, there has been no death penalty with us and I shall not introduce it."[12]

The powerful ruler also had his merciful moments, however. In 1842, a private of a model regiment deserted with the intention of seeing his mother, who was seriously ill. Although desertion was a grave offense, Nicholas closed the case by writing on the report of it the resolution: "Pardon."[13] At a great review in the late summer of 1852 he showed both fury and mercy. The Tsar was greatly pleased with the parade step of the marching regiments, but when the 5th Rifle Battalion passed the reviewing point, one of the privates left the ranks and stopped before the august personage, apparently to present a complaint. Nicholas, highly astonished and angry, delivered a sharp rebuke to the battalion commander for this unheard-of violation of discipline. Then he turned on the soldier, ordering his arrest and then his punishment, consisting of sending him "through the ranks" [the gantlet], of one thousand men, three times. The private actually went "down the green street," but suffered no ill consequences, for Nicholas gave instructions that this was to be only a symbolic punishment, with the men merely touching his back with their rods rather than beating him. After that the culprit was transferred to an infantry regiment.[14]

Another case involved one Ensign Brakkel of the Guards Jaeger regiment, who had mistakenly released from confinement an officer under arrest for a minor fault. Nicholas had him imprisoned in a fortress and intended to reduce him to a private. Before this took place, however, Gen. Ivan Skobelev, a favorite of the Tsar, interceded for young Brakkel, saying that he was fully repentant and was so broken by the disgrace to his parents that his health was endangered. Skobelev added that he was a fine, noble young man, with high and admirable feelings. The Emperor wrote on the petition: "I can't refuse old Skobelev anything; I hope that after his soldierly admonitions to the offender, out of Brakkel will again come forth a fine officer. Release him and transfer him to an army regiment with the same rank."[15]

Perhaps because of his experience with the insurgents of December,

12. "Vzgliad imperatora Nikolaia I-go na smertnuiu kazn' v Rossii v 1827 godu," *Russkaia Starina*, XL (1883), 660.
13. Mikhail Sokolovskii, "Imperator Nikolai v voenno-sudnykh konfirmatsiiakh," *Russkaia Starina*, CXXIV (1905), 420.
14. Neizvestnyi, "Za mnogo let," *Russkaia Starina*, LXXXII (1894), 110-12.
15. "Ivan Nikitich Skobelev," *Russkaia Starina*, I (1870), 539.

perhaps because of his personal inclinations, Nicholas went out of his way to make himself popular with the army. Less than a year after the suppression of the rebellious troops, the French Ambassador at St. Petersburg wrote to the Quai d'Orsay that the Tsar had neglected nothing in trying to win the attachment of the army, especially by showing himself to his troops under the most pleasing circumstances. The report added: "I think that he will be able to count on the enthusiasm that he has been able to inspire in his soldiers."[16] His favor was especially bestowed on the Preobrazhenskii regiment. This famous Guards unit was the first to come to protect the imperial family on December 14, 1825, and not one of its officers took part in the conspiracy. As a sign that he never forgot this, every year at one o'clock on the afternoon of December 14 the Tsar and the Empress, in a simple carriage, without aides, drove to the Preobrazhenskii barracks for an inspection and a sort of family reunion with officers and enlisted men, at which Nicholas expressed his special favor to this regiment. This ceremony continued as long as one of the soldiers of 1825 was still on duty.[17]

The Emperor seems to have radiated extraordinary charm upon his close associates. V. I. Dehn, son of Ivan Dehn, general of engineers who was close to the Tsar, and himself an engineer, related that he suffered much unpleasantness from the Grand Duke Michael, chief commander of the Corps of Engineers. Because he disliked the commander of the Guards Sapper battalion, Michael vented his spite upon the sapper officers, who felt little regret at Michael's death in 1849. On the other hand, Nicholas was a benevolent commander, who charmed the officers by his kindly treatment. Hence, in contrast to their attitude toward Michael, the officers sincerely and warmly loved him. From 1850 to 1853 young Dehn, now an aide de camp to the Tsar, reported daily to him at the palace—a ceremony in which he took real delight. "I loved him with all my loving soul," he wrote.[18]

But while Nicholas lavished favor upon those who enjoyed his confidence, the events of December, 1825, had left him with a persistent fear of the officers of his army. Count A. Kh. Benckendorff, head of the secret police, had a number of secret agents in the army to gather information regarding the attitude of the officers. The Ger-

16. Schiemann, II, 181n.
17. D. G. Kolokol'tsov, "Leib-gvardii Preobrazhenskii polk v vospominaniiakh ego starago ofitsera," *Russkaia Starina*, XXXVIII (1883), 291.
18. V. I. Dehn, "Zapiski," *Russkaia Starina*, LXV (1890), 78-79.

man historian Schiemann asserts that one of the many motives that impelled the Tsar into war with Turkey in 1828 was fear of the political outlook of his officers, in whom the spirit of the Decembrists still lived on.[19] That this fear had some justification was shown by the fact that on August 27, 1827, the police arrested a large number of officers who had been circulating verses of a "revolutionary" content and also copies of the letter that Ryleev wrote to his wife before his execution.[20] Even during the war with Turkey in 1828 the same fear haunted the Tsar, causing him to detail a large police force to accompany the troops in the field. One of the duties of the police was to open all letters sent by the soldiers and officers, who protested against this measure. Even the foreign officers and envoys with the Tsar's headquarters along the Danube turned in their letters to officers of the Tsar's staff for censoring. No disaffection, however, was found.[21]

Another feature of the Emperor's relations with the army was the great number of inspection trips that he constantly made, both at home and abroad. Every year he made several of these excursions, frequently starting out without warning to anyone, probably so that no preparations might be made to cover up failings and abuses. Of necessity, however, they were hasty and superficial, as the visitor often would stay for only a day or two in a city, hurriedly inspecting troops, hospitals, barracks, and other military objects, without being able to investigate with any thoroughness. The official survey of the military establishment for the first twenty-five years of his reign stated: "In unceasing activity, Your Imperial Majesty, in the course of the twenty-five years, was pleased to cover during Your August journeys: by land, 124,486 *versts*, and by sea 12,850 *versts*; of them 114,640 *versts* within the limits of the Empire, and 22,696 abroad."[22] One such journey, in 1837, was to the Caucasus—a very difficult and exhausting trip. Nicholas wrote to the Empress, however, that he was glad he had gone there, as one must know a country in order to make plans about it. "I now know more about it than all those who will wish to argue about the measures to take, for the most part of them, if not all, have not seen it and judge it like blind men."[23] As, however,

19. Schiemann, II, 210.
20. *Ibid.*, n.
21. *Ibid.*, II, 237-38.
22. "Istoricheskoe obozrenie voenno-sukhoputnago upravleniia s 1825 po 1850 god," *Sbornik Imperatorskago Russkago Istoricheskago Obshchestva*, XCVIII (1896), 317. Hereafter cited as *Sbornik IRIO*. (A verst is approximately two-thirds of a mile.)
23. Schiemann, III, 331n.

the Tsar had really seen very little of this large and diversified region, he was no more than a one-eyed man in the kingdom of the blind.

Although Nicholas was an ardent traveler, his summers were usually reserved for maneuvers and other military exercises, chiefly at Krasnoe Selo, not far from the capital. In 1835, however, he arranged joint maneuvers of his Guards with the Guards and army units of his father-in-law, King Frederick Wilhelm III of Prussia. The Russian Guards went by sea to Danzig and then marched to Kalisz, near Thorn in Prussian Poland, where on August 15 a series of drills, parades, and maneuvers took place in an atmosphere of cordial feeling. The Russian forces returned to St. Petersburg the way they had come.[24] In 1839 a Col. von Gagern accompanied the Prince of Orange to the Russian court. In his report on his observations he stressed the Tsar's extreme fondness for taking an active part in trifling military matters. "His greatest weakness is his exhausting passion for military exercizes and maneuvers. . . . If around the Russian court they speak with the greatest caution about the Emperor himself, then on this point all his adjutants admit that parades, camps, and field maneuvers [are very tiring]." On August 8 Col. von Gagern attended maneuvers of the whole Guard—forty-eight battalions and three cavalry divisions, totalling from forty to fifty thousand men. All the formations were prescribed and carefully regulated in detail.[25]

But, while Nicholas doubtless derived great satisfaction from inspections and maneuvers and from the dazzling reviews to which he gave so much attention, he doubtless felt that the real métier of the soldier is war. As he had been denied a part in the Napoleonic campaigns, it is not surprising that, when opportunity presented itself in the Turkish War in 1828, he rejected the advice of his wife and his staff and joined the army on the lower Danube.[26]

Although as early as 1826 both the Turkish and the Russian governments realized that war lay ahead, neither power made effective preparations for it. The Turks in 1828 were especially poorly prepared, as for years the Greek revolt had been exhausting the Empire's strength, a French army occupied the Morea, and in 1827 much of the Turkish fleet was destroyed at Navarino. To make matters worse, in June, 1826, the ever mutinous Janissaries revolted and the

24. *Istoriia leib-gvardii Egerskago polka za sto let, 1796-1896* (St. Petersburg, 1896), pp. 267-69.

25. N. K. Schilder, "Nemets i Frantsuz v zapiskakh o Rossii 1839 g.," *Russkaia Starina*, LI (1886), 28 and 43.

26. SVM, II, Pt. III, *Imperatorskaia Glavnaia Kvartira*, 238-41.

Sultan, with the backing of the Moslem clergy, the middle class, and many of his regular troops, proclaimed a holy war and massacred many thousands of them and their sympathizers. Those who escaped retaliated by setting terrible fires in Constantinople and other cities, although they could not maintain an effective revolt. The Janissaries had long ago ceased to be effective troops, but the new army that the Sultan was building was by no means ready to replace them. In all there were only about one hundred and eighty thousand men, of whom many were irregulars of no great value. A new force of regular infantry numbering sixty thousand promised to form a valuable nucleus of a modern army, but their discipline and training were not yet good and proper officers were lacking. There was a considerable force of artillery, but the guns pulled by oxen or poorly trained horses were clumsy and lacked mobility. The cavalry, however, with swift, sturdy horses, deserved some respect, not for their discipline, but for their mobility and speed. Nevertheless, on the whole the Turkish army was no match for the Russians, either in quality or in numbers. At first they could only try to hold along the Danube, without attempting to defend Moldavia and Wallachia, as their weak forces were spread very thin. Their main reliance was on their fortresses, the poverty of the country, the bad communications and lack of good drinking water, the climate, and disease. With a weak army and a powerless navy, Turkey had no chance of success unless someone came to their aid. The Sultan and his government realized this, but they felt their lives would be forfeit if they made concessions to the Russians and so they drifted into war.[27]

While the Russian government was not eager for war with Turkey and had no pressing territorial aims, it realized that only force could compel the Turks to free the Greeks and to permit free trade, vital to Russia, through the Dardanelles. Rights for the Serbs and greater security in the Transcaucasus also interested Russia, although these were probably of secondary importance. Nicholas had a difficult time formulating his objectives if war should come, as he did not know whether France and Britain might intervene, and there was considerable fear that Austria might oppose Russia. As late as February, 1828, Count Diebitsch, chief of the Tsar's personal staff, wrote that because they did not know how the Western powers would act, for the present they should only occupy the Principalities. As it turned out, the Rus-

27. Epanchin, I, 117-22. This work, a careful and detailed history of the military aspects of the war of 1828-1829, has supplied much of the material for this chapter.

sians achieved so little in 1828 that the powers felt no need to act, while in 1829 the Russian successes happened so quickly that they had no time to do so. But St. Petersburg was never sure how far they dared go.[28]

This state of affairs affected the Russian preparations for war, as with no definite objectives or plans it was impossible to know how far to prepare. Financial stringency was another concern, with Count Kankrin, the finance minister, seeking to keep the costs of the war to a minimum. It was only on January 20, 1828—with war only a few months away—that Count Chernyshev, minister of war, produced a preliminary estimate of 71.8 million rubles. Kankrin, however, took the position that "the more cheaply we fight, the more we raise the might of Russia." Starting from this assumption, he proceeded to object to many of the items of expenditure and finally, on April 10, he persuaded Chernyshev and Diebitsch to accept an estimate of 59.0 million instead of 71.8 million. This, of course, soon proved to be far from sufficient, but when Diebitsch and Chernyshev made supplementary proposals, Kankrin objected bitterly that they had not been included in the estimate decided on. All this made the preparation of the army for action a difficult matter.[29]

Even worse was the divided command of the army. Nominally Field Marshal L. A. P. Wittgenstein, an elderly veteran of the Napoleonic Wars, was at the head of the Second Army, in southwestern Russia, although the real authority there lay with Gen. P. D. Kiselev, the young and able chief of staff. Even he, however, had little power, as Diebitsch, acting for the Tsar, decided all matters, important and trivial. Because he, in the capital, was one thousand miles from the headquarters of the Second Army, the preparations were often faulty. Only at the last minute did he learn that it was necessary to replace many of the muskets of the Second Army, which were defective. The Russian fortresses were in poor condition and the supplies of gunpowder were insufficient because St. Petersburg did not know the real state of affairs. Wittgenstein, finding a shortage of entrenching tools for his troops, cautiously asked that as soon as war should come the authorities should obtain them "sufficiently quickly." Apparently he had been snubbed so often that he hesitated to make a definite request. There was a comedy of errors concerning the buying of

28. *Ibid.*, III, 358-62.
29. *Ibid.*, I, 351-57.

horses for the Pioneer battalions: the Tsar first gave the order to buy them, then revoked it, and then once more ordered the purchase.[30]

The Second Army enjoyed considerable popularity in Russian society, especially among the younger military men, for, unlike the stern and harsh commanders of the First Army, Wittgenstein and Kiselev were kind to their subordinates and treated them like intelligent human beings. Kiselev had much concern for the enlisted men— in marked contrast to most commanders.[31] Unfortunately, although he was very able and an extremely hard worker, he had an enemy in the person of Count Toll, who wanted his position and, failing to get it, did what he could to make his life miserable. Diebitsch, however, valued Kiselev highly and worked well with him.[32] In August, 1828, Diebitsch, in a letter to Nicholas, singled out Kiselev as his most valuable assistant. "The untiring Kiselev continues to display the same zeal and the same distinguished capabilities that you, Sire, know in him. There could not possibly be anyone better than he."[33]

Kiselev was always careful to be tactful and considerate with Wittgenstein, while at the same time he was secretly corresponding with Diebitsch about the affairs of the Second Army. During the campaign of 1828 the position of Wittgenstein was impossible, as the Tsar joined the Second Army in its advance into Turkey, taking with him Diebitsch and his own staff. At first Nicholas I conferred with the aged Field Marshal and then issued orders through Diebitsch, but before long he merely told the former about what he intended to do. This so angered Wittgenstein that on several occasions when men came to him for orders he said testily that he did not command anything. Even when the Tsar was not with the army he sent his instructions regarding the campaign to Diebitsch, practically ignoring the titular commander of the Second Army.[34] This behavior obviously did violence to the principle of concentrated command and responsibility. Moreover, the Emperor's decisions in many instances proved far from wise, so that the campaign went slowly and was marked by a number of setbacks. He was much averse to bloodshed and ordered his gen-

30. *Ibid.*, I, 316-20, 209.
31. *Ibid.*, I, 105-7; F. Fonton, *Vospominaniia. Iumoristicheskiia, politicheskiia, i voennyia, pis'ma iz glavnoi kvartiry Dunaiskoi armii, v 1828 i 1829 gg.* (3rd ed., 2 vols.; Leipzig, 1866), I, 42-45.
32. Epanchin, I, 105-8.
33. "Perepiska Nikolaia I s grafom Iv. Iv. Dibichem Zabalkanskim vo vremia russko-turetskoi voiny 1828-1829 g." *Russkaia Starina*, XXVII (1880), 765.
34. *Ibid.*, pp. 101-10, 511-26; Epanchin, I, 104-5.

The Balkan Campaigns of 1828/29 and 1853/54

erals to avoid it as far as possible, thereby greatly limiting their freedom of action.[35]

The presence of the Tsar with the advancing army attracted a huge following, for, in addition to his bemedalled staff, he had with him Count Nesselrode, Baron A. H. Jomini, a former general under Napoleon, and numerous civil officials of the Foreign Office and other departments. Moreover, all sorts of foreign personages of civil and military status went with the Russian headquarters: there were French, Prussian, and Austrian envoys, each with a large entourage, as well as lesser diplomats. Nicholas tried to run both the war and the business of the Empire from his tent.[36]

The enormous suite that accompanied the Emperor, as well as the glittering diplomatic corps, and their innumerable attendants, required over ten thousand horses to transport them and their often luxurious provisions. Thus the extravagant demands for hay and oats, of which the army had far too little, that resulted from the presence of the Tsar and his entourage played havoc with the communications of the army and helped to cause the disaster that overtook the Russian forces in 1828.[37]

The Russian campaign of 1828 was largely a failure, for which the Russian commanders (essentially the Tsar and Diebitsch) were to blame. They started late, which lost them the favorable moment to achieve easy successes, and, from reasons of economy, they used far too few men to assure victory. Even worse, they misused the ninety thousand they did have by occupying all of the Principalities without need and by uselessly attacking a number of fortresses, especially Shumla and Silistria. Although they had a strong fleet in the Black Sea, they did not use it against the key fortress of Varna until almost too late, and they were slow in bringing their powerful siege artillery into play. Fortunately for them, however, the Turks also made grave errors, while the Russian mistakes "were redeemed solely by the innate excellence of the Russian troops. The self-sacrificing obedience of the commanders, the endurance of the soldiers, their courage in suffering and their unshakable valor in danger"—these were the qualities that warded off disaster.[38]

Much the same criticism came from the elderly Gen. Adj. Prince

35. Schiemann, II, 246-49, 259.
36. Fonton, I, 68-76.
37. Helmut von Moltke, *Der russisch-türkische Feldzug in der europäischen Türkei 1828 und 1829* (Berlin, 1845), pp. 28-29.
38. Moltke, I, 229-38.

Vasil'chikov at the end of the campaign, in his "Aperçu sur la campagne de l'année 1829." He asserted that the main reason for failure was the underestimation of the Turks, which led the Russians to try to win the war with ninety thousand men. This proved woefully insufficient to take Varna, Silistria, and Shumla, and the Russians were fortunate to capture Varna, while they failed to take the other two. At the outset they mobilized only eighteen thousand men, and only five weeks later did they mobilize fifty thousand, which was still too few. They expected the fortresses to fall at their mere approach. Above all they failed to realize the strength of Shumla.[39]

At times Nicholas' conduct during the campaign was rash and dangerous. He was charmed when a group of Zaporogian Cossacks, whose ancestors had fled Russia and settled in Turkey, deserted the Turks and joined the Russian forces at Satunovo. The Tsar rewarded them lavishly. When the Russian troops began to cross the Danube, he had twelve of the Cossacks row him across, with the Cossack Ataman at the helm. This was a foolhardy venture, for the Cossacks could easily have delivered him to the Turks, who would doubtless have paid them well; but fortune smiled on him, for the Cossacks did not betray him. Next he visited the army besieging Brailov, where he came down with a bad case of fever. On his recovery he insisted on visiting a large siege battery within easy range of the Turkish artillery and by the commotion caused by his presence drew a dangerous fire from the enemy.[40]

The campaign started auspiciously with the crossing at Satunovo, where the Turks fled in panic. This enabled the Russians to besiege several fortresses that seemed necessary to ensure firm communications with Bucharest. While they masked Varna and Silistria with small forces, they began a real siege of Brailov by means of batteries and mines and soon opened considerable breaches in the defenses. When they attempted to storm the city, however, the Turks by a furious defense stopped the attacking force in its tracks. The troops refused to concede defeat for some time and kept trying to renew the assault, until finally the Grand Duke Michael, in charge of the siege, ordered them to withdraw. The Russians lost over two thousand men in this attempt, including three generals. The deteriorating position of the defenders, however, as well as "the stubborn bravery" of the

39. N. K. Schilder, "Voina Rossii s Turtsiei v 1829 godu," *Russkaia Starina*, XXX (1881), 98-99.
40. SVM, II, Pt. III, *Imperatorskaia Glavnaia Kvartira*, pp. 243-51.

Russians, induced the Turkish commander to surrender.[41] While the Russians now had a secure crossing over the Danube, they permitted the Turkish troops to march out and make their way to Silistria to fight another day.

The Russian plan of campaign called for a rapid push on through the Balkan mountains to capture Adrianople, from which they could then march on Constantinople. Before they could cross the Balkans, however, the Russian leaders felt it imperative to capture the great fortress of Shumla, as it would threaten their rear as they pushed southward. Varna was also of the greatest importance, but as they could not hope to capture it without the aid of the Russian fleet, which was attacking Anapa, at the eastern end of the Black Sea, the main Russian army, led by Nicholas, Wittgenstein, and Diebitsch, marched against Shumla, leaving a small force before Varna and another besieging Silistria on the Danube.

Although the Turks made no opposition as the Russian army marched into position before Shumla, the situation of the attackers quickly proved to be disastrous. Shumla was impregnable for this Russian army, for it was situated in a horseshoe of hills, with the Turks strongly holding the gaps through them and with free communication to the south and west. The attackers could neither storm the defenses nor starve the Turks out. Consequently, the Russians soon found themselves holding a great arc of redoubts around Shumla, while from their central position the Turks made harassing attacks on the Russian earthworks, thinly held by an army of forty-two thousand men.

It quickly proved difficult to provision this army, for it could obtain almost no food in Bulgaria, which the Turks had thoroughly stripped. Hence provisions had to come from Russia and in part from the Principalities. As long as the Russians had no port to use, their provisions had to come overland, requiring vast numbers of wagons. The Russian commanders, who had greatly underestimated the needs of this campaign, including the number of vehicles, soon found that it was impossible to haul enough provisions into Bulgaria. On September 9, Nicholas, who had recently moved from Shumla to Varna, wrote Diebitsch that he could not send him the provisions he had requested, as there were only five hundred measures of biscuits in Varna. The most that he could do was send some wagon trains of oats. In

41. Moltke, I, 96-100.

another letter on the same day he spoke of the shortage of provisions "that makes my hair stand on end" and said that they were already feeling the pinch. If ships of food did not soon come from Odessa, they would have to live on oats. The Tsar indignantly asked why the Intendant of the army had not reported this to Wittgenstein and why no one had known about it. "Here is a new illustration of the incapacity of the Field Marshal."[42]

This attempt to use Wittgenstein as a scapegoat for the impasse that Nicholas and Diebitsch themselves had created illustrates the gravity of the crisis. It was to get worse. Although shipments of provisions by sea soon remedied the shortage at Varna, it was impossible to provision the army at Shumla, which was on the verge of disaster. Hay—or the extreme lack of it—was its vulnerable spot.

When the main army had marched to Shumla in July, it had obtained enough hay for its multitude of animals by foraging along the road. They also had to depend on foraging in their new position, because it was impossible to haul enough hay for the army. The foragers, however, quickly exhausted the grass nearby, so that the mowers and their guards had to go farther and farther to find grass. After three weeks they had to go from ten to fourteen miles for it. The Turkish cavalry, with well-fed horses, frequently attacked the foragers who ventured so far. Moreover, the supply convoys soon exhausted the supplies of grass along the roads to the position at Shumla and their horses, oxen, and camels began to starve. By August the animals of the wagon trains, cavalry, and artillery began to die in increasing numbers. The troops sent out their hardest hit units, including many dismounted horsemen, while the remaining artillery horses could not haul the cannon and caissons. Many of the army's wagons were burned when the troops finally left Shumla in October.[43]

Sickness was another scourge. Before the campaign began both Wittgenstein and Diebitsch had requested forty more surgeons and large numbers of medical assistants and apothecaries for the Second Army, but Sir James Villiers, chief medical inspector, replied that it already had its full complement and he could not provide more. Repeated energetic demands and finally the intervention of the Tsar himself were required before Villiers belatedly ceased his evasion and supplied the necessary personnel.[44] Even so, the army had hospital

42. "Perepiska Nikolaia I," *Russkaia Starina*, XXIX (1880), 908-99.
43. Zatler, *Zapiski*, I, 116-18.
44. Epanchin, I, 252.

facilities for only eighteen hundred men. During the first months things went well, as there was little sickness, and the patients received good care and food. By September, however, the number of sick, which in July had been only 8,844, reached 39,824, and it continued to soar. Fever, often followed by pneumonia, dysentery, and scurvy ravaged the troops. As the medical facilities were far from sufficient, it became impossible to give the patients proper care. There was a great shortage of medical personnel, medicines were lacking, beds and linen were not available for many. Many patients lay on their overcoats on the ground, sometimes without shelter.[45]

As the Russian troops at Shumla grew weaker and weaker, the Turks, emboldened, made more frequent attacks, often with considerable success. By mid-August Diebitsch, who now was actually in command, shortened his lines by withdrawing from some redoubts. As the situation deteriorated, he attempted to lay the blame on Prince Eugene of Württemberg, husband of the Tsar's sister, who commanded an army corps under Diebitsch, and the two quarrelled bitterly. Finally, in early October after Eugene had left to join the army before Varna, the calamitous situation forced a retirement from Shumla. The troops, constantly harassed by the Turks, started with half-rations for four days. They were nine days en route, eking out their tiny supplies with damp grain collected from the fields, wild plums, and the flesh of dead oxen. Finally, the forces at Silistria sent them one day's supply of biscuits, after they had been without food for seven days. To add to their miseries, heavy rain fell, and in the resulting mud the wheels sank to the axles. Severe cold followed the rain, and of the enlisted men, who were still in linen summer trousers, two hundred froze to death. Eight hundred horses and oxen died, which forced the abandonment of four hundred wagons and their loads. Soldiers trying to help haul the cannon fell with exhaustion. Only with the help of the remaining cavalry horses was it possible to bring the guns to safety. The remnants of this army were no longer effective troops.[46]

With the Shumla campaign a complete failure and with no success possible at Silistria, Varna had become the major objective of the Russians, although here, too, their strategy had been faulty. In May and June it would have been possible to take it by a landing attack from the fleet, as the defenses were weak and the garrison small. The

45. F. K. Zatler, *O gospitaliakh v voennoe vremia* (St. Petersburg, 1861), pp. 111-16.
46. Zatler, *Zapiski*, I, 119-20.

fleet, however, was then busy at Anapa, a minor objective, and by the time it arrived in July there was a garrison of fifteen thousand good troops and the defenses were then strong. The navy blockaded the harbor and landed sailors on the dunes south of the city, while the reinforced army began determined siege operations, sapping, mining, and breaching the walls with artillery fire. This proved to be slow, difficult work, however. The Turks put up a furious resistance, marked by great bravery, heavy small-arms fire, and frequent sorties.[47]

While, in September, the siege was making steady progress, its success was far from certain. The Turks, emboldened by their successes at Shumla, bestirred themselves to move to the relief of Varna. Some Russian foragers south of the city encountered Turkish troops, and on September 10 one of the Tsar's aides, Col. Count Zaluski of the Polish army, led a force to reconnoiter. After passing through some dense woods he encountered a huge force of Turks, with artillery. Zaluski at once beat a retreat with his cavalry and four guns, leaving seven hundred men of the Life Guard Jaegers as rear guard. The Turks attacked the Jaegers and mauled them terribly, killing Gen. Gartong, their commander. Fighting their way back, the troops took a wrong turn and were cut to pieces. Eventually in some fashion slightly more than one-third of the Jaegers, most of them wounded, rejoined the army. In this affray the large army of Omer Vrione that was coming to relieve Varna made its first appearance.[48]

Nicholas and Diebitsch, who were commanding the besiegers, now realized that danger threatened. To meet it they had a force under Gen. Bistrom fortify a chain of heights less than a mile south of the Russian lines, while cavalry under Gen. Madatov (whom Paskevich had driven from the Caucasus) guarded the flank. In hopes that the main Turkish forces had not yet arrived, Diebitsch ordered Prince Eugene of Württemberg with some ten battalions of infantry, fourteen squadrons of horse, and considerable artillery, to attack the oncoming Turks. Eugene reconnoitered and found the situation highly unfavorable. Scouts and Bulgarian spies reported that perhaps forty thousand Turks, with many guns, had an entrenched camp on a hill, in heavily wooded terrain, where the Russian cannon would be at a heavy disadvantage. Twice Eugene sent to the Tsar, asking for reinforcements,

47. Moltke, I, 140-81.
48. P. A. Stepanov, "Pod Varnoiu, 10 Sentiabria 1828 g. (iz vospominaniia o leib-gvardii Egerskom polke)," *Russkaia Starina*, XV (1876), 364-76; Fonton, *Vospominaniia*, I, 161-62.

but Nicholas would not permit either Bistrom, holding a weak defense line, or Madatov, on the flank, to help. Eugene had no choice but to carry out his orders. So, believing that Diebitsch, who perhaps regarded him as a rival, had sent him to certain destruction, he advanced. His fears were soon realized. The terrain proved impossible for maneuver, and his artillery was of little use. Nevertheless, the Russian battalions attacked the Turkish fortified position at Kurtepe with great spirit, actually breaking into it for a time. The Turks, however, repulsed the Russians after terrific fighting, in which the attackers lost fourteen hundred men, including two generals, although the victors made no effort to pursue. Moltke declared: "The attack on Kurtepe appears as one of the most brilliant feats of arms of this campaign, and although it failed, through the moral impression that the bravery of the Russian troops made on the enemy, it subsequently contributed considerably to the success of the campaign. . . ."[49]

The Tsar and Diebitsch, however, regarded the outcome of the battle as a bad defeat and did not give Prince Eugene the credit due him for having escaped annihilation and for having skilfully extricated his troops from danger. Indeed, although Nicholas and Diebitsch had caused the disaster by compelling Eugene to attack in spite of his repeated warnings of danger, they did not hesitate to lay the blame on him.[50]

While the Russian high command had failed to achieve the destruction of Omer Vrione's army that would have resulted if Eugene had had a substantial force, the Turks were guilty of even greater errors. If, after Kurtepe, Omer Vrione had attacked the besiegers at Varna he almost certainly would have broken through and raised the siege. The Russians would then have had to retire across the Danube. Instead of doing so, however, the Turk sat quietly in his position for eleven days, during which he saw the Russians push the siege and eventually take the city. Then he hastily retreated.[51]

During these two weeks the besiegers steadily ate into the Turkish defenses. The defenders knew that a large Turkish army was near, but as it did nothing, their hope of aid dwindled. With their best men largely killed in sorties and their defenses about to collapse, on Sep-

49. Moltke, I, 184-95; Eugene, Prince of Württemberg, "Turetskii pokhod 1828 goda i sobytiia, za nim sledovavshiia. Zapiski Printsa Virtembergskago," *Russkaia Starina*, XXVIII (1880), 429-36.
50. Schiemann, II, 268-69; *Istoriia Egerskago polka*, pp. 221-22; Puzanov, *Istoriia leib-gvardii Grenaderskago polka* (St. Petersburg, 1845), pp. 173-78.
51. Moltke, I, 199-203.

tember 28 Yussuf Pasha with a large suite came to the Russian camp
and threw himself on the mercy of the Tsar. Isset Mehmet, with three
hundred men, retired to the citadel, threatening to blow it up, but on
the 29th he surrendered.[52]

Thus the Russian army, after so many defeats and disasters, had
won a considerable victory. It was far from decisive, as the Turks were
by no means crushed. Nevertheless, the Russian position was promis-
ing. They were firmly established south of the Danube and, with command of the sea and a suitable port through which to move supplies,
the provisioning of the army in the future would be easier. The campaign had ended in a draw instead of an outright defeat for the Russian arms. But in the light of the great hopes with which the Russians
had begun the campaign, even this was a considerable disappointment.

Another discouraging aspect of the late months of 1828 was that
disease continued to increase, so that in November there were 51,045
men sick. By the end of 1828 over 22,000 men had died—one-fifth of
all the troops.[53] The winter did not bring improvement, for the difficulty of hauling provisions made it almost impossible to correct many
of the failings. In addition, a sort of plague hit the army very heavily
early in 1829, although the mortality was not great.[54] In the first ten
months of the war (May, 1828 to February, 1829, inclusive) there
were 210,108 patients in the hospitals, 29,658 of whom died. With
the men killed in battle, the missing, and those frozen to death in the
cold of the winter, the total final losses came to about 40,000 men.[55]
The magnitude of these losses from disease did not promise well for
the second year of the war.

There was one very favorable factor—the conduct of the army
during the campaign. Moltke was high in his praise of the matériel
and the mobility of the artillery, although the accuracy of its fire was
not outstanding. The infantry had several failings—chiefly, imprac-
tical training, lack of rifles, and too heavy equipment. Nevertheless,
one could count on the orderly performance of the evolutions "and
the unshakable calm and steadfastness of the infantry in a position
once taken." The morale of the troops was excellent, for both officers
and men regarded war as an improvement of their lot.[56] The cavalry,

52. *Ibid.*, pp. 203-4.
53. Zatler, *O gospitaliakh*, p. 115.
54. *Ibid.*, pp. 116-20.
55. Epanchin, II, 51-53.
56. Moltke, I, 37-39.

however, did poorly. Moltke held that their chief weakness was the heaviness of the horses and the abundant feeding that they required, which was impossible on campaign. The Russian hussars (light cavalry) were larger and more heavily mounted than the Prussian cuirassiers (heavy cavalry). In consequence "They succumbed to the hardships of the marches and the bivouacs." Moreover, because of their heaviness, they were not mobile enough to cope with the Turkish spahis and were not suitable for scouting, outpost duty, and pursuit.[57] It is interesting to note that a discussion among young Russian officers at the end of the campaign came to much the same conclusions.[58]

Finally, Moltke pointed out the failings in strategy and in leadership that caused such meager results in the campaign of 1828, which, however, turned out better than one might have expected. He explained this as follows:

> All the mistakes were redeemed solely by the innate excellence of the Russian troops. The self-sacrificing obedience of the soldiers, their courage in suffering and their unshakable valor in danger, it was these qualities which exorcised the threatening fate at Shumla, and held the Seraskir in check, which conquered all deficiencies and all opposition at Varna and which even in defeat imposed in such a fashion on Omer Vrione that he, as though thunderstruck, remained motionless for ten days, while Varna, the bulwark of the empire, collapsed before his eyes. The measures of the field commanders must suffer the rebukes of the critics, . . . but the conduct at the siege at Brailov, the élan at Kurtepe, the perseverance in the mines and the approaches at Varna are . . . above all praise.[59]

Nicholas, who was severely disappointed in the results of the campaign, renounced his plan to join the army in 1829, as he realized that he hampered his commanders. "With me there everything goes badly: I do not want to intervene personally in affairs any more, and hence I shall not go to the army," he told his close friend, Count A. F. Orlov.[60] The able and energetic Count Diebitsch, who in 1829 replaced Field Marshal Wittgenstein as the commander at the front, enjoyed the full support of the Tsar, who adhered to his resolution to leave the conduct of operations to him. Although Nicholas often made suggestions on matters of strategy, he gave Diebitsch great latitude in carrying them out or rejecting them.

57. *Ibid.*, pp. 36-37.
58. Fonton, I, 197-201.
59. Moltke, I, 238.
60. Epanchin, II, 89.

At first the Emperor even gave up plans for further advances into Turkey. In a letter of November 1, 1828, he wrote to Diebitsch that they should avoid the mistakes of the preceding campaign in trying to accomplish too much by an offensive across the Balkans. Instead, he suggested that it would be prudent to renounce this plan and "to limit ourselves to consolidation in the regions already occupied by us and complete conquest of what is not yet in our power."[61] Diebitsch, who approved these plans, returned to St. Petersburg in December. He was especially anxious to command in the coming campaign, in which he hoped to capture Shumla. Already, however, Gen. Adj. I. V. Vasil'chikov had presented the Tsar with his "Aperçu sur la campagne de l'année 1829," calling for a new approach to the war. As a result of this, on November 19 Nicholas called a council of war, which urged a commander in chief with full power, assisted by an able chief of staff.[62]

The new plan called for taking Silistria as a first step toward pushing across the Balkans. Diebitsch, who only a few days before had opposed crossing the Balkans, with his usual flexibility accepted the new scheme, which, indeed, he had strongly advocated earlier. Actually, Silistria was not essential to the Russians, as their communications over the Danube were secure without it, and it could easily have been guarded by a corps of observation, which would have avoided delay caused by besieging it. But the Russian leaders apparently thought it a matter of prestige. Diebitsch was even very eager to capture Shumla, although Nicholas rebuked him several times for thinking of it, and eventually he dropped the idea.[63]

Diebitsch with some reluctance agreed to accept his old rival Baron Toll as his chief of staff, although he feared that Toll would not cooperate. As it turned out, they worked very well together and became warm friends.[64]

In his instructions for the coming campaign, Diebitsch ordered the commanders to train the troops during the whole winter, especially in extended order and marksmanship. He ordered that twenty ball and fifty blank cartridges per man be issued for the army, and insisted that poorly trained men get individual instruction. He also had special training for sharpshooters for tactics in broken country. At the same

61. "Perepiska Nikolaia I," *Russkaia Starina*, XXIX (1880), 919.
62. Epanchin, II, 16-23; Schilder, "Voina Rossii," *Russkaia Starina*, XXX (1881), 98-104.
63. Epanchin, III, 401-4.
64. *Ibid.*, II, 90-92.

time, however, he stressed to all that "the bayonet is the Russian weapon and that when advancing, without concern about losses, you always lose less and reach the goal of the troops—to conquer the enemy." Nonetheless, his instructions were remarkable, for in that period the usual stress was on the slow march and alignment in parades; musketry and open-order tactics were usually regarded as unnecessary.[65] Diebitsch also sought to moderate the terribly harsh treatment of the soldiers and the unnatural drill, and ordered that the commanders provide their men with fresh vegetables, bath houses, warm clothing during the spring months, fresh meat, and clean quarters.[66]

In the planning for the campaign of 1829, Diebitsch was fortunate that there was little of the constant preoccupation with avoiding even tiny expenditures that had preceded the last one. Taught by the sad experiences of 1828, the authorities felt that it was necessary to give the army what it needed, without striving for petty economies.[67] Only in manpower was there skimping. Although the special committee that had drawn up the plans for the campaign wanted to have abundant troops—some as many as one hundred and seventy thousand or two hundred thousand—Nicholas, while he realized the advantages that would flow from having a large army, believed that the experience of 1828 had shown that it was impossible to provision a great host in the Balkan theater of war. Hence it was decided to limit the army to one hundred and twenty thousand men, trusting to bold and decisive measures to defeat the Turks.[68]

During the winter Diebitsch and Toll made great efforts to solve the supply problem, amassing huge quantities of flour and oats in the border provinces and forming wagon trains to move provisions. Thanks to the fact that Varna, a highly useful port, was now available, the army could avoid the overland haul, and only the problem of moving supplies from the base to the troops proved troublesome. On the whole, there were no great difficulties in supplying the troops in the field and, once the Balkans had been crossed, the army obtained abundant food both by the capture of enemy supplies and by purchase from the inhabitants. Disease, however, proved to be a terrible foe and its effects were still felt long after the end of hostilities.[69]

65. Epanchin, II, 59.
66. *Ibid.*, II, 98-101.
67. *Ibid.*, p. 63.
68. *Ibid.*, III, 385-86.
69. Zatler, *Zapiski*, I, 121-27.

Because of very heavy snow, the grass was slow in coming up in the spring, which delayed the opening of the campaign. It was not until the beginning of May that the Russians began the siege of Silistria by erecting batteries south of the city, under whose cover they pushed approaches toward the bastions of the wall. The Turks, who outnumbered the attackers, sent large forces to establish trenches in front of the fortress, from which their fire troubled the Russian saps as they approached. The attackers, making little use of their siege artillery, continued to push ahead, although the fire from the Turkish counterapproaches slowed their advance.[70]

During the siege the Turkish Vizier, with some forty thousand men, was at Shumla, to the southwest of Silistria. Diebitsch's forces had patrols in the general direction of Shumla, but there was nothing to prevent the Turks from making sorties against some of the other Russian forces, which were in positions to the eastward, protecting the vital Russian base at Varna. Early in May the Vizier moved in force to the eastward, but, meeting strong opposition from the forces of Gen. Roth at Eski-Arnautlar, retired to Shumla. In mid-May, fearing that Silistria could not long hold out, he marched first to Pravody, expecting to proceed on to Silistria from there. At Pravody, however, he met stubborn resistance from Gen. Kupreanov's force of three thousand men, with twenty-eight guns, which was in a fortified position. For over a week the Turks made determined efforts to take Pravody, but the Russians held out very well and even received some reinforcements, with other forces near by. On May 29 the Turks lifted the siege and retired westward.[71]

This venture of the Vizier gave Diebitsch the opportunity he had been hoping for. Although his cavalry had failed to detect the sortie, the news from Pravody, as well as information from spies, deserters, and captured Turkish documents, all convinced him that the enemy had come out in force. Leaving Gen. Krasovskii with twenty-two thousand men to continue the siege of Silistria, Diebitsch with eighteen thousand troops marched out to place himself between Shumla, held by fifteen thousand Turks, and the Vizier, with forty thousand. His position was dangerous, but his advance guard crushed an attack by Turkish cavalry from Shumla, and Gen. Roth, with some fifteen thousand men, marched to join him. Nevertheless, when Diebitsch

70. Moltke, II, 294-95.
71. Epanchin, II, 200-19.

made contact with the Turkish army at Kulevcha, he was vastly outnumbered and in grave danger. The Vizier, not realizing the extent of
his own danger, delayed his advance for eighteen hours, which barely
gave Roth time enough to join his commanding officer. Timely action
by the Vizier probably would have saved his army, but he failed to
move.[72]

The day of battle at Kulevcha found the Russian forces in widely
scattered sections, while the Turks held a strong position on wooded
heights. Diebitsch, believing he had to do with only part of the Turks,
sent his advance guard of twenty-five hundred to make a reconnaissance in force. They ran into the main Turkish force, however, and in
a short time they were badly cut up. An hour later Diebitsch began
his general attack, just as the Turks were beginning their retreat. The
Russian artillery overwhelmed the Turkish batteries, exploding several
caissons, which dismayed their troops, and as the Russian infantry
attacked, the Turks fled in panic, losing all their cannon and baggage.
Many Turks were killed, and the remainder were nothing but fugitives.
The Russian losses, aside from those of their advance guard, were
slight.[73] Moltke declared that this action displayed the great moral
superiority of the Russians. "The thought of attacking an enemy almost
twice as strong, on his rocky heights immediately after a definitely
unfavorable combat, proves much regarding the decisiveness of the
leader as well as of the confidence that he could have in the bravery
of his troops. . . ." Only Russian belief in victory (and lack of confidence among the Turks) ensured the victory of the former, as the
terrain was very unfavorable to them.[74]

Although the Russian cavalry failed dismally to complete the
victory by an effective pursuit, the success at Kulevcha was decisive.
After it the Turks were beaten men who avoided battle, while the
Russians could boldly run grave risks with impunity. Nicholas I, in
his letter hailing the victory and praising the bravery of the troops,
warned Diebitsch not to delay before Shumla, but to push ahead to
cross the Balkans. The Tsar promised to send reinforcements as fast
as possible, although the problem of transporting them was difficult.[75]

Like the Tsar, Diebitsch was eager to cross the mountains, but
even Kulevcha did not completely free his hands. He had only about

72. *Ibid.*, II, 223-60.
73. *Ibid.*, II, 261-76.
74. Moltke, II, 324.
75. "Perepiska Nikolaia I," *Russkaia Starina*, XXXII (1881), 705-6.

twenty-five thousand men, of whom ten thousand would have to stay behind to watch Shumla. As reserve battalions from Russia would not arrive for months, his only reserve was Krasovskii's force. But until Silistria fell, Diebitsch could not use these troops.[76] Fortunately for Diebitsch, by June the siege was going well. By means of mining operations the Russians reached the line of bastions, which they proceeded to blow up for a considerable distance, as the siege guns, firing through the breach, worked havoc. "They achieved everything with the spade and the mattock." Once they had reached the Turkish works, they were able to complete and load each mine in twenty-four hours, firing eleven mines in eight days. In this way they compelled the defenders, who heavily outnumbered besiegers, to surrender on June 18.[77]

Even after Silistria had fallen, Diebitsch could not at once start on his great venture. On June 26, eight days later, he wrote the Tsar that there had been difficulties concerning the handling of the prisoners, the sick, and similar matters. As a result, Krasovskii's advance to the vicinity of Shumla "has unfortunately been greatly slowed and he reports that he will not be able to set out with his last column before the 29th, i.e., a whole week later than I had hoped." Even when Krasovskii did move, his march was slow, so that Diebitsch's letter of July 5 was sent from near Shumla. He planned, however, to begin his march that night. His next letter, of July 9, reported that they had reached the crest of the Balkans, with the Turkish resistance crushed.[78]

The crossing of the Balkan range, which had the reputation of being impassable for a European army, was ridiculously easy. The Turks had had no inkling that Diebitsch was planning it, and his departure during the night was not detected. The three columns in which the Russians marched had no especial difficulty in breaking through the weakly held passes. Heat and bad roads caused more trouble than did the Turks. By July 11 all the troops were south of the mountains, and part of the army was in touch with the Russian fleet. On July 12 they captured the useful port of Burgas. Diebitsch now decided to move against Aidos, an important crossroads dominating his communications with Krasovskii at Shumla. Although he approached it with caution, his troops captured it with ease. The ten thousand Turkish troops that they routed there had recently come

76. Epanchin, II, 323-25.
77. Moltke, II, 294.
78. "Perepiska Nikolaia I," *Russkaia Starina*, XXXIV (1882), 156-63.

from Shumla, sent off after the Vizier had learned of Diebitsch's march.[79]

After taking Aidos, the Russian forces were in an excellent situation, as the foe was demoralized and helpless, the inhabitants of the country were cordial, and there were plenty of supplies available, in addition to large amounts captured from the Turks. On the other hand, Diebitsch, in the heart of enemy territory, had only about thirty-five thousand men, of whom many had to be left to hold communications centers such as Aidos. An advance against Adrianople, about eighty miles away, would lengthen his communications and compel him to detach additional forces to guard his rear, at a time when the Turks might be massing to strike. The reinforcements that he greatly needed would not arrive until early August. Diebitsch wrote the Tsar that he planned to go around Adrianople by going to Kirkillissa, which would force the Turks to evacuate the former city or fight a real battle. Nicholas agreed with this scheme.[80]

Gradually Diebitsch learned that the Turks were very weak at Adrianople and his hopes of capturing it rose. In the meantime, while awaiting reinforcements, he took Iambol and Slivno, in each case dispersing about ten thousand men recently come from Shumla, of whose departure Krasovskii had sent no word. Finally, as the Turks gave no sign of strength, reserves began to arrive from Russia, all of which encouraged the commander to march on Adrianople. That this was a daring move is indicated by the fact that he had only about twenty thousand men and 110 guns.[81]

Early in August the Russian forces moved on their objective, suffering greatly from the heat and the bad roads. Sickness among the troops was increasing rapidly. By the 7th they were in sight of the city and Diebitsch, uncertain as to the proper course, reconnoitered. His decision was to attack, weak as he was, as he felt it was now or never. If he delayed, the Turks might rush up troops and prevent it. As it was, the Turkish authorities, with thirteen thousand troops, most of them regulars, and a large population of armed Moslems, could have defended the city, if the will to fight had existed. Actually, they made no preparations for defense and also did not try to withdraw to Constantinople, which suggests that, with the war coming to a close, they did not want to fight. Diebitsch had no trouble in occupying Adriano-

79. Epanchin, III, 412-16.
80. Epanchin, III, 416-18.
81. *Ibid.*, III, 419-20.

ple on August 8, and other forces took Kirkillissa, Liule-Burgas, and Midia, establishing communication with the Russian fleet in the Black Sea. Diebitsch wrote the Tsar, however, that his army was far too weak to take Constantinople, which would have to wait for another year. Moreover, the disease in his army was so devastating that the effective strength was greatly reduced. Even with the newly arrived reserves an infantry division could muster only five thousand men. Fortunately, the mortality was low and there was little plague in the army.[82] The Treaty of Adrianople, signed in September, thus released the Russian army from a most trying situation.

Compared to disease, the Turks were only a trifling problem. Gen. Grabbe correctly asserted in his diary of the campaign: "It is not so much steel as the climate, deadly for northern residents, that defends this land. . . . An army that crosses the Danube should have hospital supplies for no less than two-thirds of the effective strength in men."[83] At first the chief center of disease was Varna, the main supply center, where the plague hit during the early winter of 1829 and raged until late July, in spite of strenuous measures to halt it. In his letter of June 9 to the Tsar, Diebitsch was pleased with all aspects of his situation except for the sickness in the Principalities and Varna. "All measures have been taken, now only the hand of the Almighty can halt this scourge."[84]

Diebitsch's expeditionary force fared rather well until mid-summer, when sickness spread rapidly, even among the reserves. Moltke related that the arrival of fresh troops released two brigades that had been doing garrison duty in one of the seaports, which marched to join their corps with Diebitsch. "This was a weak reenforcement, scurvy had made fearful inroads . . . and *the whole Azov regiment on its arrival numbered only 128 men.*" The Dnieper and Ukraine regiments were depleted in like manner.[85]

The summer heat in Bulgaria and the rapid night march to Adrianople completed the devastation in Diebitsch's army. The hospital, set up in a fine Turkish barracks, had 4,641 patients by September, whose condition soon became desperate, as most of the windows and doors had been broken and mattresses, straw, and blankets were lacking. Linen for the patients did not arrive until December. In the fall

82. *Ibid.*, III, 163-64.
83. P. Kh. Grabbe, "Iz dnevnika i zapisnoi knizhki Grafa P. X. Grabbe," *Russkii Arkhiv*, XXII (1884), p. 1, Supplement, 78-79.
84. "Perepiska Nikolaia I," *Russkaia Starina*, XXXII (1881), 708-10.
85. Moltke, II, 356.

the men suffered terribly from cold and dampness and the lack of baths, which resulted in many cases of gangrenous feet. The toilets, which were not properly cleaned, overflowed and the stench was overpowering. These factors, together with the shortage of medicines, caused a very high death rate, especially when the plague set in in October. By December the men were dying at the rate of from fifty to seventy per day. When the troops went back to Russia in October, 1829, they left most of these unfortunates behind, under the protection of detachments of troops.[86]

When the remnants of Diebitsch's force arrived in Russia late in 1829, many of the troops, which still had the plague, had to go into quarantine. A number of the regiments had only enough men to form one company, and one regiment could muster only 130 men. The whole Second Corps had only seven thousand.[87]

While complete statistics on the total number of sick during the latter part of this war are not available, it seems likely that the figure far exceeded that of 210,108 in 1828. The number of men who died from disease in 1829 and 1830 was 96,722, more than three times the number of such deaths in 1828. As the number of men killed in battle was only 2,857, the mortality from sickness was thirty-four times the battle loss.[88]

Among the conclusions to be drawn from this war the first is that the Russian army, with the exception of the cavalry, was an effective fighting machine. Its successes were largely the result of the discipline, bravery, and devotion of the infantry, which, however, was weak in firepower and tactics. The artillery and the engineers, on the other hand, were probably equal in skill to those of other armies. Another deduction to be made is that war against the Turks posed very different problems from war in other areas. While their military power was quite weak, the logistical problem in a war in Turkey was highly troublesome, and the task of maintaining the health of the army was extremely difficult to accomplish. These aspects of the Russian military system were to make themselves felt, in varying degrees, in the subsequent wars under Nicholas I.

86. Epanchin, III, 327-29.
87. *Ibid.*, p. 130.
88. Zatler, *Zapiski*, I, 126-27.

CHAPTER IV. THE POLISH WAR AND THE TRIUMPH OF PASKEVICH

In the fall of 1829, at the end of the Turkish War, Nicholas I was in the fortunate position of having two victorious and famous generals. Although both had gained their glory at the expense of the Turks, whose military power was then a mere shadow of what it had been in earlier centuries, the campaigns of Diebitsch and Paskevich deserved high praise, because they had overcome the obstacles of inhospitable terrain, pestilential diseases, and difficult logistics, in addition to subduing the foe. The coming of peace left these two ambitious commanders as obvious rivals for the supreme favor of the Tsar.

With the end of hostilities against Turkey, the two generals turned to more routine assignments. Diebitsch, promoted to field marshal and given the title of Count Zabalkanskii (Transbalkan) by the exultant monarch in September, 1829, resumed his functions as chief of staff under His Imperial Majesty, in which position he had much work to do in helping to reorganize the army and put it on a peace footing. Paskevich, now Count of Erivan and viceroy of the Caucasus, had the difficult task of administering this large and loosely organized region, and at the same time of subduing the mountaineers, who were becoming increasingly hostile and better organized under fanatical new leaders who reacted sharply to the steadily increasing strength of the Russians in the area. As will be seen in a later chapter, Paskevich took part in punitive expeditions against the tribes and attempted to establish a new military policy that was designed to accomplish their eventual pacification. He also took steps to deal with the flagrant corruption in government circles, introduced needed reforms in the administration, and promoted the extension of civilization in the Caucasus. He did not, however, stay in this region long enough to accomplish much of significant value. The outbreak of the Polish Revolution late in 1830 was to draw both Diebitsch and Paskevich into this new conflict and eventually provided a final solution to the rivalry between them.

Although Polish revolutionary organizations had long been plotting to win freedom for Poland and had even planned to assassinate Nicholas I in 1826, the Polish uprising in 1830 was largely unexpected. After the July Days in France, a proclamation calling for a Polish revolution appeared in September, but the uprising was postponed. The Grand Duke Constantine, who was fond of the Poles, took no measures to repress them, and the crisis apparently had passed. The concern of Nicholas I over the events in Belgium, however, which led him to order that Poland should provide money for moving Russian troops, preceded by a Polish advance guard, to Holland, provided the spark that set off the explosion. Although Poland had made marked progress in commerce and industry after 1815 and enjoyed considerable autonomy under the benevolent, although erratic and choleric Constantine, on November 17 a revolt of radicals led by young army officers sought to kill Constantine and surround the Russian troops of the garrison, while seizing the arsenal and the city of Warsaw. The insurrection, however, was only partially successful. Constantine escaped unharmed and the Russian regiments fought off the attackers and joined Constantine outside Warsaw. Even several of the senior commanders of the Polish regiments opposed the uprising. Constantine, however, refused to crush the city of Warsaw, which was fully in the power of the radicals, as he was fond of the Poles and realized that repression would deepen their hatred.[1]

The Poles were far from united after their success, as the more conservative leaders (the Whites), realizing the precarious situation, hoped to seize power and check the revolt and then negotiate with Nicholas I for restoration of the Polish constitution. Prince Liubecki of the Administrative Council and the revered Gen. Josef Chłopicki were strongly against the revolution, feeling that it was hopeless. They, however, met sharp opposition from the Reds, headed by Joachim Lelewel and M. Mochnacki, backed by a society like that of the French Jacobins. Chłopicki negotiated with Constantine, who agreed to withdraw with his troops from Poland and to mediate with Nicholas I. The Grand Duke also released the Polish troops that had stayed with him.

1. A. K. Puzyrevskii, *Pol'sko-russkaia voina 1831 goda* (St. Petersburg, 1886), pp. 3-7.

As the revolt spread all over Poland, the Sejm assembled, and a national guard was formed. After recognizing Chłopicki as full Dictator of Poland, the Sejm dissolved. The Dictator now sent two moderates to St. Petersburg to negotiate with the Tsar, but the latter demanded full submission before making peace with the Poles, to which the delegates could not agree. After they had brought back this word, the revolutionary National Council compelled Chłopicki to break with Russia. It also set up a National Directory of five to head the government, with Prince Adam Czartoryski as the chief. On January 13, 1831, the Sejm declared that Nicholas was deposed as king of Poland. War was now inevitable.[2]

The Poles had a well-trained and effective army of about fifty-five thousand men (including reserves) and through a national levy obtained some eighty thousand more, although they rarely could put more than four divisions (sixty thousand men) in the field. They had excellent artillery, but only 146 guns at most, and they were short of powder and muskets. The regular troops, of whom Constantine was extremely proud, were well drilled and had fine spirit. As he felt, however, that "war spoils an army," he had refused the proposal of Nicholas to send part of this force against the Turks in 1828-29, although many of the Poles, remembering the glory that Sobieski had won in 1683, had been eager to take part. (Some Russian historians have held that by refusing to let his Polish forces fight the Turks, Constantine facilitated the uprising in 1830.) The high command of the Polish army lacked good generals, as most of them refused to fight the Russians or were suspected of disloyalty. Prince Michal Radziwiłł, commander in chief, was completely incapable, relying entirely on Chłopicki. Although Ignacy Prądzynski was able, he had a fiery, unstable character. Wojciech Chržanowski, however, who realized the effectiveness of the Russian forces, was a good and sensible general.[3]

Most of the Polish leaders, realizing their weakness, favored a defensive strategy, although Chržanowski proposed a quick offensive against Baron Rosen's Lithuanian Corps, which was weak and had many officers of Polish origin, in order to stir up the border areas. This scheme, which had considerable merit, collapsed in the face of Chłopicki's strong opposition. Prądzynski proposed a defensive campaign based on Warsaw and the fortress of Modlin near the junction

2. *Ibid.*, pp. 7-8.
3. *Ibid.*, pp. 9-15; E. P. Karnovich, *Tsesarevich Konstantin Pavlovich* (St. Petersburg, 1899), pp. 267, 180.

of the Bug and Vistula, with possible offensive operations as opportunity presented itself. Chržanowski offered a somewhat similar scheme. Finally, perhaps in the light of the difficulty of collecting and transporting provisions, they decided to retire slowly on Warsaw and, if they had to, to fight at Grochów. This had its dangers, for if they were defeated they would have the wide Vistula in their rear.[4]

The Russian army was by no means ready for war. There were few troops near Poland and it took considerable time to mobilize additional forces. As the Second Army, which had fought in the Turkish War, still had not fully recovered from that terrible ordeal, and the southern provinces had borne the brunt of provisioning it, the Russian authorities decided to use the First Army against the Poles, marching on Warsaw via Belostok and Brest-Litovsk. Although the First Army had not fought since 1814, the troops were supremely confident: a current saying was "The Poles will be only an appetizer for us."[5]

Field Marshal Diebitsch, whom the Tsar named as commander of the army, also was very optimistic about the campaign, which he planned to push with great speed in January of 1831, while the rivers and the ground were still frozen. This would be hard on the soldiers, many of whom would have to sleep on the ground, but he felt that speed was essential and in that way the campaign would be finished in two or three weeks. He planned to march toward the lower Vistula between the Bug and the Narew, and then, with a sudden turn to the left, push across the Bug and head for Praga, the bridgehead before Warsaw. He hoped thus to divide and crush the Polish forces and, if need be, to cross the Vistula on the ice to take Warsaw. He is reputed to have said: "If I do not succeed in ending all with one blow, then all the shame will fall on me."[6]

Diebitsch failed rather badly, however, in spite of his great numerical superiority over the Poles and his much more powerful artillery. The reason for this was the problem of provisions. Staking all on a quick, crushing blow, he refused to organize the hauling of supplies from Russia, as he was sure that this would not be necessary. Instead, he proposed to obtain the needed supplies by purchase from

4. Puzyrevskii, pp. 26-28.
5. Friedrich von Smitt, *Istoriia pol'skago vozstaniia i voiny 1830 i 1831 godov* (3 vols.; St. Petersburg, 1863), I, 306-7. This had originally been published in German in 1848.
6. *Ibid.*, 325-27, 303-4; Puzyrevskii, pp. 30-31; N. K. Schilder, "Voina s pol'skimi miatezhnikami 1831 goda," *Russkaia Starina*, XLI (1884), 386-87.

the inhabitants, and if that was not possible, to requisition them in orderly fashion. Almost immediately, however, it turned out that requisitioning was not proceeding in the correct way. Diebitsch in his orders to the troops complained that some units had commandeered peasant wagons for several days and had seized hay and provisions from the populace without payment. Before long, the disorders increased. Men straggled from their units and stripped the inhabitants mercilessly. While Diebitsch ordered stern measures to prevent these abuses, the foraging continued, often without any attempt to pay for the provisions, which infuriated the populace. The troops commandeered peasant wagons and drivers, without supplying forage for the horses or pay for the men, so that often the animals foundered and the drivers fled. All this did not produce the necessary supplies for the troops. On January 14 the military authorities issued an order reducing the daily ration of biscuits by one-half a *funt*, as the troops had food for only six days. The ration of oats for the horses was reduced by one-third.[7]

All this probably would have been of no great consequence if Diebitsch had smashed through to a quick victory, but this proved impossible, for nature was against him. At first all went well. On January 25 the army entered Poland and marched steadily ahead, encountering no resistance, to Węgrów and Siedlce. As the Poles had massed too far north, Diebitsch saw a chance to push south of them and cut their army off. A sudden, intensive thaw, however, melted all the snow and turned the roads into bogs, while the ice in the rivers became soft and unsafe. This ruined the Russian movement, for wagons and guns mired badly, and the infantry found even short marches terribly tiring. Diebitsch now decided to change his plans. On January 29, after his troops had rested for a day, he turned south, crossing the Bug, and marched toward Praga and Warsaw. After a two days' march he halted his forces for three days to rest his troops and to bring up supplies. During this halt the first news of defeats arrived.[8]

On the extreme Russian left flank southeast of Warsaw, the dashing Gen. Geismar commanded the advance guard of cavalry, with eight guns. When he encountered opposition, he divided his force, and without scouting the enemy, made a spirited attack in two columns, through

7. "Voenno-administrativnoe opisanie pokhoda Russkikh voisk v Pol'shu v 1831 godu," *Sbornik sochinenii ofitserov*, II, 175-85; Puzyrevskii, pp. 32-35. A *funt* was nine-tenths of an English pound.
8. Puzyrevskii, pp. 44-48; Smitt, I, 331-41.

The Polish Campaign of 1831

dense woods and swamp. The result was disastrous, as the Poles were more numerous and could use their force to good advantage. Geismar lost much of his force and six of his cannon, which was a terrible disgrace. At about the same time, the advance guard of the Sixth Corps was attacked by a Polish force and driven back in confusion.[9] These setbacks, while not serious, were a severe blow to Russian pride and indicated that the contest would not be as easy as had been expected.

After the rest period, the advance resumed. Although officially they now had supplies for ten days, Diebitsch on February 4 instructed his troops to requisition potatoes from the inhabitants and eat four pounds per day in place of one pound of bread. On the 13th he ordered the commanders not to pay more than the official price for provisions, which at once reduced the available supplies, as no one would sell at such low rates.[10] Nevertheless, they had enough food to push on toward Warsaw, beating off a Polish attack on the left column in a costly battle at Wawer on February 7. As the Russian advance continued, Nicholas did not try to dictate the plan of campaign, although on February 4 he wrote that Diebitsch should try to achieve victory "sans trop d'effusion de sang." He also advised against storming Praga, the fortified suburb of Warsaw east of the Vistula.[11]

The Field Marshal, however, feeling that it was imperative to bring the Poles to bay, now attempted a decisive blow at their position at Grochów, not far from the Vistula. His plan called for a direct attack on the Polish lines from the front by the two main columns, while Gen. Shakhovskoi, with the Grenadier Corps, would make a surprise attack from the right flank in order to cut the Polish retreat to Warsaw. This was to take place on February 14, but through a confusion of orders Shakhovskoi first attacked the Poles on the 12th and then, after new orders, halted his advance while the main army was entering the battle at Grochow.[12]

This confused situation led Diebitsch to begin the battle on February 13 with a direct attack on the Poles at Grochów, instead of from the left flank as planned. The Poles fought with much success, but eventually superior Russian strength drove them back, and a great

9. Puzyrevskii, pp. 48-51.
10. "Opisanie pokhoda," *Sbornik Sochinenii*, II, 193-94.
11. Schiemann, III, 97.
12. Puzyrevskii, pp. 56-69.

cavalry charge in the rear, led by Count Toll, chief of staff, almost routed the Poles. Shakhovskoi's forces were now entering the battle from the right, and energetic action by Diebitsch would have annihilated the Polish army and ended the war. Diebitsch, however, halted the Russian attacks as early darkness came, and the Poles could retire without pursuit through Praga across the river to Warsaw. Osten-Sacken repeatedly urged a decisive attack on the disorganized troops in Praga, and apparently Count Toll also wanted it, but Diebitsch either felt that Warsaw would surrender after the defeat of Grochów, or the artillery on the Warsaw walls was too threatening to attack. Thus the retiring Poles were not molested, and by one o'clock in the morning their army was safe in Warsaw.[13]

In his letter of February 14, Diebitsch reported to Nicholas that he had won a decisive battle, although he had failed to take Praga because of darkness and its numerous artillery. As soon as the ice in the river had gone he would try to cross the river higher up, according to the original plan. The Tsar, however, was not deceived, for in his letter of February 21 he regretted that the results of the battle had been so meager. He felt that at the very least the Poles should have lost all of their artillery. He advised his commander to threaten to bombard the Polish capital if it failed to surrender, and if need be, to burn part of it.[14]

After the Battle of Grochów the Russian forces remained for ten days before Warsaw, making great efforts to obtain supplies. Abundant provisions were on hand in Russia, but, because of the lack of wagons, it was impossible to move them to the army. The Russian military collected wagons and attempted to ship provisions down the Bug River to the troops, but this was not effective.[15] During this period some of the regiments had no biscuits for two days. Consequently "requisitioning," or more accurately foraging, was the order of the day. One observer stated that when the Poles tried to hide their supplies in chests and strong boxes, the troops searched them out. He saw "whole villages looted clean and abandoned by the inhabitants." In other settlements the half-starved people remained, watching

13. *Ibid.*, pp. 72-86; Smitt, *Istoriia*, I, 398-439; D. E. Osten-Saken, *Deistviia otdel'nago otriada general-maiora Osten-Saken v voinu 1831 g.* (St. Petersburg, 1865), p. 20.

14. Schilder, "Voina s pol'skimi," *Russkaia Starina*, XLV (1885), 291-92.

15. "Opisanie pokhoda," *Sbornik sochinenii*, II, 198-99; V. Aratovskii, *Obzor rasporiazhenii po prodovol'stviiu deistviiushchei armii, v 1831, 1848, 1849, i 1853-55 gg.* (St. Petersburg, 1874), pp. 28-37.

with stupefied indifference while the soldiers took away their last piece of bread.[16] On March 8 the army's general on duty wrote the Intendant General, complaining that foragers from headquarters returned from the area designated for them with almost no provisions and hay, and asked what they should do. The Intendant replied that he had no other means of provisioning and could only urge the foragers to go further afield.[17] During this period the convoys of provisions came irregularly, "and without potatoes, which they still found plentiful, they could not have maintained the army." In order to rest the soldiers and simplify the provisioning, Diebitsch distributed the troops in quarters, where the inhabitants would have to feed the soldiers.[18] The supplies obtained by foraging fell off rapidly in March, and Diebitsch then resorted to buying provisions at the current price, for hard cash. But for a long time the supply situation was desperate.[19]

During this period of inaction, the Poles opened talks for an armistice. On February 21, Diebitsch wrote to Nicholas that a Polish colonel had come to talk terms for ending the conflict. Diebitsch demanded that the Poles submit voluntarily, as otherwise Poland would be conquered by his troops. This the Polish envoy refused, asking an armistice. The emissary came to Russian headquarters on three occasions, but the talks produced no result. Possibly the Poles were merely seeking to gain time for rebuilding their army.[20]

After remaining inactive for a month, Diebitsch decided to cross the Vistula some distance to the south, so that he could then march on Warsaw from the rear. Considerable reinforcements had come or were on the way. The Guards, who, it was hoped, would be able to obtain provisions from East Prussia, and also by shipments on the Narew, would march north of the Bug. Baron Rosen's corps would hold the center, retiring on Siedlce if attacked. The main army set out on March 17 to cross the Vistula. It was a terribly difficult march, as the Polish mud—Napoleon's bête noire—was bottomless. The grenadiers, who had to help drag the guns and the wagons, fell to the ground, worn out by hunger and exhaustion. Before Diebitsch's army could reach the Vistula, however, couriers came from Baron

16. G. I. Filipson, "Vospominaniia," *Russkii Arkhiv*, XXI (1883), Pt. III, 124.
17. Aratovskii, p. 14.
18. Friedrich von Smitt, *Feldherren-Stimmen aus und über den polnischen Krieg vom Jahr 1831* (Leipzig, 1858), p. 105.
19. Aratovskii, pp. 22-27.
20. Schilder, "Voina s pol'skimi," *Russkaia Starina*, XLVI (1885), 297-301, 304, 513-17, 524-27.

Rosen with increasingly bad news. The Poles were attacking and Rosen was in danger of losing his whole force.[21]

While Diebitsch was struggling toward the Vistula, the Poles, after careful preparation, suddenly struck Rosen's advance guard at Wawer. Gen. Geismar, with six thousand men, was taken completely by surprise and outflanked by superior Polish forces. In spite of his disadvantage, he held his men together and in ten hours of fighting retired, with the loss of two guns, to Dembe Wielkie, where Rosen's main forces were. Rosen had had time to mass his forces there, although, because many of them had been scattered in quarters in neighboring villages, they were not all assembled. Rosen had about eight thousand infantry and two thousand cavalry. The Poles had three times as many, and their morale was very high. There was a fierce battle at Dembe Wielkie, in which the Russian forces were hard hit, but escaped complete disaster. They had already lost fifty-five hundred men, five banners, and ten guns. At this point, however, Skrzynecki, the Polish commander, failed to push his advantage, even though at that time (March 20), Diebitsch had not yet learned of the gravity of the situation. Rosen's forces, reinforced and regrouped, retired to hold Siedlce, the main Russian base, to lose which would be ruinous. Diebitsch, who by now was marching back with much of his army, at first hoped to strike the Poles in the rear, but as his supplies were all used up, his commanders told him the troops could not fight without food, and so he too was marching to Siedlce. The decisive battle came on March 29. Although the Poles delayed their attack and failed to co-ordinate their efforts, they almost crushed Rosen's forces. The latter held, however, and on March 30 Diebitsch's forces entered the city. The Poles, who had taken eleven captured guns, five banners, and three generals in triumph to Warsaw, had nevertheless failed to win a major victory. They had, however, wrecked Diebitsch's plans to take Warsaw. He recalled the rest of his force from the Vistula, burning his pontoons on the shore.[22]

Diebitsch now stayed between Siedlce and Warsaw for about one month, making desperate efforts to move supplies for his army from the large amounts available in Russia. The situation improved considerably, especially after the new grass appeared, but he never had real sufficiency, chiefly because of the problems of hauling what was

21. Puzyrevskii, pp. 100-12.
22. *Ibid.*, pp. 113-35; Schiemann, III, 108.

on hand. Disease was another grave problem. Much malaria developed among the troops, perhaps because they had to bivouac on damp ground, and in April and May cholera began to ravage them. While reliable statistics on this score do not exist, some estimates hold that one-third of the army was in the hospitals at this time. The cholera killed about thirteen thousand.[23]

By mid-April the army had a fifteen-day supply of provisions, which gave the possibility of striking at the Poles. Diebitsch made two attempts in April, but each time they evaded him. Polish attempts to carry the war into Volhynia and Podolia also troubled him, although Russian detachments in these areas proved able to cope with the situation.[24]

By April Diebitsch had lost confidence in himself. In his letter of April 12 to the Tsar he stated that the reverses and lack of success had "inspired in me a sort of moral timidity that was unknown to me formerly" and referred to "a constantly increasing feebleness of the nerves . . . ." On May 4 he with some justice complained of fatigue occasioned by the severe winter campaign, adding "my morale is even more crushed than my physical being." He stated that he would be quite ready to turn over the army to Count Toll, "but unfortunately he also feels that his strength is declining and has formally declared to me that he could never accept the command of the army. . . ." Diebitsch concluded that if the Tsar wished, he would do the best he could in the future.[25] His letter of April 27 complained that the corps commanders and other generals, while brave enough, could do little more than carry out orders, as they were devoid of initiative and lacked imagination to deal with developments unforeseen in their instructions.[26]

These were the letters of a hopeless man, who lacked confidence in his troops. Denis Davydov asserts that his subordinates disliked and distrusted Diebitsch, some even believing that the Poles had bribed him.[27] Epanchin, who admired Diebitsch's campaign in Turkey in 1829, accepts statements (that were common in 1831) that in 1829 and 1830 he had become addicted to drinking rum punch to excess.[28] The hapless commander also incurred the wrath of Nicholas by

23. Smitt, *Istoriia*, II, 152-53; Zatler, *O gospitaliakh*, pp. 135-46.
24. Puzyrevskii, pp. 169-92.
25. Schilder, *Nikolai*, II, 479-80, n. 423.
26. *Ibid.*, II, 481, n. 423.
27. Davydov, *Russkaia Starina*, VI (1872), 318-19.
28. Epanchin, II, 88.

his dubious reception of the latter's proposal to cross the lower Vistula at Płock, obtaining most of his supplies by shipments up the river from Danzig (letter of April 7). On April 25 the Tsar angrily replied that Diebitsch and Toll had showed by their grudging acceptance of his proposal that they were unwilling to act decisively and would not accept responsibility for its success. He declared that if they proposed to take four weeks to act and, "moreover, with the same weak indecision and disorder with which you have acted up to now, I foresee only misfortunes instead of almost certain success."[29]

In spite of the monarch's wrath, however, Diebitsch was to have one more chance. The Poles, after skilfully diverting his attention to his left flank, marched, on April 30, with about forty-five thousand men, against the Guards Corps under the Grand Duke Michael, which was advancing north of the Bug. Prądzynski hoped to destroy them and penetrate into Lithuania to destroy the Russian bases and to stimulate the guerrilla movement there. By May 2 the Grand Duke, learning of the Polish advance, made preparations for defense and informed Diebitsch of developments. The Poles, after weakening their drive by detaching twelve thousand men to guard against a possible attack by Diebitsch, drove the Russian rear guard back, but with limited success. Michael made a skilful fighting retreat and by May 9 was across the Narew, where he repulsed an attempt to cross with heavy loss for the Poles. Diebitsch, who was not sure that the main Polish army was attacking, was slow to move against them, but finally on the 8th he pushed to strike at the rear of the Poles and destroy them.[30]

Another option open to Diebitsch was to march directly against Warsaw while it was denuded of troops. He did not, however, give this serious consideration, perhaps because of the strength of the city's position. Also he probably feared the wrath of the Tsar if the Guards, under his brother, were annihilated. As it turned out, the Guards were in no great danger, but probably the risk was too great for him to follow another course.

Diebitsch, however, was too cautious for full success even on the path that he had chosen. He did not really take the offensive until May 12, and then by a roundabout road to Ostrołęka, through which the Poles would have to flee. The Poles also delayed their march, but by May 14 most of their forces were across the Narew at Ostrołęka,

29. Shcherbatov, IV, 11-14.
30. Puzyrevskii, pp. 200-22.

with a rear guard still on the left bank. The Russian forces, after marching forty-seven miles in thirty-two hours, attacked the rear guard from three sides, supported by heavy artillery fire, and quickly wiped out the enemy detachment. The grenadiers then charged the bridge, defended by two guns as well as infantry, and pushed two regiments across and set up a bridgehead. The Poles counterattacked, trying to destroy this threat, but the Russian infantry, constantly reinforced and supported by powerful Russian artillery fire from the far bank, repeatedly drove back furious Polish charges with terrible losses. By seven in the evening, the Poles were thoroughly beaten, with their army cut to pieces and disorganized. Diebitsch, however, did not realize the extent of the Polish defeat and did not pursue, largely because his troops were exhausted by their strenuous exertions of the last three days. Also once more his army was practically without provisions.[31]

Another reason for Diebitsch's caution after the battle was his concern about a strong Polish division under Giełgud, which had taken no part in the conflict. As it turned out, it had not retreated to Ostrołęka, as Skrzynecki, Giełgud's superior, had completely forgotten about him when the retreat began on May 13. Consequently, as later became clear, Giełgud, finding his retreat to Warsaw cut off, headed with his twelve thousand men toward Lithuania, where he failed to take any of the big Russian bases, and eventually had to retire to internment in East Prussia. Only a small part of his force eluded pursuit and escaped to Warsaw.[32]

Ostrołęka changed the whole course of the war, for the Polish army never recovered from it. The flower of its infantry had been lost —half of the officers, and one-third of the enlisted men, and the troops no longer had much hope of victory. Also Giełgud's forces would never rejoin the army, and when his force entered East Prussia late in June, the insurrection in Lithuania soon collapsed. Thus Russian superiority began to make itself felt and was to grow steadily. Diebitsch had recovered his spirits after the battle, and Toll, who had done wonders in combat, was his old self again. Together they prepared to move to the lower Vistula and organized a flow of supplies from East Prussia. In addition, Diebitsch stopped the requisitioning of supplies and instead purchased them at the market price for hard money. Grain cut green for forage was also paid for. Great efforts were made to collect

31. *Ibid.*, pp. 222-45; Smitt, *Istoriia*, II, 308-44.
32. Puzyrevskii, pp. 303-42.

a supply of food for twenty days and a supply train to move provisions from the stores at Grodno. New hospitals took shape. Finally, the staff took steps to prepare the crossing of the Vistula, sending off a light detachment, with staff officers, to make arrangements. Diebitsch now hoped to end the war by a rapid march to Warsaw—but instead he suddenly died of cholera on May 29.[33]

Count Toll took over the army as acting commander in chief after Diebitsch's death. He was a very effective general, with long experience, and enjoyed general respect, as he had done well in the battles of Grochów and Ostrołęka. During the first two weeks, while the army stayed at Pułtusk, awaiting the wagon train of provisions, he took no significant action, but managed to prevent the Poles from making successful attacks on detached forces in the south by demonstrative moves that suggested a new offensive. Also he sent Gen. Vlasov with a cavalry force on a successful raid along the lower Vistula. Toll was confident that he would lead the march on Warsaw, which he was sure would be decisive. On June 13, however, Paskevich, whom Nicholas had recalled from the Caucasus, took over as commander in chief.[34]

The new leader, in spite of the aura of glory that surrounded him as a result of his triumphs in Persia and Turkey, had displayed serious failings in these campaigns. The same weaknesses again appeared in Poland. An article in *Jahrbücher für d. deutsche Armee und Marine*, in 1874, stated that he acted there "with timid slowness and indecision." In addition to the understandable reluctance of a veteran commander to risk his past reputation unnecessarily, he never felt really confident and was very distrustful of all possible rivals, even junior officers. Thus, while refusing to take risks himself, he would not let anyone else win glory. He was extremely suspicious, as he was no stranger to court intrigue and imagined that he was surrounded by enemies who sought to destroy him. "When Paskevich took command of the army in Poland he met many young officers whom he had sent away from the Caucasus. He did not think of making use of them as capable, trained officers," but regarded them as enemies appointed by his foes at court. "He, of course, had many enemies; but he evidently never realized that he himself for the most part aroused people to hostile attitudes toward him."[35]

33. *Ibid.*, pp. 254-60.
34. *Ibid.*, pp. 280-302.
35. Translation in N. K. Schilder, "Fel'dmarshal Paskevich v krymskuiu voinu," *Russkaia Starina*, XIII (1875), 604-6.

When he took command of the army, he reported that the troops were "sure of themselves after the action at Ostrołęka, but distrustful of their commanders, without bread, badly clothed, dispersed, . . . so that out of the main army of 147 thousand there were only 44,000, to whom they expected in several days nine thousand men from the detachment at Brest."[36] There is in this statement some exaggeration, for the army had provisions for fourteen days, with considerable quantities coming from Prussia. The troops were probably no more ragged than any army after six months of active campaigning, and their morale was excellent. The Poles had about forty thousand men in the vicinity of Warsaw, with less than half the artillery that the main Russian force had.[37] In general, Paskevich's account of his campaign is marked by a strongly tendentious tone, as he constantly made sharp criticism of his chief of staff, Count Toll, with whom he was at loggerheads from the beginning. Toll also wrote an account of the campaign, which charges Paskevich with timidity that came close to cowardice, stubbornness, and hostility and discourtesy toward his subordinates. The two accounts are so contradictory that it is difficult to arrive at the truth.

Although the army was ready to advance to the Vistula, Paskevich insisted on remaining at Pułtusk for nine days, while the force under Muraviev (over fourteen thousand, with seventy-one guns) came up. During this time Toll and Neigardt, the quartermaster-general, laid before Paskevich their carefully prepared plan for a march from Pułtusk to Płock, on the Vistula, in four parallel columns, with intervals of about ten miles between them. He at once rejected this plan, for it would "put the advance guard under the walls of Modlin" (the Polish fortress). Holding that the forces would be so far apart that they could not support each other and that the advance guard would certainly be crushed by a Polish attack, the commander drew up new plans for the march, putting the nearest column twenty miles from Modlin and keeping the forces not more than five miles apart.[38] Instead of proceeding by main roads, however, the troops now had to march by country roads, which often were swampy, so that the troops got terribly mired and had to build many bridges and in places lay down corduroy roads. This slowed their progress greatly: instead of twenty or more miles per day, they could not do more than eight or

36. Men'kov, III, 87.
37. Puzyrevskii, pp. 345-48.
38. Men'kov, III, 88-89.

ten miles daily. At the end of the march Paskevich had to give the exhausted troops three days of rest.[39]

While they were at Płock on the Vistula, word came that the enemy was approaching—according to Paskevich, in three columns. Paskevich at once ordered a retreat to join the reserves at Osiek on the Prussian border, instead of fighting, as Toll urged. The latter stated that they had a good position and it would be shameful to retreat, for they would beat the enemy. Paskevich, however, said that they did not have the provisions for a battle and a pursuit, which would take four days, and ordered a retreat at dawn. "It was hard for me to act contrary to those behind whom was the opinion of all Headquarters. . . ." He asserted that one reason for the opposition to his views was the presence of two generals "almost expelled by me from Georgia [N. N. Muraviev and Baron Osten-Sacken]. . . . Out of envy men listened to their opinion, for my eastern campaigns had given me the right to respect; but they tried to show that my eastern campaigns meant nothing."[40]

Toll's account of this incident is that word had come from the advance guard that small Polish forces had driven in some of the Russian outposts, causing Paskevich to wish to retreat, as he felt that there might be fifty thousand Poles on the move. Toll wanted to investigate and find out how many Poles there actually were. He claimed that the Poles would never dare expose their whole army by sending it across the Vistula. The commander, however, ordered emergency measures, and himself rode to the advance guard, where he found all calm. Nevertheless, he put the whole army under arms, took them from their bivouac, and finally marched them to the rear in a pouring rain at night. Two hours after midnight on June 30 they broke camp and marched to a defensive position in the rear, in full disorganization, as if pursued by a victorious foe. The infantry and cavalry had to march over plowed fields, while the artillery and baggage went by road, often axle-deep in mud. Paskevich kept urging them on, at the double or the trot. The men often had to ford streams breast-deep. All this disheartened the soldiers, who were covered with mud from head to foot, hungry, and sleepless, for they well knew that they fled when no man pursued. Many of them came down with cholera as a result of this.[41]

39. Puzyrevskii, pp. 349-52.
40. Men'kov, III, 90-91.
41. Smitt, *Feldherren-Stimmen*, pp. 274-80.

Eventually it turned out that the Poles had not been ready to attack, and the Russians could proceed to Osiek, where they crossed the Vistula by July 8. Paskevich halted here, keeping the whole army idle while he had biscuits baked from the flour brought from Prussia. During this period, while Paskevich was worrying about destruction, Gen. Golovin, with a rather small force, harassed the Poles before Warsaw. The Polish commander, hoping to encourage his troops with a victory, sent twenty-four thousand men against him, forcing Golovin to make a fighting retreat with heavy losses. Nonetheless, he escaped destruction and his troops were by no means disheartened. This daring venture kept the main Polish forces occupied while Paskevich was slowly crossing the Vistula.[42]

As the Russian army gradually advanced toward Warsaw, the supply problem again became difficult, for the Prussians, troubled by the cholera in Poland, put a strict quarantine upon shipments over the border, which made it impossible to feed the troops from that source. Paskevich, however, handled the situation very well by sending out officials to buy Polish products for cash. This pleased many of the inhabitants, who hauled their produce to the Russian camp. German colonists in the vicinity of Łódź were especially glad of this opportunity. The army thus could obtain provisions for the whole campaign.[43]

Although Toll was eager for a rapid push on to Warsaw, where he believed the powerful Russian force would crush the disorganized enemy, Paskevich insisted on a slow, cautious advance, even though unopposed. Finally, on July 15 he moved ahead, in Toll's words "fearing at every minute an attack of the Poles." While they continued to delay, the Russian advance guard chanced to find the key position of Łowicz unguarded, and on July 21 they occupied it firmly. They had marched about eighty-five miles in fourteen days, with no fighting. Here Paskevich, instead of pushing ahead, had his troops fortify the bridgehead and awaited a Polish attack. Toll and many others wanted to march out to attack the foe, who finally occupied a position at Bolimów. Paskevich's answer was that to attack a Polish army of fifty thousand with thirty-five thousand Russians would be fatal.[44] Actually, Paskevich had considerably more than thirty-five thousand

42. I. V. Barsukov, *Graf Nikolai Nikolaevich Murav'ev-Amurskii po ego pis'mam, ofitsial'nym dokumentam, razskazam sovremennikov i pechatnym istochnikam* (2 vols.; Moscow, 1891), II, 41.
43. Shcherbatov, IV, 56-74.
44. Men'kov, III, 94.

men, but he reasoned that in attacking a fortified position the cavalry would be useless. It seems probable that the Polish army also contained a considerable contingent of cavalry, although he did not take that into account. Moreover, much of the enemy infantry consisted of untrained, poorly disciplined recruits, some of whom had scythes instead of muskets. Skrzynecki, their commander, was much opposed to attacking the Russians and it was with the greatest reluctance that he massed his army on the Bzura, opposite Paskevich, bitterly lamenting "now it remains for me to shed the last drop of blood. I shall be obedient to the general will." Instead of attacking, however, he called four councils of war, which decided only to hold the line against the Russians. The Diet, under strong pressure from the radical party, sent a delegation to Bolimów, his headquarters, with power to remove him. Finally they replaced him with Henryk Dembiński, who warmly admired his predecessor and pursued exactly the same policy. On August 2 the Polish army retired to Warsaw.[45]

Gen. G. I. Filipson, who was with the Russian forces, relates that, during the two weeks that they stayed at Łowicz, they did almost nothing. After some days Count Toll sent a Finnish rifle battalion to drive back the Polish outposts before Bolimów. As the enemy hastily evacuated this village, Toll, making a reconnaissance in force, occupied the position. An officer of the General Staff found a ford by means of which he crossed the river and pushed on into some woods, soon galloping back to say that the Poles were in full retreat. Toll at once reported this development to Paskevich, urging that they should advance immediately. The commander in chief, however, sternly ordered the Russian troops to evacuate Bolimów and to retire to Łowicz.[46]

Paskevich's explanation for the long delay was that he needed time to collect provisions and to wait for Kreutz, who, with twenty thousand men, was coming to join him. Also Gen. Rüdiger, with a considerable force, had crossed the Vistula south of Warsaw and moved nearer to Paskevich. Finally, during this period the Poles got to fighting among themselves, which weakened their resistance.[47] There is some justification for these views. On the other hand, a crushing attack on the Polish army in the field, using the full power of the

45. R. F. Leslie, *Polish Politics and the Revolution of November, 1830* (London, 1956), pp. 236-41.
46. Filipson, *Russkii Arkhiv*, XXI (1883), Pt. III, 133-34.
47. Shcherbatov, IV, 74, 81-82.

overwhelming Russian artillery against the disorganized foe, would probably have solved all problems at once and eliminated the need for a costly attack on the fortified capital.

When the Poles retreated, there was little pursuit until they were delayed by the crossing of two streams. Toll, learning of this, joined the advance guard and ordered the grenadiers to push ahead without stopping. After getting them in motion, he again joined the advance guard. The Grenadiers did not come, as he learned, because Paskevich had ordered them to take a rest period, and they remained idle, in spite of Toll's urgent requests for them to hurry. This delay enabled the Poles to get most of their troops across the river, although Toll did manage to destroy their rear guard.[48] Puzyrevskii, a colonel of the Russian General Staff, concludes that all this delay at Łowicz was not needed, as there was no shortage of provisions. "The Field Marshal, in spite of the full absence of enterprise on the part of the foe, with each step forward becomes more and more cautious and delays under various pretexts. Finally, while awaiting the arrival of Kreutz, he takes a defensive position and does not want to undertake anything." This caution gave the Poles a chance to gain time and improve the fortification of Warsaw. Fortunately for Paskevich, they opened the road to him by their retreat, although he mismanaged the pursuit.[49]

On August 5 both the Russians and Poles made reconnaissances in force, which resulted in the annihilation of a Polish force of about fifteen hundred men by the Russian cavalry. On August 6 the blockade of Warsaw began. In the meantime, on the 3rd, the radical masses of Warsaw had risen in insurrection against their leaders, whom they charged with treason, and killed several of the generals. Probably in response to this feeling, the Polish authorities sent Gen. Girolamo Romarino, with thirty thousand men, to destroy Rosen's forces east of the Vistula. The latter retreated slowly, luring Romarino away from the capital as far as Brest, in defiance of his orders not to go more than twenty miles from Warsaw. After failing, on August 18, to crush Rosen, he then withdrew toward Volhynia in the south, with Rosen in weak pursuit. Eventually his troops were driven across the Austrian border, where they were interned. Thus Romarino left Warsaw in a weakened condition, while the Russians were reaching their maximum strength.[50]

48. Puzyrevskii, pp. 379-80.
49. *Ibid.*, p. 385.
50. *Ibid.*, pp. 380-94.

The arrival of Kreutz's force and the approach of Rüdiger from the south brought the Russian strength to 86,000, with 438 guns; 70,000 of these were before Warsaw. The Poles had approximately 50,000, with much less artillery, although some of their cannon in the fortifications were heavier than those of the Russians. Their fortifications were poorly designed, being too spread out for the number of defenders. The strong redoubt of Wola was the key position. After Kreutz had arrived and Romarino had led off much of the defense force, Paskevich, who had been standing "in a strong defensive position" south of the city, decided to order an assault.[51] It was a shortage of fodder that finally "brought Paskevich out of his inactivity, by destroying all pretexts for further postponement of the assault." It was decided to attack on August 27, with Wola the first objective, but then the date was advanced to the 25th.[52]

In spite of Nicholas' proclamation to the Poles warning them that they should submit, as all hope that the French might intervene was gone, many of them refused to surrender, trusting that they could hold out until the fall rains, when the Russians would have to withdraw. They told themselves that Paskevich's army was the last effort of the Russians, and if he failed, Poland would win.[53] For his part, the Russian commander was troubled by doubts. He wrote to the Tsar that he was secretly considering what would happen if he failed to take Warsaw. If this happened, he planned to retire some distance and then return to the assault after getting reinforcements.[54]

The attack on Warsaw began with the capture of several redoubts on the flanks, and then the real attack on Wola came. In these operations the Russian artillery proved useful, massing its fire and preparing the way of the infantry in impressive fashion. In some cases the cannon won enemy positions without the infantry. The horse artillery proved especially effective, galloping into the rear of enemy redoubts, firing at close range, and even seizing enemy guns.[55]

The attack on Wola was the crucial test, as it was well fortified with bastions and a ditch. The attackers massed seventy guns against it and soon silenced its cannon, while other Russian pieces fired at the city wall behind it. The Russian infantry attacked at ten in the morning, from the rear corners and sides, and quickly broke in after heavy

51. Shcherbatov, IV, 92.
52. Puzyrevskii, pp. 395-98.
53. Shcherbatov, IV, 87-89, 93-94.
54. *Ibid.*, p. 97.
55. Puzyrevskii, pp. 412-13.

fighting. The defenders put up terrific resistance against grave odds until the victorious Russian infantry stormed the inner citadel. Thus Wola was taken in ninety minutes of very heavy fighting. By one o'clock the Russians held all the first line of defense.[56] At this point a Polish sortie against one of the Russian flank positions greatly disturbed Paskevich, although it was easily repulsed. Count Grabbe wrote in his diary that the assault could have been ended that afternoon, but Paskevich thought otherwise. Disregarding the evidence of Polish disorganization and dismay, and the eager spirit of his exultant troops,[57] he at once halted all further attacks, while keeping up the artillery fire. Count Toll strongly opposed the delay, as he felt that the momentum of the attack and the inspiration of the troops would quickly sweep aside the defenders. But Paskevich insisted on stopping the battle at three o'clock, although there was plenty of daylight for further conquests. He justified this by saying that "the men were tired." At the ensuing council of war, Count Toll made a strong plea for continuing the assault, but the other commanders supported Paskevich. This postponement, with the parley that took place the next day, gave the Poles almost twenty-four hours to recover.[58]

When the Poles wanted to continue the talks after 1 P.M. on the 26th, Paskevich broke off the parley. Shortly after the cannonade began, he was lightly wounded in the arm by a round shot, which left Toll in command. The Poles fought fiercely, with several cavalry charges, but were driven headlong by the Russian horse, while in the center there was a great artillery duel, in which the attackers gained the upper hand. When a strong Polish battery enfiladed the Russian lines from the flank, Toll sent Muraviev, with a strong force, to charge it and drove it back into the city.[59] Toll wanted to begin the major attack at once, but Paskevich ordered him to wait almost an hour. Finally at 3 P.M. the Russians stormed the defenses. Although the Poles fought with fury, in three hours the suburbs and parts of the city were in flames, and Toll ordered an attack on the city wall and the other fortifications. By ten o'clock at night much of the wall was in Russian hands, as well as the strong Jerusalem Gate, and Russian cannon were mounted to fire on the city. While the fighting was in progress, Gen. Berg of the Russian army was talking with the Polish

56. Smitt, *Istoriia*, III, 487-96.
57. Grabbe, *Russkii Arkhiv*, XXII (1884), Pt. III, Supplement, 93.
58. Puzyrevskii, pp. 400-4.
59. *Ibid.*, pp. 406-8; A. Verigin, "Shturm Varshavy v 1831 godu," *Voennyi Sbornik*, III (1860), 133-38.

leaders in Warsaw. At first they were stubborn in their attitude, but as the Russians overcame the defenders, they gradually modified their stand. Late at night they agreed to remove their army from Warsaw and Praga (although they did not promise to surrender). On the morning of August 27 the Russians occupied Warsaw.[60]

What followed was an anticlimax. The Polish army that marched over to Praga was not submissive and hoped to continue the war by joining forces with Romarino's troops, which would have raised their numbers to fifty thousand men. Upon their refusal to surrender, Paskevich would not attack them until he had been greatly reinforced. When the insurgent troops heard of the end of Romarino's force, however, they realized that there was little that they could do. Paskevich, who had followed them at a safe distance, feared that they would attack him and at first prepared for defense. Noting, however, that they were moving down the Vistula, away from the guns of Modlin, he pursued them, only to have them elude him by slipping into East Prussia. Thus ended the Russo-Polish War.[61]

"The Field Marshal after the storm of Warsaw remained. . . true to his system of expectant inactivity and . . . even took a defensive position. With a more skillful opponent, Paskevich might easily have let slip the Polish army, which, moving to the south, might have dragged out the war."[62]

This war, like the one in the Balkans in 1828-29, indicates that under Nicholas I the Russians never were properly prepared for conflict, in spite of their huge army. The attempts to fight quick and inexpensive wars resulted in grave breakdowns of communications, which ruined the plans of the commanders. Diebitsch's strategy probably would have worked well in Poland if he had had the provisions and transport to feed his army, for while the Polish troops were brave and devoted, whenever the main Russian army met them in battle, the results, as at Grochów and Ostrołęka, were disastrous for them. Finally, Diebitsch managed to solve the logistical problem and was on the way to victory, only to die of cholera. Paskevich, who took command after Diebitsch, made no attempt to fight the Poles in the field, but fled at the first hint of battle. In spite of him, rather than because of him, the overwhelming strength of the Russian forces and the weakness of the Poles brought about a Russian triumph. This, of course, does

60. Puzyrevskii, pp. 408-11; Smitt, *Istoriia*, III, 507 ff.
61. Puzyrevskii, pp. 414-35.
62. *Ibid.*, p. 436.

not prove that his system was the best. It seems probable that a good commander, such as Toll or Rüdiger, could have won the war by a single battle much more quickly and with less loss of life than Paskevich, who in the end had to undertake the costly assault on Warsaw.

The Tsar and his advisers did not digest this lesson, for while Nicholas probably had some doubts about Paskevich, he still revered him as his "Father-Commander," who had won three wars for him. Hence Nicholas heaped honors upon him, naming him prince of Warsaw. For the remaining twenty-four years of the reign, Paskevich was commander in chief of the Active Army and viceroy of Poland and had a dominant position in Russian military affairs. His jealous, suspicious nature demanded unthinking obedience of his subordinates, with the result that the whole Russian army was stamped with his system of pedantic, parade-ground training and unreasoning fulfilment of orders. It thus was no accident that in the Crimean War there were few generals worthy of their calling. Of course, Paskevich was not solely responsible for this state of affairs, but for twenty-four years he and Nicholas I set the pattern.

CHAPTER V. THE STRUCTURE OF THE MILITARY ESTABLISHMENT

Under an energetic and powerful ruler like Nicholas I, the control and administration of the armed forces naturally centered in him. As, however, not even he could handle all details, administrative machinery was necessary to perform the needful day-to-day functions of running the land forces. The Ministry of War provided much of this, although, as the organization of military affairs was not entirely logical, some aspects were in part under control that did not pass through the Ministry.

Directly under the Tsar was the Chief Staff of His Imperial Majesty, consisting of the Minister of War, the General Master of Ordnance (*Generalfel'dtseikhmeister*), the Inspector General of Engineers, the Quartermaster General, the Commander of Imperial Headquarters, the general adjutants and generals of the Suite of His Imperial Majesty, the aides-de-camp of the Tsar, and several other functionaries.[1] As, however, this staff acted as a whole only in time of war, by special imperial command, which in each case defined its duties anew, it had no peace-time administrative role, although some of its members, such as the General Master of Ordnance and the Inspector General of Engineers, had permanent functions. The persons who formed the Chief Staff of His Imperial Majesty were subordinate to the Minister of War.[2]

At the end of the reign of Alexander I, Count Arakcheev enjoyed great power. Nicholas I—no man to brook a rival—blandly stripped him of his position, although the Count continued to administer the military colonies for a while. At first the foremost military commander was Baron (later Count) Diebitsch, who was chief of staff under

---

1. Russia, *Svod Voennykh Postanovlenii* (12 vols., St. Petersburg, 1838), Pt. I, *Obrazovanie Voennykh Uchrezhdenii*, Bk. I, *Obrazovanie Voennago Ministerstva*, art. 37. Hereafter cited as SVP. Until 1828 the staff was known as the Suite of His Imperial Majesty.

2. *Ibid.*, arts. 768-70, 975.

the Tsar. As has been seen, in 1829 Nicholas assigned him to command the Russian forces in the Balkans, where he won the rank of field marshal, and in 1831 he led the Russian troops against the insurgent Poles. After his death from cholera, Field Marshal Prince Paskevich, who took Warsaw in 1831, became the military favorite of the Tsar, who called him "Father-Commander," as Nicholas while a Grand Duke had served under him. The Prince, who was in command of the Active Army and viceroy of Poland from 1832 until after Nicholas' death, had immense influence in the Russian military establishment, although he was absent from the capital for most of the period.

The Ministry of War inevitably felt these changes among the military men close to the throne. In 1826-27 an intrigue developed against Count A. I. Tatishchev, Nicholas' first minister of war. Count A. I. Chernyshev, assistant chief of staff, supported by Diebitsch, attempted to discredit the minister by sending to the Tsar an unfounded report charging Tatishchev with misconduct in an earlier position. The Tsar, while sympathetic, ordered an investigation, and eventually the Minister resigned. On August 26, 1827, Chernyshev became minister of war—a post that he held until 1853—and also chief of staff.[3] Although at first he was supported by Diebitsch, he was not firmly aligned with him, and proved agile enough to adjust successfully to the rise of Paskevich.

The new Minister at once undertook reforms in his jurisdiction, which were much needed, because of the neglect of such matters under previous rulers. In 1828 the Administration of the General Staff was combined with the Corps of Topographers under the Quartermaster General. A reform of the Commissariat Department, completed in 1829, greatly improved that disorganized body and gave much better administration of military hospitals. In 1831 the Grand Duke Michael, already head of the Artillery and the Engineers, became chief commander of the Corps of Pages and of all cadet corps. There still remained, however, division of the control over the military establishment, especially over economic matters. Chernyshev urged the Tsar to clarify the administration, and after much work Nicholas produced a new arrangement that gave more effective jurisdiction, with the Minister of War in charge of the "whole military sector; he is the one

3. Schilder, *Nikolai*, pp. 78-79; SVM, I, N. A. Danilov, *Istoricheskii ocherk razvitiia voennago upravleniia v Rossii*, 290-92.

who reports to the Sovereign concerning all parts of the military administration."[4]

Another significant development during this period was the codification of military legislation, which had been attempted under Alexander I but not completed. One of the military jurists proposed it in 1826 to Diebitsch, who supported the idea. It proved to be a long and difficult matter, as much of the original legislation dated from the time of Peter the Great. The new code appeared in 1839, containing all military enactments in effect at the end of 1838.[5]

The Ministry of War, even after its reorganization in 1832, still did not prove satisfactory, and after careful study new legislation appeared in 1836, clearly defining the structure of its various departments and setting forth their duties and functions.[6] According to this new code, the Ministry of War, through its Department of the General Staff, Inspector's Department, Medical Department, and Auditoriat Department, had jurisdiction over the personnel of the troops and of all parts of the Ministry, the movement of and supervision over all parts and persons of the military establishment, the military colonies, and the irregular troops. In addition, economic matters and military legislation came under the jurisdiction of the Military Council, of which the Minister of War was chairman. This body handled economic matters relating to the Engineering and Artillery departments, the military colonies, and the Commissariat and Provision (*Proviant*) departments.[7]

While this structure of the Ministry proved to be more efficient than any before, it had serious defects: a highly complex system, a chain of command that lacked precision, and absence of one-man control. The commander in chief of the Active Army, the commanders of the Guards and the Grenadier Corps, the General Master of Ordnance, and the General Inspector of Engineers all enjoyed the right to report directly to the Tsar and not through the Minister of War.[8] In addition, there was extreme centralization, with almost no local organs. Only the Commissariat, Provision, Artillery, and Engineering departments had local offices to serve the troops in their districts. The offices of the various departments were often in several different towns.

4. Danilov, *Istoricheskii ocherk*, pp. 297-301, 308-15. The new legislation for the Ministry of War is in *Polnoe sobranie zakonov rossiiskoi imperii* (2nd series, St. Petersburg, 1832-1916), 1832, No. 5318. Hereafter cited as II PSZ.
5. SVM, III, Pt. I, *Kodifikatsionnyi otdel. Istoricheskii ocherk*, 16-28.
6. *Ibid.*, I, Danilov, *Istoricheskii ocherk*, 316-23.
7. SVP, Pt. I, Bk. I, *Obrazovanie Voennago Ministerstva*, arts. 2-8, 10-11.
8. I. V. Bestuzhev, *Krymskaia voina 1853-1856* (Moscow, 1956), p. 23.

Troops in Khar'kov obtained their provisions in Kremenchug, while for equipment they went to Voronezh, and for arms and ammunition to the arsenal of the Artillery Department in Kiev. Moreover, these local institutions had very limited authority and all questions that arose usually could find solution only in the Ministry of War in St. Petersburg.[9]

As stated above, the Military Council of the Ministry of War was responsible for economic matters of this branch of the government. The most important part of this was the budget for the army, which—the largest single item in the national budget—amounted to approximately forty per cent of the total. Each department of the Ministry prepared its budget, supposedly with an eye toward reducing appropriations as much as possible. Next, the Accounting Section of the Chancellery of the Minister of War checked these proposals against previous estimates and the justifications for each item. The resulting budget then went to the Military Council, where, after all possible reductions had been made, the budget for the Ministry as a whole received confirmation. The Military Council was responsible only to the Tsar and no governmental agency or person had the right to give it instructions.[10]

After the Military Council had approved the Ministry's budget, it went to the Council of State's Department of Economy, where it was discussed in some detail by the elderly bureaucrats whom the Tsar had appointed to this body. The journal of this department next went to the Tsar for his confirmation and then the military estimate proceeded to the Ministry of Finance for inclusion in the state budget. This usually took place at the very end of December.[11] Although the Ministry of Finance, which always strove for reduced expenditures, had opportunity to criticize the military budget at the hearings in the Council of State, this does not seem to have been an especially searching analysis. In 1827 the consideration of the whole budget took only eight days. As the conscientious Count Kankrin, who was Nicholas' minister of finance for nearly two decades, ruefully described the budget hearings, it was much like hunting snipe: "They hunt and hunt, they aim; sometimes they hit, but most often they miss."[12]

9. P. A. Zaionchkovskii, *Voennye reformy 1860-1870 godov v Rossii* (Moscow, 1952), pp. 19-21.

10. SVP, Pt. IV, Bk. I, arts. 28, 29, 32, 47, 63, 68, 70, 73, 74; *ibid.*, Pt. I, Bk. I, arts. 978-79.

11. V. M. Anichkov, *Voennoe khoziaistvo* (St. Petersburg, 1860), p. 11.

12. I. S. Bliokh, *Finansy Rossii XIX stoletiia* (4 vols.; St. Petersburg, 1882), I, 215.

The military budget must have caused the Count a great deal of distress, for it was the chief factor that produced the chronic budget deficits of this period. While the first year of Nicholas' reign produced only a slightly unbalanced budget, the wars with Persia and then with Turkey proved extremely costly. The war in Poland still further disarranged Russia's finances. The five years of war (1827-31) caused unusual expenses of 496,298,000 paper rubles. Although indemnities from Persia and Turkey met part of this cost, they were only a fraction of the total, with the result that the Treasury was obliged to float loans in Holland, to arrange internal loans, and to increase taxes. By 1832 the Russian debt, already large, had increased from 652 million paper rubles in 1828 to 823 million.[13]

From 1832 to 1849 Russia enjoyed peace, except for the worsening conflict in the Caucasus, but extraordinary military expenses and bad harvests caused a succession of unbalanced budgets. In 1835 and 1836 both Kankrin and Nicholas undertook to prune the swollen military appropriation, over the strenuous objections of Field Marshal Paskevich and the commanders of the Separate Corps. Although a number of regiments were eliminated and other economies were made, the budget did not quite balance, and later, upon the insistence of Count Chernyshev, minister of war, Nicholas increased his appropriation by over twelve million rubles and added another twelve million in extraordinary expenditures. Thus the efforts to reduce the budget brought no result.[14]

In the decade preceding the Crimean War, the situation grew steadily worse, with the Caucasian struggle swallowing ever greater sums. Kankrin, after insistently demanding a complete end to hostilities there, resigned in 1844 when the Tsar refused to halt the fighting. Kankrin's successors were not strong enough to do even as well as he had, and deficit financing, juggling of accounts, and a mounting debt were accepted as routine matters. By the end of 1851, the total debt had risen to 400,667,799 silver rubles, or about 1,400,000,000 of the old paper rubles. Occasionally a frantic effort to cut expenditures occurred, as in 1846, but the Ministry of War flatly refused to make even a token cut. Although eventually even the Tsar insisted on reductions, they proved to be trifling.[15] The Crimean War, naturally enough, enormously intensified the growing chaos in the finances of the Empire.

13. *Ibid.*, I, 169-70, 184-92.
14. *Ibid.*, I, 193-210.
15. *Ibid.*, I, 241-90.

In this descent to Avernus military expenditures played the chief part. There were, of course, arrears in taxes caused by bad harvests and by low grain prices, and the revolutionary events of 1848 and 1849 had harmful effects on Russia's trade. Nevertheless, the conclusion seems inescapable that the military burden was more than the country could afford.

While the Military Council was thus struggling with the vital financial problems of the army, the Department of the General Staff was another highly important part of the Ministry of War. Unlike most parts of the military establishment, it did not fare well under Nicholas I. In the events of December 14, 1825, the officers of the General Staff—known as the Suite of His Majesty for Quartermaster Affairs—gained a reputation for disloyalty, although only a few of them—notably Nikita Muraviev—had been active in the insurrection. By chance, none of the top Staff officers was on hand to help suppress the movement. Thus high military circles formed the opinion that the bright young staff officers trained in the School of Column Leaders (*Kolonovozhatykh*) were unreliable. These factors, as well as the prevalent distrust of intellectuals, made a complete transformation of the Quartermaster Department inevitable. When it finally came, after having been delayed by the rapid succession of wars from 1826 to 1831, it proved to be drastic and harsh.[16]

During the Turkish and Polish wars the officers of the General Staff performed very well in planning, in providing for the needs of the armies, and in topographical work. Only under Paskevich did the General Staff officers find no welcome, as this commander, innately suspicious, disliked them. But in the Balkans and then in Poland, Diebitsch, Kiselev, M. D. Gorchakov, K. F. Toll, A. I. Neigardt, and F. F. Berg—generals with General Staff training or experience—did excellent work. The chief complaint against the General Staff was that there were too few officers to do the necessary work—which resulted from the fact that many of them were completely overloaded with paper work.[17]

In the summer of 1831, however, the situation changed sharply, to the detriment of the General Staff. Diebitsch, already losing favor in high places, died suddenly after his victory at Ostrołęka, and the Tsar called on his "Father-Commander" Paskevich to take charge of the

16. N. P. Glinoetskii, *Istoriia Russkago General'nago Shtaba* (2 vols.; St. Petersburg, 1888-1894), II, 1-7.
17. *Ibid.*, II, 19-58.

campaign. The latter, now a field marshal, quarreled bitterly with Toll, who, with a brilliant record, felt that he should have received the command. Although Toll and other staff officers deserved much of the credit for the success of the campaign, Paskevich managed to gather the laurels for himself and succeeded in getting Toll, Neigardt, and other men identified with Diebitsch to retire from the General Staff. Neigardt, who by training and experience was well fitted for the post of quartermaster general, did not receive it because of Paskevich's hostility. Instead, Lt. Gen. F. F. Schubert, head of the Military Topographical Bureau, obtained this post. As he was completely devoted to Count Chernyshev, the minister of war, and supremely interested in topography, he paid little attention to the needs of the General Staff, even neglecting it during the reorganization of the Ministry of War. As a result, the position of the staff deteriorated steadily. Finally, Schubert's neglect became too much even for the Tsar, who replaced him as quartermaster general with Berg, who had been quartermaster general of the Active Army and was familiar with staff work. In spite of his training and intelligence, however, Berg did little for the General Staff, which remained almost unchanged until the Crimean War.[18]

Under the reorganized Ministry, the General Staff was responsible for "the general distribution, quartering, movement, and activity of the military land forces" and also had charge of the Imperial Military Academy, the Topographical Department, and geodesic work. The First Section was primarily responsible for distribution, movement, and quartering of troops, assembly of troops for imperial reviews and camps, and correspondence about maneuvers and battle orders. The Second or Military-Scientific Section had as its province military statistics, history, topographic data of Russia and foreign powers, military surveys and reconnaissance, considerations of the defense and the security of the Empire, military data about border regions, questions of transportation and communications, and military science in general. The Third Section dealt with accounting matters.[19] In its administration of the General Staff, the Ministry's chief duty was to see that the troops were provided with sufficient, properly trained staff officers, as well as to spread knowledge of new military techniques and methods among the officers of the army. In time of war the duties

18. *Ibid.*, II, 59-65, 140-44.
19. SVP Pt. I, Bk. I, *Obrazovanie Voennago Ministerstva*, arts. 45-49.

of General Staff officers included mapping roads, laying out campsites, reconnoitering enemy positions, and leading troops against the foe in direct attacks, ambushes, and retirements. Planning of troop movements and battles was also part of their work. The Ministry, through the General Staff, was also required to do general strategic planning, to acquire information about potential foes, and to study military history and science.[20] From all this it appears that the higher military authorities had allotted to the General Staff the task of providing the line units with trained men who could do much of the routine administrative work which the forces of the line found it inconvenient to do. The authorities appeared to expect little of the strategic planning or other technical preparatory work for possible conflict that a competent General Staff might do to great advantage.

Because of the prevalent stress in Russian military circles on formal, parade-ground training of troops, and the almost complete disregard of realistic training for combat, there was little real service that the General Staff could perform. The various field manuals of the Russian army made almost no mention of it, although in most other respects they were very detailed and precise. Even in time of peace staff officers had little to do but learn the procedure of military paper work, study close-order drill, and do topographical work. Several efforts to publish handbooks for staff officers accomplished nothing, partly because Paskevich frowned on them. In 1848 a *Handbook for Officers in the Field* appeared, which proved highly useful for line officers, but said little about the staff. Throughout this period "firm knowledge of all intervals and distances of each battle-order was regarded as almost the last word in military science."[21]

Knowledge of the details of the prescribed formations was essential for the General Staff officers, for they had a vast amount of work preparing for reviews and maneuvers. For each they made detailed plans showing the position of the troops, the intervals between units, where they would pass in review, and other matters. They then prepared exact copies for the detachment commanders, for those conducting the review, and for their suites. In making the plans the staff officers never bothered about topographic details, but provided beautiful sketches of the position of the troops. They did not need to reconnoiter the terrain in such instances: the surveyor's transit was used merely to fix with precision the position of the troops.

20. *Ibid.*, art. 739.
21. Glinoetskii, II, 194-96.

The officers of the Guards General Staff were especially proficient at this work. They did not limit themselves to this, however, as they engaged in field trips and map problems of tactics and strategy. Staff officers of the regular army made occasional efforts to start similar activities, but they did not succeed, as their superiors had no sympathy with them, probably because of the view that terrain was not especially important to well-trained troops.[22]

On the other hand, the General Staff did a great deal of scouting and topographical work in the Caucasus. Several parties of topographers penetrated deep into hostile territory, occasionally suffering casualties. In 1838 a whole party was wiped out, together with their convoy, in Dagestan. Several officers ventured into the high mountains in disguise, only to endure captivity and other dangers. One man was tortured and sentenced to death, but because of his bravery the mountaineers freed him. Other officers of the General Staff actually commanded troops in the Caucasus, or did staff work on military expeditions against the tribesmen.[23] But the conditions in the forces in the Caucasus were not typical of the army as a whole.

In 1832 the General Staff received a new table of organization that affected it adversely. The number of generals in the general staffs of the Guards and the army was reduced from thirty-seven to seventeen, whereby the staff lost many of its outstanding generals. This greatly lowered the prestige of the staff, and its uniform did not enjoy the same respect as before. The scale of pay and promotion was quite unfavorable to the staff officers, who found it difficult to receive command of a regiment or a brigade or to rise to the rank of chief of staff of an army corps. While in 1835-40 the pay of the General Staff rose with that of the rest of the army, its situation was somewhat unfavorable and not many young officers sought to enter the service.[24]

In order to provide officers for the General Staff, a new system was adopted after the authorities had abolished the School of Column Leaders. Nicholas asked the brilliant Baron Jomini for his views on the subject. Jomini advocated an "École Centrale de grande Tactique" to teach tactics, strategy, military statistics, and military history, but no routine drill. While the Tsar approved this, the wars of 1827-29 prevented action. In October 1829 Nicholas had a commission of generals set up, with Jomini as its chairman. Although the latter tried to insist

22. *Ibid.*, pp. 196-200.
23. *Ibid.*, pp. 203-10.
24. *Ibid.*, pp. 149-67.

on wide theoretical training, Diebitsch and the other generals carried the day in favor of formation drill, whose spirit infused the new Military Academy, and through it the General Staff. "The proposals of Jomini in general did not receive August approval."[25]

While the curriculum included some fine theoretical courses such as strategy, military history, military statistics, and military geography, it was tactics, together with practical exercises, that dominated the course of study. In addition, the officers spent much time in formation drill with troops of the main arms. In general, the practical training in tactics applied the methods of the great camp at Krasnoe Selo, where the most important matter was the conditions necessary for reviews. The Academy's *Report* for 1851 stated: "The practical tendency in teaching tactics is based on the fact that the Military Academy should prepare, not so much learned officers, as capable officers for service with troops. . . ."[26]

In addition, the Academy had as its director general, Gen. Adj. I. O. Sukhozanet, an active fighting officer, who had never done staff duty. Known as a harsh disciplinarian, he dominated the scholarly side of the Academy's life as well as its administration. He insisted on a consistently strict regime for the student-officers, holding that mildness led to corruption and weakness, and forced out Baron Zeddeler, a kindly though demanding instructor, who was one of the most effective teachers. Later, Sukhozanet turned against Baron N. V. Medem, professor of strategy and military history, and after his retirement, campaigned against his successor, N. S. Golitsyn.[27] Sukhozanet made the life of the students very hard with his insistence on discipline, and termed learning in military affairs "no more than a button on a uniform"—i.e., necessary but not important.[28] Nicholas himself never valued scholarship and apparently feared that the young officers who enrolled in the Academy might be infected with liberalism. The Grand Duke Michael, who was president of the Academy, had cynically declared himself to be a foe of all learning and laughed at scholars and literary people. He never came to the Academy and never even rode past the building.[29]

25. Polievktov, pp. 327-28.
26. N. P. Glinoetskii, *Istoricheskii ocherk Nikolaevskoi akademii General'nago shtaba* (St. Petersburg, 1882), pp. 40-69.
27. *Ibid.*, pp. 95-106; N. S. Golitsyn, "Imperatorskaia voennaia Akademiia v 1834-48 gg.," *Russkaia Starina*, XXXVII (1883), 411-14, 703-12.
28. Glinoetskii, *Ist. ocherk Nikolaevskoi akademii*, pp. 95-106.
29. Filipson, *Ruskii Arkhiv*, XXI (1883), Pt. III, 149-50.

When in the highest places they held such views, it is not surprising that when P. K. Men'kov, later a well-known general and military editor, asked permission of Gen. Adj. Kleinmichel, a leading general of the Tsar's staff, for permission to enter the Military Academy, he got a cool reception. As Men'kov stated, "they looked on an officer who wished to concern himself with learning, if not with hostility, at least with extreme distrust; the authorities, as it were, avoided such officers, calling them 'learned ones'. . . ."[30]

He did, however, succeed in entering the Academy, where he found that Sukhozanet had imposed a harsh regimen upon the student-officers, who had to face an exacting curriculum, while they had only very limited recreation. In addition, their pay and maintenance were extremely meager, so that in the expensive capital they could hardly make ends meet. These conditions strongly affected the enrolment. In the first year, twenty-seven students entered, but the number declined steadily, until in 1851 there were only ten graduates and seven incoming students. As a result of this, there was an investigation by a committee of ranking officers, which recommended and secured better treatment for the students. They now enjoyed substantially higher pay and wider rights upon graduation. As a result of these improvements, thirty-seven officers entered in 1852, and almost as many in 1853.[31] The Academy now could benefit from a period of progress, but too late. The Crimean War, which created a demand for trained officers, had begun, and there were very few on hand. The fact was that in the Russia of Nicholas I there was no place for the kind of educated officers of the General Staff that Jomini had urged. Indeed, there was really no place for Jomini in the Russian service. Although he had met a cordial reception when he entered the service of the Tsar, the Russian military men soon decided that he was not sufficiently practical, in spite of his great learning and his service under Napoleon, as he had no grasp of tactics.[32] He remained in the Russian service for over fifty years, but spent much of his time in Passy, outside Paris, where he wrote numerous works on strategy.

There never was any real possibility that the Russian General Staff could achieve a dominant position comparable to that of its Prussian counterpart, which developed into a collective head of the military machine in the absence of a capable monarch. With a strong

30. Men'kov, II, 16.
31. Glinoetskii, *Ist. ocherk*, pp. 109-22.
32. Glinoetskii, *Istoriia*, pp. 270-71.

ruler like Nicholas I this was out of the question. But the Russian staff could never even fulfil what might have been its normal role—as a planning board and source of ideas for the army. With encouragement it could have done this. But Nicholas and Paskevich distrusted planners and thinkers and kept the staff from performing any but the most routine service functions for the army. It was only in the subsequent reign that a fine staff officer like D. A. Miliutin could find scope for his talents.

But while Tsar, Ministry of War, and staff were highly important in the Russian military system, they were the superstructure of the great machine, whose mass and power lay in hundreds of thousands of soldiers in gray overcoats. In the seried regiments of infantry, the dashing squadrons of uhlans, hussars, dragoons, and cuirassiers, and the batteries of grim cannon on their green carriages lay the might of Russia.

In 1826 the Active or Regular Army consisted of the First Army, in north-central Russia, with six corps of infantry and four of cavalry, and the Second, in the Ukraine, of two infantry corps and one of cavalry. There were 610,000 men in the Active Army, of whom 497,700 were infantry. In addition, various reserve, garrison, and other inactive units brought the total to 885,000 men. There were also 113 regiments of Cossacks, totaling 70,000. There were 185 regiments of infantry (including ten in the Guards, and four Marine regiments), and 143 companies of foot artillery and 30 of horse artillery, with a total of 2,076 guns.[33]

In 1830 the Second Army was dissolved, with its two corps distributed among the others. A reorganization of the army began in 1833, whereby the authorities eliminated a number of regiments of infantry and attached their battalions to other regiments as depot battalions. The latter were combined into reserve divisions (six in all), of which one was attached to each corps. The depot battalions had limited personnel and served chiefly to keep supplies of uniforms and weapons and to train reservists.[34] In all other respects the organization of the Russian army remained virtually unchanged until the end of the period of Nicholas I.

It is difficult to compare the size of the Russian army with those of other European armies, because the information is usually scanty

33. Petrov, pp. 429-30.
34. *Ibid.*

and far from precise. In 1850 the official figure for the Russian army was 859,000 officers and men.[35] In the autumn of 1854 Gen. Hess, chief of the Austrian General Staff, held that the entire Russian army consisted of 820,000 men, while Austria had 350,000, and Prussia 200,000.[36] France, with a population of 35,400,000, had an army of about 570,000, or one soldier for every 62.1 inhabitants, while Russia, a much less prosperous country, with a population of 62,000,000, had one soldier for 75.6 inhabitants.[37]

The structure of the army in large measure followed that of the Napoleonic armies, being formed of battalions, regiments, brigades, divisions, and corps. Each battalion of four companies at full strength had one thousand men, although most of them actually had about seven or eight hundred. Infantry regiments of the Guards had three battalions, those of the line had four. Two regiments formed a brigade, and each division had two brigades of infantry. One of the four regiments in each division was termed light infantry (Jaegers or Carabineers), although there was little difference between light and heavy infantry. There were six corps of infantry and one of Grenadiers, each consisting of three divisions of infantry, one light cavalry division, and one artillery division. Each corps had a battalion of sharpshooters, armed with Liège rifles, and a battalion of sappers. An infantry corps had from forty to fifty thousand men.[38]

In addition to the six infantry corps in the army, there were also Separate Corps like the Corps of Guards, stationed at St. Petersburg, which consisted of three divisions of infantry, a division of light cavalry, sappers, sharpshooters, and the artillery of the Guards Corps. The Grenadiers, another privileged body of troops, stationed south of the capital, were also a Separate Corps. The Separate Caucasus Corps consisted of two infantry divisions, a sapper battalion, a battalion of sharpshooters, Don Cossacks, Georgian, Black Sea, and Caucasus Line battalions, and artillery.[39] There were also the Separate Orenburg and Siberian Corps, each consisting of one infantry division of Line troops, together with numbers of Cossacks and other irregulars.

35. "Istoricheskoe obozrenie," *Sbornik IRIO*, XCVIII (1896).
36. E. V. Tarle, *Krymskaia Voina* (2 vols.; 2nd ed., rev. and enl., Moscow, 1950), I, 23.
37. *Ibid.*, I, 22-23.
38. SVP, Pt. I, Bk. II, arts. 7-13, 41, 44; M. I. Bogdanovich, ed., *Istoricheskii ocherk diatel'nosti Voennago upravleniia v Rossii v pervoe dvadtsati-piati-letie blagopoluchnago tsarstvovaniia gosudaria imperatora Aleksandra Nikolaevicha* (6 vols.; St. Petersburg, 1879-1881), I, 8-9.
39. A line battalion consisted of Cossacks or other irregulars who were settled as guards along a frontier defense line.

There also was a separate division stationed in Finland, consisting of Finnish Line battalions, a battalion of sharpshooters, and Don Cossacks.[40]

The main strength of the regular army, the so-called Active Army of four infantry corps, was stationed in Poland under Field Marshal Paskevich. The other two infantry corps were in the Kiev area, for the defense of the southwestern part of the Empire. In addition, the heavy cavalry and part of the light cavalry formed cavalry reserve corps of about twelve thousand men each, of which there were three: the Guards, First, and Second Reserve Cavalry Corps. These bodies, with their horse artillery, were regarded as an important reserve force to be thrown in in support of the main combat forces.

> In the organization of our troops, and especially in the cavalry, in the beginning of the 1850's the tradition of the Napoleonic times was still observed: the action of great masses of cavalry in time of battle was regarded as the best means of attaining important successes. With this end in view huge masses of reserve cavalry were constantly maintained, chiefly of heavy cavalry.[41]

The Russian army also possessed the usual auxiliary formations, such as artillery, reserve, pontoon, and engineering parks, siege trains, army hospital units, commissariat and provision detachments, and others.

In addition to the combat and auxiliary forces, there were many subsidiary units that had little or no value for use in war. Among these were the four carabineer training regiments, formed of cantonists (the sons of soldiers), which prepared these youths to be sergeants or company clerks. The Corps of Gendarmes, which served as a special police force throughout the Empire, was also nominally part of the army. The "plowing soldiers" of the military colonies were also under military jurisdiction, although they were not trained to bear arms. Then there were numerous units of cantonists: about twenty battalions, forty-eight squadrons, and six batteries. There were three military-workers' battalions, seventeen military-workers' companies, and a considerable number of movable invalid companies.[42]

An especially large force of minimal wartime value was the Corps of Internal Defense, composed of old soldiers no longer fit for active duty. In all provincial cities there were garrison battalions of one

40. SVP, Pt. I, Bk. II, arts. 41, 42, 44, 45; Bogdanovich, I, 7-8.
41. Bogdanovich, I, 10.
42. *Ibid.*, I, 18-21.

thousand men, while the county (*uezd*) towns had invalid commands, whose function, in addition to preserving order, was to receive recruits and convoy them toward their destinations. *Étape* commands had the task of convoying criminals and persons under arrest, while at the salt mines the salt commands stood guard. In 1853 there were one hundred and forty-five thousand men in the Corps of Internal Defense.[43]

In 1868 an experienced general cast a disparaging eye on the Corps of Internal Defense. It was, he said, almost useless for putting down disturbances, pursuing bandits and robbers, and for guarding prisoners and accompanying them. A few well-trained police or gendarmes could perform these tasks much more effectively at much less cost. As for putting down peasant disorders, this was usually beyond their strength, so that regular troops almost always were required. The old soldiers also made poor guards at prisons, and even, out of kindness of heart, did favors for the inmates. He concluded that in western Europe the authorities obtained much better results, at less cost, by using far fewer, able-bodied, well-trained personnel.[44]

Thus, upon examination the mighty army of Nicholas I proved to be less threatening to Russia's foes than one might think at first glance. In actual combat forces, the Tsar could put in the field not many more than Austria or France, in spite of the larger population of his realm. Of the approximately one million men in uniform in 1853, not much more than half were field troops. The rest were largely supernumeraries. Indeed, each regiment of the army had its supernumeraries, who formed an unorganized company. These were mostly artisans, such as tailors, carpenters, gunsmiths, harness-makers, blacksmiths, and clerks. One historian states that at the time of the Crimean War the infantry had supernumeraries to the amount of seven per cent of the total; the cavalry, thirteen per cent, and the engineers and artillery, twenty per cent.[45]

Nicholas I, then, had at his disposal a powerful army, but one that had weaknesses and failings. The chief of these was the absence of any effective reserve system, whereby in wartime the size of the army could be quickly increased and losses could be made good. At a time when much of Europe was beginning to move toward the Prussian system of almost universal military service for a relatively

43. *Ibid.,* I, 17-18.
44. R. A. Fadeev, *Vooruzhennyia sily Rossii* (Moscow, 1868), pp. 93-98.
45. Bestuzhev, p. 23.

short period, after which the conscripts went into the reserve and were available for recall to the colors in time of war, Russia had no such system. The most that the Tsar could accomplish was to reduce the term of service from twenty-five years to fifteen for those who had good service records. The latter were then given indefinite leave and entered the reserve for five years, with the sole military obligation of a brief training period each fall.[46] This measure, however, provided the means for only a limited expansion of the army, for a mere seventeen thousand men a year were released,[47] and many of these were not fit for further duty. Before the Russian forces marched into Hungary in 1849 to save the Austrian monarchy, the reservists were recalled to the colors. This added 177,000 men to the army. This, however, proved to be insufficient, so that Nicholas found it necessary to make a special draft of men, to the amount of 134,000 recruits.[48] Even this brief and almost bloodless war made demands for manpower that the reserve system could not meet. In the Crimean War 199.438 reservists were called up in 1853, leaving only 15,759 more for later requirements. As this did not by any means fill the need, fresh drafts brought in about 455,000 men in 1853 and 1854, and in 1855 the government made a large levy of men for 337 militia battalions (*druzhiny*) of 1089 men each, for short-term service. In all, during the Crimean War the army received 865,762 men, in addition to the 215,197 reservists that were recalled.[49]

In fairness to Nicholas, it should be said that he could not have introduced a system of universal military service in Russia without shaking the whole structure of the serf state. By law, a man who entered the army ceased to be a serf, so that universal service would have freed so many men from bondage that it would have meant the end of serfdom,[50] which the Tsar tried to accomplish but did not dare bring about, in the face of furious opposition from the nobles. In fact, he found that landowners and many of his generals were strongly opposed to the reduction of the term of military service from twenty-five to fifteen years, which they regarded as harmful to the state, for, as Gen. N. N. Muraviev-Karskii declared, the Russian villages "will

46. SVP, Pt. II, Bk. I, arts. 291, 293-96.
47. Polievktov, p. 330.
48. Petrov, pp. 431-32.
49. Bogdanovich, I, 34-37, 63-76, 170. For the decree ordering the formation of the *druzhiny*, see II, PSZ, 1855, No. 28, 994, "Polozhenie o Gosudarstvennom Opolchenii."
50. Fadeev, p. 28.

be filled with people without work and without means for livelihood, from which we may expect great disorders."[51]

Such, then, were the general outlines of the military system under Nicholas I. It was completely dominated by the Tsar, a thorough autocrat, who believed that only by maintaining rigid discipline could he avoid disaster. Beneath him was a large military bureaucracy, probably more effectively run than ever before, but still unwieldy and cumbersome. The great cost of this system was one of its distinguishing features, for, in spite of repeated efforts to achieve economies, the financial burdens that this military machine imposed on the taxpayers were crushing. It is difficult to explain the maintenance of the great military machine by purely military considerations, for Nicholas did not have great dreams of conquest, and indeed, he acquired little territory in his wars with Persia and Turkey in his early years. Moreover, Russia had nothing to fear from her neighbors, as Prussia and Austria were friendly, and Sweden and Turkey were neither powerful nor aggressive. Perhaps the explanation lies in the Tsar's great fear of revolutionary outbreaks.

Undoubtedly Nicholas feared that revolutions would again sweep Europe and believed that he, as the strongest ruler in Europe, had the duty to suppress them, lest even *his* Empire might be swept away. Indeed, in 1830 and in 1848 he did move to suppress them. Moreover, Nicholas never felt secure at home, as the Decembrist uprising in 1825 had been a rude awakening, and the widespread peasant outbreaks in his Empire displayed danger in another form. And so the powerful Tsar, believing that "gegen Demokraten helfen nur Soldaten," built a mighty army which he sought to drill and discipline into a thoroughly obedient instrument to subdue rebellion. Convinced of the need for unthinking subordination in his army, he even denied it an up-to-date, well-trained General Staff, probably lest this institution should infect his army with subversive ideas. Similarly, because of Russia's system of serfdom he found it impossible to reduce the size of his army by creating an effective system of reserves. Thus under Nicholas the Russian army remained essentially an army with some of the worst features typical of the armies of the eighteenth century and not on an equal footing with the new armies of the mid-nineteenth century.

51. Polievktov, p. 331.

CHAPTER VI. TRAINING AND WEAPONS: INFANTRY

In the light of the military thinking of the Tsar and his generals, it is not surprising that their ideas had marked effects upon the training of the troops. In normal times the climax of the year's exercises was the great review that the Tsar held—at Kalisz, at Borodino, at Chuguev, at Kiev, at Voznesensk, and at other places. A whole army corps or more massed for this event, at which formation drill and the parade march were the best way to show the troops to the Tsar. Much effort was spent in preparing for this. To obtain the best effect they sought a completely level place with all little ditches filled in and hedgehog and molehills smoothed out. Occasionally they planted trees —but only to mark the place for shouldering arms or the beginning of the parade. Thus at the time when the rest of Europe was adopting maneuvers of small units, the Russian army was concentrating on making the soldier "a beautifully marching machine," who would not spoil the orderly close formation of the massed troops. The battalions and regiments were always drawn up exactly as the official battle orders specified, in the Napoleonic dense columns, or extended battalion formations.[1]

Even when troops were about to face the enemy in battle, the same pedantic attitudes appeared. In 1827, when Diebitsch inspected the Caucasian army that was about to fight the Persians, he paid almost exclusive attention to the individual posture of the soldiers and the dressing of ranks on parade. His reports on troops had nothing to say about the tactics of the various arms, but stressed individual posture, a smooth and firm stride, the dressing of the ranks during the parade, and the elegant fit of the uniforms. When inspecting the cavalry and the artillery he was chiefly interested in seeing if the horses were sleek and well-fed and in noting their training and performance during the parade.[2] When the Tsar was with his army fighting the Turks in 1828,

1. Glinoetskii, *Istoriia General'nago Shtaba*, II, 192.
2. Shcherbatov, II, 250-51.

he regarded it as his duty to hold parades, of which there were three between June 21 and 27, followed by maneuvers on July 1, in spite of the oppressive summer heat.[3] In a similar spirit, when Prince Gorchakov reported on the condition of his troops on the Danube in 1854, he emphasized, not their fighting qualities, but their ability to maintain alignment on parade. On inspecting a newly arrived brigade he wrote: "The alignment and formation of these troops in the parade march by double companies and in close columns were so fine and precise that the men appeared ready for a review."[4]

The same formalism also ruled in the training of troops for battle. Here the infallable guide was the Regulation (*Ustav*), which set forth in great detail the various "battle orders" for the units of infantry, cavalry, and artillery, with complete disregard for conditions of terrain.[5] In the joint exercises of the three main arms, which rarely took place, the infantry, cavalry, and artillery occupied positions in the battle formation as exactly defined in the Regulation. For infantry and artillery there were five battle formations, and for cavalry there were four, although in reality there was little difference between them. In general, the troops were in three lines. In the first line the regiments took position either in battalion columns or in line formation of three ranks of men. All the battalions of each regiment were in line, with a thin screen of sharpshooters in front. The only change in this system that occurred in twenty-five years was that in the 1840's the troops had permission to form company columns, which, as smaller groupings, presented less of a target and thus would incur smaller losses. Some three hundred paces behind the first line stood the second, with all battalions in line. The third line was three or four hundred paces further to the rear, in dense regimental columns. The artillery was dispersed in separate batteries among the infantry units, with the heavier guns in front and the light pieces in reserve. Finally, the cavalry took position, in columns or in line formation. Cossacks or other light cavalry stood on the flanks of the first line, to protect the flanks of the main body.[6]

The detailed nature of these rules was extraordinary. For example, the Field Regulation for Infantry Service contained rules on all sorts of trifles that were quite unsuitable for battle-field conditions. The

3. Schiemann, II, 249.
4. Zaionchkovskii, p. 36.
5. Polievktov, p. 322.
6. Petrov, p. 447.

chapter on forming columns for attack pointed out exactly how many steps the platoon commanders should advance to regroup their units for attack, and how the columns and formations should be aligned.[7] In a *Course of Tactics* adopted in 1850 as a handbook for officers, the author emphasized the value of the Regulation for the officer, "without which he will not know what the troops can perform and what they cannot, and will not know how to give his thoughts to the troops—to command. . . ." There was no word about handling troops under fire, about dispositions, or orders. Knowledge of the Regulation would be sufficient.

The same officer, in discussing battle formations of the infantry, stated:

> When a battle formation is advancing or retiring it is necessary to observe a general alignment of the battalions in each line and to maintain correctly the intervals between battalions. In this case it is not enough for each battalion separately to keep alignment, it is necessary that the pace be alike in all battalions, so that the guidon sergeants marching before the battalions shall keep alignment among themselves and march parallel to one another along lines perpendicular to the common formation. . . .[8]

This reverence for the Regulation even appeared in the highest places. When the Emperor received word in 1849 of the successes of the Russian forces in Hungary, he ascribed them largely to the battle orders set forth in the Regulation. According to N. N. Muraviev, the Tsar added that Field Marshal Paskevich ascribed to the ruler the practical benefits from the prescribed formations, because he had insisted on adherence to the rules. "It has turned out," the Sovereign continued, "that everything we do in peacetime in training the troops is correct and necessary for wartime." Moreover, when the Tsar criticized the actions of individual commanders in Hungary, his standard for judging them was "the tactical rules established in the Regulation."[9]

While one cannot determine exactly what reasons caused the Tsar and his advisers to cling to this system, it is possible to see certain factors that influenced them. First of all, it was sanctified by success. Whereas the Prussians had kept their old system until Jena and Auerstadt, and only introduced universal military service when under

7. Zaionchkovskii, p. 34.
8. Cited by Zaionchkovskii, p. 35.
9. Cited in Polievktov, p. 329.

the French heel, the Russian system produced the armies that forced the French from Moscow and went on to fight at Leipzig and to occupy Paris. Under Nicholas I, armies of the old type continued to win battles until 1854. Suvorov's saying, "They don't court-martial a victor," applied to the Russian military machine, antiquated as it was.

Moreover, the new Prussian system was not suitable to Russian conditions. With a long frontier to defend and great areas to control, and no railroads, the Tsar had to maintain a large army *in being*, in order to meet all emergencies quickly. If the high command had to wait for reserves to organize and march to the danger spot, the war might be lost before they arrived. Furthermore, as has been stated above, as long as Russian serfdom endured, there could be no thought of universal military training. Moreover, the danger of having such numbers trained for war might raise the specter of civil war fought, not by ignorant peasants, but by trained warriors. Nicholas knew that his deadly enemies, the Decembrists, had advocated a short term of service under much milder discipline. Convinced as he was that the revolutionary spirit was still alive, he must have felt that only a long-term army, in which severe discipline had instilled an attitude of unquestioning obedience, could save Russia from chaos. Neither a short term of service, nor a system of training that stressed adaptability and individual initiative, seemed to be suited to Russia's needs, in the eyes of the Tsar.

Probably for these reasons, most of the Russian military machine was steeped in formalism, although at the Military Academy in St. Petersburg intelligent and scholarly students were devoting themselves to military science. In 1849 Capt. N. Neelov published a book on strategy in which, after giving a historical treatment of the subject, he analyzed the works of Lloyd, Bülow, Napoleon, Jomini, Wagner, Clausewitz, and others. His conclusion was that there was no precise science of war, as there were many variable elements, although there were certain basic principles to be applied according to the special circumstances in each case. Hence, he held that the wider the commander's knowledge of military history, geography, fortification, logistics, politics, and other factors that might affect a given strategic situation, the better prepared he would be.[10] It is interesting to note, however, that he estimated that railroads could never haul any signifi-

10. N. Neelov, *Ocherk sovremennago sostoianiia strategii* (3 pts.; St. Petersburg, 1849), *passim*.

cant numbers of troops, as they would not have enough rolling stock
to do the task. To move an infantry corps of twenty thousand men
would require 100 locomotives and 808 cars, or approximately all
the railroad equipment of Belgium, which was one of the European
countries with most extensive railroad facilities at that time.[11]

A study of military statistics published by Col. D. A. Miliutin
(who became minister of war under Alexander II) displayed an advanced view of military statistics and military geography, which he
grouped together. His analysis of the military geography of the
Germany of 1847 was intelligent and realistic, as it viewed most of
the lesser German states as insignificant, but had a high appreciation
of the Prussian Landwehr system.[12] On the other hand, the respected
Baron Medem, professor of tactics, clung to obsolescent theories, for
he stated that, while musketry fire could inflict considerable damage on
the enemy at from one hundred to one hundred and fifty paces, only
a bayonet could completely crush the enemy.[13] Similarly, Col. F.
Goremykin, professor of tactics after Medem, stated that in battle
musket fire was only partially effective at two hundred paces and did
not become really telling until the range was shortened to one hundred
and fifty or one hundred paces. In his view, small-arms fire was insufficient to overcome the foe. A bayonet charge, which was therefore
necessary to complete the work of the musketry, would achieve success
if made in massed strength, with dash and persistence.[14]

It is interesting to note that the same author declared that landing
operations with large armies were very difficult and, if they involved
long voyages, might be regarded as impossible.[15] This opinion remained the accepted view in Russian military circles until the French
and British forces set foot in the Crimea in 1854.

Perhaps the ideas, whether correct or unsound, that the professors
of the Military Academy held were not of great importance, for they
seem to have had little effect upon the army as a whole. As has been
stated, there were few graduates from the Military Academy, and they
did not enjoy high prestige. Also the Russian press showed little
interest in military learning, Russian military scholars rarely enjoyed

11. *Ibid.*, Pt. II, 292.
12. D. A. Miliutin, *Statistika. Pervye opyty voennoi statistiki* (2 vols.; St. Petersburg, 1847-1848), *passim.*
13. N. V. Medem, *Uchebnyia rukopisi dlia voenno-uchebnykh zavedenii. Taktika*
(2 pts.; St. Petersburg, 1837), I, 33-35.
14. F. F. Goremykin, *Rukovodstvo k izucheniiu taktiki v nachal'nykh eia osnovaniiakh i vo prakticheskom primenenii* (3 pts. in 1; St. Petersburg, 1849), I, 28-30.
15. *Ibid.*, III, 210.

the privilege of journeying abroad to investigate contemporary developments, and the dominant attitude in the Russian army was highly discouraging to military scholarship.[16]

Curiously enough, although Baron Jomini, the renowned military theorist, enjoyed little prestige in Russia because he was alleged to lack practical talents, the Russian military men eagerly adopted what they believed were his theories of strategy. Trusting that this mysterious science would win wars for them without the necessity of fighting it out with the enemy on the battlefield, they lost sight of the need to adopt up-to-date methods of combat and clung to their beloved mass tactics and fixed battle orders which were marked out for the troops on the parade grounds with the use of guidons. Forgetting that terrain could have great influence on military operations, they dealt with this complication by refusing to recognize it. Maneuvers were held on level ground, and they avoided broken and wooded locations as not suitable.[17]

This refusal to consider the realities of war influenced the uniforming of the troops. When designing the dress of the infantry, the Tsar and his assistants paid little attention to the convenience and suitability of the uniforms for field conditions, but instead sought to make them handsome and imposing. In 1826 the infantry wore tight jackets with cuffs, and high collars fastened under the chin with several hooks, with the white straps of the knapsacks crossing on the chest. Their legs were encased in leather gaiters with five or six buttons. On their heads they wore heavy leather shakos ten inches tall, visored, and adorned with brass insignia and topped by plumes nineteen inches tall.[18] Before long the gaiters and breeches gave way to long trousers worn outside the boots, and in later years a helmet of the Prussian type, with a spike on top, replaced the shako, but in other respects there was little change in the soldiers' dress.

The training of the soldiers also was highly artificial and unrealistic. They gave almost complete attention to close-order drill, in which the Russian army was outstanding. The enlisted men received their training almost entirely from sergeants, who stressed the skills necessary for reviews: the parade step—a sort of goose-step—the facings, the posture of the soldiers, and an exaggerated manual of arms. In

16. A. Andrianov, *Inkermanskii boi i oborona Sevastopolia. Nabroski uchastnika* (St. Petersburg, 1903), pp. 61-62.
17. Glinoetskii, *Istoriia*, II, 192.
18. Petrov, p. 433.

spite of the urging of the Tsar, there was little field training, which both officers and enlisted men hated as a source of extra exertion and trouble. As for musketry, that suffered almost complete neglect, as it seemed quite useless.[19] Alexander II liked to tell of Sergt. Kozhemiakin of the Semenovskii regiment, his former drill instructor, who was a perfectionist at marching. "When marching with the training step, he would put a glass full of water on top of his shako, and then marched, made the marching turns and did the facings in place, in such a manner that not a drop of water spilled." While the sergeant was performing these evolutions, "his legs in turn were raised completely parallel to the ground and the toe of his boot formed one straight line with his whole leg."[20]

The chief striving of commanders was to have their regiments achieve perfection in the parade march, with their ranks "like three strings at the moment when they are in line with the commander. . . . The parade march by regimental columns was called 'the spectacle of the gods.' "[21] Or as another writer described these achievements:

Uniformity and organization reached the point where a whole infantry division of four regiments of twelve battalions (not less than 9,000 men) formed in columns, performed all the movements, marching in step, not losing step in the turns and keeping the ideal alignment in rank and in depth. The manual of arms by whole regiments struck one by their "purity." Complete immobility and quiet in the ranks was brought to perfection. In this dead silence of the troops, in this skilful and uniform manual of arms, in unblemished formal parades, according to the views of the times, lay the guarantee of success in war.[22]

Nicholas himself was a lover of magnificent parades, but he seems to have understood that there was more to war than this. In May, 1833, he inspected a battalion of the Guards Jaeger regiment on the drill ground and later had them appear on the uneven terrain of Kamennyi Ostrov, a part of St. Petersburg, for further drill. Although they satisfied him in their regular drill, they were not skilled at taking cover, as they had been trained almost entirely on even ground. The Tsar pointed out to them how to take cover and told them not to

19. A. M. Zaionchkovskii, "Vostochnaia voina 1853-56 gg.," in Grishinskii, *Istoriia Russkoi Armii i Flota*, X, 19.
20. P. A. Dirin, *Istoriia leib-gvardii Semenovskago polka* (2 vols.; St. Petersburg, 1883), II, 168.
21. "Iz zapisok sevastopol'tsa," *Russkii Arkhiv*, V (1867), 1585-86.
22. Petrov, p. 446.

adhere always to the letter of the Regulation.[23] These variations from the usual pattern, however, were rare, and the emphasis on parades and close-order drill continued as before.

Side by side with the Russian parade-mania went underestimation of fire power and reluctance to accept technical innovations. In February, 1834, Gen. N. N. Muraviev had a chat with the Grand Duke Michael about the merits of the Robert breech-loading musket from France, which had just been tested. "I said that the introduction of this weapon would do just the opposite of what was needed," as the Russian infantry already had a tendency to fire off too many cartridges and that this habit would be intensified by a breechloader. He continued: ". . .with us troops having this weapon would cease to fight [hand-to-hand], and there never would be enough cartridges."[24] Also *Voennyi Zhurnal*, in the same year, contained a long article on the Robert and Lefauchet breech-loading muskets, which came to the conclusion that, while these weapons had great value, they could not be given to the infantry, as they would quickly fire off all their cartridges.[25] Even as late as 1855 a Russian expert wrote that Russian tests on breechloaders, including the Prussian needle gun, had disclosed technical defects. The chief Russian objection to these weapons, however, was "that the rifleman, in the confusion of battle, has the possibility of firing all his cartridges in an instant and will be defenseless. . . ."[26] The Colt revolver, which, according to a Russian officer, had proved its worth in the Seminole and Mexican wars, was finally given tests in Russia in 1854 and 1855. Only one regiment received permission to carry this arm.[27]

The lack of interest in small-arms fire that was so prevalent in Russian military thinking and that was evident in the above-cited rejection of breechloaders made itself especially felt in the training of the troops. The powder and lead that the troops received and from which they made their cartridges were only enough to provide ten ball cartridges and sixty blank cartridges per man, for the regiments of the Guards, the army, and the Caucasus Corps. The military rules sternly warned the artillery detachments that issued the powder and lead to observe this limitation strictly, for they were liable to the

23. *Istoriia Egerskago polka*, p. 265.
24. Murav'ev, *Russkii Arkhiv*, XXXII (1894), Pt. III, 149.
25. *Voennyi Zhurnal*, 1834, No. 4, pp. 201-2.
26. *Artilleriiskii Zhurnal*, 1855, No. 1, p. 43.
27. *Ibid.*, 1855, No. 5, 434-61.

Treasury for any amounts in excess.[28] For the most part, however, the rank and file rarely received ten ball cartridges, for another rule enjoined the commanders to give "to the men who will act in close formation only three cartridges per man" and to use the remainder "for training real marksmen. . . ." Moreover, the commanders were instructed to observe all possible economy in bullets, "collecting for this purpose those shot off by digging them out where possible from the banks behind the targets, and on finding them, to use them again for shooting, as there is always enough powder for training."[29] This commandment indicates accurately the position of musketry in the scale of values: these soldiers, on whose parade uniforms the government spent impressive sums, must needs grub their spent bullets out of the dirt, because the authorities begrudged the money to buy additional lead.

In vain did the Code of Military Regulations prescribe careful training of the soldiers in aiming, firing, and target practice.[30] After the Crimean War one of the major generals wrote that when training soldiers in peace time

> they usually fired blank rounds and only as an exception at targets . . . In the battalion all the attention of the men was directed to ensure that at the command "Fire!" they should pull the triggers at the same time, which indeed was performed in remarkable unison; however, no one thought to aim. . . . Firing was done in battalion volleys, and all this with blank cartridges in the air.[31]

P. V. Alabin, writing about his experiences in four wars, declared that the Russian army was by no means ready for the Crimean War. Not only did the men have smoothbore muskets that had been systematically mistreated; there were "very few men who knew how to shoot, as they [the commanders] had never carefully trained them for this art. . . ." Alabin added that often the officers never used the powder issued for this purpose, but donated most of it to neighboring landowners. "With us everything was staked, so to speak, exclusively on marching and on correct stretching forth of the toe."[32] An anonymous

---

28. SVP, Pt. IV, Bk. III, *Ob otpuskakh snabzhenii*, arts. 1106-8, 1141.
29. *Ibid.*, Pt. IV, Bk. IV, *O khoziaistve voisk*, art. 332.
30. *Ibid.*, Pt. III, Bk. I, *O vnutrennom upravlenii voisk*, arts. 751-56.
31. N. Gersevanov, *O prichinakh tekhnicheskago prevoskhodstva frantsuzov v kampanii 1855-56 gg.* (St. Petersburg, 1858), pp. 11-12, cited in A. V. Fedorov, *Russkaia armiia v 50-70 gg. XIX v. Ocherki* (Leningrad, 1959), pp. 21-22.
32. P. V. Alabin, *Chetyre voiny. Pokhodnyia zapiski* (Samara, n. d.), cited in Zaionchkovskii, *Voennye reformy*, p. 38.

military writer in 1859 alleged that many soldiers with years of service had never fired a ball cartridge, as their commanders regarded musketry training as the last item on the agenda, to be dealt with when there was no inspection in prospect and there was nothing else to teach. Many commanders, the writer stated, justified this neglect by citing the scarcity of live ammunition for training; he, however, effectively punctured this argument: "who does not know that many regiments have not even shot off the three cartridges that were issued and not rarely dumped into the water the powder that was issued to them."[33]

As for the enlisted men, they never learned to regard musketry practice as a serious matter, for all their training had stressed posture, the manual of arms, and parade-marching, and had treated practice in firing as of no real importance.[34] Hence the soldiers cared only about what was demanded during inspections, namely, neatness, posture, and marching, and regarded target practice as a whim of the commander, for they knew that most inspections did not call for practice in firing. Moreover, since the commanders spent all of the drill period on essentials and then compelled the soldiers to practice musketry during the time allotted to them for rest, the enlisted men looked on this extra demand as a punishment.[35] Holding these views, they were not above trickery at target practice. In one instance, the commander of the unit issued sixty cartridges, but when the exercise ended, they found sixty-three holes in the target: "so zealously had the carpenters drilled the target beforehand, and so cleverly covered them up with paper."[36] Another military analyst asked: "Who, for example does not know of stabbing the target with bayonets?"[37] i.e., to simulate bullet holes.

Occasionally zealous commanders made persistent efforts to improve the firing of their troops, but they usually encountered obstacles. A history of the Life Guard Dragoon regiment tells of unusual attention paid to this matter in 1827, but added: "The firing, however, could not be very successful, as too few cartridges were issued for practice, so that they used the blank cartridges left over after maneuvers, using clay bullets in place of lead ones." In 1829, when they

33. "Vzgliad na sostoianie russkikh voisk v minuvshuiu voinu," *Voennyi Sbornik*, I (1858), 12.
34. *Ibid.*
35. Zaionchkovskii, p. 33.
36. "Golos iz armii," *Voennyi Sbornik*, I (1858), 118.
37. *Ibid.*, p. 84.

again emphasized target practice, orders were issued: "In case of a lack of lead balls, clay ones should be used instead." And this practice again made its appearance in 1832 and other years. By 1837, however, when the Tsar first inspected the marksmanship of this regiment, its firing had greatly improved. "The Dragoons shot well—this was not an accident, as they had practiced, thanks to the Tsar's donation: near Orel the Sovereign had donated thirty ball cartridges per man. . . ."[38] Such an august benefaction was rare, however, and most regiments continued to be without proper target practice. It is significant that on January 13, 1854, the Artillery Department of the Ministry of War ordered that firing with clay bullets should cease, as they scratched the musket barrels.[39]

Another reason why the Russian infantryman was a wretched marksman was that his musket was a highly ineffective weapon. Until 1842 it was a flintlock, firing a round ball as much as three hundred paces, but not accurate beyond two hundred. In good weather the troops could fire about one round per minute, while in wet weather the rate of fire was slower and at times firing became impossible. The soldier had to stand to load and hence could not maintain fire from a prone or kneeling position. The ramrod was indispensable for firing, and if the soldier lost it or broke it, he was out of action. Beginning in 1845, the government had the flintlocks converted to fire with percussion caps, which greatly improved their reliability and increased the rate of fire. But this work was done slowly, with no special urgency, so that in the Crimean War some of the troops still had flintlocks.[40] The troops of the Caucasus Corps used these antiquated weapons in their battles with the Turks in 1854 and 1855.[41]

The Russian musket, whose quality was often not high, received treatment that in many cases made it practically useless for fighting. The soldiers tended to regard it as an instrument to keep glittering for parades and reviews and to lose sight of its real purpose, even to the point of giving it treatment that weakened its effectiveness as a weapon. The Code of Military Regulations of 1838 contained a set of instructions under the heading: "Harm to the musket from lack

38. M. A. Kovalevskii, *Piat'desiat' let sushchestvovaniia leibgvardii Dragunskago polka* (Novgorod, 1870), pp. 43, 50, 80, 174.
39. V. G. Fedorov, *Vooruzhenie russkoi armii v Krymskuiu kampaniiu* (St. Petersburg, 1904), p. 132.
40. Petrov, pp. 436-37.
41. M. Likhutin, *Russkie v Aziatskoi Turtsii v 1854 i 1855 godakh* (St. Petersburg, 1863), p. 398; M. I. Bogdanovich, *Vostochnaia voina 1853-1856 gg.* (4 vols. in 2; St. Petersburg, 1876), IV, 237-38.

of knowledge how to treat it," which listed a whole series of abuses inflicted upon muskets. Screws had been inserted improperly, rivets in the locks were badly placed, and sometimes the barrel had been so badly set in place that the lock failed to work properly. Some locksmiths had heated the mainspring to lessen its bend, with the result that it became too weak to activate the firing mechanism. "According to the testimony of many officers, throughout a whole campaign, many muskets were not oiled, not even the parts most liable to friction." This proved very harmful to the locks.

> Sometimes soldiers, in order that the musket should rattle more during the actions of the manual of arms, loosened the ramrod in its seat, by burning the opening with a heated ramrod, . . . and they scrape out the stock under the keeper-rings and other parts, wherever it is possible to make the musket rattle more; this also brings not a little harm to the musket by premature harm to its parts.[42]

When they called in the old muskets and converted them to percussion pieces, the inspectors detected and corrected many of these defects, but before long many of the same abuses came to light. In 1850 a set of rules for handling the percussion musket listed a number of abuses, including "scouring musket parts with emery and polishing them so that they become thin. . . ." They ordered the soldiers, when removing rust from a barrel, always to place it on a bench or other support; they were forbidden "to take the barrel by both ends and rub it on some hard substance: for by this not only are the walls made thin, but the barrel may be bent. . . ." Moreover, the rules enjoined the commanders "Not to permit them to scrape down the stock and to widen the ramrod channel in order to make the musket more noisy when doing the manual of arms. . . ."[43]

Shortly after these rules, the Tsar, in August, 1851, confirmed an Instruction on maintenance of weapons. This strictly forbade the regiments to undertake certain repairs to muskets (which they probably had been doing). Among these were: "patching up the barrel and inserting sections in it, to cover up some defect or other"; cutting down the barrel and welding on a new breech; welding broken hammers, bayonets, ramrods, or any other iron or steel parts; and making various crude alterations to the firing mechanism. The Instruction

42. SVP, Pt. IV, Bk. IV, *O khoziaistve voisk*, art. 280, Supplement IV, sec. d, par. 25-27.

43. "Instruktsiia dlia ispravnago soderzhaniia v voiskakh ruchnago ognestrel'nago oruzhiia," *Artilleriiskii Zhurnal*, 1852, No. 1, pp. 114-20.

also forbade repairing bronze fittings with solder, gluing together a broken musket butt out of pieces, and gluing the butt to the stock.[44]

These and other injunctions, however, had little effect, and the soldiers' attitude toward their muskets showed little change. In the Crimean War the remodelled flintlock muskets almost all proved to be in bad condition. As a result of long use, thin barrels were common, and some had defects in the metal, or blown barrels. The new percussion pieces were better, but had not been properly cared for. The soldiers had mistreated the locks and had failed to oil them, so that they often wore out. On some muskets the breech piece had been badly screwed on, which sometimes blocked the touch hole and made firing impossible. The soldiers had loosened the screws, keeper-rings, and seats for the ramrods, so that the pieces would rattle better during the manual of arms. During the fighting in the Crimea the muskets often received improper care, especially when men were wounded. In the Moscow regiment, out of 1,318 smoothbores inspected, 70 were so badly rusted as to be unusable, while 464 had damaged locks. Many of the others had damaged or defective barrels, defective breeches, or worn and loose bayonets. In the Butyrskii regiment, 1,400 out of 1,991 muskets received had similar defects. These were extreme cases, but other units had the same experience on a lesser scale.[45]

An incident before the Russian attack on Evpatoria in February, 1855, reveals much about the condition of the weapons of the Russian infantry. A battalion of Greek volunteers who were about to take part in the attack on the fortifications demanded Russian muskets with bayonets. To satisfy their request, Gen. Khrulev, the commander, had muskets taken from the Russian regiments and gave them to the Greeks. The latter, however, far from being satisfied, almost rioted, for the Russian sergeants had collected the worst muskets in their platoons. As a result the volunteers now had weapons with broken triggers and locks, bad ramrods and bayonets, and even cartridges filled with millet instead of gunpowder, which convinced them that the Russians wanted to have them all killed in battle.[46]

Bad as the muskets of the infantry were, their uselessness was surpassed by that of the flintlocks of the *druzhinas* (battalions) of militia

44. Russia. Voennoe Ministerstvo. Voenno-uchenyi Komitet, *Rukovodstvo dlia artilleriiskoi sluzhby* (St. Petersburg, 1853), pp. 313-14.

45. Fedorov, pp. 136-38.

46. A. A. Panaev, "Kniaz' A. S. Menshikov," *Russkaia Starina*, XIX (1877), 310-14.

enrolled during the Crimean War. The druzhina from Tambov received 216, of which 25 would fire, while the remaining 191 were completely useless. As most of them had been made between 1811 and 1815, they had defective locks, dented or cracked barrels, rotted stocks, or other failings. The Vladimir druzhina found 722 out of its 797 muskets to be worthless. Another, more fortunate unit obtained 367 effective weapons out of a total of 800. Even those that could be fired, however, failed to make hits even in the hands of good marksmen.[47]

While the infantry as a whole possessed little effective firepower, there were in the Russian army some elements of more significant marksmanship. By 1834 there were three rifle battalions—one in the Guards, one in the Grenadier Corps, and one in the regular army.[48] Eventually each corps had a battalion of sharpshooters armed with muzzle-loading Liège rifles, and later each regiment received permission to have ninety-six men armed with rifles and trained to act as sharpshooters. In 1851 the Ernroth rifle was adopted in place of the Liège type. The rifles had an extreme range of 1,120 paces, with better than fifty per cent hits on a man-sized target at five hundred paces. As they were difficult to load, however, their fire was slow. Nevertheless, in spite of the increasing interest in rifles, in 1853 the Russian infantry had only 6,198 of them—considerably less than the number called for by the table of organization.[49] Thus the existence of these small numbers of riflemen did not compensate for the general weakness of the infantry's firepower.

In spite of its ineffective musketry, the Russian army did well in the wars against the Persians, the Turks, and the Poles, for the first two were so disorganized as to be almost helpless in the field, while the Poles, who fought with great bravery and skill, were numerically weak and torn by dissension. During the Crimean campaign, however, it was another story. At the battles of the Alma and Inkerman the numerous rifles of the allied armies far outranged the Russian muskets, and even the smoothbores of the French, firing Minié balls, proved effective at long range. Allied marksmen were able to strike down Russian officers and gunners before the Russian muskets could

47. Fedorov, pp. 133-35.
48. SVP, Pt. I, Bk. I, *Obrazovanie voisk s ikh upravleniem*, art. 14, Supplement III (ruling of Jan. 7, 1834). A rifle had a grooved barrel, whereas a musket had a smooth bore.
49. Zaionchkovskii, pp. 24-25.

strike back. One of the leading staff officers at Sevastopol wrote to Col. P. K. Men'kov on the Danube:

> At the present time the greatest subject with us is stutsers [rifles]; we have powder, shot, troops, but they have not sent one stutser and evidently there is no hope of it. Seeing how, in the Inkerman action, whole regiments melted from the stutsers, losing a fourth of their men, while *they* were coming into musket range, I am convinced that they will cut us down as soon as we fight in the open. . . .[50]

In 1855 Count M. D. Buturlin, chatting with British officers who were being exchanged, heard from "young Duff" that the latter, during the Battle of Inkerman, had shuddered "to see the devastation that the Minié carbines produced in the ranks of the Russian columns," whose musket fire "did not carry half the distance to the enemy as they pressed forward."[51]

Realization of the need for rifles came to the Russian authorities immediately after the Battle of the Alma in September, 1854, but it was difficult to provide them. These weapons were made by hand, and skilled gunsmiths were rare, so that efforts to speed up their production resulted badly. Late in July, 1855, fifteen hundred rifles fabricated at the Citadel at Warsaw reached the troops at Sevastopol, only to prove unsatisfactory. A cursory inspection led to the scrapping of 216 of them, and later, more careful investigation by one of the Tsar's adjutants found that 1,490 of them had defects, some of which were of major importance.[52] The Russians made strenuous efforts to buy rifles abroad, especially in Belgium, but, in the face of pre-emptive buying by the British, they could obtain contracts for only 13,900, at high prices. Even when these weapons were made, it proved to be almost impossible to ship them to Russia, as the Baltic was unsafe, and Prussia closed her frontiers to arms shipments in April, 1855. Consequently only approximately three thousand Belgian rifles reached Russia before the end of fighting. Russian officers also attempted without success to buy rifles in Prussia and negotiated with Colt and other American manufacturers, but with no greater success.[53] Thus the Russian government was forced to rely on home production.

On November 30, 1854, the Ministry of War gave orders for 34,800 rifles to its three arms factories, and later ordered 19,700 more.

50. Men'kov, I, 255.
51. "Zapiski Grafa M. D. Buturlina," *Russkii Arkhiv*, XXXVI (1898), Pt. II, 418.
52. Fedorov, pp. 31-32.
53. *Ibid.*, pp. 14-21.

These were very large totals, which, in view of the equipment and the artisans available, were more than they could make during the period of fighting. Many more were ordered from commercial gunsmiths.[54]

In addition to the purchase and manufacture of rifles, the Russian authorities tried various expedients to improve the army's firepower. One such effort consisted of supplying Minié balls to the troops in place of round balls. The soldiers, however, found that after two or three shots the bullets would not enter the muzzle of the musket. "The soldiers forced the bullet, striking the ramrod with a stone; the ramrod bent into an arc, but the bullet would not go in. They hammered as in a smithy. The soldiers took candle ends and greased the bullets, but this did not help." As for the muskets converted into rifles by cutting rifling grooves in the barrels, they sometimes split along the rifling. "It is not surprising that in such a situation the officers were in despair, and the enlisted men raved of treason."[55]

In 1855 the army adopted the Neissler bullet—cylindrical, with a round nose, and hollow at the base, so that it would expand in the gun barrel and make a tight fit. This gave an effective range of three hundred to four hundred yards. In addition, the rifling of the percussion muskets, which used the Neissler bullet, gave reasonably good results. The Liège rifles continued in use as well. These were larger in caliber, and fired a bullet with two lugs that fitted into the rifling grooves. These weapons were effective at very great range.[56]

The introduction of the Neissler bullet proved to be a mixed blessing. After bullets of this type had been found on a French prisoner in November, 1854, the Russians at once tried them and found them effective. They made sixteen molds for them, cast two hundred thousand of this type, and issued them to the troops. On December 8 Prince Menshikov, commander at Sevastopol, reported to the Tsar that "our small-arm fire of late has been very effective, thanks to the use of the elongated bullet, . . . which carries far. This carry has greatly cheered our sharpshooters." On January 11, 1855, Count D. Osten-Sacken, commander of the Sevastopol garrison troops, wrote:

> The new bullets . . . tried by the troops of the garrison appear to be extraordinarily effective without doing any harm to the muskets.

54. *Ibid.*, p. 13.
55. N. Dubrovin, *Istoriia Sevastopol'skoi oborony*, cited in *ibid.*, p. 33.
56. *Report of Major Alfred Mordecai, Military Commission to Europe in 1855 and 1856* (Washington, 1860), pp. 157-58. 36th Cong., 1st Sess., Senate, Exec. Doc. No. 60.

The soldiers are delighted with their long range and with unusual zeal are practicing shooting. Prisoners taken from the enemy say that they have already noticed a change in our arms and that our fire has become vastly more effective.[57]

Unfortunately, although tests showed that the new bullet was much better than the Minié ball, its introduction brought new trouble. The existing sights on the muskets were not suitable to the new ranges of the shots. At first the soldiers tried to sight their pieces over a finger placed across the barrel, but that was a crude expedient. Obtaining and installing suitable sights turned out to be an almost impossible task during the remaining months of fighting. Obtaining accurate molds for casting the bullets was extremely difficult, as these projectiles had a very complicated shape and there were few machine shops in Russia able to make the molds.[58]

Even worse was the fact that muskets using the Neissler bullets frequently burst. As a result of this, on June 11, 1855, the commander of the artillery sent a special report to the new commander in chief, Prince M. D. Gorchakov, on this subject, asking that a special staff officer be assigned to investigate. The report contained the following excerpts:

> With frequent firing, in spite of the fact that the bullets have been greased, the barrels clog up, so that after 10 rounds the bullets enter the barrel badly, as a result of which the musket bursts in its upper part. . . .
> In the 10th division, when the French bullets have been used the barrels have frequently burst. . . .
> In the 6th, 9th, 10th, and 11th divisions there are no bullet-molds at all as yet. In the remaining divisions there are. . . some, . . . but the greater part of them are either not suitable or have become unusable from use.[59]

Shortly thereafter the commander of artillery sent Prince Obolenskii, an aide-de-camp of the Tsar, to investigate. He found that the molds sent to the Crimea were of two different calibers. One of these was too large to fit the musket of official caliber, although the projectiles were suitable for muskets with enlarged bores. Hence it was necessary to sort out the bullets and make sure that each division had the bullets and the bullet molds suitable for its muskets.[60]

57. Fedorov, pp. 78-81.
58. *Ibid.*, pp. 86-89.
59. *Ibid.*, p. 90.
60. *Ibid.*, pp. 90-91.

Thus, while Russian musketry made some improvement during the Crimean campaign, it was impossible in such a short time to correct the failings of decades. Although the Tsar increased the number of sharpshooters in each company of infantry to twenty-four in September, 1854, and in January, 1855, to twenty-six,[61] the shortage of rifles made these changes impossible to carry out in full. During the war the number of rifles acquired was 135,360, of which 91,723 were made in Russia, and 6,735 were converted smoothbores. The balance were imported.[62] As has been already stated, however, a considerable number of these proved to be defective, so that the number of riflemen ready for combat probably did not increase greatly. It is noteworthy that in the Battle of the Chernaia River, on August 4, 1855, of the 102½ battalions in action, only three were rifle battalions, and they were much reduced in strength.[63] It seems safe to say that throughout this crucial conflict the Russian infantry—the backbone of the army— was at a grave disadvantage because of its antiquated tactics and weapons.

61. *Ibid.*, p. 30.
62. Zaionchkovskii, p. 28.
63. N. . ., "Neskol'ko zamechanii po povodu stat'i: 'Vzgliad na sostoianie Russkikh voisk v minuvshuiu voinu,'" *Voennyi Sbornik*, I (1858), 286.

CHAPTER VII. TRAINING AND WEAPONS: CAVALRY, ENGINEERS, ARTILLERY

While Nicholas I was extremely proud of his "incomparable infantry," he probably took even greater delight in the magnificent cavalry that he displayed at annual reviews. There were fifty-nine cavalry regiments of approximately one thousand men each, which formed twenty cavalry divisions of about four thousand each. The greater part of the mounted units consisted of light cavalry—hussars and uhlans—in regiments of eight squadrons of from one hundred and twenty to one hundred and fifty men. The uhlans carried sabers and lances; the hussars, carbines as well as sabers. The dragoons and the Guards horse grenadier regiment had eight squadrons armed with sabers and light muskets and bayonets, and two squadrons of lancers. These regiments fought either as infantry, while the mounted lancer squadrons guarded their flanks, or on horseback. Finally, there were the cuirassiers. These were large men in steel breastplates and helmets and carrying heavy swords, mounted on powerful horses. Their purpose was to make a shattering charge that would sweep all before it and decide a stubborn battle.[1] The basic battle formation of the cavalry was extended order, aligned in two ranks. Columns were used for purposes of maneuver or other movement. Finally, there was the rarely employed open order, in which the ranks were twenty-five paces apart. This was for use in attacks or in flanking operations in which the firepower of the cavalry would be important.[2]

It must be said, however, that the cavalry, like the infantry, did not receive proper training for war. Before 1825 the officers of the Iamburg Uhlan regiment—a crack unit—had so little knowledge of the evolutions that before any regimental exercise the colonel summoned the squadron commanders to headquarters, and there they rehearsed with checkers the formations for the coming exercise. Like-

1. Medem, pp. 40-47.
2. *Ibid.*, pp. 47-54.

wise, they had "no conception" of training maneuvers. If it was believed that the Tsar might order maneuvers, it was the duty of officers of the General Staff to make up in advance the most exact and detailed program of the maneuver and to study it with the troops. "We rehearsed maneuvers exactly like a ballet. On the field men with guidons were stationed and the highly detailed description showed the movements, not only of regimental or brigade columns, but even of squadrons." The authorities regarded it as necessary, in order to study the planned maneuver, to call in the commanders of all detachments down to and including those of double squadrons and to explain to them, orally and in writing, both the general and the detailed movements. Even with these precautions, however, the unit commanders often did badly, as they lacked an understanding of real war. When Nicholas I came to power he made strenuous efforts to change this senseless state of affairs, but his efforts, labors, and demands "did not succeed quickly and everywhere in combatting the established routine."[3]

In truth, the new ruler himself continued for some time to stress non-essentials. When he inspected the Iamburg Uhlan regiment in May, 1827, he paid particular attention to the riding of the officers and men and was much astonished when he saw to what a degree of perfection they had brought manège riding. He did not, however, examine them on their knowledge of outpost duty and scouting, or their use of weapons. "You have led before me a whole regiment of riding-masters!" he said to the commander of the regiment. He was so pleased with this skill that after the review he awarded five silver rubles to each enlisted man and bestowed various promotions on the officers.[4]

In similar fashion, when the Second Army was on the eve of its campaign against the Turks in 1828, it did not receive training that was suitable for wartime conditions, but was directly contrary to them. "Thus, for example, they almost never practiced the cavalry in performing scouting duty, did not train them on long marches, and did not teach them how to spare the horses but at the same time to require work of them. . .," and in general did not develop in them habits necessary in war.[5] Similarly, when the Iamburg Uhlan regiment

3. V. Krestovskii, *Istoriia 14-go Ulanskago Iamburgskago Eia Imperatorskago Vysochestva, velikoi kniazhny Marii Aleksandrovny polka* (St. Petersburg, 1873), pp. 499-500.
4. *Ibid.*, p. 385.
5. Epanchin, I, 84.

was about to march against the Polish insurgents in 1831, its colonel issued detailed rules for the campaign, which, however, specified nothing about tactical matters, advance- and rear-guard work, patrols, guard duty, and scouting, but dealt with trifles. He told the officers how to instruct orderlies on restdays; how to preserve the flesh of the horses; how to lay down their caps and other belongings at night. Also he had them drill their men on keeping their pikes at the same level, by reviewing them every night, at a walk, a trot, and a gallop, paying especial attention to the pace of the horses.[6]

Another failing of the Russian cavalry was that they were heavy and not agile. A group of Russian officers after the campaign of 1828 against the Turks mentioned that even the Russian light cavalry was really like heavy cavalry. The horse carried a large saddle, an overcoat, a kettle, a bag of biscuits, a sack of oats, and often a bundle of hay, to say nothing of pistols, saber, carbine, and cartridge-box. Consequently the Russian horse was like a pack animal compared to the lively Turkish mounts.[7]

Under such conditions it is not surprising that the Russian cavalry at times performed poorly in war. In 1828 it lost most of its horses from lack of fodder—although in large part this resulted from improper logistical planning at higher echelons. In addition, there was inexcusable carelessness. On January 13, 1829, Gen. Kiselev reported to Count Diebitsch that in some units "the horse-blankets have completely rotted," which he ascribed to the fact that "throughout the campaign for a very long time they did not unsaddle the horses."[8] This was bad, not only for the blankets, but for the horses as well.

During the campaign of 1829 the Russian cavalry, fully supplied with fresh horses, failed almost completely to provide Diebitsch, the new commander, with knowledge of the enemy. When the Turkish Vizier left his stronghold of Shumla, Diebitsch learned of it from spies, scouts, and Turkish deserters, but not from his cavalry. On one occasion the Turks sallied forth, but the Russian patrols did not discover them until they were less than two miles from the Russian positions. In fact, the cavalry patrols failed repeatedly to learn of the movements of large bodies of Turkish troops, although the Russian horse had full opportunity to range far and wide. Against the Turks this did

6. Krestovskii, p. 399.
7. F. Fonton, *Vospominaniia. Iumoristicheskiia, politicheskiia, i voennyia pis'ma iz glavnoi kvartiry Dunaiskoi armii, v 1828 i 1829 gg.* (2 vols.; 3rd ed., Leipzig, 1866), I, 200-2.
8. Epanchin, I, 84.

not matter greatly, but against more effective foes such negligence might have been costly.[9]

In the Polish War of 1831, the Iamburg regiment did very poorly, committing almost all the military sins. They were careless and noisy on outpost duty and on occasion went to sleep, so that the Poles could approach at will. When they foraged for provisions they stole and looted, which, of course, infuriated the peasants. In encounters with the Poles their shots almost never hit anyone, although at times they blazed away for an hour. Drunkenness and disorder were common, and even a sergeant got drunk and went off for days, and got off almost scot-free.[10]

In combat the Russian horse did little better. On one occasion the Iamburg Uhlans caught up with a Polish unit by galloping for a *verst*, only to have their prey escape, as the uhlan horses were worn out by their exertions. And in general, they never achieved real success during this entire campaign. "... we must admit that in the Polish campaign, *as cavalrymen* we did very little, almost nothing, and in this respect we only reaped the worthy fruits of the system that had taken root in our regiment since 1819"[11]—by which the author probably meant the stress on manège training and parades.

The Polish cavalry proved incomparably more vigorous than the Russians and differed from them "in initiative, enterprise and the spirit of boldness in the field and not of the parade ground." On one occasion a whole Russian corps of three cavalry divisions was for three hours prevented from crossing a bridge by a company of Polish infantry—"and held up solely because they didn't think to dismount two or three squadrons and with their pikes drive out the trifling handful of the enemy." Later, at the Battle of Grochów before Warsaw the Russians made a magnificent cavalry charge that gravely disordered the Polish forces, but it was not supported by other cavalry forces and the Poles escaped destruction. Moreover, this attack was much delayed because "our cavalry regarded the roadside ditches and field drains as impassable obstacles to them and were able to cross over to the point of attack, in deep columns of three, only over a little bridge built by sappers."[12]

In two minor wars, then, the Russian cavalry had displayed its

9. *Ibid.*, III, 396-97.
10. Krestovskii, pp. 400-11.
11. *Ibid.*, pp. 484-85.
12. *Ibid.*, p. 497.

ineptness in the face of the foe. They should have taken these lessons to heart and mended their ways—but nothing of the kind occurred. The Iamburg Uhlan regiment is a case in point. Forgetting its disappointments while chasing guerrillas in the Lithuanian forests, it quickly slipped back into its rut. As soon as it arrived at its station in Warsaw, the chief concern became the appearance of the horses of orderly officers at headquarters, on which the colonel issued a mound of detailed instructions. Scouting and outpost duty were again forgotten.

> Again the manège, again the arranging of darkness and warmth in the stables, the plucking of manes and of fuzz under the jaws. . ., again feeding to satiety, fourth and fifth measures of oats, feeding with a special warm mash of beer and barley, again advice not to give the horses prolonged movements, to avoid fast paces and to develop, even in the manège, shortened paces. . . . And for what? Because, "if we presented bad orderly officers to our superiors the regiment might most quickly of all lose its standing."[13]

As before, the cavalry had almost no target practice. In addition to riding in the manège and cleaning equipment, all the free time of the men was swallowed up by care of the horses. In some regiments, to protect the horses from catching cold when going from the warm manège to the stables in cold weather, they put blankets or soldiers' overcoats over their necks, and in winter they usually gave the horses warm water to drink. To beautify them they pulled long hairs out of the horses' faces and clipped their pasterns. If, however, the regiment was quartered in a rural area, there was little of this in the winter. But in any case, cavalry drill ordinarily consisted of a detailed inspection of the seat of the officers and men at a walk, a trot, and a gallop, then of several formations according to the Regulation, and finally, the parade march.[14]

When the cavalry had to march for any distance, it did so at a walk, as trotting was strictly forbidden. At the end of the day the horses, all hot and caked with dust, were held for two hours in the stable, without water, and with their saddles and blankets still on. This was supposed to save the horses and keep them from catching cold. To go one hundred *versts* (about sixty-six miles) they took about ten days, as the commanders did only ten or twelve *versts* per

13. *Ibid.*, p. 490.
14. Petrov, pp. 446-47.

day and set aside two or three days for resting. When they were required to go long distances, with marches of twenty or twenty-five *versts* per day, the squadrons barely dragged their feet into camp, and moreover, went some five *versts* dismounted. They also took several rest periods en route, so that they reached camp only at nightfall. A cavalry regiment would take four weeks to go from St. Petersburg to Moscow—a distance that it could easily march in ten days.[15]

A Capt. von Höpfner of the Prussian army who was with the Russian forces that took part in the joint maneuvers with the Prussians in 1839 at Kalisz, mentioned this practice of the Russians in his report to his superiors. They usually had two rest days a week, while the usual length of the day's march was not over three leagues, (thirteen and one-half miles). They extended the duration of the daily march to an excessive degree, in the infantry through long pauses for rest, in the cavalry through frequent dismounting and travelling on foot. "The Russian officers regard it as extremely harmful to trot on the march; in order, however, not to make the horses stiff by constant walking and not to overburden them, they feel it advantageous to take care to have the riders march on foot."[16]

In June, 1845, as the Iamburg regiment was proceeding to maneuvers, the squadrons separated to go to their various encampments. The captain of one detachment, finding a bridge across a river clogged by a wagon train, led his unit to the bank of the river and with them swam across. He halted in the middle of the shallow stream and reviewed them as they passed in calm and perfect order. A general, however, who was lunching in a nearby cafe, became panic-stricken on seeing this daring move and shouted that that crazy man would lose his whole squadron. When he rushed to stop the fording of the river, he found the squadron in order on the bank, cheerily responding to the thanks of its captain. The general, however, severely punished the officer for needless risk to his force, sending him to the guardhouse for a week and depriving him of promotion.[17]

While Nicholas I loved military pageantry and praised and promoted commanders for the fine appearance of their troops, he also realized that his cavalry needed toughening and more realistic training. At one of his reviews he stressed the absurdity of the shortened paces used by the cavalry, especially when a regiment of dragoons,

15. Krestovskii, pp. 498-99.
16. Schiemann, III, 438.
17. Krestovskii, pp. 503-4.

dismounted and advancing as an infantry battalion, caught up with galloping cavalry, and when a battery of horse artillery, at a ceremonial trot, ran into the rear squadron of the regiment ahead, which was parading at a gallop. The Tsar called together the commanders of the cavalry units and lectured them on the incorrectness of the shortened paces. At reviews in 1833 and after he did the same thing in regard to "impassable" obstacles. The cavalry marvelled beyond words when the Sovereign personally led them in dense columns across a sheer gully and when he made whole regiments in extended front jump in full career across roadside ditches. "In our youth this seemed impossible," admitted one of the old cavalrymen.[18]

The Tsar insisted on holding reviews of this type, which very gradually exerted some influence over the cavalry, as he had them perform dashing line exercises, using fast paces only. The commanders of the cavalry, who did not realize the purpose of this, "were much embittered by such fire and speed," as it cost them dearly in dead horses. Probably the most famous example of these reviews was the extensive one held at Voznesensk in 1837.[19]

The review in 1837 took place along the Bug River in the southwestern Ukraine, with 351 squadrons of cavalry, 18 horse batteries, and 28 battalions of infantry with three field batteries. On the first two days there were cavalry maneuvers, with the corps of dragoons playing a leading role. Then on the morning of August 23 the Tsar sounded the alarm in camp, with the boom of warning guns.[20] As Gen. N. N. Muraviev-Karskii described it,

> all the troops collected very rapidly, and maneuvers began for the cavalry. The day was hot, all the movements were made at the trot and the gallop, from which the horses, already worn out from the previous reviews, suffered greatly. The field behind the troops was like a field of battle: fallen horses, hurt and sick men returning to camp in a multitude; in all, yesterday alone, 140 horses died and eight men were hurt.

He added that for several days horses died as a result of this alarm exercise. "The heat of the 23rd cost up to 700 horses, which fell from heat and weariness."[21]

18. *Ibid.*, pp. 497-98.
19. *Ibid.*, p. 501.
20. V. A. Potto, *Istoriia Novorossiiskago Dragunskago polka, 1803-1865* (St. Petersburg, 1866), pp. 153-54.
21. "Iz zapisok N. N. Murav'eva," *Russkii Arkhiv*, XXXII (1894), Pt. III, 511-12.

Strenuous exercises of this type seem to have had little immediate effect on the commanders, who apparently regarded them as an unfortunate whim of the Tsar and made no effort to toughen their regiments. But in time Nicholas' insistence compelled them to pay more attention to cavalry evolutions and they learned to dash from one part of the field to another. Moreover, by insisting on rapidity of action the Tsar was stimulating initiative, keenness of mind, and flexibility. He would often present his troops with an impromptu tactical problem, which they then had to solve under his watchful eye.[22]

On the other hand, the importance of the shock treatment that the Tsar gave to his troops could not accomplish miracles, especially as it occurred for only a few days each year. It is significant that the Iamburg Uhlans came under the command of an intelligent and conscientious cavalryman only in 1854. Col. Likhachev at once imposed strict discipline on his officers, and above all, stressed proper military training such as outpost work, mastery of their weapons, scouting, and proper battle tactics and theory. He relegated formal training in the manège to a secondary position. ". . . this was the *first* commander in our regiment who, after long years and a whole series of predecessors, set the regiment upon the right road, pointed out to it the true aims and problems of the fighting cavalryman, gave it new direction, spirit, and training."[23] Unfortunately, this refreshing change occurred only at the eleventh hour, for the Crimean War was upon them. It is sad to think of the waste of precious time and manpower that had been going on for decades before this regiment came under the control of an effective soldier. And it seems quite probable that the experience of this one regiment was fairly typical of the Russian cavalry of this time.

Of all the Tsar's cavalry, probably the dragoons were his favorites. They caught his attention by their effective role in the taking of Lublin in February, 1831, during the Polish War, and he rewarded them lavishly for this success and never forgot them.[24] In 1833, as part of the general reorganization of the cavalry he created a corps of dragoons, of two divisions, each with four regiments of ten squadrons. Their training, according to the concepts of the period, was superb, as their riding was almost perfect and they performed as infantry as

22. Krestovskii, pp. 502-3.
23. *Ibid.*, p. 589.
24. A. M—v, "Otryvki iz pokhodnykh zapisok o voine v Pol'she," *Voennyi Sbornik*, III (1860), 79.

well as the infantry regiments of the Guards. Actually, however, their evolutions were not suitable for war, so that they were neither good cavalry nor good infantry. The corps, ten thousand strong, was schooled to dash headlong and then halt suddenly. At once, before the dust had settled, they transformed themselves into beautifully aligned massed infantry battalions with drums beating and with their flanks covered by squadrons of lancers. At another signal, the horse-holders would gallop up and in an instant the battalions became splendid cavalry regiments. This, of course, made a fine showing, which is what counted in those piping times of peace. Their infantry training "could be of little use, as dragoons, in this respect, should be assigned for action in broken country, or in other cover, where it is not well-aligned masses that are needed, but an accurate bullet."[25]

At the great review at Vosnesensk in 1837 the Dragoon Corps was in its glory. During the first day, in a simulated attack on a city, the dismounted dragoons made an attack as infantry. The next day, the dragoons held the center of the stage. After the artillery had taken up position, with squadrons of lancers on the flanks, up the center galloped the dragoons, who suddenly halted, dismounted, formed battalions, and fired at targets. All this was "performed with astonishing precision." The next day came the alarm and the hurried assembly of the regiments, in which the horses of the dragoons suffered heavily from the heat. On the whole, however, the dragoons won much applause. The Russians were delighted with their unique performance, which no other army could match. Not even a German lecturer on tactics, who asserted that this was not the way to use dragoons, could dampen the enthusiasm.[26] Nicholas was particularly impressed with their shooting, which showed the results of earnest practice.[27]

Again, at the imperial inspection of the troops in 1850 at Belaia Tserkov' in the Ukraine, one of the features was the maneuver of the Dragoon Corps. After they had performed several evolutions, the whole corps was drawn up in a formation of dense regimental columns facing the Tsar. He gave the signal: "Attack!" whereupon the whole mass dashed toward him for three hundred paces over broken ground. At the end they halted and stood without one pike wavering. Nicholas

25. K. Detlov, "Neskol'ko slov o dragunakh," *Voennyi Sbornik*, II (1859), 395-96.
26. Potto, pp. 153-56.
27. P. A. Ivanov, *Obozrenie sostava i ustroistva reguliarnoi russkoi kavalerii* (St. Petersburg, 1864), p. 289.

was so delighted that, passing along the front, he said to one of his generals: "Only I could make such an attack!"[28]

While this must have been an awe-inspiring sight, it would appear to have had little value for war. But the dragoons seem also to have learned some of the true craft of the soldier. In 1854 one of their regiments joined the Caucasus army and quickly showed its value. When a number of Turkish irregulars tried to harass the Russian forces, a platoon of dragoons rode out toward them, dismounted and formed in open order to drive them off. One of the Caucasian officers wrote: "We must do them justice: they had all the actions of good riflemen. The soldier seeks a hillock, a little bush, he catches hold of it, crawls up, doesn't shoot wastefully; evidently, he does his work with love and knowledge. . . ." The observer added that the dragoon gave his musket good care and that it shot well. He closed his account with a wish that other troops sent from Russia would prove equally effective.[29]

In spite of this example, the evidence clearly indicates that the majority of the Russian cavalry were trained for parades and reviews rather than for war. The unimpressive performance of the mounted troops in the Crimean War, which will be discussed in later chapters, supports this conclusion. The Don Cossacks, however—who, as irregulars, were really not part of the army, although they served with it in its wars—had none of the glitter and show of the army regiments and were not trained for parades, but for scouting and outpost duty. Nonetheless, for very different reasons from the regular cavalry, they were not effective soldiers and did not enjoy an especially good reputation, as indicated below.

The Cossacks were farming people who enjoyed a special status, as they had much larger tracts of land than the ordinary peasants, paid no taxes, but were all obligated to do military service. While there were several different groupings of Cossacks, only those of the Don and some of the Caucasus Line were attached to the regular army, as the others were settled as frontier guards along dangerous sections. The Don Cossacks had the duty of doing military service for twenty-five years, starting at twenty years of age. They served in regiments of nearly one thousand men or in batteries of artillery for periods of three years outside the Don area, and then returned to their homes,

28. Potto, pp. 199-200.
29. Esaul, "Pokhodnyi dnevnik," *Voennyi Sbornik*, III (1860), 337.

also for three years, although in time of war they had to serve as needed.[30] As, however, the army required the services of more and more Cossacks, they usually had to return to duty before the end of their three-year periods at home.[31]

Although the literature of the period of Nicholas I has little to say about the treatment of the Cossacks in the army, what there is indicates that they were looked down upon and abused. A. L. Zisserman, one of the noted military historians of the Caucasus, tells of a colonel who wished to requisition a horse for his travelling companion. When he demanded one at a Don Cossack post in the Caucasus, the *uriadnik* (sergeant) politely objected that they supplied horses only for journeys along the main road, while the colonel was heading for some remote spot. The colonel jumped up, shouted to the *uriadnik*: "You (*ty*) dare to argue!" hit him in the face and then kicked him out the door. He then repeated his demand for a horse, threatening that if he did not get it, "I'll flog the scoundrel to death!" He immediately received the horse. Zisserman says that this was characteristic of the times.

> The Don Cossacks of that time played the saddest, most degrading role, and they were regarded as messengers, grooms, lackeys; on their horses they hauled everyone and everything, even packs of baggage of staff officers. Blanks of open orders [authorizing] to take Cossack horses and a convoy were at the disposition almost of any clerk, and one can imagine how they abused them; for some trifle, even not of official business, but simply on some private matter, the Cossack had to ride often for several hundred *versts*, without receiving a penny for food, and feeding himself for several days practically on the donations of his half-starving brethren at the posts. And this continued for decades. . . .[32]

Since the military authorities had such a scornful opinion of the Don Cossacks, it is not surprising that the morale of the latter was often low. One officer who knew and admired them stated that, while the enemy did not respect them, this was because the Russian commanders did not know how to use them properly. Suvorov was able to use Cossacks to storm Turkish forts, and Admiral Serebriakov, by giving them encouragement and opportunity to win easy success, developed the Cossacks serving under him into dreaded foes of the

30. SVP, Pt. I, Bk. I, *Obrazovanie Voisk s ikh Upravleniiami*, arts. 1941-43, 2036.
31. Bogdanovich, *Istoricheskii ocherk*, I, 300.
32. A. L. Zisserman, *Dvadtsat' piat' let na Kavkaze (1842-1867)* (2 vols.; St. Petersburg, 1879), I, 185.

Caucasian tribesmen.[33] Indeed, in 1854 a force of Cossacks displayed great bravery in a battle with the Turks near the Danube. Although the Turks outnumbered them, the Cossacks held them off for hours until Russian reserves could attack the Turkish flank, when the Cossacks also attacked. Under this double onslaught the Turks fled.[34]

This instance, however, was not typical of the Don Cossacks, who were not regarded as effective fighting men. One reason for this probably was the fact that the muskets that they carried were partly flintlocks and in part percussion pieces, but almost all of them were reconditioned weapons. As a result of complaints about the bad quality of their firearms the authorities made a general inspection of them in 1855, which disclosed that their muskets were usually assembled out of parts made at various times: the lock was made before 1800, the barrel was more recent, and the other parts were of various types. They probably were highly unreliable, as shown by the fact that they sold for two silver rubles or less, whereas new muskets cost thirteen rubles.[35]

But while the commanders looked on the Cossacks as far inferior to the regular cavalry as fighting men, these irregulars had great value for their skill in scouting, outpost work, and carrying messages through enemy territory. An officer who commanded some of them in 1831 stated that they deserved their fame, for

> There is no one anywhere shrewder, quicker, and in some cases, bolder and more rash than they; but they are not distinguished by firmness. To die, standing uselessly in one's place, according to their views, is not valor. Heroism with them is regarded as high merit; but they see it only in daring, in bold raids, in an unexpected attack on the enemy. To evade the enemy, by any means whatever, they regard as a good deed and not a disgrace; the Cossack knows that as long as he is alive he will think up a thousand ways to harm the enemy, and hence he saves himself assiduously.[36]

After a victorious battle the value of the Cossacks showed itself, for they were untiring in pursuit of a retreating enemy. Unlike the cavalry horses, those of the Cossacks were hardy and could endure long marches, and their riders could often pursue the enemy for great distances. They also were excellent on outpost duty. In 1854, in the

33. Filipson, *Russkii Arkhiv*, XXII (1884), Pt. I, 334-35.
34. P. Alabin, *Pokhodnyia zapiski v voinu 1853, 1854, 1855, i 1856 godov* (2 vols.; Viatka, 1861), I, 88-90.
35. Fedorov, pp. 135-46.
36. M—v, "Otryvki iz pokhodnykh zapisok," *Voennyi Sbornik*, III (1860), 49.

Danube campaign against the Turks, some pickets consisted of two cavalrymen and one Cossack. According to an officer who commanded there, the Cossack, being careful by nature and with a strong instinct of self-preservation, was well suited to outpost service. "He does not doze on his post, but uses all his inventiveness in order to see or hear an approaching enemy, so as not to be killed or taken prisoner." The soldiers, however, did not realize the importance of their assignments and the need for caution. Hence it was advantageous for them to stand watch with the Cossacks, for they developed, became more ingenious, more alert mentally. Above all, from the Cossacks they learned the importance of advanced posts, which made them more effective cavalrymen.[37]

Another characteristic of the Cossacks was their zeal in obtaining booty. This was so well known that the Code of Military Regulations contained definite rules for the disposition of the captures of the Cossacks. They also warned that booty meant only the property of the armed enemy and did not include the property of unarmed inhabitants, seizure of which would be grounds for severe punishment.[38] There is reason to think that the Cossacks did not always observe this rule. In 1828 a Cossack patrol with the Russian army captured four Turkish civilians and took them to army headquarters without taking a sum of money they had. Nicholas I was so pleased by "this unselfish action" that he issued a special order to the army announcing that the Cossacks had been given a reward of double the sum owned by the Turks and declared his special approval to the Cossacks' commander.[39] The Cossacks in question thus received a reward for not doing what they were forbidden to do. The Tsar's emphatic expression of gratitude suggests that others had not been so forebearing.

There is other evidence of the acquisitive tendencies of the Cossacks. In 1831-32 a force of Cossacks quartered in a village of military colonies lorded it over the villagers, compelling them to kill their chickens, sheep, and even cows, and demanding great quantities of butter with their meals, with the result that the villagers were ruined by their eight-month stay. When on patrol they never missed a chance to stick a young pig with their lances and carry it home for dinner.[40] When the Russian army moved into Hungary in 1849, the

---

37. "Desiat' mesiatsev na Dunae," *Voennyi Sbornik*, I (1858), 525-26.
38. SVP, Pt. I, Bk. II, *Obrazovanie Voisk s ikh Upravleniiami*, arts. 274-89.
39. Epanchin, III, 426-27.
40. L. A. Seriakov, "Moia trudovaia zhizn'," *Russkaia Starina*, XIV (1875), 168.

Cossacks were pleased with the fertile countryside, asking one of the officers, "Please, your honor, is it possible to look for things there?" When questioned, they discreetly explained that they meant to forage for oats, "but the real sense of it was simply to loot."[41]

When the Crimean War came, the Cossacks displayed the same enterprise. Driven headlong by the charge of the British Light Brigade at Balaklava, they soon recovered and at once set about their favorite work, catching and selling the fine English horses left riderless after the charge.[42] They also found other opportunities for gain, for on September 30, 1854 a Gendarme officer in the Crimea reported to Count Orlov that all villages near the Russian camp had been stripped, the homes of the landowners had been looted and everything in them smashed and broken, and some even burned by the Cossacks. They even stole carriages and sold them for a trifle or carried them off to their regiments. This occurred because the Cossack regiments sent foragers out, who took everything without payment, and simply looted.[43]

Some of the Cossacks were apparently not averse to making slaves, for the Code of Military Regulations of 1838 carried a stern injunction "to all officers, *uriadniks*, clerks, and Cossacks of the Don Host, that they, on returning from service to the Don, under no circumstances should dare to import any outside person of either sex, of whatever status they may be."[44]

The morality of the high Cossack commanders also was not above reproach. Lt. Gen. G. I. Filipson, in a passing reference to Lt. Gen. N. S. Zavodovskii, who was Ataman of the Black Sea Cossack Host for a number of years from 1828 on, remarked that he had never been court-martialled, "which was almost unprecedented."[45]

While the Russian infantry and cavalry were not really ready for war because of poor training, the engineers and artillery were in good condition. The engineers, as previously indicated, did much building of fortifications. In the Crimean War the sea forts of Sevastopol completely barred the allied fleets from the harbor and

41. M. D. Likhutin, *Zapiski o pokhode v Vengriiu v 1849 g.* (Moscow, 1875), p. 42.

42. S. Kozhukhov, "Iz krymskikh vospominanii o poslednei voine," *Russkii Arkhiv*, VII (1869), No. 7, 2133.

43. N. F. Dubrovin, *Vostochnaia voina 1853-1856 godov; obzor sobytii po povodu sochineniia M. I. Bogdanovicha* (St. Petersburg, 1878), p. 175.

44. SVP, Pt. I, Bk. II, *Obrazovanie voisk s ikh upravleniiami*, art. 1926, Supplement, "Polkovye instruksyii dlia Voiska Donskago."

45. Filipson, *Russkii Arkhiv*, XXII (1884), Pt. I, 365.

endured their heaviest bombardment almost unscathed. Maj. Richard Delafield, USA, in his report on military affairs in Europe in 1854-55, said that Cronstadt (Kronstadt), Sevastopol, and Cherbourg were the strongest in Europe, "and the works of the first (viz: Cronstadt) [are] superior in execution and material, and not inferior in design, to any others in Europe."[46] Maj. Delafield, after a lengthy discussion of the defense measures at Kronstadt and St. Petersburg, summed up his observations thus:

> Such were the formidable defenses that for two years set the Allies at defiance, and protected the city of St. Petersburg. It cost the Russians great exertions and some treasure, and the Allies far greater. Russian skill and ingenuity kept pace with that of the Allies; every new expedient on the part of the latter soon became known to the former, and her engineers, as capable in every way as those of France and England, with a ready talent to turn everything to advantage, were not long in adopting some counteracting defensive means.[47]

This opinion coincides with that of a Russian military historian, who stated that their engineers had had frequent practice in numerous wars in conducting sieges and fortifying positions and hence had developed extremely effective methods of siege and defense. Gens. K. I. Schilder and E. I. Totleben were leaders in their profession. During the Crimean War the latter showed great talent by brilliant innovations and skill at active defense.[48]

Much of this engineering skill stemmed from the work of A. Z. Teliakovskii, who in 1839 and 1846 published two outstanding books on the subject of fortification. The author, a graduate of the Engineering School, gained practical experience from participation in sieges and in erecting fortifications during the Russo-Turkish War of 1828-29. After teaching the subject of fortification in military schools for several years he produced his books, which went through three editions in Russia and were adopted as textbooks in the military schools.[49] Later, these works were translated into almost all European languages, and the *Spectateur militaire* recognized their importance. In 1854-55 the French engineers at Sevastopol used his methods,

46. Maj. Richard Delafield, *Report on the Art of War in Europe in 1854, 1855, and 1856. From his Notes and Observations Made as a Member of a "Military Commission to the Theater of War in Europe,"* (Washington, 1860), 36th Congress, 1st Session, Senate, Executive Document No. 59, p. 26.
47. *Ibid.*, p. 36.
48. Petrov, p. 450.
49. *Iz istorii russkogo inzhenerskogo iskusstva* (Moscow, 1952), pp. 95-108.

which had been taught at the St. Cyr Military Academy. And in 1852, when Napoleon III was courting the favor of Nicholas I, he sent a de luxe French edition of Teliakovskii's work to the Tsar as an Easter gift.[50]

The essence of Teliakovskii's teaching was that, unlike the leading French and German engineers, who espoused a single, universally applicable principle of fortification, he rejected formalism and insisted on a special approach to each problem as it arose. In his volume on permanent fortifications, he preached the necessity of an active defense, with frequent counterattacks by the infantry, and stressed the need to have inner defenses to fall back to after the main works had been breached. He also taught that the bastions of a fortress should be largely infantry strongholds, with much of the artillery concentrated in batteries on the flanks or in the rear. In his text on field fortifications (1839) he emphasized the value that well-placed earthworks had for a defending force, although he was careful to say that they were only adjuncts to the tactics and strategy of the combat forces and not an end in themselves.[51]

Although Teliakovskii's texts on fortifications were widely used in Russian military schools and were well regarded abroad, he encountered the opposition of highly placed persons in Russia. Apparently because of this, he played little role in the Crimean War and was compelled to retire while he was still in his prime.[52]

Nicholas I himself also played a large role in the development of Russian engineering, for even greater than his love of maneuvers and parades—if indeed this be possible—was his passionate addiction to military engineering and fortification. In 1818 he had taken the post of inspector general of engineers, at a time when these forces were composed largely of foreigners, as few Russians could obtain the proper training for this service. The following year he founded the Chief Engineering School, which in time made it possible to rely on Russian engineers and to eliminate dependence on foreigners.[53] When he became Tsar, Nicholas undertook to build a vast series of forts for the defense of the western frontiers of the Empire. Under his exacting guidance, which reached even to minor details of construction, the

50. Tarle, II, 109-10.
51. *Iz istorii*, *loc. cit.*
52. *Ibid.*
53. N. K. Schilder, *Graf Eduard Ivanovich Totleben. Ego zhizn' i deiatel'nost'* (2 vols.; St. Petersburg, 1885-1886), II, 545.

engineers built a number of strong works in Poland and Lithuania, as well as others in the Caucasus and in Central Asia. He also rebuilt many of the existing fortresses, from Kronstadt and Reval on the Gulf of Finland to Kiev, Izmail, and Sevastopol in the south.[54]

It would be difficult to conceive of a more expensive interest than this one. Year after year he poured great sums into construction, even going so far as to sanction expenditures without obtaining the necessary estimates of the Engineering Department. Occasionally, under extreme pressure from the Minister of Finance he curtailed some items, but he usually managed to find some special funds to cover them.[55]

In addition to this outpouring of funds, he loved to bestow gifts on officers of engineers. Gen. I. Dehn, commander of engineers of the western army, who was the Tsar's chief instrument in constructing fortresses, received from him an estate of 2,000 *desiatinas* (about 5,400 acres) and 538,600 rubles. Frequently Nicholas granted a group of officers who had completed the building of a fortress, an award of an extra year's pay. In 1838, when Gen. Schilder of the engineers went on a mission abroad, the Emperor gave him five hundred gold pieces and a lieutenant who accompanied him received two hundred more. It became a fixed rule that engineer officers sent to the Caucasus received an extra year's pay plus travel allowances.[56]

The Russians were also well advanced in other aspects of military engineering. After citing a report that the French Engineering School at Metz had used an electric spark to detonate mines, the editor of *Voennyi Zhurnal* (*Military Journal*) in 1832 stated: "with us, during the present summer, . . . at Krasnoe Selo mines have been set off with complete success by means of a conductor of a Volta galvanic apparatus, at a distance of 200 *sazhens* [1,400 feet]."[57] In fact, during the extensive mining operations during the siege of Sevastopol in 1855, the Russians set off all their mines by electricity, with much better results than the French, who continued to use ordinary fuses.[58] The Russians also planted many land mines in the ditch before their

54. Polievktov, p. 333.
55. G. Timchenko-Ruban, *Ocherk deiatel'nosti Velikago Kniazia i Imperatora Nikolaia Pavlovicha kak rukovoditelia voenno-inzhenernoiu chast'iu* (Vol. I only; St. Petersburg, 1912), pp. 116-23, 368-70.
56. *Ibid.*, pp. 149-53.
57. *Voennyi Zhurnal*, 1832, No. 5, p. 188.
58. Polkovnik Frolov, *Minnaia voina v Sevastopole v 1854-1855 gg. pod rukovodstvom Totlebena* (St. Petersburg, 1868), pp. 163-64.

fourth bastion, which caused some trouble to attacking French soldiers. These were tarred boxes of gunpowder which, when trod upon, exploded through the breaking of a glass tube of sulphuric acid, which, coming into contact with potassium chlorate, ignited it and caused the charge to explode.[59]

Like the engineers, the Russian artillery was an elite service, training its officers in special schools or accepting the top graduates from the cadet corps. As its pay was also better than that of the infantry,[60] its prestige was high. While its training, like that of other arms, stressed correctness of the evolutions and the parade march, and in the horse artillery, *élan* and dash, it stressed target firing, at which it did well.[61] Its proportion of hits compared favorably with those of French and Prussian batteries at roughly similar ranges, although the varying sizes of the targets used makes exact comparison impossible.[62]

The Russian artillery had both foot and horse batteries. Somewhat less than half of the foot batteries were field or heavy artillery, with four twelve-pound cannon, of 4.8 inch caliber, and four half-*pud* (18-lb.) howitzers with six-inch bore. The howitzers, with shorter barrels, were for lobbing shells at the enemy and for firing grapeshot at short range. The cannon fired round shot, shell, and grapeshot at short range. The light batteries, including most of the horse artillery, had 6-lb cannon (3.76 inch bore) and quarter-*pud* (9 lb.) howitzers. The heavier guns had an extreme range of almost twelve hundred yards, while the lighter ones carried as far as nine hundred yards.[63]

Because of the ineffectiveness of the firepower of the infantry, the Russian army relied heavily on the fire of its artillery to disorganize the foe and prepare the way for the charge of the infantry. In the wars with the Persians, the Turks, and the Poles, and later in Hungary, the Russians had great numerical superiority in artillery and in most cases, greater skill as well. At the Battle of the Alma in the Crimea the fire of the Russian artillery was successful in checking the French advance on the left flank, but, without proper infantry support, it suffered severely from the French sharpshooters, who picked off gunners and horses from long range. Eventually the guns had to withdraw, but

59. Delafield, pp. 109-10.
60. *Rukovodstvo dlia artilleriskoi sluzhby*, p. 939.
61. Petrov, p. 447.
62. *Rukovodstvo dlia artilleriiskoi sluzhby*, pp. 577-88.
63. Medem, I, 80-83; Zaionchkovskii, *Vostochnaia voina, Prilozheniia*, I, 478-79.

nonetheless they inflicted much heavier losses on the enemy than did the fire of the infantry.[64]

One result of this encounter was that many of the Russian generals no longer had confidence in light artillery, which they termed useless, but demanded the heavier field guns.[65] As it happened, Russian military designers had already developed a 12-lb gun of lightened weight for firing from a light carriage and for hauling by six horses. A number of these cannon were supplied to the army, and many of them came to the Crimea. There were few opportunities to use them, however, in the latter part of the Crimean campaign.[66]

Opinions of non-Russians about the Russian artillery, while not many have come to light, indicate that it enjoyed respect. Maj. Mordecai, U.S.A., in his report on European military affairs, stated that its weapons were much like the usual weapons of European armies. He found that the Russian gun carriage had admirable features, as its construction gave it "great facility of turning." He added: "in rapidity and compactness of movement the maneuvering of the Russian artillery leaves nothing to be desired."[67] From S. J. G. Calthorpe, British staff officer in the Crimea, comes a report of a conversation with a Russian colonel, probably during a period of truce. The colonel expressed great admiration for the British infantry, but declared that the Russians had finer artillery. Calthorpe could not admit this, although he stated that "in the scientific part of that arm I think they are equal, if not superior to us."[68] Gen. Daniel Lysons went even further in his tribute to the Russian artillery. In his letter of November 13, 1854 (after the Battle of Inkerman) he wrote: "The French are getting reenforcements, so we shall be able to hold our own against anything. If it were not for their powerful Artillery, we could drive them [the Russians] out of the country, but in that branch they are far superior in every way to us."[69] Whether these remarks refer to the field artillery or to that of the besieged fortress is not clear.

64. G. D. Sherbachev, "Vospominaniia o nachale krymskoi kampanii v 1854 godu," in N. F. Dubrovin, ed., *Materialy dlia istorii Krymskoi voiny i oborony Sevastopolia* (5 vols.; St. Petersburg, 1871-1874), II, 472-75.

65. "O legkovesnykh orudiiakh," *Artilleriiskii Zhurnal*, 1860, No. 5, pp. 143-44.

66. "Ob ispytanii mednoi 12-fun. oblegchennoi pushki," *Artill. Zhurnal*, 1854, No. 6, p. 445.

67. Mordecai, *Military Mission to Europe*, p. 130.

68. S. J. G. Calthorpe, *Letters from Headquarters; or the Realities of the War in the Crimea* (2 vols.; London, 1856), II, 35.

69. Daniel Lysons, *The Crimean War from First to Last. Letters from the Crimea* (London, 1895), pp. 130-31.

Maj. Mordecai in his report remarked that the Russian fortress artillery seemed to be on a par with that of other countries. He found their gun carriages to be good, especially those of wrought iron, which were better than those used elsewhere. He also mentioned that the Russians had ingenious devices for pointing the guns without exposing the men to enemy fire.[70] Maj. Delafield also was enthusiastic about the wrought-iron chassis and carriage for emplaced cannon. He declared that there was no other system better adapted to American coastal defense "than this wrought-iron *tubular* one of the Russians." He stated that English and French models of cast-iron or wood "break into fragments when hit by one shot, whereas the wrought-iron tubular carriage may be shot through and through in many places without destroying its efficiency."[71]

Finally, Col. Charles Auger, author of *Réflection général sur le siège de Sébastopol*, stated that this contest indicated that the Russian artillery "is completely on an equal footing with all the other European armies, and is not lagging behind the most recent successes."[72]

In addition to the conventional forms of artillery in the Russian army, there also were units of rocket troops, rather on an experimental basis. The Russians had begun testing them in 1812 and decided that, although they had certain attractive features, their inaccuracy, especially in a wind, made their value doubtful.[73] In 1849, Col. Goremykin, in his manual on tactics, wrote that their value was questionable, although they had been used to advantage in India and on the Austrian frontiers.[74] The Russians used rockets with success in the Caucasus in the 1850's,[75] and with great effect against Turkish irregular forces in 1854.[76] At the siege of Silistria in the Danube campaign of 1854, rockets proved to be very valuable, as they could be used in the trenches at short ranges where it was impossible to bring cannon. They were especially useful against sorties of Turkish infantry and

70. Mordecai, pp. 121-23.
71. Delafield, pp. 13 and 15.
72. Cited in Weigelt, *Osada Sevastopolia, 1854-1856*. Perevedeno po Vyso-chaishemu poveleniiu (St. Petersburg, 1859), p. 333. The author was a captain of artillery in the Prussian army.
73. "O zazhigatel'nykh raketakh (Kongrevskikh)," *Voennyi Zhurnal*, 1828, No. 3, pp. 121-28, 144-46.
74. Goremykin, I, 161.
75. Bobrovskii, IV, 420 and 422.
76. Polkovnik Fersman, "Opisanie srazheniia pri derevne Kiuruk-Dara, 24-go iulia 1854 goda," *Artill. Zhurnal*, 1855, No. 3, p. 235.

cavalry.[77] On the other hand, they were not used in the siege of Sevastopol, apparently for lack of appropriate targets.[78]

From this consideration of training and weapons of the chief branches of the Russian army it becomes apparent that because of concentration on external appearance and a neglect of the main functions of the army, most of the troops had to respond to senseless demands from their commanders, from which the military capacity of the army suffered. In those services such as the engineers and the artillery, where the technical nature of their activities compelled a more realistic system of training and where intelligent and enthusiastic men could pursue their callings with a minimum of interference, the results were highly successful. From this the conclusion emerges that the Russians were by no means inferior in military ability and that only an outmoded and poorly conceived system prevented them from achieving significant successes.

But while most of the army continued to be hampered by unsuitable training methods, in the Caucasus a very different system existed. Here, in the face of a hostile population, which fought with great fierceness over a difficult terrain, the commanders could not apply the formal methods in use in the Active Army and the Guards. Instead, they were forced to develop, by trial and error, a system of operations suited to the extraordinary conditions of the region. This was to be a long and difficult task.

77. "Ob upotreblenii boevykh raket pod Silistrieiu i pri gorode Babadage," *Artill. Zhurnal*, 1855, No. 2, pp. 130-34.

78. G. D. Shcherbachev, "Dvenadtsat' let molodosti. Vospominania," *Russkii Arkhiv*, XXVIII (1890), Pt. I, 244 and 249.

CHAPTER VIII. THE WAR IN THE CAUCASUS

Throughout the reign of Nicholas I, both during the wars with Persians, Turks, Poles, and Hungarians, and during the periods of peace, the war in the Caucasus continued, gaining rapidly in intensity until the late 1840's, when it slackened slightly. It was a costly and exhausting conflict, involving a considerable part of Russia's military strength, and during the Crimean War it threatened to increase greatly the magnitude of Russia's defeat. Thus a study of the military history of the period cannot pass it by.

The Caucasus mountains form an almost impassable barrier from the Black Sea to the Caspian, as they rise almost from the shore to reach heights higher than the Alps. On the west there was no road along the Black Sea coast, as the mountains and the swift rivers rushing down to the sea, with their swampy estuaries, made travel almost impossible. Through the center ran the Georgian Military Highway over the lofty and wild Dariel Pass, from Mozdok to Tiflis— a difficult and dangerous route, never completely safe from the wild tribesmen living in valleys on both sides of it. A passable road ran through Derbent on the Caspian to Baku and the Moslem lands between the Caucasus and Persia.

The great mass of mountains had numerous valleys inhabited by many peoples speaking many languages. Most of these tribes were Moslems, warlike and fiercely independent, and increasingly hostile to the steadily growing power of the Russian Empire. The Russians surrounded the Caucasus on three sides. To the north they held the Kuban and Terek rivers by means of Cossack settlements, compelled always to be ready to take to arms to drive off raiding bands of tribesmen or to ride off to intercept their retreat and release the captives that they led off into slavery. Garrisons of troops held strategic positions in order to drive off enemy raiders and to pursue them into the mountains to wreak vengeance on their *auls* (villages). Russian garrisons also manned forts in the Moslem regions along the Caspian

Sea and south of the main range, as well as in Armenia and Georgia. Their position south of the Caucasus was somewhat shaky, however, until the victories of 1826-29 made it clear that their armies were too much for Persians and Turks. Even so, at any sign of real weakness a host of enemies would rise up, for even many of the Georgian nobles and princes opposed them and plotted against them, to say nothing of Turks and Kurds and Persians who dreamed of recovering lost lands and looting the Russian possessions. The Turks, who still held much of the Black Sea coast of the Caucasus, also were in contact with the mountaineers, with whom they traded weapons and other goods and to whom the tribesmen sold their wares, as well as girls for the slave markets of Constantinople.

While Russian military power was sufficient to keep the peace along the Persian and Turkish borders, no real peace could exist with many of the mountain tribes. Fortunately for the Russians, the tribes were so diversified that for long there was no unity among them and the Russians could deal with them in detail. In general, there were four main groups of mountaineers. In the western Caucasus, between the Dariel Pass and the Black Sea, the Kabardinians and other tribes, whom the Russians called Cherkessy, opposed the Russians in the Kuban region and on the coast, but rarely attacked Georgia. They had little in common with the peoples of the eastern Caucasus. In the low, heavily wooded mountains or foothills north of the main range lived numerous tribes of Chechens, warlike and always ready to raid Russian settlements. They were rather prosperous farmers, growing considerable quantities of corn (maize) and other crops. They were generally hostile to the Russian settlements north of the Terek River. In the high mountain valleys and the lowlands along the Caspian shore lived the Dagestany. They were highly warlike, although the coastal societies had become less so than their mountain brethren. In the 1820's the Russians managed to keep them fairly quiet by a policy of winning the friendship of the khans and other nobles where possible and using grim punitive measures against those who were hostile. Finally, there were the Lezgins, in the remote valleys of the highest range of the mountains northeast of Tiflis. Not many decades before they had terrorized all Georgia by their raids up to Tiflis itself. By the second quarter of the nineteenth century, however, Russian forces protected the Georgians from Lezgin depredations, although they had by no means renounced violence.

During the period when Ermolov was in power, he managed to keep the region under control with only twenty-eight thousand troops, in addition to the numerous Cossacks in settlements. He developed a sound, systematic approach. In addition to the traditional policy of establishing a fortified Cossack line, he built a few large forts in advance of the line, from which forces could strike at raiding parties and make punitive expeditions against hostile auls. He constructed roads and bridges to facilitate movement of the troops, which, to some degree, also aided the beginnings of commerce with the tribesmen. He also was scrupulous in his treatment of friendly chiefs, giving them honor and presents and respecting their ways, although he appointed resident officials to supervise them. Courts were set up where the inhabitants could bring their disputes. In the Chechen regions, Ermolov undertook to cut wide clearings through the dense forests and built roads, so that hostile auls were no longer safe. All this was not too difficult, as the tribes were divided and often carried on feuds with each other, and their fear of the Russian troops and especially their artillery was lively.[1]

By 1826 the situation was changing rapidly. As Russian power grew in the Caucasus, the mountaineers began to forget their feuds and to present a more unified opposition, especially as they were learning to fight the Russians and were losing their fear of cannon. In this atmosphere, muridism, an active religious movement, developed. While much of its appeal came from the preaching of a holy war against the infidels, its precepts of equality of all followers aroused sympathy among the independent peasants, who resented the power of their princes, many of whom were in league with the Russians. Authority under this movement would reside with a group of murids, with unlimited power, who swore to live by the *Tarikat* (a set of special rules, calling for life in imitation of Mahomet). One Mullah Mahomet began to preach this movement in 1823, but as it appeared to be merely an obscure Moslem sect, the Russians, involved in war with the Persians and the Turks, paid little heed.[2]

In 1825 the Chechens, supported by other tribes, rose in rebellion, and many of the Kabardinians were eager to cast off Russian control. Early in 1826 Ermolov led an expedition into the Chechen country, defeating their forces and burning their villages, although his forces

1. D. I. Romanovskii, *Kavkaz i Kavkazskaia voina. Publichnyia lektsii, chitannyia v zale Passazha, v 1860 godu.* (St. Petersburg, 1860), pp. 212-15; 311-25.
2. *Ibid.*, pp. 309-18.

encountered fierce opposition when they went back. Another expedition resulted in the burning of the Chechen stronghold and other settlements. At this they lost heart, as they suffered terribly from cold and hunger, and made their peace with the Russians. By the end of May, 1826, the Russians dominated all Chechnia and had roads cut through the forests in several directions.[3] It is significant that as early as 1825 the Chechens used cannon against Ermolov's troops, although on a very limited scale.[4]

During the Persian and Turkish wars the mountaineers gave relatively little trouble. When the Lezgins, encouraged by the Persian onslaught, raided toward Tiflis, Ermolov quickly marched against them and subdued them without fighting, compelling them to give hostages for good behavior. Paskevich, however, criticized this moderation. In his letter to Diebitsch of December 27, 1826, he complained that his rival had not wiped out "the last refuge of the mountaineers of Zakatala."[5] The Russian victories against the Persians and the Turks did much to discourage fresh uprisings in their rear, so that Paskevich could concentrate his attention on his operations in the field.

By the end of 1829, however, the strength of muridism, preached by Kazi-Mullah, a disciple of Mullah Mahomet, had increased greatly. He called for a holy war against the Russians and all pro-Russian Moslems, with particular attention to the khanate of Avaria, in central Dagestan. Here he failed, however, as the grandmother of the infant Khan inspired her followers and beat off Kazi-Mullah's bands, who retired with Shamil, his leading disciple, to his stronghold of Gimry.[6] This was only the beginning of the conflict, which now spread to the Lezgins. The Russians easily subdued their first outbreak and in 1830 moved high into the mountains to build a fort that would block their exit into the lowlands. While the work was in progress, however, a sudden onslaught of the foe overran a Russian battalion which, losing four guns, made a disorderly retreat down the mountain. It required a general attack by heavy forces of troops to break the Lezgin resistance and compel them to swear loyalty to the Tsar.[7] Also in 1830 Paskevich personally led a big expedition into the land of the Shapsugs in the western Caucasus, where his troops had several brushes with the

3. Bobrovskii, IV, 165; Zubov, *Podvigi*, I, 255-85.
4. Zubov, *Podvigi*, I, 240-43.
5. Shcherbatov, II, 142 and 152.
6. Romanovskii, pp. 320-25.
7. Bobrovskii, IV, 174-85.

natives and destroyed many auls. All this, however, had no well-conceived purpose, although three small fortifications were built. The chief result of this incursion was to arouse the previously divided Adygei tribes to unite against the Russians.[8]

By this time the Tsar expected great things of Paskevich. On March 21, 1830, Count Chernyshev transmitted to the latter the monarch's will "that the beginning of military activities against the mountain tribes hostile to us should not be at all postponed, so that in the course of the coming summer and fall it may be possible to carry out successfully all the proposed plan of subduing the mountaineers."[9] The General, however, took the position that it was impossible to bring the conflict to a speedy end, as the situation was so uncertain. He mentioned various disturbing phenomena, such as the appearance of Kazi-Mullah in Dagestan, his influence upon the Chechens, and the hostility of many of the Cherkessy. His plan was to make limited gains against the enemy, especially by creating a new fortified line of settlements south of the Kuban, to bar the Turks from contact with the interior.[10]

Paskevich, however, spent very little time on Caucasian affairs, as the Tsar called him to St. Petersburg and he later joined the army in Poland. Nevertheless, in spite of his limited knowledge of the situation in the mountains, he enjoyed the reputation of an expert regarding this region, and for years his opinions carried great weight in the capital. Indeed, his plan of operations calling for the chief effort in the western Caucasus became the basis for Russian policy. His major project was to build a new line of fortifications and a road south of the Kuban, anchored on a new fort at Gelendzhik on the Black Sea, with the other end at Olginskoe, near the Kuban. The purpose of this was to sever the connection of the Turks with the mountaineers, as well as to provide a new line of departure for offensive operations.[11]

Gen. Vel'iaminov, one of the ablest generals in the Caucasus, protested energetically against this scheme, especially Paskevich's plan for a battue of the mountaineers between the Gelendzhik line and the Kuban, which never took place. Most of the project proved to be a sad failure, for the work of settling Cossacks along this line was not

8. Filipson, *Russkii Arkhiv*, XXI (1883), Pt. III, 192.
9. Shcherbatov, III, 244.
10. *Ibid.*, pp. 247-50.
11. P. M. Sakovich, "Georgii Vasil'evich Novitskii. Biograficheskii ocherk. 1800-1867," *Russkaia Starina*, XXII (1878), 296; Shcherbatov, III, 285-86.

soundly carried out, and in three or four years the line no longer existed.[12]

This was the beginning of the Russian plan to control the western Caucasus, which became the main effort from 1832 to 1839. By the Treaty of Adrianople this coast passed to Russia, and the government, fearing to lose it in a new war, set out to establish firm control there. Baron Rosen, who became viceroy in 1831, sceured the Tsar's approval for a system of forts along the coast, to bar the Turks and the British traders and compel the mountaineers to trade with Russia.[13] The Tsar had high hopes of establishing strong commercial ties with the mountaineers, for he ordered Rosen to pacify them by opening trade with them and by developing all possible resources of industry in order to establish firm economic bonds with them, "so that with time they may be joined by mutual advantages and needs and form one whole [with Russia], without any traces of forced union."[14] These instructions, however, caused confusion, for there was a contradiction between the policies of conquest and conciliation, especially as the Tsar demanded full subjugation of the tribesmen while, at the same time, he sternly rebuked leaders of punitive expeditions.[15]

For almost two decades Russian policy emphasized the holding of the coast of the Black Sea by means of a string of small forts. In 1834 and 1835 strong forces of troops marched south along the shore to build a road for supplying the forts. This, however, proved to be an almost impossible task, in view of the terribly wild country, the torrential mountain streams, and the miasmic swamps at the mouths of many of the rivers.[16] Several of the forts had no connection with Russia proper, but received their supplies and reinforcements from Russian warships and steamers in the Black Sea. During the winter months they were completely isolated. Nicholas was keenly interested in this effort. When one of the generals reported the need to build a fort at a certain river crossing, the monarch dug out of the files a sketch made at a reconnaissance of the location three years before. After studying the drawing, he marked on it the spot for the fort, and then ordered a special messenger to gallop it two thousand *versts* to

12. Sakovich, *ibid.*, p. 299; Filipson, *Russkii Arkhiv*, XXI (1883), Pt. III, 193-94.
13. G. Kazbek, comp., *Voennaia istoriia gruzinskago grenaderskago E. I. V. Velikago Kniazia Konstantina Nikolaevicha polka, v sviazi s istoriei Kavkazskoi voiny* (Tiflis, 1865), pp. 141-47.
14. Zisserman, *Istoriia*, II, 23.
15. *Ibid.*, p. 26.
16. Kazbek, pp. 145-47.

the Caucasus, so that the entrenchment could be built according to his wishes.[17]

Most of the nineteen coastal forts were useless and indefensible. Lt. Tornov, who visited many of them, spoke of one redoubt, "if one can call with this name the disorderly pile of mud marking the spot on which should be the breastwork," where the one company of soldiers lived in huts made out of brush and reeds which were "literally sinking in the mud." He added: "It is difficult to know for what need the redoubt was built at Ilora, which protects nothing but the soldiers defending it; and why they were here, and to the number of only one company, it was still less possible to explain. . . ." He stated that at that time the authorities made a number of such mistakes. "They unceasingly occupied places without any need, built fortifications not adapted either to the terrain or to the nature of the war, they stationed in them garrisons too weak to keep the inhabitants in fear, . . . and to the mountaineers they left . . . only opportunities to steal from and kill Russian soldiers."[18] The fort at Gagry was dominated by mountains on three sides, with the sea on the fourth. "The Cherkessy killed soldiers with muskets within Gagry, firewood and forage were obtained only by fighting. For months at a time they were fed only on salt meat and bread, grits, and potatoes. Vegetables, fresh meat and poultry were regarded as the greatest rarities." As Gagry had no land communications, its provisions came by sea at stated intervals. It had one rooster and two hens.[19]

When Gen. Filipson visited the Black Sea forts, "the frightful sickness among the troops struck me." Intermittent fevers, which were raging, usually ended in a convulsion or a stroke. If they lasted a long time, they often turned into scurvy and ended with death from bloody fluxes. Disease was especially rampant in Gagry and Sukhum. Near Tuapse, the garrison of Vel'iaminskoe had no fresh meat and scurvy was raging. A tent, partly concealed, held the bodies of unburied dead.[20] In the fort at Sukhum "the men had the sickly look of unhappy victims doomed to eternal fever, from which half of them died every year. They knew this, and it cannot be said with a calm spirit, but uncomplainingly they endured their fate, not ceasing to

17. Filipson, *Russkii Arkhiv*, XXII (1884), Pt. I, 339.
18. F. F. Tornov, "Gergebil'. Iz vospominanii," *Russkii Arkhiv*, II (1881), Pt. II, 425-26.
19. F. F. Tornov, *Vospominaniia Kavkazskago ofitsera* (2 pts.; Moscow, 1864), II, 59-60.
20. Filipson, *Russkii Arkhiv*, XXI (1883), Pt. III, 317.

perform their grievous duty with the submissiveness characteristic of the Russian soldier."[21]

These conditions paved the way for the fall of the Black Sea forts in 1840 during a general uprising of the Cherkessy tribes. Fort Lazarevskoe, the first, was overrun on February 7—an event that aroused great enthusiasm among the mountaineers, who swore to end the domination of the Russians or die trying. The result was that Vel'iaminskoe and Mikhailovskoe fell not long after. Nikolaevskoe, which had been reinforced and put in excellent condition, nonetheless fell on March 31, and the attackers also took Sviatoi Dukh. The Abinskoe fortification beat off its attackers, however,[22] as did two of the others.

The defense of the Mikhailovskoe fortification was greatly honored in the Russian military establishment, for the garrison, after retiring to the inner citadel, refused to surrender. By agreement, one of the soldiers blew up the powder magazine, killing all his comrades and many of the enemy. In commemoration of this deed, his name was kept on the list of the first company of his regiment, and at roll call, the first man after him always answered: "Died for the glory of the Russian arms in the Mikhailovskoe fortifications."[23]

After these disasters the Russian authorities sent in strong reinforcements which occupied and rebuilt several of the forts in much stronger condition, and also burned a number of auls in the vicinity. Reserve forces were set up and the navy provided a squadron of vessels to maintain communications. All this, however, proved a useless expense of money and manpower, for in 1854, with the Crimean War looming up, the Russians evacuated all of these forts.[24]

Thus this system of subjugating the Caucasus, which originated with Field Marshal Paskevich and was warmly supported by Nicholas I, proved to be a dismal failure. In other parts of the region, as well, the Russian efforts proved little more successful, for only in the Lezgin area did the fortifications and troops maintain an uneasy peace. When in 1831 Baron Rosen succeeded Paskevich as commander in chief in the Caucasus, Kazi-Mullah, although checked, was powerful and gaining rapidly in strength. His preaching of social justice for the masses

21. Tornov, *Vospominaniia*, I, 30.
22. P. Kh. Grabbe, "Raport k Grafu Chernyshevu," *Akty Kavkazskoi Arkheograficheskoi Komissii*, IX, 251.
23. *Ibid.*, p. 265.
24. Filipson, *Russkii Arkhiv*, XXI (1883), Pt. III, 344.

in the Caucasus won him a great following, which enabled him to strike first at the fortress of Vnezapnaia, which held out, and then at Derbent, on the Caspian, where it was only with the greatest difficulty that hastily gathered forces repulsed him. In September, 1831, Baron Rosen's subordinates tried to hunt him down, but he escaped to the Chechens, who, along with the Ingush, gave strong support. He evaded the pursuing Russian forces and with one thousand picked men raided and looted Kizliar, the administrative center of the Terek region. This greatly encouraged the murids, who raised new bands and accomplished several successful raids. During these operations the Russians followed no definite system except along the Black Sea coast. Rosen was following the program of Paskevich, who, indeed, was freely prescribing for the situation in the Caucasus. Rosen enjoyed no freedom of action and had to await instructions from St. Petersburg. Finally, in July he received the plan approved in the capital, calling for an expedition to punish the Chechens for their hostility, to be followed by a drive against Kazi-Mullah and his followers. A force of nine thousand men moved first into Chechnia, proceeding in a war of destruction in which "the movements of the Russian troops were marked by piles of ashes and the flight of infuriated inhabitants into the wooded foothills of the Black Mountains. Wiping out over sixty unsubmissive auls in seven weeks," the expedition passed through the country, receiving the submission of over eighty settlements, and then in October went to its base in Dagestan.[25]

On October 1 Baron Rosen proceeded with a strong detachment into central Dagestan. At first all the tribesmen submitted, giving hostages and pledging loyalty, but soon reports came that Kazi-Mullah and Shamil had fortified Gimry and Irganai in the impassable mountains beyond. The Russian sappers had to build a road along the sheer cliffs before the troops could approach. At first the troops were repulsed, but by a turning movement they avoided the main defenses and stormed the walls of Gimry with great success. Some of the murids and their followers tried to hold out in the fortified houses, but artillery fire soon drove them out and the infantry bayonetted the survivors. Thus died the Imam, Kazi-Mullah. Shamil, however, escaped.[26]

This success of the Russian arms, which Nicholas I hailed in a special message to the troops, made a deep impression on the moun-

25. Bobrovskii, IV, 200-3.
26. *Ibid.*, IV, 203-8.

taineers, but only for a brief time did it cool their ardor. Hamzat-Bek, a disciple of Kazi-Mullah, soon revived muridism, and by June of 1834 he had control of most of Dagestan. Only Avaria, under the old grandmother of the Khan, still defied him and held off his force of twenty thousand. Hamzat-Bek now used deceit to gain control of the young Khan and his brother and killed them, and later killed off their grandparent. Avaria now came under Hamzat-Bek. One of the embittered Avarians, however, managed to kill him in September, 1834, which opened the path for Shamil to take control of the mountaineers.[27]

By this time the doctrine of muridism had spread everywhere east of the Military Highway, arousing the mass of peasants to oppose the Russians and their leaders and nobles who collaborated with the infidel. The murids, sworn to complete obedience to their Imam, had managed to kill many of the former magnates and establish a system of general equality under Moslem law. Shamil, a disciple of Mullah Mahomet, stepped into the place of Kazi-Mullah and built up a strong regime among the mountain peoples. Most of the tribes promised him complete obedience and support in war. A tax system went into effect, and the tribesmen accepted the obligation of universal military service. Shamil, a brilliant administrator and warrior, enforced this through the murids, who provided local officials and judges. Although there was no regular army, the mountaineers had a gunpowder factory, a foundry for casting cannon and projectiles, and a small force of artillery. Thus there now was a unified opposition to the Russians, as the consolidated population of the Caucasus, from near Derbent to the Military Highway, sought to repulse their blows. If the troops destroyed an aul, the women and children were fed by other tribes until the next harvest. When the Russians advanced, villages were evacuated, and when they had passed, "peaceful" auls were at once fortified. Thus for the first time the Russians met a unified and co-ordinated reaction against their penetration of the area—one that they were not prepared to cope with.[28]

At first, however, Shamil remained quiet. The Russians had installed a new Khan in Avaria and stormed several of the hitherto impregnable mountain positions. Many of the tribes submitted to the

27. Romanovskii, pp. 329-33; M. I. Shishevich, "Pokorenie Kavkaza. Persidskiia i Kavkazskiia voiny," in Grishinskii, VI, 72-73.
28. Romanovskii, pp. 334-47; R. A. Fadeev, *Shest'desiat let Kavkazskoi voiny. Pis'ma s Kavkaza* (St. Petersburg, 1899), pp. 29-37.

Russians or accepted rulers installed by them. For the time being the people of Dagestan were terrified by the power of the Russians and remained quiet during 1835.[29] In 1836 Shamil, who had done little during the past year, again became active, and Baron Rosen ordered an expedition to destroy his power. In 1837, after the Avarians had asked for a Russian garrison as protection against Shamil, Gen. Fezi provided one and then pushed on to attack Shamil's fortress of Akhulgo. Shamil, however, took refuge in the most inaccessible position of Tilitl. Fezi nevertheless pushed on and bombarded it. When he was ready to storm it, Shamil asked for peace talks, which Fezi mistakenly granted. Shamil formally "submitted" and once more upper Dagestan seemed peaceful.[30]

With the eastern Caucasus apparently under control, the Russian authorities now devoted most of their attention to the western Caucasus, where the forts on the Black Sea were constructed. In Dagestan and Chechnia they had no systematic plan, relying on expeditions to crush the main centers of resistance and frighten the tribesmen. This policy gave Shamil a chance to reorganize his forces and to fortify anew his stronghold of Akhulgo, high in the mountains. In the spring of 1839 Gen. Golovin, the new commander in chief in the Caucasus, ordered Gen. Grabbe to march against it. The latter, after first subduing the Chechens, advanced against Shamil's refuge by an almost impassable mountain road, fiercely defended by large bands of tribesmen. It took three weeks to reach the objective. Even when he stood before it, so well had the mountaineers done their work that it was impossible to storm it, and the artillery could not destroy it. Grabbe's force of nine thousand had to undertake a regular siege, building batteries on all sides of the town, which consisted of New and Old Akhulgo. Approaches were made with much difficulty over the rocky terrain and the besiegers, frequently fighting off attacks from large forces of tribesmen in their rear, had to bring in heavier guns and cross the river to surround the town before they could make much progress. Finally Grabbe ordered an assault on July 16, only to suffer a repulse with the loss of 875 men. So the siege operations went on, with the sappers building a closed gallery close to New Akhulgo for a fresh assault. Shamil, seeing defeat approaching, started peace talks, but they broke down. On August 17 the Russians

29. Grzhegorskii, *Russkaia Starina*, XII (1875), 548-50, 653-54.
30. Shishkevich, "Pokorenie Kavkaza," in Shirinskii, VI, 73.

stormed into New Akhulgo. Shamil again talked of surrender, sending his son as hostage, but once more the talks failed. A new assault on New Akhulgo failed for a whole day, but finally Shamil and his men fled to the old town, which the Russians quickly stormed. The defenders fought to the last, with women fighting beside the men, and very few would surrender. Even after the houses had all been taken, desperate men continued to fight on for a week in caves underneath. Shamil and a small band escaped, apparently broken and discredited men. The Russians could boast that they had sought out the enemy at his strongest point and had broken his resistance. They now placed residents in the leading communities of northern Dagestan and apparently could feel that this region was secure.[31]

While this was a great victory, it was not an easy one. The attack itself lasted eighty days and cost about 500 dead, 1,722 wounded, and 687 badly bruised with stones. Gen. Grabbe was overly confident after his success, claiming that Shamil's head was not worth three hundred rubles. The Imam, he declared, would find no support or shelter, either in the mountains or the valleys; "nowhere can he find a place more inaccessible than Akhulgo, and the bravest adherents have now sacrificed their lives for him. His party has been completely wiped out; the murids, left by their chief, died one after the other, one beside the other." Nicholas, however, was somewhat skeptical, for while he rejoiced in the defeat of Shamil, he regretted that he had escaped and feared new underhandedness from him.[32]

The Tsar's fears were more than realized, for in the next few years the Russian position deteriorated seriously. The commanders did little to follow up their victory, neglecting to build roads and strong forts. Attempts to impose a permanent administrative system on the Chechens, one of the most peaceful of the Caucasian peoples, infuriated them, for Gen. Pullo, commander in this region, acted in highhanded fashion. Hoping to demonstrate Russian authority to them, he insisted on collecting one usable firearm from each ten families—a demand that would by no means disarm them, but convinced them that this was but the first step of many intended to leave them naked to their enemies. Pullo's subordinates enforced this requirement ruthlessly, with sad results. "From this time the very name of Pullo became a

31. D. A. Miliutin, *Opisanie voennykh deistvii 1839 goda v severnom Dagestane* (St. Petersburg, 1850), pp. 29-132.
32. Zisserman, *Istoriia*, II, 154-55.

synonym of oppression and injustice in Chechnia."[33] Many of the Chechens seem to have believed that the Russians intended to enserf them and to subject them to conscription. D. A. Miliutin, after serving on Grabbe's staff, wrote that the Russians must convince the mountaineers that under them their religions, customs, and property would be safe. "Up to now we have not acted in this spirit in the Caucasus. This compels them to look on the Russians as plunderers come to them for their enrichment, exactly as the Mongols once were for Russia."[34]

As a result of these factors and the encouragement derived from the capture of the Black Sea forts from the Russians, the Chechens rose in the spring of 1840 and Shamil established his administration over them. In the fall, Gen. Grabbe marched in and wreaked devastation throughout their land, but this did not bring them to submission, but only infuriated them the more. At about the same time, the Khadji-Murad incident led to the loss of Avaria, the one strongpoint of the Russians in Dagestan. Khadji-Murad, chieftain of Avaria, for long had been a fierce opponent of Shamil and had denied him control of this region. In 1840, however, the Russian leaders, suspecting him of dealing with the Imam, seized him and sent him in chains—a terrible disgrace—to headquarters at Temir-Khan-Shura. Somehow he managed to escape, fled to Shamil, and at once became a ferocious and daring enemy of the Russians, who for a time lost Avaria. Shamil now was fully dominant over much of the eastern Caucasus.[35]

In the next two years, the Russians accomplished little, building a number of small forts in Dagestan and making daring but ineffectual raids to terrorize the mountaineers. Shamil's strength and boldness grew, aided by several able and daring leaders. The Russians, although considerably reinforced, lacked unity of action, for Gen. Grabbe, commander in the Left Flank (Chechnia) was bitterly at odds with Gen. Golovin, his superior, repeatedly appealing over the latter's head to St. Petersburg. In the summer of 1842 Grabbe moved with a force of nine thousand men through the Ichkerian forest to destroy Shamil's base at Dargo in Chechnia, only to run into disaster. He had to return to his base with the loss of 1,900 men, one gun, and vast supplies. A later attempt also failed. These developments caused the authorities in St. Petersburg, who controlled the commanders in the

33. *Ibid.*, p. 157.
34. P. A. Zaionchkovskii, ed., *Dnevnik D. A. Miliutina*, (2 vols.; Moscow, 1947-1950), I, 10-11.
35. Bobrovskii, IV, 321-23; Shishkevich, in Grishinskii, VI, 81-82.

Caucasus, to concentrate on the eastern regions instead of the western Caucasus.[36]

Nicholas I sent Count Chernyshev to study the Caucasus situation, with the result that at the end of 1842 the Tsar replaced Gen. Golovin with Gen. Adj. A. I. Neigardt, quartermaster general of the imperial staff, to carry out the new plan of operations worked out in the capital. This proved to be an unfortunate choice, for the new appointee felt himself unfitted for the post, which he had undertaken only as a result of the Tsar's insistence. He had never served in the Caucasus, did not know the leaders there, and had no knowledge of its peculiar problems. He did not wholly sympathize with the plan that he had to carry out and for whose almost inevitable failure he would receive the blame.[37]

In 1843 the Russians held Avaria, the key to all upper Dagestan, by means of eleven fortifications. Khunzakh, the main point, high in the mountains, had a garrison of two companies. Most of the other positions were towers held by thirty or thirty-five men, or at most one company, with two or three cannon. All of them were very weak positions, subject to fire from nearby heights and extremely vulnerable to artillery fire. The garrisons were gravely weakened by disease, with nearly one thousand cases annually—fevers, typhus, scurvy. They were always overworked, as they had to do guard duty, build roads, repair the forts, forage, or cut firewood.[38] In the lowlands the Russian situation was little better. The main position was Temir-Khan-Shura (now Buinaksk), commanding several vital roads, including the route for bringing in provisions for the whole region. It was damp, crowded, and fever-ridden, and in summer the heat was stifling. Hence the mortality was great: in the last half of 1842, out of perhaps 4,000 men, 544 died. The ditch and the wall were weak and not properly protected by artillery fire, as cannon were few, and some of those on hand lacked proper platforms. Its port was Nizovoe (Makhachkale), through which passed the provisions brought from Astrakhan. Its ditch was half filled in and its wall was crumbling, while a foe on the nearby heights could shower it with fire. Both its climate and drinking water were very bad, so that disease was prevalent. In 1841, out of its garrison of 430, some 127 died in the last five months. Kazi-Yurt, commanding a main river crossing, had a comparatively healthy

36. Shishkevich, pp. 82-84.
37. Glinoetskii, *Istoriia*, II, 225-26.
38. Zisserman, *Istoriia*, II, 243-48.

climate, but its walls and ditch were so weak that it was practically defenseless. Only two or three of the Russian forts had any real strength.[39] Thus, although the Russian troops had been reinforced, their position was highly vulnerable.

Suddenly, late in August, 1843, Shamil struck at one of the smaller forts. A battalion that marched to the rescue was surrounded and cut to pieces, and other relief forces were almost annihilated. In two weeks the Imam's forces took six forts and inflicted losses of fifteen hundred men on the Russians, who also lost twelve field guns and a number of fortress guns, as well as large quantities of ammunition and provisions. Two Russian generals had to take refuge with their forces in Khunzakh, high up in Avaria, where Shamil besieged them and devastated the pro-Russian parts of the region until a relief expedition rescued them, leaving a garrison under Col. Passek in this mountain post. Next, a powerful force of tribesmen struck at the important position of Gergebil, on the road between Khunzakh and the Russian base at Temir-Khan-Shura. Two generals moved to aid Gergebil, but, finding that they were too weak to break through Shamil's forces, sent off for additional troops. The reinforcements failed to arrive in time, and so, although the defenders of Gergebil could see Russian bayonets a short distance away, the siege continued and a few days later Gergebil fell. The relief expedition, terribly dejected that they had failed to save their beleaguered brothers, had to fight their way back to safety at Temir-Khan-Shura. Passek's force now was completely isolated at Khunzakh.[40]

While Khadji-Murad watched Passek, Shamil moved his forces in early November around Temir-Khan-Shura to strike at Nizovoe, the port of entry for the whole Dagestan force, and thereby to starve out the Russians at Temir. On November 8 the tribesmen appeared before the pitifully weak position at Nizovoe, held by 346 men with five guns, three of them without carriages! The attackers, building batteries and trenches, pushed steadily to storm the defenses. When they were on the very verge of success, with the defenders completely exhausted, Gen. Freitag came to the rescue. The mountaineers tried to destroy his force but were lured into a trap and crushed, fleeing in complete disorder. Freitag, after inspecting the fort, evacuated it, burning the supplies and sending off the civilians in ships. The Russians still held

39. M. Ia. Ol'shevskii, "Kavkaz s 1841 po 1866 god," *Russkaia Starina*, LXXIX (1879), 287-90.
40. Tornov, *Russkii Arkhiv*, XIX (1881), Pt. II, 426-57

Temir-Khan-Shura, with a weak garrison, but Shamil now controlled all Dagestan and could put thirty thousand men in the field. He delayed in attacking Temir, however, and failed to capture it.[41]

Passek's position in Khunzakh now was hopeless, for he could get no aid from the lowlands, with Khadji-Murad barring the way, and Shamil preparing to attack Temir-Khan-Shura. Consequently, on November 16 his force evacuated Khunzakh, to the despair of its people. In their rage they actually pursued and fought the retreating Russians. Passek, however, led his troops through difficult mountain terrain to the position at Zyrany, in the Lezgin country, where his troops skilfully fortified their refuge and beat off attacks. Running low on provisions, they were reduced to eating horsemeat—a step that their officers had great difficulty in persuading them to take. Almost one month later, Gen. Gurko came to the rescue, and Passek with his two battalions advanced to meet them, thus ending the siege.[42]

Thus the Russians were able to hold only a few posts in the lowlands like Temir-Khan-Shura. All upper Dagestan backed Shamil, and most of the Chechens were with him, although the Russians had some forts there. Not for decades had Russian prestige been so low. Nicholas, however, sent in heavy reinforcements late in 1843, and 1844 was to see fresh efforts to restore their power.

As usual, the authorities in St. Petersburg worked out the plans for 1844 and communicated them to Neigardt. Whereas earlier he had been forbidden to take the offensive and had followed a largely passive defense, now his orders were "to crush Shamil's power at one stroke." This proved impossible, for Shamil successfully evaded battle, and when Neigardt with superior forces had an opportunity to attack him, he did not do so, but tried a flank movement, which Shamil again eluded. Thus, although the Russians successfully dominated all southern Dagestan and broke the power of Daniel-Bek, a trusted Lezgin officer, who suddenly defected to Shamil with his followers, they failed to harm or discredit Shamil.[43]

Late in 1844, the Tsar sent Prince M. S. Vorontsov, an elderly and much respected hero of the Napoleonic Wars, as viceroy and commander in chief in the Caucasus, to subdue and pacify the region. Nicholas added: "I regard the task as a matter that may last not less

41. Zisserman, *Istoriia*, II, 310-16.
42. *Ibid.*, II, 321-35.
43. Bobrovskii, IV, 347-56.

than three years."[44] The monarch gave him wide powers and as the whole Fifth Corps was now under his orders, as well as the usual veteran Caucasus troops, he expected great things of his appointee. The latter, however, began his duties under much the same handicaps as his predecessors, for, instead of approving Neigardt's proposal for limited gains followed by careful consolidation—a plan that the experienced Caucasus generals favored—Nicholas drew up his own highly detailed plan for 1845. Essentially it called for powerful simultaneous drives by two strong forces to smash the Imam's bands and occupy and hold Andi, in the Chechen country, which was Shamil's main base. The Tsar based his whole scheme on this feat, which, he wrote: *we must and can do*."[45] The able Prince M. Z. Argutinskii held that it was really the same as the plan for 1844—a huge raid into Shamil's area, which would cost heavily and not be decisive, while on the retreat back to safety they would suffer heavily.[46] And that was the way it turned out.

Although Vorontsov protested against this plan, which he wanted to postpone for a year, the monarch demanded that he carry it out, as the Fifth Corps, which had reinforced the Caucasus Corps, would soon be returning to Russia proper. "In a word, it is evident that the Sovereign was firmly convinced both of the infallibility of his plan and of the impossibility of some unorganized mountain bands fighting against our regiments," especially when led by Vorontsov.[47]

Early in June the advance started, through country so difficult that the sappers had to construct the road for the force to travel over. All went well at first, with the troops easily driving the enemy off and winning a position high in the mountains. At this point a terrible blizzard hit them, and for seven days they had to remain immobilized, deep in snow, without fuel or warm food. Almost five hundred men were frostbitten. Yet discipline held and the men were in good spirits. On June 11 they were able to resume their advance, and, moving through a narrow pass, they came down to Andi and other villages, all of which Shamil's men burned as they left.[48]

After staying in Andi for nearly a month, while the troops built

44. M. S. Shcherbinin, *Biografiia general-fel'dmarshala Kniazia M. S. Vorontsova* (St. Petersburg, 1858), p. 213.
45. "Zapiska imperatora Nikolaia o voennykh deistviiakh na Kavkaze," *Russkaia Starina*, XLVIII (1885), 209-12.
46. Zisserman, *Istoriia*, II, 388-91.
47. Zisserman, *Dvadtsat'*, I, 71.
48. Zisserman, *Istoriia*, II, 400-8.

forts along the line of communication, they marched through the grim Ichkerian forest to Dargo, Shamil's new base. The advance guard went ahead very rapidly, only to be cut off from the main forces. The main body had to take barricades of heavy trees that blocked the road, each one with heavy fighting, in part along a narrow, exposed ridge. They encountered twenty-three barricades in about a mile and a half. Finally, by eleven o'clock at night they reached Dargo, where hot food was waiting. Before they could eat it, however, enemy fire smashed the kettle. The next day they realized the seriousness of their position, for enemy cannon in the woods beyond the river fired down into the camp, and the Russian gunners were unable to silence them. Moreover, their provisions were already very scanty and it was almost impossible to bring in more over the dangerous road over which they had come. On July 10 a cannon shot in the distance having announced the coming of a convoy of provisions from Andi, Vorontsov sent a strong column under the experienced fighting generals Klugenau and Passek to meet it. After some time the column sent back word that it had fought its way to the convoy, losing many men and two guns, and they expected great difficulty on the return trip, burdened as they were with many wounded, a big pack train, and numerous beef cattle. Their fears were realized. The tribesmen, sensing victory, attacked with abandon, slashing with their swords into the center of the column, and killed Passek and many other soldiers. They also concentrated on the pack animals, killing many, so that their bodies at times blocked the road. They also killed many of the artillery horses. Finally, when all seemed lost, a battalion from Vorontsov's force came to the rescue and the convoy was able to join the main body. During the fighting 1,421 men had been put out of action, and three guns were lost. Although the soldiers were not daunted by their experience, Klugenau and other experienced officers, realizing that the "biscuit expedition" had brought back only food enough for three days and that the army now had hundreds of wounded to look after, feared that all was lost.[49]

Prince Vorontsov, who also appreciated the grave predicament of his forces, decided to leave the next day, but by a different route, to the north and northeast. He had sent a daring messenger to Gen. Freitag to lead a force to the rescue. At first their retreat met little opposition, as the enemy did not expect it to take the direction it did.

49. Baron A. P. Nikolai, "Iz vospominanii moei zhizni. Darginskii pokhod 1845 goda," *Russkii Arkhiv*, XXVIII (1890), Pt. II, 257-67; Zisserman, *Istoriia*, II, 427-35.

The rear guard, however, had to fight heavily as it withdrew. Somewhat later the long, narrow column, with eight hundred wounded, marched through the forest into a deep ravine, with wooded mountains on each side, and it cost them heavy losses to drive the enemy from his barricades. At one point the Russian forces became separated and lost contact with each other. As the enemy slashed into the column, cutting down some of the wounded, tremendous confusion developed, with some panic. The foe, however, feared that it was a trick and withdrew, permitting the Russians to escape complete disaster. Two days later they experienced the same dangers, but survived to reach a clearing, where they camped, under enemy artillery fire, to await the coming of Freitag. After two days of waiting, during which their food and ammunition ran very low, Freitag's force came into view. The next day Vorontsov's troops fought their way through to Freitag, and, although the rear guard still lost heavily from the attacks of the enemy, Shamil soon gave up the pursuit. If Freitag had come one day later, probably Vorontsov's whole force would have been lost.[50]

In his report to Nicholas, Prince Vorontsov presented these events as a normal campaign, in which the objectives set had been captured, although the foe evaded decisive action. He concluded that it was useless to try to crush the enemy at one blow, but instead they should follow a slow, systematic policy of occupying Chechnia, and in Dagestan should fortify and hold the main rivers, thus consolidating their hold on the lowlands as a first step. The Tsar wrote on this report: "I agree with everything; I completely share the opinion of Prince Vorontsov. I leave it to him to act as he sees fit."[51]

Thus the realities of the situation had compelled a return to a modified form of the system of Ermolov. The Russians fortified the river lines protecting coastal Dagestan and maintained control of the mountain areas in the south. The country of the Chechens now became the scene of the decisive struggle, as the Russian forts threatened them and Shamil was unable to protect them from Russian reprisals, although they in turn harried the Russian settlements across the Terek. In June, 1846 Prince Bariatinskii led a force into the heart of Chechnia, burning the ripening crops and reconnoitering areas never before visited. As Shamil's forces were elsewhere, the Chechens were unable

50. Nikolai, *Russkii Arkhiv*, XXVIII (1890), Pt. II, 269-77; Zisserman, *Istoriia*, II, 450-51.
    51. Zisserman, *Istoriia*, II, 457-60.

to defend their homes against this incursion. Many of them lost hope of expelling the Russians, and a few of them fled their homes to settle under Russian protection, where Shamil's vengeance could not reach them.[52] In mid-December, 1846, Gen. Freitag made a surprise raid into some remote settlements in Chechnia, destroying much property and further proving to the people how vulnerable they were to the Russian arms.[53]

The ax now became the chief instrument for subduing the Chechens. During the months when the trees were bare, Russian forces in great strength marched into the forest and, while strong patrols and artillery kept back the tribesmen, numerous axmen cut down broad belts of trees and burned them, so that avenues of approach gradually penetrated the heart of the country. This inexorable advance, which cost little in casualties, left the settlements exposed to Russian attack even in the summer. This brought the population to the verge of despair and, as forts were built in key positions, they began in greater numbers to accept the peace and security that submission brought.[54]

The Russians also achieved a significant success in April, 1846, when Shamil, with a strong force of Chechens and Lezgins, pushed across the Georgian Military Highway into Kabarda, in the western Caucasus, in an effort to incite the Kabardians to strike against the Russians. While this appeared to be an extremely dangerous threat to Russian power in the Caucasus, it failed completely. Few of the Kabardians rose, while the others remained in their homes or retired into the mountains. In the meantime, the Russian troops massed to cut off Shamil's retreat. The Imam realized his danger and beat a hasty retreat, covering one hundred miles in thirty-six hours. If he had delayed for two days it would have been too late. This event showed that the Russians were in no danger in the western Caucasus, so they could continue to follow their policy of systematic conquest of Chechnia and Dagestan.[55]

Prince Vorontsov did not, however, at once halt his expeditions to capture Shamil's fortified positions. In 1847 he planned to take Gergebil and Salta in lower Dagestan, largely for reasons of prestige.

52. A. L. Zisserman, "Fel'dmarshal kniaz' A. I. Bariatinskii," *Russkii Arkhiv*, XXVI (1888), Pt. I, 120-21.
53. Bobrovskii, IV, 384.
54. Glinoetskii, *Istoriia*, II, 248-52; Bobrovskii, I, 373-74.
55. Bobrovskii, I, 371-72.

A sizable force marched to Gergebil and, after the batteries had breached the wall, the Russian infantry stormed the settlement. Here, however, they found themselves in heavy crossfire, and as repeated charges failed to take the aul, they finally ceased their attacks, retiring with the loss of six hundred men. In order to redeem himself, Vorontsov now pushed on Salta, where the defenders again inflicted heavy losses on the Russian troops. Finally, the tribesmen slipped away by a hidden path, leaving the Russians to destroy the aul. Actually, it was an empty victory, for its capture did not weaken Shamil's position, and the two sieges had cost the Caucasian army over two thousand casualties.[56] In 1848 Vorontsov's forces again moved against Gergebil which, in spite of the massed forces of Shamil and his long-range cannon fire, the Russians bombarded heavily. This time the defenders slipped away, leaving the Russians the satisfaction of completely destroying the village. The next year the Viceroy moved against Chokh, another fortified position. A heavy bombardment ruined the settlement but failed to silence the defenders, so that eventually the attackers withdrew without attempting to storm it. This annoyed the Tsar, although he did not rebuke Vorontsov for the vain losses of about six hundred men.[57]

Edified by the events of these years, Vorontsov did not need the anger of the Tsar to make him realize the worthlessness of the former policy, and from 1850 on the large-scale raids ceased. In Dagestan and on the Lezgin Line on the southern slope of the mountains, the Russian forces maintained a defensive posture, with only occasional small counterattacks. In the area of Dagestan also, the program was to control and consolidate, rather than to expand. In fact, even many of the old Caucasus commanders gave up hope of conquering the whole region and were content to hold on, only occasionally building a new road toward the mountains or constructing a new fort.[58]

But while the western Caucasus was fairly quiet, and only minor actions occurred in Dagestan and on the Lezgin Line, in Chechnia there was great activity. The Russian forces under Prince Bariatinskii steadily cut the forests, thereby exposing increasingly large numbers of auls to destruction. Shamil sent in large forces of Lezgins and Dagestany to help the Chechens in their defense, but Russian strength and

56. Zisserman, *Istoriia*, II, 19-22; Nikolai, *Russkii Arkhiv*, XXIX (1891), Pt. II. 138-52.
57. Zisserman, *Istoriia*, II, 55-58.
58. Fadeev, *Shest'desiat let*, pp. 37-38.

tactical skill usually overcame them with little difficulty. Dismayed by the devastation inflicted by the forces of the infidel and furious at the inability of Shamil to protect them, many of the Chechens began to consider making their peace with the Russians and resettling on lands provided by them, although their hatred of the invaders had not abated. Shamil's murids, however, still inflicted death on those who attempted to flee to the enemy, and only under strong Russian protection were they safe. More and more of them risked the penalties, especially as the Russian commanders provided detachments to protect them as they left their homes.[59]

In 1852 so many Chechens had resettled under Russian protection that Prince Bariatinskii organized a system of courts, with elected judges under a Russian presiding officer. Nicholas I also wanted the Chechens to have a role in their own defense, and so a militia system took shape, with good results.[60] By the end of August, 1852, the situation in Chechnia was so well under control that Prince Vorontsov marched all through the land with a small force, parading his troops in sight of the enemy, without a shot being fired. Another sign of success was that when Shamil's forces tried to attack a Chechen settlement under Russian protection, the friendly tribesmen beat off their attackers with considerable loss to the foe.[61] These phenomena indicate that the Russians were rapidly winning control over the Chechens and that these important allies of Shamil would soon be lost to him, which would deprive him of much manpower and also of highly important food resources. It thus seems probable that if the Crimean War had not taken place, the Russian forces would have been able to complete the conquest of the Caucasus much earlier than they actually did.

The war with the Caucasian mountaineers thus proved to be a severe test for the military system of Nicholas I, and indeed, one that was almost too great for it. While the difficulties in large part stemmed from the new unity and fanatical determination of the inhabitants under the leadership of the murids, they also in large measure proceeded from the incorrect approach adopted by the Tsar and his advisers. The fall of Ermolov and the rise of Paskevich meant that the rational system of the former, based on long experience in

59. Bobrovskii, IV, 406-8.
60. Zisserman, *Istoriia*, II, 126-27.
61. *Ibid.*, pp. 143-45.

this region, would give place to various doctrinaire projects founded upon superficial understanding of the situation. Thus, instead of devoting attention to Dagestan and the Chechens, for a full decade they chiefly sought to control the Black Sea coast by a series of sorry forts, most of which fell in 1840. In the meantime, the authorities had no effective policies to halt or contain the rise of muridism, with the result that in 1843 the Russians almost suffered expulsion from the Caucasus and only the heroism and skill of the troops themselves prevented this. Finally, after repeated fumbling by commanders controlled by St. Petersburg, the Tsar had to call on the elderly Vorontsov, a leader of the old school and a warm friend of Ermolov, to avert disaster. Eventually he worked out a variant of the Ermolov system to regain some of the lost ground. Backed by an unprecedented number of troops, Vorontsov began to constrict the enemy, slowly consolidating defense lines around the latter's position and reducing the Chechens to submission by a systematic cutting of the forest. In 1852 this program was well advanced. If a somewhat similar approach had been adopted two decades before, how much blood and suffering might have been avoided!

Probably the army as a whole could have benefited from the lessons of these three decades of conflict in the Caucasus. The conditions of fluid mountain warfare taught the commanders there to stress mobility and agility rather than parade-ground technique and to value soldiers with initiative and *élan*. The cavalry of the Caucasus Corps were inured to difficult marches over defiles and ridges and to fighting in dense forests. The infantry were never able to demonstrate the value of good musketry, as many of the regiments in the Caucasus continued to use outmoded flintlocks, while the mountaineers sometimes had excellent British weapons. But the troops could climb up mountain sides under a rain of falling boulders and knew how to storm strongly held barricades of tree trunks or to carry them by a bayonet charge from the flank. With excellent co-ordination of all arms, the forces of the Caucasus were able to perform wonders.

Instructive as this experience was, it had little influence on the rest of the army. The Caucasus regiments rarely if ever served in Russia proper, while the units of the Active Army were seldom detailed to the Caucasus and at most for brief periods only. After Paskevich, the veteran commanders of the mountain region spent their entire careers south of the Don. A few served with the main army, but only in subordinate positions. Perhaps the greatest interchange between the two military forces came from the detailing of dashing young cavalry officers to the Caucasus for a year or two, where they hoped to find adventure, win medals, and receive mention in despatches after some battle in the mountains. But the intellectual baggage of these young bloods on their return to their regiments consisted chiefly of anecdotes and colorful tales of mountain campaigns, while most of them gained little military insight from their often exciting experiences. Indeed, the conviction was firmly rooted in upper military circles in Russia that the Caucasus was merely a lively sideshow and that the methods and practices in use there were completely valueless in modern warfare in European areas. While the French in Algeria and the British in India probably gained experience that had some effect on their respective military systems, the Russians absorbed little or nothing from their experience in colonial warfare.

CHAPTER IX. THE OFFICERS OF THE RUSSIAN ARMY

Although the fact is sometimes forgotten, an army is an organization of human beings, deriving its virtues and deficiencies from this human material, who therefore are worthy of study. While the enlisted men of the Russian army were, of course, far the most numerous category, they were completely subjected to the officers and generals, who imposed their will upon the masses of the soldiers. This chapter, therefore, will discuss the officer personnel—their origins, education, training, and lives. Subsequent chapters will deal with the rank and file.

There were three sources from which the Russian army derived its officers. The first of these, in prestige if not in numbers, was the military schools—the Corps of Pages, the Noble Regiment, the School of Guards Sub-Ensigns, the Engineering and Artillery schools, and the cadet corps. Most of the officers, however, were young nobles who obtained their commissions by serving as volunteers with the regiments of the army until they qualified for commissions. Finally, there was a very small number of peasants or other men drafted into the army who, by long service, good conduct, and strenuous exertion, managed to secure commissions.

During the reign of Nicholas I the army needed from two thousand to twenty-five hundred new officers annually to fill the vacancies in the peacetime officer corps of some thirty thousand. The military schools supplied only about one-sixth of the amount. Moreover, almost half of the graduates of the military schools went to the Guards and to the Engineering and Artillery schools. Somewhat over one-third of the cadets became officers in the infantry and cavalry of the army, while a small number with bad records received assignments to the garrison troops or the line battalions. In the early 1850's officers from the cadet corps amounted to not more than twelve per cent in the army infantry and twenty-five per cent in the cavalry, while the number of officers who had served as volunteers or *yunkers* (officer candidates) with the regiments attained eighty per cent in the regular infantry and two-thirds in the cavalry.[1] The third category of officers was that of the enlisted men who had served twelve years in the ranks as sergeants or, rarely, received promotion for distinction in battle. In the infantry these officers formed about seven per cent of the total and in the cavalry, five per cent.[2]

Most of the officers were nobles. Nearly half of them were from hereditary noble families, while over one-third were "personal" nobles, of lower status. The rest were of humble origin or came from the intellectuals. In the 1850's perhaps one-tenth of the officers had university education, or had graduated from special cadet schools or lycees. Thirty per cent had secondary education in cadet schools or gymnasia. The majority, however, had had little or no schooling and were barely literate. While these men could make lives for themselves in the army, Nicholas strongly encouraged the graduates of lycees and universities, holding out to them the rare privilege of obtaining commissions after serving only six months with the regiments.[3]

First place among the military schools belonged to the Corps of Pages, whose membership—16 kammer-pages (the senior group), 133 pages, and 15 externs—[4] came from the sons of military and civil officials of the first two classes in the table of ranks, and also sons of the most notable Moslems of Transcaucasia who had won the favor of the Tsar by special services. The latter personally approved the admission of the pages, who were from ten to fourteen years of age.[5]

The School of Guards Sub-Ensigns and Yunkers also enrolled only children of high nobility, approved by the Tsar and the commander of the regiment they wished to enter. If they passed the rigorous examinations set, they then enrolled in the regiment chosen. Only thirty-eight were accepted annually. They took a two-year course stressing military subjects and history, mathematics, Russian, and French. Those who graduated then became officers in their regiments,

1. "K istorii voenno-uchebnoi reformy Imperatora Aleksandra II-go," *Russkaia Starina*, LIV (1887), 354.
2. *Ibid.*
3. Neizvestnyi, *Russkaia Starina*, LXXXII (1894), 120-21.
4. SVP, Pt. I, Bk. III, *Obrazovanie Voenno-Uchebnykh Zavedenii s ikh Upravleniiami*, art. 317.
5. *Ibid.*, art. 672.

while those who failed were commissioned in the army or became yunkers in army regiments.[6]

None of the writers discussing the military schools of this period has much to say about life in the Corps of Pages, probably because the small numbers of the pages and their residence in the imperial palace gave them little scope for pranks and adventures, even if they sought such diversion. The youths in the School of Guards Sub-Ensigns, however, were an unruly lot, drawn from wealthy families from all over Russia. Many of them had brought serfs with them as lackeys. Exposed as they were to the numerous temptations of the capital and amply provided with money, they easily turned to carousing and debauchery, which produced scandalous behavior and brutality. Although the authorities forbade them to go to restaurants and resorts of low repute, they did so nonetheless, or held drinking bouts in the homes of relatives or in rented rooms. In the dashing hussar tradition, the cavalry yunkers were the worst carousers, sometimes ending a spree by a visit to a public dance hall, where they tried to pick fistfights with the habitués. Maj. Gen. Sutgof, the head of the school, in the 1840's, in time managed to correct many of these failings by ruthless measures against the worst offenders, while appealing to the better natures of those who were not beyond hope.[7] The sub-ensigns and yunkers also misbehaved when they marched out to reviews or to camp at Peterhof. They were quartered in peasant homes, which gave them the opportunity to have great drinking bouts and orgies.[8] In addition, the older students terrorized the younger ones, asserting their despotic authority with their fists—a practice that the author asserts was prevalent in all military schools of the time, especially the Artillery School. The upper-class students compelled the younger ones to act as their servants in a fashion much like the "fagging" in the British public schools. Ridicule, and even sheer cruelty, made the lives of the youngsters miserable. Some complained to the school authorities, but for this their fellow-unfortunates gave them severe beatings. In time, however, Gen. Sutgof managed to moderate the brutality and the use of fists and tried to persuade the students to treat each other decently.[9]

Even more than the preceding schools, the Noble Regiment had a

6. *Ibid.*, arts. 1394-1420.
7. "Shkola gvardeishkikh podpraporshchikov i iunkerov v vospominaniiakh odnogo iz eia vospitannikov 1845-1849 gg.," *Russkaia Starina*, XLI (1884), 205-13; 441-42.
8. *Ibid.*, p. 449.
9. *Ibid.*, pp. 215-16.

poor reputation. Its first battalion contained students from provincial cadet corps who had finished their studies but required further military training, and noble volunteers who had been educated in gymnasia and had certificates of good conduct. The second battalion was a sort of catchall, as it accepted overage or rejected candidates for the Corps of Pages, the School of Guards Sub-Ensigns, the Engineering, Artillery and Naval schools, and the various cadet corps. The age of admission was from fourteen to sixteen.[10] It was filled with lazy young nobles, ignorant and uninterested in learning, and so vicious that nearby residents were afraid to go out on the street at night. About 1840, the Grand Duke Michael picked Gen. N. N. Pushchin to reform the regiment, giving him full power to act. He used this power to good effect, winning the reputation of a martinet, but changing the whole nature of the regiment in five years. Later on, he was recognized as a kind and fair man, who treated decent students like members of his family. When he died in 1847 many of his former charges mourned him sincerely.[11]

As a means of preparing officers for the army, the cadet corps were much more important than the institutions already considered. In 1825 Russia had five cadet corps with four hundred instructors and fifty-three hundred students. Nicholas, however, felt that the army needed far more trained officers and in 1830 issued new bylaws for the cadet schools. In 1832 the Grand Duke Michael took charge of them and set out to expand and improve them. Thanks to substantial sums that the government provided and to donations by the nobility, new cadet corps arose in a number of provincial towns.[12] Until 1830 there were vacancies for all applicants, but after the reform of 1830 the number of those wishing to enter rose rapidly, so that in 1832 there were six hundred who failed to gain admission. Several new corps opened their doors in 1834, but the number of applicants grew faster than the number of places. In 1845 there were seven thousand candidates, which was larger than the total number of students in all the cadet corps. Hence new rules had to be adopted,

10. SVP, Pt. I, Bk. III, *Obrazovanie Voenno-Uchebnykh Zavedenii*, arts. 683-690.
11. Kartsov, I, 48-50.
12. "K istorii voenno-uchebnoi reformy imperatora Aleksandra II-go," *Russkaia Starina*, LIV (1887), 347. Another writer states that there were seven cadet corps at the accession of Nicholas, in addition to the Corps of Pages and the Noble Regiment. F. V. Grekov, *Istoricheskii ocherk voenno-uchebnykh zavedenii 1700-1910* (Moscow, 1910), pp. 9-10.

which provided for selective admission.[13] Throughout this period these institutions became increasingly dear to the hearts of the nobility, who found them an excellent way to provide for their sons and start them on a career. In fact, there were cases where parents refused to readmit into the family circle sons who had been dismissed for poor work or bad conduct.[14] Both nobles and government provided much money for the cadet corps, so that their number increased from five in 1825 to twenty-three in 1855, with eighty-three hundred students and fourteen hundred instructors. Undoubtedly they provided a much better education to the army officers than ever before, but the cost was very high—over six thousand rubles per cadet in the 1840's.[15]

According to the Code of Military Regulations, all young nobles of the Russian Empire and of the Kingdom of Poland had the right to appointment to the cadet corps, as did the sons of Caucasian princes and nobles, and of Georgian and Tatar nobles. The Finnish Cadet Corps admitted only the sons of distinguished Finnish parents. As a rule, generals and army officers had preference for their sons, as did high civil officials, while the sons of civilian landowners often had difficulty in gaining admission, especially those of Polish parentage. There was no cadet corps in Poland after 1831.[16] Although children might enter for preparatory training at six or seven, the cadets enrolled at ten or older and graduated at eighteen.[17]

The regulations provided that every year the viceroy of the kingdom of Poland should appoint four young Polish nobles to each of five of the cadet schools, and an unlimited number of older ones to the Noble Regiment. There also were ten places in the First Moscow Cadet Corps for sons of Polish insurgents, although only as vacancies occurred.[18] In view of Paskevich's harsh attitude toward Polish nationalism, he probably made these appointments from Polish youths whose loyalty to the Tsar was certain, while the sons of the insurgents of 1831 could look for little favor at his hands.

13. M. Lalaev, *Istoricheskii ocherk voenno-uchebnykh zavedenii podvedomst-vennykh Glavnomu ikh upravleniiu, 1700-1880* (2 vols.; St. Petersburg, 1880-1882), II, 57-59.

14. Neizvestnyi, *Russkaia Starina*, LXXXI (1894), 173.

15. "K istorii voenno-uchebnoi reformy," *Russkaia Starina*, LIV (1887), 347 and 352.

16. SVP, Pt. I, Bk. III, *Obrazovanie Voenno-Uchebnykh Zavedenii*, arts. 671, 673, 674, 675, 678, 679, 682.

17. *Ibid.*, arts. 673 and 778.

18. *Ibid.*, arts. 722-23, 728.

Once enrolled, the cadets took a general course for four years, with great stress on mathematics, along with history and geography, Russian grammar and literature, and French and German. The curriculum put much emphasis on religion, with special arrangements made for non-Orthodox students. In the two upper years the cadets began to take more military subjects: tactics, fortification, gunnery, topographic sketching, and military history, and also physics and chemistry and higher mathematics.[19] Nicholas was much interested in the cadet corps and sought to attract fine teachers by offering excellent salaries and other advantages.[20] While not all of the teachers did good work, most of them seem to have been devoted to their profession and inspired the youths with a desire for learning.[21]

The authorities also placed much emphasis on drilling the cadets in posture, marching, and the manual of arms. All winter they spent each afternoon on this and on formation drill. Before parades and reviews they practised company and battalion drill and various evolutions, in the *manège* in bad weather, or outdoors when it was fine. In the First Cadet Corps (which was an elite school) the cadets were enthusiastic about drill, with a keen spirit of rivalry. As the second and third companies rarely participated in reviews and summer camp, they contested fiercely to secure this honor. In the upper classes the cadets sought the honor of serving as orderlies to the Tsar and as honorary guards.[22] The Grand Duke Michael, who was head of all the military schools from 1832 to his death in 1849, zealously inspected their military accomplishments and verified all details of their skill. The cadets of the corps in St. Petersburg were especially under his eye, and at summer camp he had individuals take command of units during drill, and occasionally he would call night alarms to test the training of the cadets.[23]

The Grand Duke, however, did not succumb completely to the passion for drill that was then prevalent. After noting that many students were discharged for reasons of health, he recognized that

19. I. I. Rostovtsev, *Nastavlenie dlia obrazovaniia vospitannikov voenno-ucheb-nykh zavedenii. Vysochaishe utverzhdeno 24 dekabria 1848 goda* (St. Petersburg, 1849), pp. 13-42.
20. Grekov, p. 10.
21. Neizvestnyi, *Russkaia Starina*, LXXI (1894), 189. This author has extremely harsh things to say about many of the officers who were in charge of disciplinary matters at the cadet corps. Also Grekov, pp. 12-13.
22. M. Ia. Ol'shevskii, "Pervyi kadetskii korpus, 1826-1833," *Russkaia Starina*. IL (1886), 87-90.
23. Grekov, p. 13.

"such diseases are often caused and intensified by frequent prolonged formation drills which are not suited to the strength of young persons" and ordered the directors of the schools "as far as possible to adjust the formation activities of the students to their physical strength."[24]

The rules for running the cadet corps repeatedly emphasized the importance of moral training of the students, the aim of which was "to make the students virtuous and pious."[25] The rules urged the heads of the cadet corps to "try to instill in the souls of the students so that they will not part with them all the rest of their lives" suitable feelings such as: "fear of God, piety, a feeling of duty, limitless loyalty to the Sovereign, submission to superiors, esteem for elders, thankfulness, and love of one's neighbors." These principles were explained in a long series of injunctions urging those in command to teach by personal example, by stimulating love of honor, and finally, by rewards and punishments.[26]

In 1848 Nicholas confirmed an Instruction for the education of military students, which stated the following principles:

> Training should be based on love of God, on reverence for the rulings of His Holy Church, on filial loyalty to the Throne, on unselfish love for the Fatherland, on soulful realization of family and social duty, and on the contemporary condition of learning in the enlightened world.[27]

Some of the officers on duty sought to follow these precepts, with good results: mention has been made of Pushchin and Sutgof, who brought unruly students under control by a judicious combination of severity and kindness. P. P. Kartsov, a student at the Novgorod Corps, found Gen. Borodin, the director, a stern but kindly man, who, when he left the institution, took farewell of them in terms of real affection. The officers who ran the school under him also were fine, upright men, of simple ways.[28]

Unfortunately, others were less admirable characters. The decrees of Gen. Sukhozanet, chief director of the cadet corps in 1834, display the ruthless severity for which he was noted. When a student of the First Cadet Corps received fifteen blows with the birch for not having corrected his sloppy attire when called upon to do so by the

24. *Ibid.*, p. 14.
25. SVP, Pt. I, Bk. III, *Obrazovanie Voenno-Uchebnykh Zavedenii*, art. 850.
26. *Ibid.*, arts 853-872.
27. Grekov, p. 20.
28. Kartsov, I, 29-30.

officer of the day, Sukhanozanet had him birched once more, in the presence of the cadet corps. A disappointed cadet had muttered a threat to desert when his commander refused to let him transfer to another unit, for which the officer had punished him with fifty blows of the birch. When the general learned of this, he forbade the student to graduate for an indefinite period, although he was on the point of receiving his commission.[29]

Sukhozanet was soon replaced, but many of the officers who were in charge of the students as well as serving as drillmasters were little better. They were mostly men of narrow outlook, who knew little and cared less about the natures of children, but sought merely to enforce submissiveness and outward good conduct. At times the students protested strongly against their preceptors, and there were cases in which such protests achieved results, because of the sympathy of kindly corps directors or because some of the students had influence in high places. But in many cases the results were tragic, for they sometimes ended with a lively student being driven from the corps, to serve as a private in the Caucasus or in a line battalion in the steppes of Central Asia. Nicholas himself supported the officers. In one such instance the authorities expelled a cadet, sending him to serve as a yunker in an infantry regiment. The Tsar, however, changed the order to read "to serve as a private."

Flogging was the favorite punishment of these officers. On one occasion an officer found a cadet whose slate did not have its wooden frame and, angered by such sloppiness, sent him to the guardhouse to be flogged. The cadet, in terror, escaped from his guards and, seizing a knife, cut his own throat. Another cadet threw himself down a three-story staircase, nearly killing himself. Another deserted to escape flogging, but was captured. Upon his return under guard they flogged and expelled him.[30]

While there were brutalities in the lives of the cadets, they also had lighter moments. Their living accommodations, while not luxurious, were fairly comfortable. Even while living by drumbeat they had recreation and amusements in addition to duties. During the winter the authorities at the Novgorod Cadet Corps brought in jugglers with trained animals, magic lantern shows, and a circus. There also was abundant reading material in the library. The students also could

29. Gershenzon, pp. 80-81.
30. Neizvestnyi, *Russkaia Starina*, LXXXI (1894), 179-88.

amuse themselves by listening to the tales of old soldiers, some of whom had taken part in famous battles. Their officers and teachers often joined in their amusements—games, choral singing, and plays, which became quite elaborate, even attracting visitors from the surrounding region. In the winter there were costume balls, in which the senior students took part.[31] The Grand Duke encouraged this sort of activity. With his approval the authorities published a semimonthly magazine to provide the cadets with reading, with one copy free for each five cadets. He also entertained outstanding cadets of the corps in the capital, or sent them theater tickets. He also organized excursions to his villa on Kamennyi Ostrov or to Pavlovsk. At his advice the corps directors encouraged the students to organize plays, dances, and games, and the directors often provided the students with music and concerts.[32]

Perhaps the cadets had need of these civilizing influences, for many of them were rough, and some were even brutal. In the 1830's the First Cadet Corps had a number of "old cadets," too stupid to earn promotion, but kept on until they were discharged at eighteen to go to army regiments or garrison troops. They fought with their fists and were guilty of various other offenses, for which the authorities flogged or imprisoned them, but rarely expelled them. The younger students were often mistreated by the older students, who beat or kicked them and otherwise abused them, so that some of them fell sick from it, and some even died.[33] In the Novgorod Corps a new student, attacked from the rear, pursued his assailant and paid him back in kind, only to be seized by the officer of the day, who treated him as a troublemaker. It was only with some difficulty that he escaped a severe flogging.[34] In 1837 an even more serious incident developed in the Second Cadet Corps in St. Petersburg. A newly assigned officer did not know of the weaknesses of the students and failed to post sentries against the bringing in of contraband. As a result, a number of the students were able to smuggle in quantities of vodka, on which they became royally drunk. Although the officer did not report this offense, his superiors learned of it. They did not, however, wish to have a public scandal, and so "they dealt with it on the quiet, sobering

31. Kartsov, I, 34, 37.
32. Grekov, pp. 13-15.
33. Ol'shevskii, *Russkaia Starina*, IL (1886), 66.
34. Kartsov, I, 33.

up the offenders by scourging them with a hundred or more birches."[35] Probably if this case had come to the attention of the Tsar it would have had grave consequences.

In spite of the unruly nature of some of his charges, the Grand Duke, who, rumor had it, was harsh and brutal, displayed considerable fondness for the youths under him. On the eve of the opening of the Novgorod Cadet Corps, he went into the dormitory of the cadets and, gathering them around him, began to joke with them and even encouraged them to toss him in the air! On the following day, however, Michael was formal and correct at the ceremonies marking the opening of the cadet corps. Nevertheless, in the evening he invited a dozen of the cadets for dinner and chatted with them freely.[36] On his other visits to the Novgorod institution he also mingled with the students in informal fashion, asking them to drink tea with him and chatting and joking gaily.[37]

Nicholas himself also took great interest in the cadets, especially in their summer encampment at Peterhof, where he repeatedly reviewed them and observed their conduct on maneuvers. The imperial family often visited their camp, and every Sunday invited them into the palace gardens. Nicholas himself treated them like friends, inviting them to the palace, joking with them, and otherwise showing his cordiality. He even encouraged his sons to give them fruit and cakes. On one of the last days there was a gala event—the storming of the fountains. Each unit in turn marched to the foot of the cascade of fountains and then clambered up through the torrents of water to the imperial party waiting on the terrace at the top. The Tsar and the Empress gave generous prizes to the winners, amid general rejoicing and informality.[38]

These events had a very impressive effect upon the cadets, who came to feel that they were indeed favored sons of the fatherland and cherished warm feelings of affection for their ruler.

Finally, the day of graduation arrived. It was a solemn occasion, beginning with a full-dress church parade, with a liturgy and a requiem for former cadets who had died in battle. The graduates then took their oath, after which the chaplain performed a *Te Deum* of farewell and gave an inspiring address. Then the corps proceeded to the

35. Men'kov, II, 15-16.
36. Kartsov, I, 25-27.
37. *Ibid.*, p. 29.
38. *Ibid.*, pp. 51-53.

manège, where the remaining cadets paraded to band music before the newly commissioned officers. A banquet followed, with the graduates as honored guests. Lastly, there were long farewells to teachers, officers, and comrades. This was an occasion calculated to leave the graduates with warm and pleasant memories of their schooling.[39]

Graduation day was not a time of rejoicing for all the senior students, however, for not all of them received attractive assignments. Promotion into the Guard was the reward that awaited the outstanding graduates, while others who had distinguished themselves in their studies went to the Engineering or Artillery schools. Those of more modest achievements obtained commissions in the regular army. As for those of poor records in conduct and in learning, their lot was the Line battalions or the Corps of Internal Defense. Cadets whose health did not permit them to serve in the army received civil-service positions according to their capabilities. Finally, the most hopeless of the cadets in conduct and in learning became sub-ensigns or yunkers in army units, to serve up to three years before they might receive commissions.[40]

Perhaps because of the special expenses and the extravagant way of life characteristic of the cavalry, officers commissioned to this arm had to present sufficient guarantee money to "show that they have sufficient means and can maintain themselves in the cavalry without need. . . ."[41]

At least one cadet who was eager to become a cavalryman met strong disapproval from the head of his corps and the officer directly above him. The latter regarded cavalrymen as good-for-nothings— drunkards and showoffs in red uniforms. The very word *hussar* was almost a term of reproach in his eyes. But the cadet insisted on joining the cavalry, in spite of dissuasion and the certainty of slow promotion.[42]

But while the cadet schools furnished most of the noted officers in the Russian army, who entered service with a fair military education and a fine knowledge of marching, riding, and formation drill, by far the greatest number of officers began their careers as volunteers who served as sergeants or yunkers in army regiments. These youths were of several types. Probably the most numerous were those entering with

39. *Ibid.,* I, 54-55.
40. SVP, Pt. I, Bk. III, *Obrazovanie Voenno-Uchebnykh Zavedenii,* art. 778, 805, 818-19.
41. *Ibid.,* art. 778.
42. P. V. Zhukovskii, "V obraztsovom kavaleriiskom polku, 1844-1845," *Russkaia Starina,* LV (1887), 155-56.

noble status. They might qualify for commissions after serving as sergeants for two years if vacancies developed, although if no vacancy occurred they had to wait longer. Those who qualified as university graduates could obtain commissions after three months' service as sergeants, and university students without degrees needed only six months to qualify. The students received their commissions promptly even if no vacancies existed. Volunteers from middle class and intellectual families needed four months of service to qualify for commissions, while déclassé nobles (*odnodvortsy*) had to serve six years as sergeants.[43] A special limitation on the promotion of yunkers in the cavalry regiments required them to present "definite proof that they have the means to maintain themselves in those regiments in proper manner."[44]

Most of the yunkers came to the regiments without proper schooling. Many were students dismissed from the gymnasia for poor work, or who had had to leave because of lack of funds. Others had had some sort of home education from tutors or other instructors. Many of them were pampered youngsters unfit for any career or spoiled sons of generals and other officers. The army at least offered them a livelihood, while those with ability could make good careers. Regimental life, however, provided neither the facilities for education nor a real military training. Many of them, already accustomed to idleness and sometimes to debauchery, found themselves with no compulsion to study or to occupy their minds, while their commanders, busy with other duties, lacked the facilities to keep control "of a mass of youths with perverted tendencies, careless scapegraces, or those who had become completely lazy from inactivity and idle life." The commanders had to use threats and punishments to compel these lost souls to exert themselves, but often this did not achieve much and the young men used their energies in evil ways and sank ever deeper into the mire.[45] Count Rüdiger, who in 1856 was commander of the Guards Corps, wrote to the Minister of War about the lack of educated officers in the army, which he ascribed to the practice of commissioning yunkers. The latter, he stated, enter the army unprepared "and not only cannot develop themselves, but being constantly among enlisted men, lose what little knowledge they had." He pointed to the fact that over the winter, when the troops were in quarters in the villages, the yunkers "spend the winter months in complete idleness, without any

43. SVP, Pt. II, Bk. I, *O pokhozhdenii sluzhby po voennomu vedomstvu*, art. 503.
44. *Ibid.*, art. 539.
45. "K istorii voenno-uchebnoi reformy," *Russkaia Starina*, LIV (1887), 357.

supervision over their morals, in a circle of soldiers or villagers. . . ." In the cities the situation was little better.[46]

There was, to be sure, an examination that the prospective officers had to pass, which, as specified in 1844, called for Russian grammar and composition, a reading and writing knowledge of French or German, arithmetic, including long division, general and Russian history, and some knowledge of geography.[47] They also were required to know the Regulation on formation drill for the company and the battalion, but there was no mention of tactics, fortification, or gunnery. In fact, Peter the Great's Regulation of 1716 was considerably more rigorous than that of 1844. Moreover, the examiners did not even satisfy the program of 1844.

> In the staff they issued fictitious certificates to known ignoramuses, with satisfactory comments. It had to be thus, in spite of the stern circulars of the Inspector's Department. . . . For a long time the commanders had been accustomed to look on such slackness through their fingers, if only the formalities were observed.[48]

One officer did raise objections to this criticism of the yunkers, claiming that they did have to pass stiff examinations, although not in military science. Moreover, the yunker knew the life of the soldier more intimately than the officer from the cadet corps, as "he has had to sleep with the soldier on the same bench and to eat with him out of the same bowl."[49] Against these views, however, there is the observation of D. A. Miliutin, later a most effective minister of war. He stated that most officers had had neither a military nor a general education. After serving among the soldiers for a period they were promoted to officers "without any examinations, and of military science there was none." Neither the young nor the old officers had any understanding of the tactics of their arms to say nothing of other military knowledge.[50] Similarly, in 1857 Col. Sabler, chief of staff of the 2nd Grenadier Division, wrote to the Ministry of War that the yunkers were examined according to the rules of 1844, "in which there is not one of the military sciences. These young men, after serving the

46. *Ibid.*, p. 350.
47. II PSZ, 1846, No. 17887.
48. "K istorii voenno-uchebnoi reformy," *Russkaia Starina*, LIV (1887), 357-58.
49. S. V—skii, "Ob ofitserakh armeiskikh pekhotnykh polkov," *Voennyi Sbornik*, II (1859), 416-17.
50. Ms. in Lenin Library, Moscow, Fund of D. A. Miliutin, XIII, 318, quoted in Fedorov, *Russkaia armiia*, pp. 176-77.

required period, are promoted to officers, having gained knowledge only of the drill regulations."[51]

Some of the commanders not only pointed out the faults of this system, but actually tried to do something about it. After the Hungarian War of 1849, a few farsighted and experienced generals (Count Rüdiger, Dannenberg, Lüders) undertook to group together the yunkers in each regiment to teach them military knowledge essential for an officer. They recalled the yunkers' schools that once had existed in the First and Second Armies and hoped to make promotion of yunkers impossible unless they graduated from such schools. However, the yunkers' groups proved unruly and created grave disturbances. Also it proved difficult to provide the money, teachers, and supervisors necessary for their training. And finally, many Russian commanders saw no need for any special measures, reasoning complacently that the Russian army was easily overcoming its foes without these changes.[52]

Thus to the end of the reign of Nicholas I the Russian army continued to obtain most of its officers from yunkers, with most of those from the cadet corps going to the Guards and other elite troops and supplying only a small number to the regular army. There also were the relatively few officers who made their way up through the ranks. Their way was not easy, for they had to serve twelve years as sergeants before they could become eligible for promotion. In addition, if they had ever been punished corporally by order of a court or by regimental order, they thereby became ineligible for a commission. The educational demands made of them were not severe: they had to be able to read and to write from dictation, and also to have firm knowledge of all drill up to and including battalion drill. The regulations also demanded that they had served in regular army units and had taken part in campaigns.[53]

Most of these men of humble origin (known as "bourbons") had not been conscripts of peasant origin, but, as sons of soldiers, had been trained in the harsh school of the battalions of military cantonists, where they had received training for posts as sergeants. They usually made officers who were thoroughly submissive to their superiors and gratified their wishes. Commanders often cherished the bourbons, to whom they could entrust command of supernumerary units or other

51. Cited in Zaionchkovskii, *Voennye reformy*, p. 29.
52. "K istorii voenno-uchebnoi reformy," *Russkaia Starina*, LIV (1887), 359.
53. SVP, Pt. II, Bk. I, *O prokhozhdenii sluzhby po voennomu vedomstvu*, arts. 503-6, 527.

positions that produced income for the commander. "According to the concepts of the times concerning the military economy, men of such a stamp were especially useful: they knew how to cover up, and very well understood their interests." Some of them made satisfactory careers for themselves.[54] A very few rose to fairly high ranks. Gen. Ivan Skobelev, who enjoyed the favor of the Tsar, was of this type. But the difficulties in the way of the average enlisted man made attainment of a commission almost impossible. In the infantry "bourbons" formed about seven per cent of the officers and in the cavalry, five per cent.[55]

Detailed statistical data on the origins of the officers of individual regiments are rare. What information is available, however, supports the conclusion that most of them originated as yunkers. In 1841 the Erivan Life-Grenadier regiment had forty-four officers of yunker origin, or forty-seven per cent. Thirty-one per cent had come from cadet corps, twenty per cent had risen from the ranks, and one had come as a volunteer.[56] During the three years of the Crimean War the proportion of yunkers and volunteers entering the army increased greatly, chiefly because the cadet corps could do little to expand their output of officers. During this time, 18.7 per cent of the new officers were from the cadet corps, while 69.2 were promoted yunkers and volunteers. Only 12.1 per cent came up from the ranks.[57] And in 1857 —two years after the death of Nicholas I—in the four regiments of a fairly typical infantry division, only 65 of the 481 officers were graduates of cadet schools. The contingent of yunkers numbered 347, while five had graduated from universities, and 13 had finished gymnasia. Finally, 51 had risen from the ranks.[58]

Throughout the reign of Nicholas I, then, the Russian army derived most of its officers from the contingent of poorly educated and poorly prepared yunkers. Although the cadet corps were training more officers than ever before, and probably giving them a broader education than in previous periods, the best cadets went into the Guards and the Engineering and Artillery schools, while the mediocre ones entered the regiments of the regular army. Another small group of officers consisted of former enlisted men, barely literate, although they prob-

---

54. "K istorii voenno-uchebnoi reformy," *Russkaia Starina*, LIV (1887), 354.
55. *Ibid.*
56. Bobrovskii, IV, Prilozheniia, 195.
57. "K istorii voenno-uchebnoi reformy," *Russkaia Starina*, LIV (1887), 355.
58. "Vzgliad na stepen' obrazovaniia Russkikh ofitserov v armii," *Voennyi Sbornik*, I (1858), 149.

ably knew the details of company life intimately. As many of the best military men of the times stated, this was a highly unsatisfactory way of staffing the army, and it seems probable that the ignorant and poorly trained officers were one reason for the defeat in the Crimea. From these poorly schooled ensigns and cornets came the captains, majors, and colonels, and some of the generals, who continued to display the same weaknesses and failings that they had originally had. As they often could not surmount these handicaps, the results for the army were unfortunate.

CHAPTER X. THE LIFE OF RUSSIAN ARMY OFFICERS

For the newly commissioned officer, gaily leaving the cadet corps and journeying in his brand new uniform to join his army regiment, a far from encouraging prospect opened before him, for, unless he had personal resources, he was doomed for long to an existence marked by poverty and boredom. The officers of the Guards and other elite corps fared much better, as they had the exciting life of the capital or other large cities to amuse them and, if they had enough money, could live very well. But the ordinary officer in one of the regular regiments, whether he had been trained in a cadet corps or had learned smatterings of his trade as a yunker, faced a bleak future on low pay. In 1850 the annual pay of infantry officers ran from 209 silver rubles for ensigns to 238 for first lieutenants, 307 for captains, 336 for majors, and 502 for colonels. In the artillery, engineers, and heavy cavalry the pay was about ten per cent better.[1] By 1860, five years after Nicholas I, the pay of the Russian officers had risen by from ten to twenty per cent, but even so, a Russian colonel's pay was about one-half of that of an Austrian or French colonel, and only one-third of a Prussian colonel's pay. A Russian lieutenant general's pay was little more than one-third of that in the other armies. The Russian officers also received allowances for food, as did those in most other armies.[2]

While these pay scales were far from munificent, the officers enjoyed other perquisites that provided substantial supplements to the rates of pay. The officers had the right to quarters, or, if they were not available, to quarter allowances. The laws provided that the local authorities were obliged to furnish a colonel with seven rooms for his use and that of his clerical assistants, as well as stables for five horses.

1. V. A. Vladislavlev, *Pamiatnaia kniga voennykh uzakonenii dlia shtab i ober-ofitserov* (St. Petersburg, 1851), pp. 510-14.
2. Anichkov, p. 218.

Majors and lieutenant colonels might demand four rooms, while company officers had the right to two rooms each and stabling for two horses. They were entitled to these accommodations from the population, whether on temporary duty in a locality or on permanent winter station. The municipality also had the duty of providing heat and light for its military guests.[3] The officers were also permitted to have orderlies to serve their needs. Ensigns and lieutenants had one each, while captains and majors might have three, and a colonel had six. Often these orderlies were serfs brought from the officer's estate, although if he owned less than one hundred male peasants he could obtain orderlies from the enlisted men of his unit. The orderlies, whether soldiers or serfs, wore uniforms and received their food and maintenance from the government.[4] Furthermore, the government furnished hay and oats to the horses of the officers, with cavalry and artillery commanders favored in this respect. But even an infantry major might draw rations for two saddle horses and two harness horses, while cavalry and horse-artillery colonels enjoyed the right to provisions for three saddle horses and four harness horses.[5]

The government also provided free medical care to officers[6] and granted pensions to them and their widows and families. These pensions were not abundant, however, for those who served from twenty to thirty years could expect only one-third of their pay upon retirement, while only those who served more than thirty-five years were able to retire on full pay. Those who were incapacitated by wounds or illness received pensions after shorter terms of service.[7]

Neither army regulations nor the descriptions of army life say much about the marriage of officers. This was permitted, with the approval of the regimental or other commander, who merely had to ascertain that the officer was free to marry and to consider the "propriety" of the union.[8] Most accounts of army life, however, indicate that only if a young lieutenant had considerable private means or married into a rich family could he afford to wed. There probably were few such fortunate beings in the line regiments of the army. In spite of the fact that the officer received a subsistence allowance and

3. Vladislavlev, pp. 534, 538, 543, 602-3.
4. *Ibid.*, pp. 569, 587-91.
5. *Ibid.*, pp. 577-78.
6. *Ibid.*, pp. 591-92.
7. *Ibid.*, pp. 767-70.
8. *Ibid.*, pp. 856-58.

free quarters and other rights for his family,[9] most of the junior men apparently could not afford to marry. Officers probably married fairly late, after they had risen to ranks that provided them with considerable income, or after they had inherited property or had been able to make an advantageous match.

Even during their years of bachelorhood, the younger officers probably lived poorly, unless they had private means. In August, 1855, Gen. Adj. Count Rüdiger wrote in a memorandum to Alexander II that he did not see how the officers lived on their pay, as in 1855 the pay of both colonels and ensigns was much less than it had been in 1801, while since that time prices had risen considerably. As a result, the Count stated, the officer had to abandon all thought of moral development and to surrender "to brutal enjoyments which ruin his personal dignity." This state of affairs led many able officers to leave the service, while the stupid and incapable stayed on, side by side with those who, by devious means, hoped to obtain a command that would offer opportunity for illicit gain. "A regiment and its revenues are the apogee of the glory dreamt of by an army officer. . . ." Such an officer felt fully justified in securing this compensation for years of privation and "he makes no secret of such calculations and . . . speaks of them in the circle of officers with revolting cynicism." Moreover, as no such opportunities were open to the brigade and divisional commanders, whose salaries were meager, "the greater part of the regimental commanders, far from desiring it, fear to be promoted to the rank of general."[10]

Like army officers the world over, some of the Russians were fortunate enough to obtain assignments in locations that provided gay social life and an abundance of amusements. A young artillery officer whose battery was stationed in Moscow in 1834 later wrote of the wonderful life that opened before him, enlivened by joyful hospitality to young officers, who frequently found themselves guests at fine dinners, balls, and other entertainments. Although their incomes were scanty, they never felt pinched by poverty.[11] Regiments quartered in provincial towns also could count themselves fortunate, for here, too, there were balls and dinners, although often the limited number of

9. *Ibid.*, p. 866.
10. SVM, I, N. A. Danilov, *Istoricheskii ocherk razvitiia*, Prilozhenie 8, 47-49.
11. Men'kov, II, 13.

interesting people curtailed the possibilities of stimulating social inter-course.[12] Even wintering in the villages of central Russia might be fairly pleasant, if the neighboring landowners proved hospitable.

Many regiments, however, found much less satisfactory billets for the winter. An officer quartered in the western Ukraine found the local landlords—most of them Polish—not interested in the society of Russian officers, while, because of the widely scattered villages in which the squadrons were quartered, the officers rarely saw each other, so that for a large part of the year they found themselves doomed to solitude and boredom.[13] Similarly, officers of a regiment that wintered near Kiev found their village domiciles dirty and forlorn, with the people half asleep and the children unclean and uncared for. On entering the miserable hut that was his temporary abode, the officer might encounter a piglet that, squealing, dashed between his feet. The walls were bare and the air was foul, partly because of the presence of pigs and poultry. The summers were pleasant enough, but the fall and winter, when blizzards or mud made excursions almost impossible, were filled with "frightful, inexpressibly boring days." Cards soon lost their interest, leaving little but drinking coffee and sleep to pass the time. When the post brought belated newspapers and magazines life suddenly became interesting, but once the exiles had read and reread and discussed these welcome benefactions, bore-dom once more ruled.[14] Another described the lot of the officer in winter quarters in even more gloomy tones: "cast off in winter to a distant village, sometimes in a chicken-house, he sees no one but the parish priest; and even this does not fall to the lot of all of them." Visits to landlords offered little escape, in part because the officer lacked the money for such trips, and partly because he was not certain of a cordial welcome. Hence he almost certainly became accustomed to an idle, coarse life in solitude and tended to sink into apathy.[15]

The boredom of life in winter quarters, however, could be re-lieved by furloughs—usually of fifteen days, granted by the regimental commanders. Longer leaves of twenty-eight days or even four months required a petition to the divisional or corps commander, who prob-

12. I. O., *Vospominaniia ofitsera zakavkazskoi armii (1853-1856)* (St. Peters-burg, 1857), p. 2.
13. Dragunskii ofitser, "Vospominaniia o Kavkazskom pokhode 1853 i 1854 goda," *Voennyi Sbornik*, III (1860), 137.
14. I. O., pp. 2-5.
15. V—skii, *Voennyi Sbornik*, II (1859), 418-19.

ably made the officer present some justification for the request.[16] For those who were welcome at the home of a landowner or could afford to travel, these vacations must have been a blessed relief from the boredom of quarters in a primitive village. In addition to the usual furloughs, the regulations authorized longer ones, usually for reasons of health or pressing family reasons. Moreover, officers who had been on campaigns against the enemy and who had had at least eight years of service, had the right to receive indefinite leave for the above reasons, during which they were assigned to the reserves and drew no pay.[17]

Finally, for those who found themselves unsuited to military life, there was the right to leave the service "at their own wish and discretion." Young nobles and volunteers who, serving as yunkers, had not won commissions, were obliged to serve for at least twelve years. University students who had entered service as volunteers might, however, leave it at any time.

These regulations applied to the whole of the Russian army, including the troops in the Caucasus. In other ways, however, the situation of the officers there was different, although hardly better than that of their brethren in the Russian provinces. In the Caucasus Corps, the troops were kept together as garrisons, sometimes in isolated and dismal mud forts. Even the larger posts lacked the amenities, and the officers degenerated. In one regiment an observer reported that the junior officers were sunk in debt and debauchery, even though their colonel forbade them further credit and ordered the regimental treasurer to sequester their pay. This did not prevent them from getting further credit from their tailors, by assuming a bill for thirty rubles in order to receive twenty in hand. Similarly, they used the same device to obtain from the sutler the supplies for a night of heavy drinking. They went around in rags, without overcoats, and fed themselves on charity or from the common kettle of the enlisted men, by permission of their company commanders. Punishments had no effect, as all they thought of was cards, drinking, and debauchery in the dens of the town. The author adds that, to make matters worse, these were essentially fine lads and good soldiers in action, who had come to such a pass because of the low level of education and morals prevalent in the Russian army. The author added that this particular regiment was

16. Vladislavlev, pp. 466-68.
17. *Ibid.*, pp. 484-88.

by no means unique, as this state of affairs was widespread in the Caucasus troops and, indeed, in the forces stationed in Russia proper.[18]

Cavalry officers especially had a tradition of wild and frivolous conduct suitable to the cornets and subalterns from the *jeunesse dorée*. When Prince A. I. Bariatinskii joined a cuirassier regiment as a cornet in 1833, his tour of duty "was, in keeping with the current cavalry mores, a series of carousals, pranks, of idle civil life." Far from regarding this as a serious defect, the higher military authorities looked on it with amusement, "as consequences of youth and *élan* characteristic of a military man in general and of a cavalryman in particular."[19] Even if they did not misbehave, the young hussar and uhlan officers rarely paid much attention to their military roles—from which, indeed, their squadron commanders often willingly excused them—but spent much of their time at the estates of hospitable landowners.[20] On the other hand, there was little uniformity in regimental life. As the personality of the colonel had much to do with the spirit in the regiment, a command stationed in the province of Poltava might have an attitude toward its military duties and a way of life quite unlike those of a regiment near Kherson, no great distance away.[21] The statements of well-informed observers of the period under consideration nonetheless indicate that in general the lives and the habits of the officers were not conducive to an effective military establishment.

As a preceding chapter has indicated, the men who attained commissions in the Russian army, either after graduating from cadet corps or after serving with the regiments as sergeants, brought to their new positions little sound military training or knowledge. Most of them seem to have obtained few additional military qualifications during their first decade and more as officers. It is not surprising that a commissioned yunker, who had only the most rudimentary education when he received his promotion, was unlikely to devote himself to intensive study of military science. Isolated in remote villages over the winters, without books and without stimulus from fellow officers, whom he rarely saw, the young officer gradually became accustomed to a lonely and idle existence. After ten years of this he forgot what little he might

18. Zisserman, *Dvadtsat' piat' let*, II, 101-3.
19. A. L. Zisserman, *Fel'dmarshal Kniaz' Aleksandr Ivanovich Bariatinskii. 1815-1879* (3 vols.; Moscow, 1889-1891), I, 20.
20. Potto, pp. 162-63.
21. M. Zolotar'ev, "Zametki o sovremennom sostoianii nashei kavalerii," *Voennyi Sbornik*, I (1858), 21.

have learned in his earlier years, so that he ended up coarser and more ignorant than he started. "The correctness of this fact will scarcely be disputed by anyone."[22]

The officers trained in the cadet corps usually did little to set an example of military scholarship to their fellow officers. There were few of them in the average line regiment, and their youth and inexperience often led them to conform to the established pattern. There were few books available, and the ensign or cornet lacked the money to buy them. Neither his commanders nor his fellow officers gave him encouragement to study, and his efforts rarely brought more rapid promotion. Indeed, a former first sergeant, who was barely literate, might even secure advancement ahead of him.[23]

The same situation obtained in the cavalry, where the officers completely lost touch with scholarly work. Not only did they fail to derive visible advantage from it or encouragement from their superiors, but they knew that their comrades resented their efforts to distinguish themselves. The other officers branded them as "the deserving," and loved to play practical jokes on them. The regimental and divisional commanders were too busy to notice a man's efforts to study, while his squadron commander might even resent his efforts on the grounds that a studious officer might be a dangerous rival. As much willpower and determination were needed to keep on studying, it is not surprising that there were almost no significant works written on cavalry service. Indeed, when the average officer was given command of a squadron, he had little knowledge of how to meet his responsibilities, and either relied on his first sergeant or tried to handle his men by bullying and bluster. When, after another decade or more, he received command of his regiment, he still was unfitted for his responsibility.[24]

In marked contrast to the generally low level of intellectual life in most army regiments was that in the Iamburg Uhlan regiment. In 1847 well over half of its officers had been educated in cadet corps or in gymnasia, and two-thirds of them knew at least one foreign language. The regiment had a dance orchestra, a church choir, and an officers' club boasting a billiard table, a piano, and chess tables. There was a fine regimental library with newspapers and magazines, as well as books on military history and numerous literary works. The officers

22. V—skii, *Voennyi Sbornik*, II (1859), 419.
23. "Vzgliad na stepen'," *Voennyi Sbornik*, I (1858), 150-52.
24. Zolotar'ev, *Voennyi Sbornik*, I (1858), 23-24.

also enjoyed pleasant and stimulating relations with the landowners and other social groups in the vicinity.[25]

While there appears no reason to doubt this attractive picture of the life of the officers of the Iamburg Uhlans, it probably was far from typical of the usual regiments of the army. This was an elite regiment, many of whose officers probably had private means to enable them to provide the amenities mentioned, most of which were out of the question for officers who had no income but their pay. It is probably true that, as the majority of the sources that have been cited indicate, most of the officers of the ordinary regiments of the army lived lives that were boring and dismal and sometimes even brutish, and for most of them there was no study of military science or technique to raise their military knowledge above the level of mere competence on the drillfield.

Grim as this characterization is, it coincides with the views that Count Rüdiger presented to Alexander II in 1855. He stated that many of the officers from cadet corps were fine, but, far from increasing their knowledge while in service, they lost all contact with learning and, after ten or fifteen years "reach a stage of total ignorance and complete *abrutissement.*"[26] A. L. Zisserman, who had a long term of service in the Caucasus Corps, lamented the unenlightened attitudes of the officers of the Dagestan regiment. "Neither books nor newspapers, there were no interests at all, except the narrowest, everyday, petty ones!" They talked only of such matters as assignment, promotion, headquarters gossip, and fantastic rumors about their regiment. To be sure, there were some who were more intelligent and did some reading, but these were very few and these were "drawn into this mire." Only expeditions and campaigns enlivened the group, but after these activities they relapsed into the same stagnant ways.[27] He mentioned one major of this regiment as a common type in the 1830's, "who could march with a full glass of water on his helmet without spilling a drop; but under the helmet there was nothing to look for." The good major had no interests outside drill and routine duties except hope of promotion. And yet, for all his pedantry and strictness, he was "a simple, kindly man, and at times likeable in his way."[28] Traveling with a colonel of the General Staff, Zisserman found him to

25. Krestovskii, pp. 508-10.
26. SVM, I, N. Danilov, *Istoricheskii Ocherk*, Prilozhenie 8, 45.
27. Zisserman, *Dvadtsat' piat' let*, II, 21-22.
28. *Ibid.*, p. 14.

be even less prepossessing than the major. Angered because a special messenger in a coach had passed them, the colonel cursed his driver, and when the latter mentioned that his team had a heavier load to pull than the other, beat him furiously with his fists and covered him with a string of barrackroom curses. When they arrived at their destination, however, the officer's wrath had cooled, and he sought to redeem himself by giving the driver a ruble note.[29]

A Prussian captain who for a time was attached to the Russian Third Corps during the joint maneuvers at Kalisz in 1835 found that, while the higher officers were sophisticated and sociable, they were dissipated, dishonest, arrogant, and prone to intrigue. The lower officers were ignorant, but retained the native Russian goodness and kindliness. The Prussian concluded that the failings in the Russian army were so deep that the Tsar could not easily and quickly eliminate them, as the whole system needed basic change. He believed that a shortage of funds, established habits, the lack of culture of the Russians, and the size of the army, all would hinder or prevent reforms.[30]

Probably a factor partially responsible for the low level of the Russian officers was the harsh and often brutal attitude of their superiors. In 1822, shortly before the accession of Nicholas, Field Marshal Wittgenstein issued an order to the Second Army:

> I have noticed that in some regiments of the 14th division the regimental commanders treat their officers very harshly, forgetting the proper esteem for a noble person [and] permit themselves the use of expressions not compatible with the treatment that each officer has the right to expect from his superior. Strictness and harshness, punishment and insult are entirely different things. . . .[31]

Prussian officers who were able to observe the Russian army at close range in 1835 were horrified by this phenomenon. One reported: "On the second exercise day I saw a general ride up to a battalion commander who had made a mistake in drill and with gestures and words treat him as with us rarely happens to a noncom."[32] Capt. von Höpfner remarked on the mercilessness of superior officers to their subordinates. He mentioned how the general commanding the Third Corps had the impudence to address a colonel as follows, because of a minor mistake

29. *Ibid.*, I, 186-87.
30. "Bemerkungen über das Kaiserlich Russische dritte Corps im Lage bei Kalisch," cited in Schiemann, III, 268-69, 444.
31. Epanchin, I, 111.
32. Schiemann, II, 443.

in drill: "You are a colonel? You are a s - - t." The same general was shameless enough to rebuke Gen. Martynskii, close to the guard of honor and under the windows of Field Marshal Paskevich, because of insignificant mistakes in etiquette: "You sleeping-cap, you old woman, you won't stay a general with me for long!"[33]

In 1841 N. Kutuzov, in a memorandum that he prepared for the Tsar on the condition of Russia, said much the same thing. He stated that the Russian army was brilliant on the surface, but within it bore the seeds of decay. He warned that its moral strength was in danger of collapse because of a loss of esteem of the enlisted men for their commanders, without which the army could not function. "This loss has occurred from the prejudicial treatment by the higher commanders of the officers and generals subordinate to them: before the formation and at other gatherings of enlisted men they curse them, shame and insult them." Kutuzov added this caused proud and self-respecting men to leave the army, while it greatly weakened the esteem that the enlisted men should have for their officers.[34]

From these poorly trained, ignorant officers, insulted by their commanders, came many of the colonels and generals of the Russian army, who rarely rose above the milieu that had produced them. At the close of the Russo-Polish War of 1831, Denis Davydov, famed partisan leader of 1812, wrote his memoirs of the Polish War, in which he deplored the type of commanders produced by the system of parade-ground training in the Russian army. Such a system, he warned, had as its result that the army became "gradually filled only with coarse ignoramuses, who with joy devote their whole lives to study of the details of military regulations. . . ." Thanks to this, the Russian army, in the perfection of its drill, exceeded all others. "But my God! What are the majority of the generals and officers, in whom is killed the striving for education, as a result of which they hate all learning?" He warned that this system prevented gifted men from advancing "out of the level of ignorant mediocrity. . . ." He warned that if this tendency continued Russia would be at a loss to meet some future crisis. "Woe to her if at that time when the activity of intelligent and informed men shall be especially necessary for her, our government

33. *Ibid.*, III, 441.
34. N. Kutuzov, "Sostoianie gosudarstva v 1841 godu," *Russkaia Starina*, XCV (1898), 523.

will be surrounded by a crowd of ignorant men, stubborn in their ignorance."[35]

P. K. Men'kov, a very able officer, wrote in his memoirs in 1848 that poor nobles made careers in the army by patiently and humbly enduring poverty and hardship until they could become commanders of regiments, at which point they hastened to steal from the soldiers enough to make up for their former privations. He stated that he had seen a poor officer, barely able to feed and clothe himself, reach a profitable position, and at once all was changed. In less than a year he was excellently dressed, had a horse and carriage, rugs, and luxuries, and gave champagne to his guests. Men'kov added: "The scanty up-bringing of the officers, their life in sorry quarters, the demands of service, rough treatment by superiors, and mental inactivity and idle-ness have killed all social ideas in them, have stifled high feelings."[36]

In 1846 Men'kov gave biting characterizations of two generals that he knew. One was commander of the Ekaterinburg infantry regi-ment, who had won this post by serving out his time in absurdity and patience. His characteristics were a resigned consciousness of his worthlessness, greediness for profit, and love for formation drill, which was the means that had raised him to importance. The general, Men'kov said, looked on his regiment of four thousand men as a living estate: "he runs it, wrings it and squeezes it in order to exact as much as possible of that essence without which a general's rank is nothing and which is called money."[37] The second was Gen. N—v, commander of the Tobol'sk regiment. Like Sir Joseph Porter, KCB, he had risen to his rank through patience alone, for he had not served in a single campaign. After an undistinguished career, through curry-ing favor he became commander of the regiment, where he proved to be a bad regimental officer. He soon learned to extract his profit out of everything, while at the same time bewailing his excessive decency and unselfishness. His worthlessness had not prevented him from achieving the rank of general; "from his regiment, a living income-property, he has drawn all that could be drawn, and now he has a secure situation; all this came to him as if in recompense, a reward for all his sufferings, which fate had promised him."[38]

Another officer had a very different experience. Assigned as aide

35. Davydov, *Russkaia Starina*, VI (1872), 26-27.
36. Men'kov, II, 108-9.
37. *Ibid.*, II, 73.
38. *Ibid.*, II, 89-90.

to a Gen. Vishnevsky, he was invited to dine with the latter and his wife, whom he found to be fine people.

> When you think and remember how many goat-generals I have met during my service, how many swine I have seen among these big cattle, how can one not wonder when he meets with a good person, kindly, educated, with a good mind, and noble, and this man is a general, and this general is your commander, who sets forth his orders sensibly and courteously! This is really a marvel in the Russian army, one's eyes cannot believe it. The Russian general should certainly be long-nosed, big-bellied, and the stupider the better; he must without fail shout at his subordinates, especially when many people have gathered to watch the drill, and right away they will magnify him: "There is the commander—and it's very clear what an important person! See how he dresses down the little officers!"[39]

Count Rüdiger, in his memorandum of August 11, 1855, to Alexander II, dwelt at some length on the causes of the sorry condition of the general officers of the Russian army. By the accession of Nicholas I, the fine generals of the Napoleonic Wars were gone and no suitable replacements came up after them. While the commanders of the Corps of Guards and of the Caucasus Separate Corps had the opportunity to distinguish themselves, after 1831 Field Marshal Paskevich, commander of the Active Army, and his staff dominated all the others. The commander in chief, a proud, suspicious man, and his staff, created in his image, began to control in detail the internal matters, not only of corps, but even of divisions and of regiments. The choice of a temporary cantonment, the distribution of training exercises, and similar matters, were all decided directly by orders from the Field Marshal and his staff. The slightest disagreement with such an order, even if in the interests of the service, "exposed a corps commander to the greatest unpleasantness. Like his sergeant, they asked of him only blind obedience." The corps commander, compelled to execute orders from above without question, demanded the same from his divisional commanders; the latter in turn demanded the same conduct from the brigade and regimental commanders.

With the commander in chief holding such views, "the slightest tendency to an independent idea, the slightest freedom of opinion, were treated as a crime." If a general, not wishing to take the

39. K. A. Obninskii, "Pokhodnyia zametki," *Russkii Arkhiv*, XXIX (1891), Pt. III, 394.

responsibility of carrying out a measure which deviated from the views of his chief, pointed out the difficulties present in the execution of the order received, they immediately treated him as an arguer, and used all possible means to get rid of him, "so that the ranks of talented generals began gradually to thin, and they were replaced for the most part by incapable men, faithful sectarians of the military code and having no aptitude except to transmit orders and excelling solely in training the soldiers to march."

Such practices, so Count Rüdiger stated, had resulted in a lack of good generals in important positions, as such men rarely received advancement. There was a lack of real care for the interests of state, for the interference of the commander in chief and his chief of staff had destroyed all initiative in his subordinates. Finally, the perfection of the troops was only superficial, in line formations and in marching, and no one paid proper attention to marksmanship, the use of skirmishers behind cover, or outpost duty. "From the battalion commander to the corps commander, all nourish the firm conviction that their reputation depends solely on the irreproachable alignment of the soldier and his degree of perfection in the art of marching."[40]

Count Rüdiger was correct in laying much of the blame for the lack of effective generals at the door of Field Marshal Prince Paskevich, Nicholas I's "Father-Commander," for this man for a quarter of a century wielded vast power over the Russian army. Nonetheless, the Tsar himself cannot avoid a substantial share of the guilt for this state of affairs, for in large measure his views coincided with those of the Field Marshal, on whom he lavished his favor. Nicholas, in whose veins there was far more German blood than that of the Romanovs, was himself a military formalist and Paskevich, knowing this, maintained himself in favor by supporting ardently the harsh absurdities of the outmoded military system that the Russians had learned from the Prussians, but which the Prussians had already discarded.

As Nicholas was more German than Russian, so that he always felt at home in his father-in-law's Prussia, it is not surprising that, along with Russians, many Germans rose to high positions under him. His first military favorite, I. I. Diebitsch, was born in Prussia and was educated in a Prussian cadet school. He commanded the Russian army in the second year of the Turkish War, winning laurels by crossing the Balkan mountains and taking Adrianople, for which Nicholas made

40. SVM, I, Danilov, *Istoricheskii Ocherk*, Prilozhenie 7, 36-38.

him a count and field marshal. In the Polish campaign of 1831, Diebitsch commanded the Russian forces until his sudden death from
cholera. Prince Eugene of Württemberg, brother-in-law of the Tsar,
also commanded Russian troops in the Turkish War, although he fell
from favor, as he felt, because of Diebitsch's intrigues against him.
Probably, however, most of the numerous Germans whose names
figure so prominently in the military history of the period were not
natives of Germany, but were Baltic Germans, whose families had
lived in Estonia and Latvia for centuries.

While the names of many Germans have already appeared in the
preceding chapters, the list is still very long. It includes Rennenkampf,
Schmidt, Freitag, Osten-Sacken, Kliuki von der Klugenau, Wunsch,
and Baumgarten. Others were Baron Hoven, Kapherr, von Wenzel,
Budberg, Dannenberg, von Manteuffel, Grabbe and Lüders. It would
be easy to extend the roster to great length, but this is not needed to
prove that officers of German stock played a very important role in
the army.

A natural result of the prevalence of Teutonic officers was that
many of the Russians were envious and resentful. In 1839 a Russian
officer told Col. von Gagern: "Germans are not liked in our army. . .;
they are intriguers, egoists, and support each other, like links of a
chain. In the army they are nicknamed 'Lieber Bruder' [sic] because
they call each other this." He felt that the Germans enjoyed favor in
high places, which aroused much resentment. In addition, the Germans
were pedantic drillmasters. The Russian revealed another reason for
the success of the Germans. "True, the Germans serve punctually, they
have education, . . ." but he termed them proud, careful to please, and
prone to help their relatives into good positions. "The Russians possess
more character; they are not educated and frequently they treat their
subordinates with merciless severity, but on the next day they smooth
all this out. . . . The Russians steal, but they do not hoard money and
they live openly. . . ."[41]

Another Russian officer asserted that the Germans had an Eleventh
Commandment—to help one another to get ahead and to repulse the
Russians. The Germans must be courteous, careful always to smile,
always be patient, submissive to superiors, kind to subordinates—but
destroy them when possible. Not all Germans were like that, however. He termed Gen. Freitag a marvelous man. Col. F. K. Zatler

41. Schilder, "Nemets i frantsuz," *Russkaia Starina*, LI (1886), 42-43.

was a fine intendant, and Col. Weimarn was an excellent officer— "happy the commander in chief and the army which list several Weimarns in the general staff." Still, the majority of the Germans, he felt, were ambitious, ruthless, insidious, and clannish.[42] One of the noted opponents of the German influence in the Russian army was Gen. A. P. Ermolov, a hero of the Napoleonic Wars, who afterward commanded the Caucasus Corps until Nicholas replaced him with Paskevich in 1827. Ermolov, who was highly popular in the army, was widely known as an enemy of the Germans.[43]

While there were many officers of German stock in the Russian army, those of French origin were rare. One noted example was Count A. F. Langeron, who emigrated from France in 1789 and fought in the Russian army against the Swedes in 1790. In the Russo-Turkish War of 1828-29, he commanded the Russian troops in the Danubian Principalities.[44] A Count Choiseul and the Marquis de Gramont, probably French émigrés, were aides of Gen. P. D. Kiselev, chief of staff of the Second Army in 1828. A. O. Duhamel and Fanton de Verraillon were General Staff officers in the Russo-Turkish War, while Gen. A. K. Guerois of the engineers was in charge of siege operations at Brailov.[45] Strangely enough, Duhamel, in spite of his Gallic name, came from one of the Baltic families.[46] M. L. Fanton de Verraillon, however, was the son of a French revolutionary émigré. He had received his military training in Russia.[47] Guerois, who was the son of a French architect who had come to Russia in the reign of Catherine the Great, was a favorite of Nicholas I and an adjutant general in 1828.[48] Several officers with French names served in the Russian army in the Crimean War in 1854-55, although their families had probably come to Russia long before and had been assimilated into the Russian nobility. Maj. Gen. Villebois, who was wounded in the Battle of Inkerman,[49] seems to have been a descendant of N. P. Villebois, who served in the Russian navy under Peter the Great. Lt. Col. de Gervais, who was in command of the 2nd bastion at Sevasto-

42. Men'kov, I, 28-35.
43. Kartsov, I, 84.
44. "Pis'ma Nikolaia I-go," *Russkaia Starina*, XXVII (1880), 767. Langeron's biography is in *Entsiklopedicheskii Slovar'* (41 vols. in 82; St. Petersburg, 1896), XVII, 329.
45. Fonton, I, 46, 56.
46. *Russkii biograficheskii slovar'* (25 vols.; St. Petersburg, 1896-1918), VI, 740.
47. *Ibid.*, XXI, 21-22.
48. *Ibid.*, V, 95-96.
49. Bogdanovich, *Vostochnaia voina*, III, 138.

pol in June, 1855,[50] appears to have been descended from one of three brothers of that name who came to Russia from Prussia in the eighteenth century. They were almost certainly of Huguenot stock, as the Russian records state that they were "of the Reformed faith."[51] Finally, a Col. de Saget commanded a light battery at the siege of Kars in 1855.[52] No further information about him is available.

Another contingent of non-Russian officers in Nicholas' army consisted of graduates of the Finnish Cadet Corps, mostly Finns of Swedish stock, who seem to have gravitated to the General Staff. Seven of them served in the Caucasus, including Maj. Gens. I. I. Nordenstam and B. E. Indrenius, and Lt. Gen. Kroierus.[53] A. L. Zisserman, historian of the army in the Caucasus, mentioned Col. (later Gen.) Indrenius, "who belonged to the category of officers of whom they said among us: 'honorable as a Swede.' " He added that all the officers from Finland "were distinguished by their puritanical honor, their conscientious attitude toward their obligations," as well as a degree of pedantry, poor knowledge of Russian, marked capabilities that won them advancement, and a modest way of life. "These were to the highest degree useful laborers and assistants in all branches of military service."[54] Gen. N. N. Muraviev (Karskii) also thought highly of the Finnish officers. I. I. Evropeus, himself from Finland, tells of a dinner to which Muraviev invited him, at which the guests were all Finnish officers. The host served them champagne, drinking a toast to their health and that of Finnish officers in general with whom he had served. "I have found in them strict performance of service, honorable and unselfish men . . . . I drink a second time to your health, gentlemen!"[55]

A considerable number of officers also came from peoples of the Caucasus area, from which, as has been said, a number of young nobles went to Russian cadet corps. In addition, in the 1830's provision was made for receiving poor young Caucasian nobles and sons of other distinguished classes in schools set up with each battalion, where they received general education and learned Russian. As many as ten of such children, from nine to fourteen years of age, might come

50. *Ibid.*, III, 377.
51. *Russkii biog. slovar'*, VII, 35.
52. Bogdanovich, *Vostochnaia voina*, IV, 298.
53. Glinoetskii, *Istoriia*, II, 260-63, *passim*.
54. Zisserman, *Dvadtsat' piat'*, II, 5-6.
55. I. I. Evropeus, "Nikolai Nikolaevich Murav'ev," *Russkaia Starina*, XI (1874), 184.

under the guardianship of each battalion commander, and fourteen were assigned to the Dragoon regiment. Upon reaching the age of seventeen, they ceased their schooling and were free to enter military or civil service.[56] The Erivan Grenadier regiment was one of the Caucasus units that had such youths. In 1837, with permission of the Tsar, it set up a school for twenty-five boys, which later, under Count Vorontsov, expanded to a total of one hundred. This school did much to provide the regiment with native yunkers, who were promoted to officers for bravery in action. In this manner the regiment obtained almost two-thirds of its officers.[57]

Several of the officers from Transcaucasia rose to high rank in the Russian service. One of the early ones was Prince Bagration, a Georgian, who won great fame for his dash and courage during the Napoleonic Wars, dying in the battle of Borodino in 1812. Prince V. G. Madatov was another Georgian, who began his service under Paul I and rose to lieutenant general after service in several wars.[58] Prince Andronikov, who was descended from King Solomon of Georgia, was another lieutenant general. While he was not especially intelligent, he was kindly and thoroughly courageous and enjoyed the esteem of all who served under him.[59] Prince Bebutov, an Armenian, was educated in the Corps of Pages and served first in the Guards and later in the Caucasus. A dashing commander without great military talent, he was intelligent, and was pleasant to his subordinates and won the devotion of the soldiers by his friendly ways. While much of his career was undistinguished, fortune smiled on him in 1853-54, as he won two remarkable victories over the Turks.[60]

The preceding chapter has already referred to opportunities given to young Polish nobles to enter Russian cadet schools. In addition, others were accepted as yunkers with Russian regiments. This was probably true during the 1830's, and on August 29, 1846 the Tsar decreed that Polish nobles of the kingdom of Poland who had passed the necessary examination might enter service with the Grenadier Corps and the first six infantry corps, although in no regiment should the number of Poles exceed half the number of Russian nobles.[61]

56. SVP, Pt. I, Bk. III, *Obrazovanie voenno-uchebnykh zavedenii*, arts. 1747-1762.
57. Shabanov, II, 120-21.
58. *Zhizn' general-leitenanta kn. Madatova* (2nd. ed.; St. Petersburg, 1863), p. 3.
59. P. D. Rudakov, "Dva epizody iz voiny 1853-1856 gg. v Aziatskoi Turtsii," *Russkaia Starina*, XL (1883), 532.
60. *Ibid.*, pp. 531-32.
61. II PSZ, 1846, No. 20, 367.

Moreover, in 1842 Nicholas published a long decree in which, after expressing indignation at the failure of the Polish nobles of the western Russian provinces to serve the state in either the army or the civil service, he stated: "Such hostile feelings to the duty of a nobly born nobleman can no longer be tolerated. Hence We command:

The sons of nobles of non-Orthodox landowners of the said provinces, to send away to service for enrolling as sub-ensigns or yunkers, . . ." provided such nobles or their wives had no less than one hundred souls (i. e., male serfs). Exceptions were made for only sons, those unfit to serve, and those who wished to enter civil service in Russia proper.[62]

It is not surprising to find some hostility to Poles in the Russian army. In 1827, Ganglebov, a Decembrist, reported from the Caucasus that the garrison of Vladikavkaz consisted in large part of Poles "of the lowest sort."[63] In 1847 Prince Vorontov, viceroy in the Caucasus, ordered an investigation into charges that Polish soldiers, and especially an Ensign Zalieski, alleged to be a fanatical Polish nationalist, had had treasonable dealings with the mountaineers. Nothing apparently came of the charges, however.[64] In general Polish officers fared well in the Caucasus Corps, where there was a tradition of kindly treatment for political exiles. In the Siberian and Orenburg corps, however, a more hostile attitude toward them prevailed.[65]

This same author mentioned meeting a Col. Potocki, who was aide to Count Vorontsov, who, with his wife, liked the Pole. The colonel, originally an exile of 1831, was unofficial guardian of all Poles in the Caucasus forces. He was "an educated man, standing in this respect immeasurably higher than many of the personages of that time." Many of the Russians, however, did not like him, as they regarded him as an intriguer.[66] Another Pole came to the Caucasus as a private, sent into exile from the gymnasium for having read nationalistic verses. "Like many of his compatriots in the Caucasus, he found most cordial good will and support." Eventually he received a commission and, proving to be a good soldier and a kind and modest man, at length became commander of a regiment.[67] Another Polish

62. *Ibid.*, No. 26, 190 (April 21, 1842).
63. Ganglebov, *Russkii Arkhiv*, XXII (1884), Pt. II, 235.
64. Zisserman, "Fel'dmarshal Kniaz' Bariatinskii," *Russkii Arkhiv*, XXVI (1888), Pt. I, 435-36.
65. Zisserman, *Dvadtsat' piat' let*, II, 56-57.
66. *Ibid.*, I, 130-31.
67. *Ibid.*, II, 118-19.

colonel commanded a regiment on the critical Left Flank of the Caucasus line, where he was known as a fine fighting man and a hard drinker. As colonel he went to the Orthodox church with his regiment and crossed himself in the Orthodox manner, although later under his cloak he crossed himself in Catholic fashion.[68]

In 1848 the Iamburg Uhlans came under a Polish officer, who, in addition to the usual *manège* training, gave his men practice in outpost work and scouting and instruction in use of the saber and small arms, with excellent effects. Unfortunately for his career, he brought in numerous Polish officers and yunkers and gave them rapid promotions and other special favors. This resulted in his removal in 1854.[69]

Polish origin did not prevent a capable soldier from reaching high rank, although it may have hindered the rise of some. Gen. O. P. Zhabokritskii, of a Polish noble family of the province of Kiev, had a noted career in the Russian army. He began his active military life in 1812 and fought at Leipzig, Rheims, and near Paris. In the Polish campaign of 1831 he was in several of the major battles and near Siedlce distinguished himself by effective rearguard actions for a whole day against vastly superior Polish forces. By 1847 he was a major general. During the Crimean War he commanded a division at Sevastopol and did well at the Battle of Inkerman where, in command of the reserves, he covered the retreat of the Russian forces. He was made a lieutenant general for distinguished conduct.[70] These achievements, however, did not prevent Prince Vasil'chikov, one of the better Russian generals, from suggesting that when Zhabokritskii, already quite elderly, gave up his command on grounds of illness, it was partly because he felt that his post was too great for his strength, and also "it may be because he, a Pole, did not greatly sympathize with the war against the French. . . ."[71]

Other observers gave more favorable accounts of the activities of Polish officers in the Crimea. Zisserman lists among the heroes of Sevastopol "a desperate Polish-born sapper yunker" who was active in the most dangerous places during the siege and who volunteered to lead an especially hopeless attempt to occupy a French position. Zisserman adds: "Many Polish-born, officers and soldiers, served in

68. Filipson, *Russkii Arkhiv*, XXII (1884), Pt. I, 371.
69. Krestovskii, pp. 562-75.
70. *Russkii biog. slovar'*, VII, 1.
71. V. I. Vasil'chikov, " 'Sevastopol'.' Zapiski," *Russkii Arkhiv*, XXIX (1891), Pt. II, 229.

Sevastopol with the dazzling bravery for which this people has been famous of old."[72] Similarly, in 1855 Count Rüdiger in his memorandum to Alexander II declared that "a large part of the best officers of the line is composed of Poles" and asked that the "rigorous prescriptions" against them should cease, "all the more since I can testify that in the recent developments [the Crimean War] they have conducted themselves very reasonably . . . ."[73]

The Russian officer corps, then, contained men of several national origins and probably was less homogeneous than those of most European armies. While this may have been somewhat harmful, because of the friction between the native Russian officers and those of German and Polish origin, this dissension does not seem to have been serious. In fact, the army may have benefited somewhat from the presence of the non-Russians, as some of them were better educated than the mass of Russian officers and probably helped to raise the general level of the military technique of the forces. Nevertheless, the effect of this leaven was slight, as the evidence indicates that most of the army officers of this period had had little education and during their service added to this modicum little more than a thorough knowledge of the superficialities of formal drill needed for parades and reviews and were poorly prepared for the realities of war. Thus, in a period when modern military technique was becoming increasingly important in other armies, the majority of the officers of the Russian army lacked the skills necessary for success on the battlefield. For these failings both the backwardness of the Russian social system and the senseless military regime favored by Nicholas were responsible.

72. A. L. Zisserman, "Zametki o krymskoi voine," *Voennyi Sbornik*, II (1859), 390n. and 391n.
73. SVM, I, Danilov, *Istoricheskii ocherk*, Prilozhenie 6, 31.

CHAPTER XI. CORRUPTION IN THE ADMINIS-
TRATION OF THE RUSSIAN ARMY

In the preceding chapters there has been mention of the corrupt actions of some Russian army officers. These abuses, which were not a new phenomenon in Russian life, were in part a consequence of the poor pay and other deprivations that the officers encountered, and also derived from a poorly organized system of provisioning and supplying the army, which made it easy to obtain illicit gains. These improprieties appear to have been quite extensive and they doubtless affected the efficiency and morale of the army. For these reasons it seems advisable to present a detailed study of this side of Russian army life.

In time of war the troops in the field obtained their provisions directly from the army command, which secured them by purchase or requisitioning. Under peacetime conditions, however, the task of feeding the troops in Russia proper was under the jurisdiction of the Provision Department of the Ministry of War,[1] although the Active Army, in Poland and the western provinces of Russia, had its own Field Intendant Administration, and the Caucasus and other Separate Corps had Field Provision Commissions. These various administrations acted with considerable independence, drawing up their own estimates of the cost of provisioning their troops, which they then sent to the Provision Department for inclusion in the budget.[2] For the most part the various corps and army commanders did not try to obtain and distribute provisions to the troops, which would have been almost impossible in the light of the great distances, the primitive roads, and the absence of a capable central bureaucracy. Instead, the generals had their intendants set fixed prices for the foodstuffs and left it to the regimental commanders to purchase their supplies at prices not above those officially set. The regimental commanders had full freedom in

1. SVP, Pt. IV, Bk. I, *O zagotovlenii snabzhenii*, arts. 6-7.
2. Anichkov, pp. 91-92.

making contracts with suppliers of food. The Provision Department's officials approved the contracts and issued the sums called for to the regimental quartermasters.[3]

In such arrangements the colonels had full discretion in providing for their regiments, as any savings achieved by buying provisions at less than the fixed price might be retained by them with no questions asked. The quartermaster, who actually handled the transactions, was responsible directly to the colonel. Likewise the captains in command of the various companies, to whom the colonel distributed the provisions, had no way of controlling or limiting his actions, even though they might be illegal.[4] In this way an unscrupulous colonel had ample opportunity to enrich himself at the expense of the enlisted men. As late as 1856, a report to Tsar Alexander II by Gen. Adj. Glinka stated that the regulations gave the regimental commanders such opportunities for gain that many a one had become a purveyor as skilful in business matters as any private merchant, through years of enriching himself "at the expense of the unit he commands." Supervision of the higher commanders over such transactions was only a matter of form and in no way limited the profiteering of the colonels. Glinka concluded: "The abuses in the provisioning sector are too well known for there to be need to discuss them extensively here."[5]

The simplest form of the abuse to which Gen. Glinka referred was for the colonel to buy food of inferior quality for his men, or to buy less than the required amount. In 1856 a young Russian officer, writing in the leading military periodical, termed this "soldier-robbing." In spite of the efforts of the government to prevent this, he added, "with us the soldier is constantly burdened by constant, uninterrupted thievery."[6] In addition, the commander could simply steal funds set aside for the needs of the soldiers. In each regiment there were special sums derived from savings of the soldiers, from awards made them by the Tsar after successful parades, from earnings by the men during spare time, and from the pitiful savings of deceased soldiers. These moneys, most of them intended to buy extra meat, vegetables, and other supplements to their diet, were kept in the regimental strongbox. Two commanders of the Iamburg Uhlan regiment systematically appropriated these funds over a period of years,

3. *Ibid.*, pp. 92-93, 102.
4. *Ibid.*, pp. 397 and 440.
5. SVM, I, N. A. Danilov, *Istoricheskii ocherk*, Prilozhenie 10, 62-63.
6. "Golos iz armii," *Voennyi Sbornik*, I (1858), 81-82.

with the result that in 1853 many of the men fell ill with dropsy and other diseases induced by scanty and poor food. When one of these colonels died, investigation disclosed that he had taken 2,956 silver rubles of the soldiers' money.[7]

In St. Petersburg, where the Guards and other troops were concentrated in barracks, it was possible to feed them from food supplies obtained by the Provision Department, instead of food obtained by the individual regiments. But here, too, improper practices occurred. Gen. Glinka, in his report to the Tsar referred to above, stated that it was fairly common for the Provision Department to require that the troops accept a certain proportion of damp and moldy flour along with that that was in good condition. He cited two instances of this in the year 1854 alone. In the first case, the Guards and Grenadier Corps had to accept 13,940 sacks of spoiled flour, to be mixed with good flour. Toward the end of the year a second order required the troops to accept 2,298 additional sacks of wet flour. Glinka pointed out that, while the flour was inspected by a doctor, an officer, and an official of the Provision Department and found fit for food, this was largely a superficial investigation. Moreover, by the time that the last of the dampened flour had reached the troops—sixteen months later —it probably had fermented much more and may well have been highly injurious for the health of the soldiers. This bad practice occurred, Glinka stated, because an official of the Provision Department and the contractor of one of the leading noble families were in difficulties and wished to solve their problems by passing the damaged flour on to the troops.[8]

Gen. Glinka stated that this was common practice in the army and that the above instances were fairly typical. An even worse episode was reported from besieged Sevastopol in 1854. According to A. A. Panaev, aide to Prince Menshikov, in November and December of that year there was extreme difficulty in hauling provisions for the defenders, because of the terrible condition of the roads. Finally a considerable quantity of biscuits were hauled in at the cost of super-human exertions. On one occasion during this period, Menshikov and Panaev rode past some soldiers who, for their noon meal, were taking out of their messkits "some sort of liquid, like coffee, and lifting out fragments, black as coal." Menshikov ordered Panaev to dismount

7. Krestovskii, pp. 574-75.
8. SVM, I, Danilov, *Istoricheskii ocherk*, Prilozhenie 10, 63-65.

and try it. When the latter did so he found that the mixture consisted of biscuits recently delivered, which smelled to high heaven and rasped the throat. Menshikov, angered, said that undoubtedly the intendants had sent on from the Southern Army in Bessarabia the same rotten biscuits that Gen. Gorchakov had already rejected as unfit. Unfortunately, there was no way to remedy the situation, as, because of the grave shortage of provisions, there were no biscuits to replace the spoiled ones. "But what a trick the Intendancy of the Southern Army has played on me; they have skillfully taken advantage of our need."[9] It should be said, however, that Gen. F. K. Zatler, intendant of the Southern Army, strongly denied the truth of this statement.

The system of supplying the troops with uniforms, boots, and equipment was another source of profit for dishonest commanders. The accepted practice was for the Commissariat Department to issue to each regiment the requisite quantity of materials (cloth, leather, and metal parts), which were then made up by craftsmen of the regiment. The soldiers themselves made their own boots, underwear, and shirts. Uniforms and overcoats, however, required more skilled work, and hence each regiment had its own tailor shop, filled with enlisted men from the ranks—at least twenty from each company— detailed for this work. For the most part they received little or no pay for this, and in addition had to march in their companies at reviews, for which they received intensive training. The small sums of money issued for the sewing of the uniforms were largely used to buy buttons, insignia, and other ornaments.[10] For each soldier the regiment received material for two shirts per year, in addition to twenty-five silver kopecks for a third, and the cloth for one pair of drawers. It also received the leather for two pairs of boots and two extra soles for each man. The Commissariat issued cloth for uniforms, which should last two years, and for overcoats, with a three-year term. Helmets, cartridge-boxes, belts, knapsacks, and other equipment were issued in completed form, for the most part once every ten years.[11]

As in the French and Prussian armies, the uniforms and items of equipment had fixed terms of service. If the item of equipment did not last out its term, the soldier was punished. If, on the other hand, he made it serve longer than the period set, he received no reward for his care. "On the contrary: with the imperfect organization of the regi-

9. Panaev, *Russkaia Starina*, XIX (1877), 287-90.
10. Anichkov, pp. 504-5.
11. *Ibid.*, pp. 163-65.

mental administration, a dishonest commander is offered the possibility to derive personal, illegal profit from the carefulness of the soldier." In addition, the official terms of service did not always correspond to the actual life of the articles. If articles received hard wear, especially in bad weather or active service, they often wore out before the time set, especially if the quality of the materials was inferior. This was especially true for boots and underwear. With a review in prospect and the company commander insisting that everything must be in perfect order, the soldier might become desperate and resort to theft to fill his needs, as he would surely suffer if he did not have the proper equipment when the review took place.[12]

At times the wearing out of the soldier's equipment was a result of the dishonesty of his commander. Instead of insisting on the issue of first-grade materials by the Commissariat, the dishonest colonel could readily obtain second- or third-rate materials, for which he would receive rebates from the Commissariat, as he would sign a statement that he had received goods of the best quality. The Commissariat officials, who had bought the inferior goods from conniving contractors, had collected the full price for first-grade goods from the government, and thus both colonel and Commissariat officers would profit by the acceptance of poor-grade goods. The troop units were by no means innocent in this peculation. "On the contrary, the initiative of all abuses of the Commissariat belongs to them: if they would obtain their articles honestly, this would eradicate abuses in the Commissariat itself." Unfortunately, the author added, in few armies did the establishment of a Commissariat prove "to be so bankrupt as with us."[13]

The report of Gen. Glinka to Alexander II referred to above dealt with this problem. It told the same story. Two thirds of the articles bought by the Commissariat went directly to the troops, while the rest, of high quality, were properly recorded and became part of the Commissariat's stores. He, too, laid the blame on the troops:

> The troops are so filled with greediness for money that they do not willingly accept good supplies. Part of them, more moderate in their demands, receive average supplies and in return for this get a moderate rebate in money and in kind. Those, however, whose objective is solely the acquiring of money, receive very bad articles, but for this they receive a very considerable rebate in money and in kind.

12. *Ibid.*, pp. 149-51.
13. *Ibid.*, p. 172.

In addition, they turn the rebate in kind into cash and thus the soldier gets bad articles and the commander and the treasurer get money.[14]

Glinka named the specific amounts of the rebates received. For one thousand *arshins* of wool, worth sixty rubles, the regiment received a rebate of seven rubles and also seven *arshins*, worth forty-two kopecks, or twelve and one-half per cent. Leather for one pair of boots, worth eighty kopecks, brought a rebate of seven kopecks, or eighteen per cent. A helmet priced at ninety kopecks carried an eleven per cent rebate, while a sheepskin overcoat costing two rubles seventy-five kopecks provided a rebate of forty kopecks, or fourteen per cent.[15] Thus, at the expense of the national treasury and of the enlisted men themselves, the Commissariat officials and the regimental commanders obtained tainted income.

In addition to these sources for illicit income, the cavalry had additional opportunities, from the purchase of horses for remounts, and above all from the buying of forage. While the Provision Department might have supplied the regiments with forage, it rarely did so, as the buying and moving of quantities of oats, hay, and straw would have been complicated and difficult. Hence the regiments themselves handled this matter. Twice a year the regimental commanders through the divisional commanders presented the corps commanders with the prices at which they would agree to feed their horses. The corps commander, armed with a price list from the Provision Department, then established the prices for forage. In theory, he could reduce the prices suggested by the colonels to reasonable levels, but in actuality this was rarely done. If the colonels refused to feed their animals at the lowered prices, the task of supplying forage would then fall to the Provision Department, which was extremely reluctant to do this. Hence the corps commander usually accepted the prices suggested by the colonels and merely demanded that they feed their horses well.

The colonels usually set their prices for forage well over the market price—sometimes double the current rate. While they explained that they could not foresee accurately the future price developments and had to protect themselves against sudden price

14. SVM, I, Danilov, *Istoricheskii ocherk*, 60-61.
15. *Ibid.*, pp. 61-62. An archin was twenty-eight inches.

increases, the real reason probably was to obtain extra income.[16] The Provision Department had no reason to object to this system, for it everywhere retained two per cent or more of the sums that it dispensed, and thus it stood to benefit by the high prices approved for the cavalry regiments.[17] The colonels also were satisfied with the amounts they had received. They did not retain all the profits, however, as they had to turn the actual purchase of the forage over to the squadron commanders. The latter demanded as large a share of the gains as possible, while the colonels sought to keep as much as they could. After much bargaining, a satisfactory bargain was struck. The captains, who were usually in grave financial straits, looked on their squadrons as valuable income-properties and sought to recoup their debts and save a nest egg for old age. The other officers of the regiment, both the majors and the junior officers, had no share in these transactions and remained in financial straits and often had little to do with the affairs of the regiment. The colonels were the chief beneficiaries of this arrangement.[18]

The results of this were unfortunate for the cavalry. The colonels enriched themselves and spent money on the outward aspects of their regiments. At reviews the horses were sleek and fat, the uniforms clean and new, and the regimental band made a good show. The enlisted men replied to questions with loud shouts of satisfaction with their condition. Hence the inspector would thank the colonel for having done well with his regiment.[19] The divisional and corps commanders would sign the books every month, attesting to fine condition of the regiments, although those who were intelligent must have realized that the situation was not good, for the generals themselves were products of the same system and in their hearts knew that it was a false one.[20]

Confirmation of these statements came from the German officer Gagern who was in Russia in 1839. He reported that in army circles "They figure that each regiment must bring to its commander a minimum of 8,000 rubles," which was to come from forage and remounting "which are entirely left to them." His informants told him that the higher commanders, such as those of cavalry divisions, received a

16. A. S., "Zametki o prodovol'stvii kavalerii furazhem," *Voennyi Sbornik*, II (1859), 138-40.
17. *Ibid.*, p. 144.
18. Zolotarev, *Voennyi Sbornik*, I (1858), 30-34.
19. *Ibid.*, pp. 28-29.
20. A. S., *Voennyi Sbornik*, II (1859), 144.

share of this income.[21] Prussian officers who took part in joint maneuvers with the Russian army in 1839 told of the commander of the Nassau Uhlan regiment who was imprisoned for two weeks in the guardhouse and then suspended from service for embezzlement of funds assigned for purchasing horses. An officer of this regiment, who was attached to the Prussian 6th Cuirassier regiment, was very critical of his colonel, not because of his peculation, but because he had been so grasping that the squadron commanders had received almost no share of the profits (presumably from the purchase of hay and oats).[22]

Although the engineer officers were among the best-trained men in the Russian army, some of them also proved to be corrupt. In 1843 Gen. Filipson had a lieutenant colonel of engineers under him draw up the estimates for some construction work. For some reason the officer used a new set of prices for materials, whereby the cost of the work was reduced by about one-third. Perhaps he figured that he had already made enough money by the use of the former inflated prices, for he soon retired, and, according to common talk, with a fortune of four hundred thousand rubles. By 1851 he had reached the standing of a rich landowner.[23]

In his memoirs Gen. V. I. Dehn, a noted engineer, relates that in 1853, when he ordered a colonel of engineers to construct a fortress at Bendery, the latter commandeered numbers of Bulgars and Moldavians and drove them to work, without pay and with no concern for their feeding. Dehn, learning about this, appealed to his superior to do something for the unfortunates, but to no purpose. Finally, on returning to St. Petersburg, he told the Tsar of the situation. Nicholas, astonished that Dehn's pleas had had no effect, ordered that the workers were to be paid fifteen kopecks per day. Dehn, however, expressed doubt that they ever received this pay.[24] Another example of carelessness with state money on the part of the engineers was uncovered by Gen. N. N. Muraviev when he came to the Caucasus late in 1854. After viewing the site for a proposed bridge over a river, he asked for estimates as to its cost. One engineer officer set a figure of twenty-four thousand rubles, while another named twelve thousand. The local commander thought it would cost about six thousand. Muraviev then investigated and found that there was plenty of timber,

21. Gagern, *Russkaia Starina*, LXV (1890), 331.
22. Schiemann, III, 443.
23. Filipson, *Russkii Arkhiv*, XXII (1884), Pt. I, 360.
24. Dehn, *Russkaia Starina*, LXV (1890), 555.

which the troops could cut in the nearby forests. Likewise the troops could provide the necessary skilled workers. Thus iron for bolts would be the only item of expenditure. After figuring the required quantity of iron, Muraviev announced that the bridge could be built for six hundred rubles—and it was. This was the first time that anyone had questioned the estimates of the engineers. Probably the latter had been able to do all their construction work on the basis of their highly inflated figures, which must have provided them with abundant opportunities for illegal profit.[25]

Even the artillery, the elite force of the Russian army, was not entirely free from corruption. An officer of twenty-five years of service related that often in his time he had heard the officers tell with pride how the gunners had sallied forth at night to raid the haystacks of the peasants or of landowners, so that the battery horses could be well fed. They also made marches from village to village to seize oats from the peasants. These things, of course, happened with the knowledge and consent of the officers, who took pride in the initiative of their subordinates.[26]

One of the worst concentrations of corruption in the Russian military system was in the hospitals. In 1860, a Maj. Gen. Krasik presented a report concerning them to the committee for improving the military medical administration and the military hospitals. His conclusions were that most of them made an excellent impression in respect to cleanliness and order, and the government spared no expense on them. Underneath this fine exterior, however, lay all sorts of failings, both medical and economic. His report, of course, dealt chiefly with the situation that obtained five years after the death of Nicholas I, but, convincing evidence indicates, these abuses were by no means new, but had existed in the 1830's and 1840's, and probably long before that. Gen. Krasik held that one of the chief causes of the evils was the appointment of chief doctors who rarely had special medical knowledge or worth, but who obtained their eminence by seniority or influence. As a result, the chief doctors for the most part could not exert effective control over the staff doctors, whose conduct became marked by "laziness, carelessness, and mistakes." Moreover, most chief doctors were interested in supplementing their incomes, which

25. I. S. Kravtsov, "Kavkaz i ego voenachal'niki," *Russkaia Starina*, L (1886), 572-73.

26. N. N., "Mysli o chastnoi i sluzhebnoi zhizni artilleriiskikh ofitserov," *Artilleriiskii Zhurnal* (1857), No. 2, pp. 73-74.

they did by securing an indirect income (i.e., graft) out of caring for the sick, "so that they are more interested in their own concerns than in caring for the patients." The staff doctors, with such examples before them, also placed their private interests above their duty. Many did not try to visit daily each of their two or three hundred patients, but built up private practice on the side, in addition to violating their official obligations in various other ways. To make matters worse, there was a lack of properly trained and conscientious medical assistants to administer medicine promptly, and even the orderlies did not know how to look after the sick. As for the apothecaries, they, too, had their failings: they often dispensed small amounts of medicine or port wine, while entering in their books that the full amounts had been issued.[27]

According to a Soviet military historian, Sir James Villiers, Bt., a Scot, who was personal physician to Nicholas I, deserves much of the blame for this state of affairs. Although he lived in Russia for fifty years, he never learned to speak or write Russian. Nevertheless, he was chief inspector of the Medical Department of the Ministry of War and president of the Medico-Surgical Academy. Vain and haughty and surrounded by foreign careerists, many of them incompetent, he would not tolerate criticism and fought the rising Russian medical men and drove them out of his hospitals. He quarreled fiercely with Dr. N. I. Pirogov, a brilliant Russian surgeon. Villiers cared nothing about military medicine and let it go to rack and ruin.[28] Doubtless there is much truth to this assessment, and yet it does not seem that it is correct to lay all the failings at the door of Villiers. The whole system of Russian military medicine was so filled with inefficiency and corruption that probably the best administrator in the world could not have singlehandedly corrected these failings.

As early as the 1830's the military hospitals in the Caucasus were filled with abuses. Gen. G. I. Filipson stated that the regimental lazarettes, of which the commanders were proud, cost vastly less to operate than the hospitals, "which for long had been the favorite field for the robbery of an endless multitude of institutions, beginning with the Commissariat Department and ending with the hospital inspector."[29] This view received support from the testimony of Gen. Chai-

27. SVM, III, *Glavnyi Voenno-Sanitarnyi Komitet*, Pt. II, Prilozhenie 5, 173-75.
28. Fedorov, *Russkaia armiia*, p. 63.
29. Filipson, *Russkii Arkhiv*, XXI (1883), Pt. III, 273.

kovskii, who reported to the investigating committee that in the 1830's several conscientious and experienced doctors in the Caucasus had told him that if they wished, the staff doctors could reduce the number of patients in the hospitals by one-third. As the doctors were eager to keep the good will of the chief doctor in order to receive good recommendations from him, they sought his favor by an extremely small discharge of cured cases. Chaikovskii asked his orderly and some sergeants, all of whom had been in hospitals, about the discharge of cured patients. They told him that a doctor would come into the ward, half full of recovered patients, and would ask loudly: "Who wishes to be discharged?" Two or three men, who were bored by the idle existence, would come forward, the doctor would discharge them, and the rest, many of them healthy, would stay on. The reason was that those who handled the hospital payments were eager to keep an especially large number of patients, because of the profitable rebates they received from the contractors who furnished the supplies for the hospital. "Not for nothing did hundred-mouthed rumor at that time declare a large hospital to be the equivalent of a large estate." He asserted that the supervisors and commissars bought their places from the Commissariat officials at fixed prices, and paid rent on them.[30]

This sort of grafting seems to have been especially widespread. Another witness testified that when he inspected hospitals he, unlike most inspectors, went to them right away, without giving the authorities a chance to cover up their misdeeds. He always found that there was a sharp discrepancy between the number of patients listed in the books and drawing rations, and those who were actually there. The missing patients usually turned out to be healthy men, servants of the hospital officials or artisans of some sort. When presented with the irrefutable evidence, the commander was in dismay, for he had to act, and yet he did not dare discharge the head doctor, the staff doctors, and the hospital officials, as the hospital would be left without personnel, for the supply of doctors, especially, was very limited. So he usually contented himself with a stern order threatening the culprits with dire penalties unless they mended their ways. This usually was effective for a few days, after which matters resumed their normal course. Once, however, the inspector's report resulted in the dismissal of the head doctor and the inspector. He had found the hospital full of patients, with two doors wide open: one for admissions, the other

30. SVM, III, Pt. II, *Glavnyi Voenno-Sanitarnyi Komitet*, Prilozhenie 7, 189-90.

leading to the cemetery. The door for recovered patients had not been opened for a long time. He found that sixty "convalescents" were constantly maintained on special diets with beef and wine—among them men acting as servants to the hospital officials.[31]

Another incident of this sort occurred when the authorities, tipped off by an informant, sent an officer to make a sudden inspection of a hospital where allegedly the number of patients on the books was larger by twenty persons than the number of men actually sick. The officer discovered that the patients numbered nineteen less than the number entered in the books. An hour and one-half later he went, together with the inspector and the head doctor, to verify his findings. This time the correct number were in the beds. The inspecting officer, however, recognized one of the men in bed as the sergeant who had earlier taken him through the wards. In the time between inspections the sergeant and eighteen other men had hastily doffed their clothes, put on hospital garb, and jumped into bed.[32]

Even in the capital the military hospitals were in miserable shape. In 1841 Dr. Pirogov was appointed to manage the surgical division of the Second Military Hospital in St. Petersburg. He found it in frightful condition, with from sixty to one hundred beds in each ward, filled with patients with most varied diseases, unventilated and malodorous. The patients did not receive effective medical care, as the "medicines" issued by the pharmacy were useless substitutes for the real medicines. Thieving was open and flagrant. "The supervisors and commissars lost several hundred rubles at cards every day. The meat contractor before the eyes of all distributed meat to the homes of the members of the hospital office. The apothecary sold his supply of vinegar, poisons, and so on, on the side."[33]

Profiteering from the buying of provisions for hospitals was one of the most common forms of corruption. A high official of the Provision Department reported to the Minister of War that in 1838 he had observed a group of invalids from an army hospital enjoying themselves in a resort in the capital. The women were dressed in velvets and furs. The leader, a sergeant, ordered five bottles of champagne and boasted of his "warm place" under the Commissariat, which brought him an income of five hundred rubles a month, more

31. *Ibid.*, pp. 188-89.
32. *Ibid.*, Prilozhenie 3, p. 162.
33. SVM, VIII, Pt. II, *Glavnoe voenno-meditsinskoe upravlenie*, Prilozheniia, 285, 256, cited in Fedorov, *Russkaia armiia*, p. 63.

even than the hospital inspector. "We operate thus: when there is an order for six *puds* of fish, we issue only two *puds*, and instead of sixty pitchers of milk only twenty—there's our income." Another flagrant example involved the purchase of fifteen thousand lemons for one hospital in Stavropol, at from ten to fifteen and one-half kopecks each —which were very high rates. Later some ten thousand of the total were charged off as rotten, although the investigator believed that they had never been bought, as this quantity far exceeded the number of lemons imported at Stavropol in any year. It seems likely that the whole transaction was fraudulent and that the money for the lemons lined the pockets of the hospital officials.[34]

Another example of profiteering came from a hospital in the Stavropol area. The hospital administration informed the Commissariat Commission that the roof over two of the wards was leaking. An army engineer was sent to make an estimate of the repairs, which he set at three thousand rubles. This figure seemed to be too high, so a new estimate was asked. It came after several months, but instead of being lower, it was for thirty thousand rubles. After fresh protests and delays of six months—while the patients lay in leaky wards— another estimate came, this time for sixty thousand. Finally the engineers had the work done by a contractor, who received fifty thousand rubles for it. The patients in this hospital, however, were more fortunate than those in one in Poti. In 1837 the building collapsed, killing twenty-seven patients and injuring more than seventy. This resulted in a court-martial of the commandant, the head doctor, and the supervisor.[35]

In 1847 these same hospitals again became the scene of an investigation. After word from the Tsar that they were filled with vast corruption, Prince Vorontsov, the viceroy of the Caucasus, sent a young officer, Vladimir Tolstoi, to investigate. On his mission he found many of them in disgraceful condition. He especially remarked on the hospital on the Black Sea Line, which had made contracts for a vast quantity of firewood at over ninety rubles per cubic *sazhen* (a *sazhen* is seven feet). The enormity of this price was made clear by the fact that in the nearby town of Anapa the hospital office bought logs from the mountaineers at about ten rubles per *sazhen*.[36]

34. *Ibid.*, III, Pt. II, *Glavnyi Voenno-Sanitarnyi Komitet*, Prilozhenie 3, 160-62.
35. *Ibid.*, Prilozhenie 7, p. 189.
36. Vl. Tolstoi, "Kniaz' M. S. Vorontsov," *Russkii Arkhiv*, XV (1877), Pt. III, 298-99.

A quite different abuse came to light during the Russian campaign in Hungary in 1849. One of the officers regularly visited a nearby field hospital and chatted with the patients. He became quite friendly with a certain Cossack, whose condition seemed to grow worse rather than better. On being questioned, the Cossack said that he had made the mistake of entrusting his funds to the *fel'dsher* (medical assistant), who, he now believed, was trying to kill him for his money. The officer made the *fel'dsher* return the gold pieces, and from then on the Cossack recovered rapidly. The officer tried to persuade the patients to deposit their money at the hospital office, as then they would surely get it back. The patients, however, distrusted the hospital authorities and preferred to keep their money in leather sacks under their knees. There were cases where the hospital orderlies who came at night to check on the sleeping patients tried to steal their little sacks, although they rarely succeeded, as the patients or their neighbors detected them.[37]

The Crimean War of 1853-56 uncovered a vast number of defects in the Russian military system, including many weaknesses and abuses in the hospitals. A whole series of examples were presented in Gen. Krasik's report to the committee for the improvement of the military medical administration and the military hospitals. One of these was having the hospital laundry done by contractors, usually at highly inflated rates. In one group of hospitals that did this, the cost of laundry per patient was from seven to ten times what it was where the hospital had its own laundry. Occasionally hospitals would make contracts to have an unusually large quantity of laundry done, from eighty-five to one hundred thirty-seven pieces per person per month. The normal amount in nearby hospitals was fifty pieces per patient per month, so it was strongly suspected that much of this excess washing was never done, but merely charged to the government, so hospital officials could pocket some of the extra costs. The time-honored device of padding the issue of hospital rations again appeared, and often the hospital administration would order a large number of the rations to be of special types, requiring beef, wine, milk, and other more expensive items. In one hospital where this was done, most of the patients were seriously ill with typhus, malaria, cholera, and other grave ailments and hence were unable to eat beef. Even in the giving

37. A. L. Vernikovskii, "Vengerskii pokhod 1849 goda. Vospominaniia armeiskago ofitsera," *Russkii Arkhiv*, XXIII (1885), Pt. III, 525-26.

of medicines there was deception: on occasion, apothecaries would substitute inexpensive medicines for the more costly ones prescribed by the doctors. The report, which was very detailed, concluded:

> In spite of the number and extreme diversity of the individual forms of the abuses, which cover almost the whole sphere of treasury expenditures on the hospitals, there were well grounded reasons for supposing that there were even greater forms of thieving, established more or less legally, and, moreover, outside the hospitals, actually in the Commissariat Commissions and even in the Department of the Ministry of war.[38]

Regrettable as were these widespread indications of corruption in the military hospitals, which undoubtedly resulted in much increased mortality among the unfortunates who became patients in them, they certainly showed that enterprise and ingenuity were not lacking in imperial Russia and proved the validity of the Russian saying: "Give me the control of only one state-supported sparrow and I'll live in comfort."

In contrast to these devious and involved forms of corruption, there were several cases of simple embezzlement involving high military men. Late in 1846 the Tsar uncovered a series of cases of this sort. He found it necessary to dismiss Gen. Adj. Prince Trishchatnyi— of his personal staff—and Gen. Dobroshchin of the Guards for this offense. An especially flagrant case was that of Gen. Klevetskii, chief of the St. Petersburg police, who stole 150,000 rubles provided for the maintenance and forwarding of 17,000 recruits to the Caucasus Corps. These unfortunates were sent off anyhow, without proper clothing and provisions, with the result that half of them died on the way.[39]

This outrage was followed by the death of Prince N. A. Dolgorukii, general adjutant and governor general of Khar'kov, who left two letters to the Tsar. The first begged Nicholas to support his family, which the Tsar did with a pension of four thousand rubles to his wife. The second admitted that he had stolen forty-three thousand rubles from the funds of an orphan asylum. This news greatly mortified the sovereign, but he did not punish the offender's family for this defalcation.[40]

In 1853 there was disclosure of the embezzlement of over one million rubles from the funds of the Committee for the Wounded.

38. SVM, III, Pt. II, *Glavnyi Voenno-Sanitarnyi Komitet*, Prilozhenie 5, 175-84.
39. Schiemann, IV, 119.
40. *Ibid.*

The culprit, a civilian, poisoned himself, so the Tsar's wrath turned against Gen. Ushakov, chairman of the committee, and the other generals and the admiral who were its members. Ushakov was dismissed from service and imprisoned for six months for carelessness in his trust; the others received lesser punishments. The anger of the Tsar soon cooled, however, and before long they were reinstated.[41]

A variety of other sorts of impropriety also existed in the Russian army. In 1829, G. I. Filipson took command of a company containing many married soldiers, most of whom proved to be heavily involved in smuggling liquor to sell to the soldiers—a practice that he termed "a very great evil, although very often encountered in the troops." Where it appeared, fairness and discipline became impossible, the enlisted men fell into debt, became accustomed to a disorderly life, and ruined their health, drinking vodka to forget their woes. Filipson suggested that it had become established because one of the last commanders, heavily in debt, had diverted the moneys of his company, holding up payment of pay and equipment money, which many soldiers never received. As he was known as a cruel man, there were no complaints against him, as the soldiers feared reprisals if they objected.[42]

In 1841, N. Kutuzov, one of Nicholas' aides, presented him with a memorandum on the unfortunate state of the army, which included an absence of probity in the Ministry of War.[43] While he failed to present specific evidence to support this charge, there were numerous indications that the morality of the army was weak. In 1849 the Fifth Corps, returning from the campaign in Hungary, reached Brody in Galicia, a free port. Here the officers were approached by Jewish merchants, who urged them to accept consignments of goods to take into Russia in their baggage, where they would be duty free. After the goods had been sold in Russia at a substantial profit, the officers and the merchants should divide the proceeds. Most of the young officers indignantly refused such proposals, but some made substantial gains either by collaborating with the merchants or by personally buying the sugar, tea, Holland linen, and other goods easily sold in Russia. It was common talk among the officers that Gen. Cheodaev, commander of the Fifth Corps, had made an especially large venture of

41. Sokolovskii, *Russkaia Starina*, CXXIV (1905), 398-99.
42. Filipson, *Russkii Arkhiv*, XXI (1883), Pt. III, 115.
43. Kutuzov, *Russkaia Starina*, XCV (1898), 523.

this sort, filling all the wagons of the corps staff with sugar and tea, which were hidden under the papers of the staff archives.[44]

Occasionally retribution fell upon the culprit. When Nicholas I visited Sevastopol in the fall of 1852, he heard reports that for years the lieutenant general there commanding had been drawing money for the firewood, food, and clothing for four thousand prisoners, although there were only two thousand. The Tsar, according to the reports of the British Ambassador, promptly degraded the commander and threw him into prison, in spite of the intercession of Prince Vorontsov.[45] This practice of profiting from "dead souls" also existed at lower levels. In 1854, when Col. Likhachev took command of the Iamburg Uhlans from Gedroits-Iuraga, he found that there were sixteen men carried on the rolls who had either died or been discharged at earlier times. Nevertheless, the commander had continued to draw rations and equipment money for them. It turned out that earlier, under Col. Kutuzov, there had been many more, but Gedroits had quietly written most of them off. After an investigation, Col. Likhachev, on instructions from the divisional commander, removed all these names from the lists.[46]

Even in the Guards, stationed in St. Petersburg, the commanders abused their powers. A report on the heating of the barracks of the Guards Reserve Corps stated that, while the importance of fresh air in barracks was common knowledge, "who does not know that. . . firewood is one of the chief sources of income of their commanders?" Because the latter wished to profit in this way, the barracks were poorly heated, with dire consequences. A visit to the barracks at night during the winter months would prove this: with all the doors and casement windows tightly closed, "the visitor will be struck by the stench and the dense vapors spread through all the rooms." Improper heating was definitely a cause of sickness and death, as it resulted in a lack of ventilation. Thus the men breathed foul air, which infected their respiratory organs. To support this statement, the report presented statistics of the losses from death and disease in the Guards Reserve Infantry Corps in 1855. The general loss of men amounted to about 10 per cent, and 4.6 per cent of this came from pulmonary diseases. The report concluded with the remark that the official rules

44. P. V. Alabin, *Chetyre voiny. Pokhodnyia zapiski v 1849-53-54-55 gg. i 1877-78 gg.* (3 pts.; Samara, 1888), I, 159.
45. Schiemann, IV, 270.
46. Krestovskii, p. 576.

for firing barracks stoves were excellent; "but they are nowhere observed, for they are too contrary to the profits of the commanders of the units. . . ."[47]

While corruption in the army was no rarity, it seems to have been especially widespread in the Caucasus, perhaps because the region was so remote from the seat of government and because it was difficult for the local administration to exercise control over troops widely dispersed over a vast and difficult terrain. For a long time, matters went their usual way, but in 1837, with the arrival of Nicholas I on one of his favorite inspection tours, an explosion occurred. The Emperor heard such convincing charges against one of his own aides-de-camp, Prince A. L. Dadianov, that he summarily disgraced him. In spite of the fact that Dadianov was son-in-law of Baron Rosen, viceroy of the Caucasus, the Tsar, at a public review in Tiflis, stripped the culprit of his insignia and, without the formality of a trial, sent him off, in the custody of a Gendarme officer, to prison in a fortress in Russia. Three years later a court-martial tried and convicted Dadianov of grave offenses, but Nicholas released him from prison, although he remained in disgrace.[48]

Investigation of Dadianov's conduct disclosed that he had been misbehaving for several years. Above all, he had used the enlisted men of his regiment as farm hands and laborers for years at a time, paying them little or nothing and completely neglecting their military function. Thanks to this virtually unpaid labor, the Prince had amassed large sums through farming operations, construction of mills and other commercial buildings, the cutting of great quantities of hay on the lands of neighbors, and other highhanded actions. He had even compelled the wives of soldiers to mow hay for him, and when they protested that they had to neglect their infants, he had them flogged, including one in the last stages of pregnancy.[49] Nicholas wrote to Field Marshal Paskevich about his observations in the Caucasus, laying especial emphasis on the weakness of Baron Rosen and the resulting abuses. "In the troops they have also gone to extreme limits. In a word, there is no sphere where they have not gone to extremes!"[50] Ten days later he wrote: "The general infection of greed—what is most

47. SVM, I, Danilov, *Istoricheskii ocherk*, Prilozhenie 10, 65-66.
48. A. P. Berzhe, "Imperator Nikolai na Kavkaze v 1837 g," *Russkaia Starina*, XLIII (1884), 391-93.
49. Bobrovskii, IV, 305-15.
50. Shcherbatov, V, Pt. II, 330.

terrible of all—has even reached the military sphere to an unbelievable degree, so that I was even compelled to make an unheard-of example of my own aide-de-camp."[51] It is interesting to note that Filipson, who had served for some time in the Caucasus, observed that Dadianov "was not a bit worse than the other regimental commanders," but the Tsar chose to make an example of him.[52]

After the downfall of Prince Dadianov, which also led to the downfall of Baron Rosen, matters did not improve in the Caucasus, but disintegrated. Abuses, highhanded conduct, and extortion continued, so that "Col. Daniel-Bek of Mekhtulina of the Grodno Hussar regiment, one of the local people most loyal to the Russian government, abandoned his fine estate, the support he received, and his high position in the area and fled to Shamil [the enemy commander]."[53] Prince Vorontsov, who eventually became viceroy, took strong measures to clean up the corruption. One of his first measures was to halt the sale of Russian gunpowder to the hostile mountaineers, especially after the Russian forces had discovered some of it in the captured enemy fortress of Dargo.[54] Actually, this does not seem to have been a serious matter, as Filipson states that the mountaineers made better powder than the Russians had or bought a superior English product. His explanation for the traffic in powder is that the troops in the Caucasus received more than they wanted, as target practice made no sense with the worn-out flintlocks that the troops carried. Hence they got rid of it by giving it to friendly natives, who sometimes sold it to the foe. Some of the troops even dumped the powder in rivers.[55] Another situation that drew the attention of Prince Vorontsov was the relationship between a commander and his sutler. Because the latter had promised to carry a full supply of goods, no matter how few the troops were, the commander helped his trade. As soon as the sutler began to trade in an area, the commander sent in troops, with orders to close all rival shops in the vicinity. This enabled the merchant to charge triple prices to the local people, although he sold to the soldiers at the regular price. Vorontsov quickly ended this arrangement.[56] It appears that Vorontsov was one of the better viceroys in the Caucasus,

51. *Ibid.*, p. 333.
52. Filipson, *Russkii Arkhiv*, XXI (1883), Pt. III, 254.
53. Tolstoi, *Russkii Arkhiv*, XV (1877), Pt. III, 296-97.
54. *Ibid.*, p. 296; A. L. Zisserman, "Bariatinskii," *Russkii Arkhiv*, XXVI (1888), Pt. I, 437.
55. Filipson, *Russkii Arkhiv*, XXII (1884), Pt. I, 478.
56. Tolstoi, *Russkii Arkhiv*, XV (1877), Pt. III, 296.

for, although he sometimes made mistakes, he made strenuous efforts to eliminate abuses in this region, and the evils in the armed services that formerly flourished unchecked began to diminish under him.

This chapter presents considerable evidence to show that widespread corruption existed in the Russian army and continued at least until the end of the reign of Nicholas I. Lest the reader should think that the situation was deteriorating under him, it is necessary to state that corruption of this sort had been widespread before his reign and may very well have assumed much greater proportions during the opportunistic reign of Catherine II and under Alexander I, except as occasional high-minded commanders like Rumiantsev and Suvorov sought to check it. For all his faults, Nicholas had a much more serious attitude toward his responsibilities than his predecessors and introduced many reforms in the military system. While these were far from sufficient, they were probably the first among the efforts to clean up the Augean stables that resulted in the Army Reform of 1874. One such step was an improvement of the accounting of the troops, which in 1826 was almost non-existent. The existing chaos, of course, permitted almost unlimited abuses. After a committee appointed by the Tsar had grappled with this problem for some time, on August 15, 1833, a new Regulation was issued, simplifying the paper work of the troops and making their accounting procedures more definite and precise. Thus for the first time the Ministry of War could establish some check on the manpower of the troops.[57]

At the same time, the Provision Department of the Ministry of War was reorganized. In 1835 it received a new table of organization, which provided considerable increases in pay. The following year new rules for handling the work of the department and its subdivisions appeared. Above all there was a basic change in the negotiation of contracts, which eliminated many of the previous failings. This resulted in great savings, which enabled the Tsar to make several increases in the amount of meat supplied to the troops. By 1850 almost nine times as many men got meat rations as in 1826. The cost of rations per man, however, had increased by only 22.9 per cent.[58]

The Tsar also took the Commissariat Department in hand. In 1826 it was in a sorry condition, with an immense backlog of unfinished business, and its officials unable to cope with the demands on

57. "Istoricheskoe obozrenie," *Sbornik IRIO*, XCVIII (1896), 327-28.
58. *Ibid.*, pp. 342-47.

them. Nicholas proceeded to clear away much of the overdue back work, but could make no fundamental reform until after the Polish War of 1831. In 1832 the department received a new table of organization, which provided a small increase in personnel, while increasing the salaries over three times. New rules for making contracts, adopted in 1838, greatly simplified and clarified the procedure of bidding. The buying of military supplies became more effective, as it now proved possible to purchase them at prices below the maximum set by the government, while the quality of the commodities furnished improved substantially.[59]

Thus in the second quarter of the nineteenth century the economic aspects of the Russian army presented a somewhat contradictory picture. On the one hand there was the corruption known of old, although perhaps on a somewhat reduced scale. On the other, there were probably greater efforts than ever before to limit abuses and an organization and a procedure that were somewhat more effective in achieving these objectives. In many ways this resembled the general development of the nation during this period. At times, the old order, with all its abuses and failings, seemed to persist unchanged. But, often almost unnoticed, Russia was advancing and overcoming its weaknesses. Sometimes the government aided this progress, at other times the progress was in spite of, rather than because of the government, as growing popular forces exerted themselves. In this often halting advance, the Russian army shared.

59. *Ibid.*, pp. 354-60.

CHAPTER XII. THE LIFE OF THE ENLISTED MEN

Important as the officers of the Russian army were, with their superior education, status, and wealth, the real strength of the troops lay in the masses of enlisted men—privates, corporals, and sergeants —drawn from the ranks of the working people. Conscription was the method used to obtain them. It was not, however, universal military service for brief periods, as in the Prussian army, but selective conscription of a small portion of the populace for long periods. Although military service *for life* had ended, in 1825 the conscripts faced terms of service of twenty-five years (twenty-two in the Guards). This burdensome obligation fell chiefly upon the privately owned serfs, the state and crown peasants, and town laborers, and other categories who had to pay the poll tax.[1] Men were liable to draft at twenty years of age, but not all were taken at twenty, and indeed, they remained liable to call until the end of their thirty-fifth year. The draft calls were made to the village communes, which thereupon picked the conscripts from the eligible men, in some sort of order, from the families of the village.[2] Since there were many exemptions of persons because of class status, and because the more wealthy families in the villages could often save their sons from call by bribery and other influence, the burden fell heavily on the lowest social groups. In 1848 about one-fifth of the inhabitants of European Russia were exempt, which increased the burden on the remaining families.[3] Another inequity of the system was the provision that men called for service might procure "volunteers" to serve in their place, of course for considerable sums.[4] The volunteers, whom the people termed "hirelings," were usually men of low moral caliber and often

1. Russia, *Svod Zakonov Rossiiskoi Imperii* (15 vols.; St. Petersburg, 1832), IV, Bk. I, *Ustav Rekrutskii*, arts. 3 and 8.
2. Petrov, p. 422.
3. *Ibid.*, p. 423; N. M. Druzhinin, *Gosudarstvennye krest'iane i reforma P. D. Kiseleva* (Moscow, Leningrad, 1946), I, 336-38.
4. *Svod Zakonov*, IV, Bk. I, *Ustav Rekrutskii*, arts. 304-5, 310, 314.

proved to be mere bounty jumpers. There were from ten thousand to twelve thousand each year.[5]

One of the worst features of the conscription system was that groups of townsmen or communes of state peasants had the right to send any man off to the army as a recruit if he had proved troublesome or unreliable in paying taxes "because of stubbornness." Landowners might send off any of their serfs at their discretion, without regard for priority in the normal order of selection. This could be done at any time.[6] This privilege, which the landlords insisted on retaining, proved very useful in getting rid of rebellious peasants. In somewhat similar fashion, the courts used the army as a prison without bars for religious offenders—"schismatics of all sects in general who have been detected in enticement, turbulence, or disobedience." The courts also sentenced Jews of bad conduct who did not pay their taxes, and student apothecaries dismissed for bad conduct, to serve in the army, along with "vicious men, vagabonds and criminals."[7] Thus with reason the Russian people looked on induction into the army as almost equivalent to penal servitude for life and bewailed as dead their sons whom the army took. Often they never saw them again. Nicholas I realized the severe burden that military service proved to the people and sought in various ways to lighten it, in part by compelling additional categories of people to submit to it. Beginning in 1827, the Jews were made to perform military service on the same basis as other subjects. From 1834 on, he extended the obligation to the inhabitants of the kingdom of Poland, the townsmen of the western provinces of Russia, the Little Russian (Ukrainian) Cossacks, and in 1835, the military colonists. He also divided the Empire into two conscription zones, in which the draft was made every second year, alternately. The vast majority of the conscripts, however, still came from the Russian peasantry.[8] During the twenty-five years from 1826 to 1850, the army inducted 2,087,507 men, at an average rate of almost 80,000 per year. The proportion of available men taken declined from one out of sixty-seven in 1826 to one out of 87.5 in 1850.[9]

5. Petrov, p. 424.
6. *Svod Zakonov*, IV, Bk. I, arts. 322-25.
7. SVP, Pt. II, *O prokhozhdenii sluzhby po voennomu vedomstvu*, arts. 273-80.
8. "Istoricheskoe obozrenie," *Sbornik IRIO*, XCVIII (1896), 329.
9. *Ibid.*, p. 331-32.

One of the worst features of Russian conscription was the drafting of Jews, according to the law of August 26, 1827. While it stated that the Jews should perform this obligation on the same basis as the rest of the population, there were certain special provisions for them. Rabbis, merchants, highly skilled artisans, and Jewish farmers were exempt, although the sons of rabbis were not. Jewish students who did excellent work in the public schools could receive permanent exemption by obtaining certificates of excellence. The Jewish communities selected the recruits from those of their number who enjoyed no exemption, taking them between the ages of twelve and twenty-five years. Jews presented as recruits out of turn were acceptable at thirty, if physically fit, and those not fully suitable for the army service were acceptable up to thirty-five, if they were skilled in trades like shoe-making, carpentry, cooperage, locksmithing, glazing, painting and barbering. One escape from conscription open to some was to hire a Jewish substitute; this, of course, helped only the more wealthy Jews.[10]

Service in the Russian army had special terror for the Jews, for, in addition to the hardships that any recruit would encounter, they would be compelled to live among strangers, often hostile, and to accept a way of life completely alien to their religion and their traditions. As a result, when conscription time came, the probable recruits fled to the forests or the swamps or to distant cities. But if their evasion proved successful, this would merely shift the burden to others of their community, and hence special agents tracked down the fugitives. If adults were not available to fill the quotas, children of twelve years were seized, and often younger ones, of eight.[11] One recruiting officer had to keep the young Jewish recruits under close supervision until he could send them off in a party, under a special officer and guards, to their destination.[12] Melancholy fates awaited them. In 1835 Alexander Herzen, on his way to exile, met a party of these Jewish children, some only eight years of age, on the march. The talkative officer in charge disliked his assignment, as one-third of them had already died and he expected that half of them would not reach their destination—"they just fall like flies." He added: "Well, you know, these Jewish boys are so puny and delicate. They can't stand raising dust for ten hours, with dry biscuits to live on.

10. *Svod Zakonov*, IV, Bk. I, *Ustav Rekrutskii*, Prilozhenie II, arts. 1-65.
11. S. M. Dubnow, *History of the Jews in Poland and Russia, from the Earliest Times to the Present Day* (3 vols.; Philadelphia, ca. 1918-1920), II, 18-23.
12. SVP, Pt. II, Bk. I, *O prokhozhdenii sluzhbe po voennomu vedomstvu*, art. 208.

Again, everywhere strange people, no father, no mother, no caresses. Well, then, you just hear a cough and the youngster is dead."[13]

Perhaps those that died on the road were more fortunate than those that survived, for the latter entered the schools of cantonists, which were known for extremely cruel treatment of their inmates. Although the Code of Military Regulations contained detailed provisions for permitting Jewish soldiers to observe the ceremonies of their religion,[14] it is highly likely that in these schools, where the authorities did not treat Russian youths like human beings, young Jews suffered far worse. S. M. Dubnow states that the latter suffered especial torments under the sergeants, who tried to convert them to Orthodoxy, by means of starvation, denial of sleep, thirst, flogging, or outright torture. Most of those who survived accepted baptism in the end, which relieved them of only part of their sufferings.[15]

While the Jewish boys whose destination was the cantonist battalions were perhaps the worst sufferers of all, the lot of adult Jewish conscripts, who were sent to army regiments as recruits, was little better. There many of them had to endure mockery and abuse because of their religion and way of life, in addition to the harsh treatment that fell to the lot of all recruits. A Jew in the Russian army often bore a heavy burden.

Indeed, for all recruits—even those who were Russian and of the Orthodox faith—the introduction into army life was a hard one. For married men, whether Jewish or Christian, it was especially painful, because of the added grief at being torn from wives and children, whom they rarely saw again. The rending sorrow of parting was made worse by the knowledge that the lot of a conscript's wife was dreadful. If she stayed on with her husband's family, she probably was treated like a parasite, with the womenfolk nagging and reminding her that she "was eating another's bread." Frequently, also, the fathers-in-law forced their attentions upon the young women widowed by the army, so that the Russian language contains the term *snokhachestvo* to describe this illicit relationship. Small wonder that the soldier's wife soon fled into the world. The more fortunate became domestic servants or workers in textile mills. Others eventually forgot their husbands and found new mates, while some were forced into prostitution to

13. Quoted in Dubnow, II, 24-25.
14. SVP, Pt. II, Bk. I, Prilozhenie 11, to art. 261.
15. Dubnow, II, 26-27.

avoid starvation. Only rarely could the soldier and his wife maintain a normal life.[16]

In 1855 an officer travelling to the rear with a convoy of convalescents had a conversation with a soldier of fifty-five who had re-enlisted after his term of service, as he found he could not live in retirement. He had not heard from his wife and children for twenty years. ". . . when a man becomes a soldier the first thing that is known to you is that it is difficult to return, and you say farewell to your family as if it were forever, because the severed crust does not fit back on the loaf." So, after grieving for a time, he had forgotten. As for his wife, she had written several times and had sent him a shirt, and then the letters came more and more slowly and finally nothing at all. "Indeed, from that time I don't even know if she is alive." Eventually the army discharged him as too old, and the author met him going home to his village, with seven rubles in his pocket, to live out his days, alone in the world.[17]

When the conscription call came, the authorities set up induction centers in the cities, headed by a receiving officer. A Gendarme officer, a force of the Internal Defense Corps, under an officer, doctors, and barbers also were present. A Recruit Session (*Prisutstvie*) composed of civilian officials had the function of deciding which of the proposed recruits should be inducted.[18] After the recruit had had a physical examination and had met the other requirements, the chairman of the session indicated his acceptance by uttering the word *lob* (forehead), whereupon a sergeant took the man to a barber, who shaved the front part of his head. The session accepted men who were not fit for full duty by assigning them to auxiliary service. In such cases the barber shaved the back of the head.[19]

Once the recruits had been accepted, the receiving officer had a priest administer the oath to them and then formed them into groups (*artels*), each member of which would be responsible for the conduct of the others, especially in case of flight. Detailed rules provided for the uniforming, feeding, and care of the men, with special emphasis upon kindly treatment and absence of cruelty toward them.[20] If, however, the recruits were guilty of offenses such as drunkenness, fighting,

16. P. Brant, "Zhenatye nizhnie chiny," *Voennyi Sbornik*, III (1860), 358-60.
17. Skorov, "Riadovoi Zinoviev," *Voennyi Sbornik*, III (1860), 432-40.
18. SVP, Pt. II, Bk. I, *O Prokhozhdenii Sluzhby*, arts. 179-80.
19. *Svod Zakonov*, IV, Bk. I, arts. 255-56.
20. SVP, Pt. II, Bk. I, *O prokhozhdenii sluzhby*, arts. 202-10, 215, 224.

small thefts, and first attempts at flight, the officers in charge had the duty to punish them with rods, up to fifty blows, before all the recruits. For more serious offenses such as two and even five attempts at flight, the punishment would be running the gantlet, through five hundred men from two to seven times.[21] If a recruit sought to escape military service by intentionally mutilating himself, the penalty was public punishment with whips from twenty-five to fifty blows; if he had inflicted a major mutilation on himself, he was then to go to perform auxiliary military service, to a penal battalion, or to permanent settlement in Siberia.[22] Obviously, from long experience the military authorities had learned that in dealing with the recruits they had to do with desperate men.

After the recruits had been collected, the officers of the Internal Defense Corps formed them into parties of varying sizes, from one hundred fifty to five hundred men each, according to plans worked out in the Inspector Department of the Ministry of War. These then set out for their respective destinations, accompanied by troops of the Internal Defense Corps.[23] The basis for distributing the recruits among the various branches of the service was largely their physical characteristics. The tallest and best formed men, not less than five feet ten inches in height (except in unusual circumstances), went to the Guards. The Grenadiers and infantry took average men from five feet three inches to five feet ten, the light cavalry took men of light build, while the artillery and engineers demanded powerful men; the engineers required that they could read and write.[24]

The reforming hand of Nicholas I, which dealt with so many aspects of military life in Russia, also extended to the handling of recruits. In 1831 he replaced the complicated, confused rules concerning them with a full Recruit Code, which clearly defined all the topics dealing with the treatment of recruits. The Tsar especially introduced changes to preserve their health, chiefly during their movement to their regiments. They should have comfortable and suitable uniforms; they were to be well fed; and while marching to their regiments they were to have every third day as a rest period, with more rest on very long marches. Nicholas ordered that the recruits were to go to nearby regiments, in order to avoid long journeys, and even urged moving

21. *Ibid.*, arts. 249-57.
22. *Svod Zakonov*, IV, Bk. I, art. 468.
23. SVP, Pt. II, Bk. I, arts. 225-30.
24. *Ibid.*, arts. 263-67.

them by wagons or by railway if this proved advantageous. Finally, in the late 1840's, he ended the practice of shaving the foreheads of the recruits. These measures brought good results in reducing the number of deaths and desertions among them. In the first ten years of his reign, there was one death for 483 recruits, and one desertion per 130. In the period from 1835 to 1850, the deaths had declined to one per 1,737, and the desertions to one per 833. These were substantial improvements.[25]

Once the recruits had arrived at their regiments, their training began. The Code of Military Regulations specified that for a week they were to have no formal training at all, in order to permit them to get adjusted to their new life, "under the protection and guidance of their tutors [diadki—old soldiers assigned to individual recruits], corporals, and sergeants," after which their instruction should begin, "patiently, carefully, and without the least overdoing." The instructors were enjoined not to curse, ridicule, or abuse the men, and when their superiors felt it necessary to punish, the penalties should be moderate and well justified to the culprit. Recruits should retain this status for not longer than six months.[26]

While these rules seem to have been sensible and humane, the men who had the task of training the recruits for the most part used a quite different system. In the early years of Nicholas' reign, at least, there was much harshness and brutality.[27] An account of the actual instruction of recruits in 1831 presents a grim picture. "Who does not know . . . the measures that were used . . . in training recruits? Rods and birches were regarded as necessary appurtenances of formation drill, and it seemed unthinkable to make a soldier out of a muzhik [peasant] without using whole wagonloads of these pedagogical aids." With the arrival of the recruits the camp became "a sort of stick-and-fist academy, where the beating of the men began at reveille and ended with taps." Latvian and Chukhny recruits, completely ignorant of the Russian language, had an especially severe time, as they did not understand the instruction or "the wisdom of military science."[28] These accounts both pertain to the early period of Nicholas' reign, and it has not been possible to find any that would show whether the system

25. "Istoricheskoe obozrenie," Sbornik IRIO, XCVIII (1896), 329-31.
26. SVP, Pt. III, Bk. I, O vnutrennem upravlenie voisk, arts. 638-45.
27. Epanchin, I, 15.
28. A. K. Gribbe, "Kholernyi bunt v novgorodskikh voennykh poseleniiakh v 1831 g.," Russkaia Starina, XVII (1876), 513-14.

of training recruits had improved by his later years. As will be seen, however, the treatment of the enlisted men in general did not show appreciable improvement during this period, so that probably recruit instruction did not moderate greatly.

While almost all the enlisted men entered the army as conscripts, there were some who entered military service as cantonists, at earlier ages, and then later joined the army, usually at eighteen. Most of the cantonists were sons of soldiers, who were "liable, as a result of their very origin, . . . to military service. . . ." This included all children of enlisted men at the time of their military service, sons of former Polish soldiers who were in Russian service, all illegitimate sons of soldiers and soldiers' wives and daughters, and most sons of discharged soldiers. Jewish youths of tender years who were taken for military service also became cantonists until they reached the age of eighteen. In addition, the authorities sent many orphans and children without proper support to the cantonist battalions, some at the age of eight or nine.[29] In addition to military training, the cantonists received education in reading and writing, arithmetic, geometry, military criminal law, and military problems. The older ones were taught various trades, such as tailoring, shoemaking, joinery, cooking, and baking. The younger ones learned to knit stockings or sew underwear. In addition, the St. Petersburg battalion of cantonists trained specialists such as telegraphers, musicians, topographers, and skilled engineers and artillerymen. Others were trained as auditors' assistants or as clerks.[30]

While the cantonists received educations, which few of the ordinary enlisted men obtained, the cantonist battalions were known as "the stick-academies," from the notoriously cruel treatment of the youths. In 1844 Gen. Filipson visited Baron Zeddeler, inspector of all the cantonist schools and battalions, who told him that there were more than 224,000 soldiers' sons, fit to serve "if only they lived through the barbarous training in the schools of military cantonists, where they systematically beat them and with a sort of soulless indifference destroyed them by cold, hunger, and increasing corporal punishment. This was called Spartan training, which should prepare hardened warriors."[31]

L. A. Seriakov, a member of the Academy of Arts, began his

29. SVP, Pt. II, Bk. I, *O prokhozhdenii sluzhby*, arts. 64-66, 73-83.
30. *Ibid.*, Pt. I, Bk. III, *Obrazovanie voenno-uchebnykh zavedenii*, arts. 1492, 2537-49, 1560-91, 1600-9.
31. Filipson, *Russkii Arkhiv*, XXI (1883), Pt. III, 155.

active life as a cantonist at the age of nine, when he became a singer with one of the army regiments, and then, at twelve he was sent to sing with a divisional choir, where he attended school and learned reading, writing, and arithmetic from a former seminary student. At fifteen he went to a half-battalion of cantonists where, because of his fine handwriting, he became a clerk and also a singer. Here life was truly hard. To please their brutal commander, his whole room of youths had to get up at two in the morning to scrub the floor, 210 feet long, on hands and knees with rags and cold water. At five they washed and dressed and began a long day of drill and classes. Drill was harsh and brutal. When practicing marching they had to stand in line on one foot, with the other leg extended and the chest arched, until the commander verified the precise alignment of the legs. If a man's chest did not protrude sufficiently, they jabbed him in the back with their fists, or the instructor kneed him in the back. If this failed to achieve results, at night they would bind the youth to a plank, with his shoulders drawn back.[32]

This half-battalion trained the youths either to be army clerks or for the carabineer training regiments, from which they went out, after three brutal years, to all the regiments of the army as model sergeants. The four carabineer regiments were filled largely with cantonists, "men who had been through fire and water, because in training them they almost in a literal sense regarded it as possible to torture nine out of ten to death, provided this tenth man survived as a model."[33]

After two years of this, perhaps because he had received fine training in artistic drawing from a gifted teacher, Seriakov became teacher of drawing and algebra at a school of cantonists. He also served as first sergeant of a company and every second day was the battalion sergeant major. It was almost unbearably hard work, as he was responsible for two hundred and fifty boys of from seven to fifteen. If a cantonist fell asleep in class, or had dirty buttons, he was to blame. Once a cantonist's boot broke open during drill, exposing his toe, whereupon the battalion commander raged against the sergeant, even calling for birches, and the latter was fortunate in escaping with a mere two weeks in the guard house on bread and water. He, in turn, felt forced to be savage in his treatment of the sergeants under him. If, in making rounds, he found some of the cantonists

32. Seriakov, *Russkaia Starina*, XIV (1875), 173-78.
33. *Ibid.*, p. 178.

playing cards and drinking vodka, he waked up their sergeant by striking him in the teeth, and sometimes he beat his cheeks until the blood ran. This was the way things were—it was each man for himself and he had to avoid punishment. He knew that for any slip-up he might receive two or three hundred birches, for nothing.[34]

During this period there were two desertions, and it was Seriakov's task to track down the men and bring them back. The penalty for this was five hundred birches apiece, after which they took the victims to the lazarette. When they had recovered, they were sent to penal companies.[35]

While the battalion commander was a harsh man, Gen. Andzhikov, commander of the brigade, was "a fierce beast in the full sense of the word." Once he entered the company room and, after looking carefully at the floor, shouted: "Battalion commander, company commander! What is this? I can't move!" There on the floor lay a tiny pebble, the cause of all the outcry. Then he looked to see how the cantonists aligned themselves at their cots. If a man did not do so properly, the general had a habit of immediately striking the delinquent with his full hand, and on one occasion, when he struck the extreme cantonist on the right flank, ten others also fell to the ground.

After about three years of this existence, Seriakov managed to secure assignment to St. Petersburg as a topographer, to which he marched, under heavy guard, with a convoy of prisoners. When he arrived there, a young man of twenty, his real life began, because, thanks to his artistic talents, he secured favorable notice and eventually was admitted to the Academy of Arts. This was truly an escape from darkness into light.[36]

Frightful as the life of the cantonists was, that of the ordinary enlisted man was not much better. For mistakes in drill or other failings the officers applied what they lightly termed "the toothpick"— which was a blow in the face. All drill and training of the soldiers was attended by unrestrained beatings. "To teach and to beat, to beat and to teach were at that time synonyms. If they said: teach him well —this meant: give him a good thrashing. For teaching they put to use fists, scabbards, drumsticks, and so on. Flogging with birches was practiced comparatively rarely," for this required more time and inter-

34. *Ibid.*, pp. 178-80.
35. *Ibid.*, p.182.
36. *Ibid.*, pp. 182 ff.

fered with the drill, while the fist and the drumstick were always at hand. While the officers sometimes beat the soldiers, it was chiefly the sergeants and *fel'dfebels* (first sergeants) who gave the beatings. They themselves had been beaten innumerable times, and now it was their turn to use the same methods. Likewise, the officers had been beaten at home and in school and so they beat the soldiers, believing that this was the only way to train them and that discipline demanded it.

The sergeants and *fel'dfebels* who were graduates of the "stick-academies"—the cantonist battalions—were the most ruthless applicants of this method. One such *fel'dfebel* moved along a company in formation, halted before a young soldier. "What are you frowning for? How many times must I teach you that you must look your superiors cheerfully in the eye!" The *fel'dfebel* accompanied this shout with a hard slap. The soldier somehow screwed up his eyes in an effort to look cheerful, but without satisfying his tormentor. "Look more cheerful! More cheerful, I tell you, you blockhead!" continued the *fel'dfebel*, raining blows on the man. Somehow the latter blinked his eyes and formed his lips into a painful grimace that satisfied the *fel'dfebel*, who moved off. An old veteran standing beside the young soldier tried to console him with the words: "That's what real service means, brother: they beat you and won't let you cry."[37]

Beatings by officers might be just as senseless. On December 27, 1827 an aide reported to Gen. P. D. Kiselev, chief of staff of the Second Army:

> I regard it as a duty to inform your Excellency that the treatment of the soldiers by Maj. Gen. Tarbeev is frightful! At the reviews made by him in his brigade they bring the soldiers out at nine o'clock, and sometimes at eight, and only let them go home in the late twilight. Extreme punishment by beating with sticks is administered each time to a whole platoon together; the soldiers, going out to drill, know beforehand, in numerical order, which platoon will catch it.[38]

Episodes like these led the Prussian Capt. von Höpfner, who had been with the Russian army in its maneuvers in 1839, to hold that anyone who knew the Russian army must conclude that both "officers and privates must wait for war with yearning." He added: ". . . no army in the world loves war for war's sake as does the Russian army; not for the sake of honor, fame, love of the fatherland, or of some other

37. Neizvestnyi, *Russkaia Starina*, LXXXII (1894), 110-11.
38. Epanchin, I, 111.

powerful motive, but solely for their own liberation from an unbearable situation."[39]

This treatment of the soldier seems to have continued until after the Crimean War. Prince N. K. Imeritinskii told in his memoirs of seeing Maj. Gen. Zherkov, commander of the Preobrazhenskii Guard regiment, use the "toothpick" against the soldiers of this crack unit. "His fist was huge, and he acted with this fist in very original fashion: with his knuckles he thundered on the neck, the back, and the cheekbones of the guilty man, and sometimes the knuckles travelled along a whole rank and threw back, like a cannon-ball, a whole half-platoon . . . ."[40] On one occasion, part of this regiment was drilling in a gloomy *manège*, when Zherkov informed one of the company commanders that he had three "dancers" (men whose posture was incorrect) in the third platoon. The captain could not detect the culprits, so Zherkov said calmly: "Permit me, I'll go to them at once!" He pushed into the middle of the column and, "in deathly silence, they heard how the commander's fists thundered against all three dancers." The lesson was a grim one, but, according to the author, after it the drill proceeded perfectly.[41]

In 1855 the situation had not changed, for an officer wrote in his diary:

> For a mistake in drill to thrash the soldier with the scabbard or the iron ramrod, so that they carry him off to the lazaret on his cloak —that meant nothing. To knock out some of his teeth with the guard of the saber, so that the soldier should look more cheerfully at his commander and hold his head higher, or to bore his back with the saber, so that the soldier throws his chest out—this means to know posture and how to train a soldier. If the soldier after such beatings coughs and spits blood, then he is glad. "Glory to God, your honor; in the fall they will assign me to the unfit."[42]

Even as late as 1858 a young infantry officer wrote in the leading military journal to complain about the use by the officers of "a deeply immoral and senseless phrase: 'For the Russian soldier the stick is necessary; he does not understand good words.' "[43] Another wrote of

39. Schiemann, III, 442.

40. Kn. N. K. Imeretinskii, "Iz zapisok starago Preobrazhentsa," *Russkaia Starina*, 1893, cited in Gershenzon, p. 81.

41. *Ibid.*, pp. 86-87.

42. K. A. Obninskii, *Russkii Arkhiv*, XXIX (1891), Pt. III, 338.

43. "Golos iz Armii," *Voennyi Sbornik*, I (1858), 79.

worthless officers "who apparently achieve wonders in teaching the soldiers the manual of arms and a broad stride by means of the 'toothpick' and kicks."[44]

According to the military regulations, the enlisted men had opportunities to voice complaints against mistreatment by their superiors. The brigade, division, and corps commanders had the duty of making inspectors' reviews of the regiments under them, so that each regiment was inspected six times a year, with the chief concern being the financial condition and the state of the equipment and other government property. At such occasions the rules called for removing the officers and non-commissioned officers from their units and then the inspectors asked the men whether they had any complaints against their commanders, either on grounds of cruel treatment or of failure to give them the supplies and money they were entitled to. In this way, if the men had serious grievances, they might receive redress. But the men well knew that unless their complaints were important and based on impressive evidence, it was safer not to utter a word of dissatisfaction. Indeed, the regulations expressly stated: "If the men bring unfounded complaints, as sometimes happens because of troublesome men among them, then after pointing out that they demand something they should not, the ringleader is to be punished as an example at once, before the whole company."[45] The enlisted men well knew that it was wiser not to voice complaints, and the inspectors were chiefly interested in observing the formalities, unless some grave failing showed up in the condition of the men and equipment or in the financial accounts. Hence "According to long established custom in our army the persons inspecting the regiments each year in their accounts presented everything in fine shape, pointing to minor defects, as it were, according to the established order."[46] The enlisted men also in most cases observed the formalities. Well coached beforehand to answer the inspector in his own words, to the question, "Are you satisfied with everything?" they replied: "We're satisfied with everything, your excellency." Asked: "Do you receive everything?" their answer was: "We receive everything, your excellency." Once, however, an inspecting general turned out to have a sense of humor, for he asked the men: "And do the commanders feed you with sugar buns?" and

44. *Ibid.*, p. 84.
45. SVP, Pt. II, Bk. I, *O vnutrennem upravlenie voisk*, arts. 792, 800-6.
46. Bobrovskii, IV, 31.

the men promptly echoed him: "They feed us with sugar buns, your excellency."[47]

Although the inspections of the regiments gave the soldiers almost no relief from harsh treatment at the hands of their superiors, many of them did obtain a measure of relaxation through the practice of quartering regiments in rural areas for seven or eight months of the year, when rain and cold and muddy roads made life in camp and maneuvers impossible. The men were often lodged in widely dispersed localities, so that, except for a period when each company or squadron was on duty at regimental headquarters, there was little or no work for them to do. In fairly prosperous Russian provinces, the soldiers got on well with the peasants, in whose households they lived, often helping them with the farm work. Except when on duty they wore peasant clothes.[48]

In order to compensate the peasants for the burden of feeding the soldiers, the military regulations provided that the regiment should issue to them the full ration of two and one-half *funts* of flour and one-quarter of a *funt* of grits per day. These provisions usually went to the funds of the village commune, which used them to pay taxes; they rarely went to the householder who fed the soldier. In many of the more prosperous villages the inhabitants renounced all provisions from the regiment and fed the soldiers gratis. When this happened, the regiment could sell the unneeded provisions and apply the money to the artel funds, which during the summer months enabled the soldiers to eat more meat and fish. It was not the individual peasants, however, that renounced the soldiers' provisions, but the township officials,[49] who for reasons best known to themselves took this step. But in any case, in the more prosperous of the Russian provinces the soldiers lived quite well in winter quarters.

Relatively few of the soldiers, however, had their winter quarters in these areas, as strategic considerations required the stationing of large elements of the army near the western frontiers. In 1851 the government made an effort to equalize the burden of quartering the troops, by levying a universal quartering tax, which was used to recompense the localities that had to maintain troops temporarily quartered there. This tax did not by any means cover the cost of

47. "Iz ocherkov nedavnei stariny," *Russkii Arkhiv*, 1871, cited in Gershenzon, pp. 89-90.
48. Krestovskii, pp. 516-20.
49. Anichkov, *Voennoe khoziaistvo*, pp. 85-86.

quartering the troops and was distributed chiefly to the towns.[50] Thus, as before, the peasants of Bessarabia and the Lithuanian and other western provinces, which were miserably poor, bore the main burden.

While this state of affairs was bad for the peasants, it also was very bad for the health of the soldiers. In his memorandum to Alexander II, Count Rüdiger pointed to the evils of quartering the soldiers in the western provinces, whose peasants were ruined and among whom illnesses were rampart because of their poverty and poor nourishment.[51] An officer of the General Staff wrote that after the bad harvests in the western provinces in 1844-46, the mortality among the troops stationed there increased noticeably.[52] Another officer wrote in 1858 that it was very hard on the troops to have to share the miserable peasant diet of boiling water, onions, and very black bread, usually made with bran and the bark of trees.[53] In another passage this same officer explained that the diseases in Lithuania were not a result of the west or southwest wind, as was often alleged, but were the consequence of bad harvests.

> Who has seen the ruined huts of the local population, its degenerating, feeble, weak cattle, who has tried its bread, always mixed with chaff, and in bad years with tree-bark, who has seen, how with the first appearance of spring grass whole villages spread out on the meadow, quarreling over each little blade for their own nourishment, who, finally, has heard at night the groaning of sufferers ending their existence without shelter, he, even without investigating the causes, and even leaving aside the Jews, on whom they always blame it, will say only that the climate does not cause it.[54]

The conclusion necessarily follows that, while soldiers in more prosperous locations lived fairly well in winter quarters, those in the poor western provinces benefited little from their winter's rest.

Another way in which the soldiers gained respite from the terrors of the drill-field was through the labor on construction projects in which they sometimes took part. In 1841, some eighteen regiments performed work of this sort, and by 1843 the number had increased to twenty-eight. By 1847 only seventeen regiments were so engaged. While such work was in process, two-thirds of the men drilled and

50. *Ibid.*, pp. 223-31.
51. SVM, I, Danilov, *Istoricheskii ocherk*, Prilozhenie 6, 28.
52. Il'iashevich, "Statisticheskoe izsledovanie smertnosti v nashei armii," *Sbornik sochinenii ofitserov*, II, 33.
53. N. Obruchev, "Iznanka krymskoi voiny," *Voennyi Sbornik*, I (1858), 469.
54. *Ibid.*, p. 462.

stood guard in nearby towns, while one-third labored. This change in their routine was not, however, an unmixed blessing, as often the men had to arise at one o'clock in the morning in order to reach their jobs by 4:30. Hence the men were tired when they began work. In addition, the work-sites were often very unhealthy. On several of the projects the troops so engaged had an illness rate of forty per cent or more, while the 17th division, which in 1843 worked on the Moscow-Volga canal, had 49.8. In 1841 the troops working at Sevastopol and the eastern shore of the Black Sea had a morbidity rate of 96.1 per cent.[55]

Disease was a constant factor in the life of the Russian soldier, to a much greater degree than in other European armies. One reason for this was the fact that the Russian troops were actively in combat to a greater extent than any other army, except possibly that of Her Britannic Majesty. In 1826 the Persians attacked in the Transcaucasus, and after their defeat the Russian forces, both in Asia and in Europe, were at war with the Turks. The Transcaucasian forces escaped without grave losses from disease, in part because they lived in camp, often in high mountain areas. Although they suffered an epidemic of the plague in 1828, prompt measures brought it to a speedy end. Only in the deadly swamps of Georgia did disease take a heavy toll. In 1828 the total losses from battle and disease were not over thirty-two hundred out of a force of twelve thousand.[56] In the Balkans at first there was little disease, but, by the autumn months, about half of the army fell victims to fever, dysentery, typhus, and other disease. Over one-fifth of the total (22,023 men) died of disease, while battle losses were slight. In 1829, although the Russian forces won a series of victories, they were ravaged by disease, which laid low almost three quarters of their number. In 1829 almost half of the army died. More died in 1830, after hostilities had ended, bringing the total of deaths from disease in the three years to 118,745.[57]

The Polish campaign of 1831 was another costly episode, largely because of hopes of a quick and easy victory, which led to insufficient preparation of hospital facilities. A combination of effective Polish resistance and difficult logistics dragged out the war, during which the troops fell victim to cholera and other diseases. Only 7,122 were killed

55. Il'iashevich, in *Sbornik sochinenii*, II, 39.
56. Zatler, *O gospitaliakh*, pp. 128-33.
57. *Ibid.*, pp. 111-27.

in action, while wounds and sickness carried off over 85,000 men, bringing the total deaths for the eight-month period to 93,000. No good figures are available for the other medical losses in this war; it seems safe to say, however, that over two hundred thousand men became sick but survived.[58]

No detailed information is available concerning the losses of the Russian forces in the Caucasus area during the reign of Nicholas I from disease, but they must have been large, far more than from the swords and bullets of the enemy. In the mud forts at the mouths of the rivers along the Black Sea coast, the men died at a rapid rate from the fierce malaria that almost no one escaped. In other garrisons malaria was not so prevalent, but dysentery, typhus, cholera, scurvy, and respiratory diseases undoubtedly inflicted heavy losses. This was a steady drain on the Russian army from the beginning to the end of the reign of Nicholas I. In 1859, the first year for which figures are available, the cases of disease amounted to 1,437 per thousand, which means that everyone was sick at least once, and about half were sick twice in the course of a year.[59] Probably the rate was even higher for the period of Nicholas I.

In 1849 the Russian army embarked on its three-month campaign in Hungary. Once more strong hopes led to insufficient medical preparations, as Field Marshal Paskevich sent hospital equipment for only 4,350 patients, although for an army of 360,000 men the rules called for beds for 36,000 men. For the most part the Russian forces used Austrian hospitals and personnel, supplemented with Russian surgeons and supplies. This proved to be far from sufficient, as in July a cholera epidemic struck, carrying off thousands of soldiers on the march. In all, 57,193 Russians entered the Austrian hospitals, while many more filled Russian lazarettes. A total of 10,253 men died, 7,414 of them from cholera.[60] In this campaign only 708 men were killed in battle, and 2,447 were wounded.[61]

In addition to the disease among troops on campaign, those on duty within the Empire also took sick in large numbers. In the first twenty-five years of the reign there were 16,022,875 cases of disease, of which 1,028,650 died. Cholera proved to be the most deadly malady, followed closely by typhus and typhoid fevers, and diarrhea.

58. *Ibid.*, pp. 135-46.
59. Il'iashevich, in *Sbornik sochinenii*, II, 43-44.
60. Zatler, *O gospitaliakh*, pp. 147-61.
61. P. M. Andrianov, "Vengerskii pokhod v 1849 godu," in Grishinskii, VI, 160.

Intermittent fevers were the most common ailment, although they did not cause many deaths.[62]

In the decade from 1841 to 1850, the number of sick averaged 655 per thousand. The military statistician who presented these figures, however, held that they were too low, because the soldiers quartered in peasant households, with little supervision for more than half the year, were very reluctant to report themselves sick, but tried to cure themselves with peasant remedies. Only when the case became grave did it come to the attention of their superiors.[63]

The death rate in the Russian army before the Crimean War was unusually high, averaging 37.4 men per thousand, and probably was higher, because of incomplete reporting, whereas other European armies of the period had death rates of about 20.0 per thousand, about double that of the civilian population of the same age group. The death rate in the Russian army was often above that of the total Russian population, which was one out of 27 or 28 persons (35.0 or 36.0 per thousand). The death rate of the population from twenty to forty years of age was not over 12.0 or 13.0 per thousand. Thus the deaths in the army were three times as great as those in the corresponding civilian age groups. The chances of dying in the army were three times as great as among civilians. This excessive death rate in the army compelled the drafting of from thirty-two thousand to thirty-six thousand recruits a year to maintain it at strength, whereas with a death rate of 15.0 per thousand in the army, a draft of only 13,500 recruits annually would have been enough.[64]

The high death rate in the army was not caused by the climate or any other local factor, as, except for high infant mortality, the death rate in Russia was not much greater than elsewhere. It was a result of the organization, economy, and system of training of the army itself. "In scarcely any of the European armies did the soldier find himself in a more unfavorable position than our Russian soldier. . . ."[65] This was particularly true of the recruits. "It is well known that our recruits have died especially in the first period after they entered service. It could not be otherwise. . . ." The despair, the strangeness of the new situation, and above all, the brutal treatment that the recruit experienced often cost him his life. Proof of this is given by the Cau-

62. "Istoricheskoe obozrenie," *Sbornik IRIO*, XCVIII (1896), 371-74.
63. Il'iashevich, in *Sbornik sochinenii*, II, 42-43.
64. *Ibid.*, pp. 6-7. These figures do not agree with those cited on p. 234 *supra*.
65. *Ibid.*, pp. 7-8.

casus reserve division which, situated in a fine location, with plenty of room, for the years 1842-52, had a death rate that averaged 44.6 per thousand, almost certainly because it received numerous recruits for the Caucasus Corps. In 1842 its death rate soared to 95.6 per thousand, probably because it had just received a large draft of recruits.[66]

Another factor contributing to the high death rate was the system of quartering the troops upon the peasantry. When there was a bad harvest in the fall, the worst effects of it made themselves felt in the spring, when the peasants' supplies of food were practically exhausted. Since the soldiers ate the fare of the peasants they, too, would have to endure privation in the hungry spring months. This produced an especially high death in the first half of the year, 13 per cent higher than that in the last six months. ". . . moreover, in our army, as in others as well, one-quarter of all the dying are tuberculous."[67]

There was considerable variation in the death rates of the different parts of the army. The Active Army, which formed three-quarters of all the troops, had a mortality rate higher than the rest of the army, except for the invalid companies and the Corps of Internal Defense, which contained many old soldiers. The Caucasus Corps had an especially high death rate, averaging about 67.0 per thousand, which was caused almost entirely by deaths from disease: only 5.8 per thousand annually were killed by the enemy.[68] Within the regular forces, the infantry had the highest mortality, with the cavalry and artillery the lowest.[69]

By 1851 and 1852, after the effects of the Hungarian campaign had disappeared, the mortality rate in the army declined,[70] probably as a result of reforms in the treatment of recruits, better feeding in the army, and efforts to improve the hospitals.

Throughout his reign Nicholas devoted much attention to reform of the military hospitals. In fact, nine months before he came to the throne he investigated and punished abuses in one of them. During his reign he frequently visited the hospitals, usually unexpectedly, and he required his aides to do the same. His reign produced several important pieces of legislation on hospital matters, especially a Regula-

66. *Ibid.*, pp. 9-10.
67. *Ibid.*, pp. 17-18.
68. *Ibid.*, pp. 25-33.
69. *Ibid.*
70. *Ibid.*, p. 11.

tion for the permanent hospitals, in 1828. In all, the Ministry of War issued forty-three directives or regulations pertaining to hospital affairs during the reign of Nicholas. Unfortunately, the Tsar's efforts to eliminate the corruption in hospital accounting, did not, as has already been seen, end such abuses, and if anything, increased greatly the paperwork and red tape. Nevertheless, probably in no preceding reign had so much been done to improve the medical care of the soldiers. Indeed, by 1851 the number of hospitals had risen from 95 in 1825 to 189, or had practically doubled.[71]

Helpful as these reforms of Nicholas I were, like others that he made in the military system, they were limited by the social conditions of the times and did not eliminate the causes of many of the abuses against which he struck. Moreover, the improvement in the lot of the enlisted men that occurred in the early 1850's was soon reversed by the Crimean War, which, especially in the last two years, produced such a complete breakdown of the medical service that mortality from disease in the army again increased drastically. The subsequent chapters on the Crimean War will deal with this topic.

Another significant reform introduced by Nicholas I was the reduction of the term of military service from twenty-five to fifteen years for men with records of good conduct, who were put on "indefinite leave" for the balance of the term, with the obligation to perform six weeks of service each year with the troops. They were subject to recall to active duty in time of war.[72] This law, which was published in 1834, applied to drafted men of the Russian Empire, but did not apply to supernumerary troops, and cantonists (including Jews). Soldiers in these categories had their term of service shortened to twenty years, instead of fifteen.[73] In 1839 the provision for indefinite leave was extended to enlisted men of the kingdom of Poland who in 1831 voluntarily entered the Russian army.[74] In addition to the shortening of the term of service, in 1834 the Tsar decreed that men who had served for ten years with good-conduct records might receive permission to go on short-term leave of from twenty-eight days to five or six months. Also men released from hospitals in

71. SVM, III, Pt. II, *Glavnyi Voenno-Sanitarnyi Komitet*, 12-35.
72. SVP, Pt. II, Bk. II, *O prokhozhdenii sluzhby*, arts. 1204-5.
73. *Ibid.*; Dobrovol'skii, comp., *Rukovodstvo zakonovedeniia. Polnoe rukovodstvo dlia voenno-uchebnykh zavedenii* (2 vols.; St. Petersburg, 1853-1854), II, 197-98.
74. II, PSZ, 1839, No. 12794.

weakened condition were to have long furloughs so that they might recover their strength.[75]

In 1842 *Russkii Invalid*, the army newspaper, published statistics showing that from 1833 to 1842, inclusive, 149,235 men had been released from service on indefinite leave. Almost all of them had taken up farming, either for themselves, or helping relatives. About ten per cent had not yet established themselves. Only a handful—less than one-tenth of one per cent, had been brought to trial for various causes.[76] This evidence strongly supported the Tsar's statement in a decree of January 25, that the system had worked very well.[77]

On the other hand, voices were raised against this innovation. In his gloomy report on "The Condition of the State in 1841," Gen. Adj. N. Kutuzov said that it presented "the greatest revolutionary danger" for Russia, as the peasants would be burdened by taxes to feed these idlers. He declared that with his own eyes he had seen how they wandered over the face of Russia, especially in summer. They went from village to village where there were church holidays and three-day drinking bouts. Only a few of these men settled down and, as they had no ties or loyalties, they would present a real danger to the state. He feared "this huge mass of idle men, knowing how to handle weapons, and drawn by some Cromwell or other to destroy the existing order!" He added that these men would prove of little value in time of war, as they would have spent years in idleness and would not accept discipline and duty. Moreover, the shorter the term of service, the more men would have to be drafted and trained, which would cost the country dearly.[78]

This criticism does not seem sound. For one thing, the country was not flooded with idle veterans, as the number of men released from the army was not over fifteen thousand per year, from an army of one million men. Moreover, unless the statistics in *Russkii Invalid* were incorrect, the number of furloughed soldiers that came to trial in court was so small as to indicate that very few of them were leading peasant revolts. Perhaps a more valid criticism of the measure was that it did so little to ease the burdens of the soldiers. Real relief for them did not come until after the Crimean War, in the series of measures that culminated in the Army Reform of 1874.

75. SVP, Pt. II, Bk. II, *O prokhozhdenii sluzhby*, arts. 1162-63.
76. *Russkii Invalid*, No. 25, Jan. 31, 1842, p. 96.
77. *Ibid.*, No. 21, Jan. 27, 1842, p. 80.
78. Kutuzov, *Russkaia Starina*, XCV (1898), 525-26.

Even when a man received his indefinite furlough from the army his future was not brilliant. Probably few of them could have saved any appreciable amount from their private's pay of two rubles eighty-five kopecks per year. Even a sergeant drew only four rubles five kopecks per year.[79] Usually when he received his discharge all that the soldier could count on was his share of the money in the artel fund (a group savings account in the keeping of the regimental administration). It consisted of any money that the soldier might have deposited with the artel; money received as rewards: sometimes the Tsar would bestow a ruble on each man of a regiment after an especially successful review; money deducted from his pay by decision of the soldier; and money he had earned by doing hired work. Each soldier was supposed to have at least seven rubles fifty kopecks in the artel fund, and some had more.[80] For most soldiers this was all the money that they had when they left the service.

As for the men incapacitated by wounds or disease, there was some provision made. If not badly crippled, they served on invalid commands, where they received state rations and soldier's pay. Men who were severely wounded or crippled, and to some extent their families, had the right to the aid of the Alexander Committee for the Wounded, founded in 1814. It sought to secure positions for them, or to have them assigned to the Chesme and Izmailov Old Soldiers homes, founded under Nicholas I, or to have them stationed as caretakers at the monuments of the War of 1812. Nicholas broadened and systematized the protection furnished old soldiers, but at the end of his reign the shortage of funds reduced the amounts available.[81]

The assistance provided for old soldiers improved considerably during this reign in comparison with what it had been under previous rulers, when veterans sometimes had to beg in the streets for bread. On the other hand, as was the case with most of the reforms of Nicholas I in the realm of military affairs, it was not sufficient to change the rule that the lot of the soldier was a hard one, from the day he put on his uniform to the end of his days.

79. II PSZ, 1840, No. 14116.
80. Anichkov, pp. 416-17.
81. Dobrovol'skii, II, 234-35; SVM, XIII, D. I. Berezhkov, *Aleksandrovskii komitet o ranenykh*, 94-95, 128.

CHAPTER XIII. INDOCTRINATION

One of the most surprising aspects of the Russian army of the period of Nicholas I is that somehow it developed an *élan*, an *esprit de corps*. The enlisted men who composed it, who had been torn from home and family, often forever, who suffered brutal treatment at the hands of sergeants and officers, and on whom lay crushing burdens of privation and disease, would seem to have been most unpromising material for building an army that had spirit. Yet from it such an army was formed, although it is difficult to explain how. This chapter is devoted to an attempt to suggest by what means the military authorities accomplished this feat.

The first conclusion that becomes clear is that the latter made no attempt to present organized, systematic printed propaganda to the enlisted men. In a country where the overwhelming majority of the people were illiterate and where no effort to train the soldiers to read and write was possible, it would have been a waste of time and money to try to indoctrinate the soldiers by means of the printed word. Moreover, unless the government could present the soldiers with free copies, it was practically impossible for them to obtain reading matter, as the tiny pay that they received did not permit the buying of books and periodicals. Probably for these reasons the army newspaper *Russkii Invalid* contained little but official announcements of promotions, transfers, and assignments, and similar matters, along with a small quantity of world news. There also were occasional articles on technical military developments. Only rarely were there articles written in what purported to be the language of the common soldier and expressing his views. These compositions, which related experiences of old soldiers in former wars, breathed patriotic fervor, religious zeal, and eagerness to smite the enemies of the Great White Tsar. They probably entertained and perhaps inspired the officers who read them, but like the rest of the paper, probably almost never reached enlisted men. In similar fashion *Voennyi Zhurnal* (*Military Journal*), the military magazine for most of Nicholas' reign, had no material for popular consumption, but contained articles on military history and technical developments, with only an occasional article on the value of religion for the soldier. Much more popular in nature was *Chtenie dlia soldat* (*Reading for Soldiers*), which began in 1848 and continued on into the reign of Alexander II. It contained short stories, poems, episodes from Russian military history, proverbs and sayings, and much religious material that preached the sacredness of the soldier's duty to faith and fatherland. This periodical also probably had officers as its reading public, as, for the reasons cited above, doubtless very few enlisted men ever saw it.

Probably the most effective writer of inspirational material for the rank and file was Gen. I. N. Skobelev, who entered the army as a private and served for twelve years in the ranks. Commissioned in 1804, he fought all through the Napoleonic Wars, rising to the rank of colonel in 1813. He died as a general of the infantry in 1843. He had a number of articles in *Russkii Invalid* which were published as a volume in 1833 with the title of *Podarok tovarischam* (*A Gift to Comrades*). A second volume in 1839 bore the title: *Besedy Russkago invalida, ili novyi podarok tovarishcham* (*Talks of a Russian Old Soldier, or a New Gift to Comrades*). According to a highly enthusiastic review in *Voennyi Zhurnal*, by command of the Tsar the authorities distributed both the *Podarok tovarishcham* and its continuation, *Vecher chesmenskikh invalidov* (*An Evening of the Old Soldiers of Chesme*), "in a sufficient number of copies in the military educational institutions, in the battalions of military cantonists, in the troops of the Guard and the army. Both books form a full theoretical and practical course of the soldier's life."[1]

The first of these, which was typical of Skobelev's writing, took the form of letters of enlisted men in 1812 to a friend. They were full of expressions of loyalty to the Tsar and religious sentiments: the soldier had been chosen from birth to defend the fatherland and would attain heaven by death in battle. The writers told of their colonel's speech to them, telling them that they and God were the sole hope of the Tsar, and that they must defend the churches of Moscow and the fatherland against the invader. To this they had answered: "You always were our own true father; we love you. Command us: we are ready for death." The writers asserted that the Russian troops should

1. *Voennyi Zhurnal*, 1851, No. 1, p. 152.

follow the example of Minin and Pozharskii and Dmitrii of the Don and other heroes of the past. Declaring that the Tsar, not Kutuzov, had been the savior of Russia by standing firm in the face of the foe, they lavished extravagant praise on Alexander, telling of the delight of the troops when he appeared before them.[2]

This was a rare example—if not the only one—of mass distribution of inspirational printed matter to the troops. While Skobelev had couched it in a style that had considerable appeal for the troops— the religious and patriotic themes were cleverly interwoven—it is, however, questionable how effective this effort was. Although the cadets and in part the cantonists may have read these books, very few of the enlisted men of the army could read. Many of the sergeants were literate, but the reading aloud of material of this sort does not appear to have been a feature of their relations with the privates. Therefore, these propagandist efforts probably had little direct effect upon the great mass of the soldiery.

Skobelev also published a book of orders of the day that he issued to recruits and soldiers who served under him from 1834 to 1836. This volume, however, seems to have had very little circulation and hence his proclamations, in their printed form, must have had no significant effect upon the troops.

In addition to the works of Skobelev, there were a few others of the same sort. In 1835 Viktor Lebedev published a small volume, *Pravda Russkago voina* (*The Truth of the Russian Warrior*), which was printed by subscription of seventy-four generals and officers of the Guards. Its theme was a fervently patriotic recital of the might of Russia, the merits of "the autocratic Sovereign, blessed and protected by God," and his warriors—generals, officers, and enlisted men —eternally loyal to their banner and to their oath. Two decades later, during the Crimean War, a book of anecdotes about the brave deeds of Russian soldiers in that conflict made its appearance in Moscow.[3] These works, however, like the others already mentioned, probably had little influence on the rank and file.

Proclamations, orders of the day, and other utterances of commanders to their troops probably achieved more than written indoctrination, especially where the commander was admired and respected

2. I. Skobelev, *Podarok tovarishcham, ili perepiska russkikh soldat v 1812 godu* (St. Petersburg, 1833), *passim*.
3. Viktor Lebedev, *Pravda russkago voina* (St. Petersburg, 1835); *Doblestnye podvigi russkikh voinov v voinu s Anglo-Frantsuzami i Turkami* (Moscow, 1855).

by the soldiers and had the gift of arousing their enthusiasm through imaginative words that had the ring of sincerity. The great Suvorov had had that gift, and although there were no Suvorovs in the reign of Nicholas, a few generals such as Skobelev, A. P. Ermolov, P. D. Kiselev, K. F. Toll, A. N. Lüders, and especially K. A. Khrulev in the Crimean campaign, showed ability to inspire their men. Most of the generals, however, either lacked the confidence of their subordinates or apparently had little talent for inspirational utterances. Thus it seems likely that appeals of this sort were not especially efficacious in building up *esprit de corps.*

To a considerable degree Nicholas I himself proved effective in presenting himself to the masses of soldiers as their friend and benefactor who had their interests at heart and was always trying to eliminate failings and abuses in the military machine. He loved to organize vast military spectacles at which he appeared in superb uniforms and with his fine military bearing, tall figure, and clear, resonant voice, seemed every inch the soldier-monarch. In the great reviews and parades of thousands of troops in resplendent uniforms, enlivened by gleaming banners, prancing steeds, and martial music, many of the soldiers must have felt that they were members of a noble fellowship sworn to perform the holy duty of protecting faith, fatherland, and the White Tsar, the Anointed of God. Moreover, Nicholas knew how to be gracious and winning and in his orders of the day could praise and encourage them and win their confidence. Furthermore, when reviews and inspections went well, he gave generous rewards. From the coronation ceremonies at Moscow in 1826 each soldier of the Iamburg Uhlans carried away nearly eight silver rubles given them by the Tsar. The next year he again reviewed this regiment and, delighted with their horsemanship, gave each man five silver rubles.[4]

In 1839, on August 26, there was a great celebration at the consecration of the monument on the battlefield at Borodino. The assembled troops heard the Tsar's order of the day, reminding them how in 1812 the Russian troops had fought for faith, Tsar, and fatherland. God had punished the evildoers, who had left their bones all the way to the Neman, and the Russian forces had pursued the remnants even to Paris. After proclaiming eternal glory to the men of 1812, Nicholas told the assembled troops that now *they* were the hope and support of the sovereign and of Russia and should follow the

4. Krestovskii, pp. 383 and 385.

example given at Borodino. Then, after a church procession in the presence of the Tsar, Metropolitan Filaret of Moscow performed the *Te Deum*. Next, two hundred and seventy cannon thundered in salute and the voices of one hundred and twenty thousand men roared hurrah! The Tsar personally escorted the banners off, and then returned for the review.[5] At this celebration, Nicholas, well pleased with the dragoons, granted them large rations of meat and liquor and bestowed on them almost eighteen thousand silver rubles.[6]

Badges of merit and decorations were another means of indoctrinating the enlisted men with zeal and loyalty. Ten years of good conduct won a man a stripe, and for twenty years he received three stripes and the Badge of Distinction of St. Anne, which brought the holder exemption from flogging and double pay while in service, and a pension of full pay upon retirement. Men who distinguished themselves in battle received the coveted silver Cross of St. George. In addition to the prestige that it carried, it brought the holder an increase of one-third of his pay and an increased pension for his widow when he died.[7] After the capture of Varna in 1828, the Tsar granted 184 Crosses of St. George to the men of the Guards Grenadier regiment alone.[8] To the force of Col. Passek in the Caucasus, which in 1843 had made an outstanding defense of their position against overwhelming odds, Nicholas granted one hundred and fifty Crosses of St. George.[9] And in 1854 P. Alabin wrote in his diary: "Today. . . they gave the St. George's crosses to the enlisted men who especially distinguished themselves in the action of June 25 . . . . This time the Prince sent 104 George crosses to the enlisted men . . . ."[10]

Perhaps the most effective means of indoctrination of the soldier was a sort of catechism appended to the regulations, with the title of "Memorandum booklet for enlisted men." This document, in the form of questions, with lengthy answers, was the basis for intensive drill of the enlisted men by their sergeants. This study, which was known as *"punktiki,"* was not to the soldiers' liking, but it was rigidly required. The answers to the questions, which the soldiers had to learn by heart, contained insistent instructions as to the duty of the soldier and the

5. Potto, pp. 168-69.
6. *Ibid.*, pp. 442-43.
7. SVP, Pt. II, Bk. II, *O nagradakh vo vremia prokhozhdeniia sluzhby i pri otstavke*, arts. 112, 144, 147, 239, 255, 356-57.
8. Puzanov, p. 187.
9. Zisserman, *Istoriia*, II, 341.
10. Alabin, *Pokhodnyia zapiski*, II, 237.

necessity for blind obedience to superiors. The first question, "What is a soldier?" had as its answer a long discourse stating that a soldier was one "on whose powerful shoulders lies the obligation, dear to soul and heart, to defend the holy Faith, the Tsar's Throne, and the native land; to strike down foreign foes and to wipe out domestic enemies, . . . A bad son of the Church cannot be a son of the Fatherland. . . ." To be a good soldier, the man must "love God, Sovereign and Fatherland; submit blindly to the Commanders; be brave and fearless in battle; perform all deeds of service without complaint, with submissiveness, with zeal, with good will, and bear with Christian patience all hardships. . . ."

The next questions called for definitions of the various kinds of enlisted men, including the recruit. His first obligation, the answer stated, "is to observe exactly the oath given before God; to have full trust in his Commanders, as in fathers who love their children and unceasingly care for them."[11]

Question 6 dealt with the sentry. He, according to the required answer, "is obliged sacredly to fulfil his orders; . . . and he should rather die than leave the post where he is, without orders to do so." There followed a series of examples of the proper performance of duty by a sentry. In 1806 as a soldier in a small town stood on guard before the treasurer's office, a fire swept the town, threatening to burn his house and family. When urged to go to the rescue, he replied: "If God and good people don't save them, let them burn, for I shall not leave my post." Later the flames threatened to engulf him, but he still stood fast, answering advice to flee with the word, "But God! and my oath!" He escaped with his life, although his home was burned, and presumably his family with it. When the Tsar learned of his devotion, he gave him his discharge from service with a gift of five hundred rubles and an annual pension.

In 1834 a sentry at the Artillery Laboratory in St. Petersburg refused to leave his post, although fire threatened to burn his sentry box. Generals and officers ordered him to leave, but he replied that he could go only ten paces from the sentry box, and he stayed on until he was removed by the officer of the guard. "Private Kuliabin showed by his conduct how firm the Russian soldier is in the holy oath given to God and Sovereign, and he resolved to burn rather than to violate

11. SVP, Pt. II, Bk. I, *O vnutrennem upravlenii voisk*, Prilozhenie k st. 248.

his duty. . . ." For this observance of his duty the Tsar rewarded him liberally.[12]

Regarding the nature of the oath, the answer in the catechism was that it "is a pledge given before the face of God on the cross of the Savior and on His Holy Gospel: to serve God and Sovereign with faith and truth; unconditionally to submit to commanders; patiently to endure. . . ; not to spare the last drop of blood for Sovereign and Fatherland. . . ." As for rewards for fulfilling the oath, "Who is true to the holy oath and lays down his life on the field of battle, will receive from God the Heavenly Kingdom; and who returns from war alive will have glory and the grace of the Sovereign." Finally, this passage quotes the words of Suvorov: "Friends! Fear God; love the Sovereign; remember the oath; obey your commanders. Act bravely, and all will fall before you. God is with us, and who is with them?"

A section on the importance of the banner and the obligation of each soldier to defend it with his life was followed by extensive examples of supreme devotion by various Russian soldiers and a statement of the rewards that the soldier might receive. Finally, after setting forth the requirement that each soldier should learn firmly the names of all persons of the Emperor's family and the names of his commanders, including the commander in chief, and their quarters, and information about his regiment—the catechism ended with a tribute to the musket and the bayonet. "The bayonet is invincible in the hands of the Russian soldier! Against it no enemy strength will stand; but it is necessary for each one to know also how to shoot accurately. The musket for the soldier is his constant friend and comrade, who protects his life and opens the road to victory and glory."[13]

This catechism, which was painstakingly drummed into the heads of the soldiers by their corporals and sergeants, probably was the most effective method of indoctrination that the men encountered. They disliked the task of learning it, but they had no choice; and the phrases that they eventually learned became part of their mental equipment—an ideology that helped to make them accept the new life of the soldier.

Another important part of the indoctrination of the enlisted men was the example and the teaching of old soldiers, who had grown

12. *Ibid.*
13. *Ibid.*

accustomed to army life and felt a pride in momentous deeds that they had had a part in. In time this feeling of pride in the traditions of their regiment and the army's victories over the enemy made the new men identify themselves with it. Friendships and sympathy with fellow-soldiers also helped in time to build up a feeling of group loyalty, both to their regiment and to army and country as well. Finally, there were the soldiers' proverbs. "The bullet will find the guilty man" and "No man can escape death, but no one has to die twice" were sayings that induced fatalism and stoicism in the face of danger. And the proverb, "Prayer to God, and service to the Tsar, are never in vain" assured them that the good soldier would surely receive his deserts.

It is obvious that through all these efforts at indoctrinating the rank and file there was great emphasis on the religious influence. While much of this was a natural result of the Orthodox traditions of Holy Russia, the authorities also consciously used religion to strengthen the loyalty and devotion of the soldiers. The officer's handbook in use in 1850 reminded the commanders that they must support the religious feeling of the soldiers by giving a strict example of performing the rituals of the church and of punishing those who violated them, "not forgetting . . . that religion is the sole consolation, refuge, and hope of the soldier in all dangers. For the Holy Church and the Orthodox Tsar he cheerfully goes to a thousand deaths in the firm trust that beyond the grave this sacrifice will not remain without reward." For this very reason, the commanders should strive to secure good and effective priests as chaplains with the troops to instill cheerfulness and trust in God in the men. Nothing, the book asserted, could so raise the morale of the soldier as could the magnificent rituals of the church. To convince oneself of this, "one need only look at them when preparing themselves for battle and accepting in deep silence the holy blessing, with the singing of the majestic hymn, "Save, O Lord, Thy People. . . ."[14]

The army regulations contained precise rules on religious observance. The regimental commander had an obligation to see that all men under him should make confession and receive communion once a year and perform all the obligations of the Orthodox faith. The regimental priest should say mass every Sunday in the church and on the regiment's saint's day. The rules required all officers to

14. Vladislavlev, pp. 39–40.

enter the church with the men and not to leave before the end of the service.[15] The regulations also provided for the rights of Jews and Moslems to have religious worship performed by their respective clergy on their holy days,[16] but, as the vast majority of the soldiers were Orthodox, the emphasis was strongly on the favored position of their church. As for the Old Believers and sectarians (the latter had a variety of faiths, most of them mystical in nature and vaguely resembling Protestantism), they received grudging toleration if they were not actively hostile to the official church and if they performed their military duties. Most of the Line Cossacks of the North Caucasus and the Kuban were fanatical Old Believers, and there also were Molokane, Dukhobors, and other sectarians among them. As they proved to be "the best, bravest, and most trustworthy regiments,"[17] they were let alone.

There are innumerable instances of religious observance in the Russian army. In 1827, during the campaign against the Persians, the Carabineer regiment held its saint's celebration on St. Peter's day, deep in Armenia.[18] In 1828, in the campaign against the Turks, Gen. Bistrom, on taking command of troops besieging Varna, brought with him a large ikon of St. Nicholas the Wonder-worker, which he always took with him on campaigns, "and placed it on the barbette of Redoubt no. 2; before it a lamp constantly burned. All the soldiers who passed by crossed themselves, praying to the All-Highest for victory." Later, after beating off an attack of the Turks, the troops held a *Te Deum* of thanksgiving. Before the ceremony, Gen. Bistrom, with bared head, "indicated to them the ikon of the holy St. Nicholas at Redoubt no. 2 with the words: 'Pray! Here is the one to whom we owe this victory!' "[19] Capt. Helmuth von Moltke, who was with the Russian forces in the Balkans, observed: "The soldier held strongly to religious ceremonies and crossed himself at every meal, also in each camp a tent was set up as a church and daily mass was read."[20] On December 6, 1839, Gen. V. A. Perovskii, in command of an expedition in the far-off steppes of Central Asia, wrote to a friend that, in spite of a temperature of 27 degrees below zero Fahrenheit, they performed a *Te*

15. SVP, Pt. III, Bk. I, *O vnutr. upravl. voisk*, arts. 372, 375, 380.
16. *Ibid.*, arts. 386-94.
17. Filipson, *Russkii Arkhiv*, XXII (1884), Pt. I, 380.
18. Bobrovskii, IV, 103.
19. P. Voronov and V. Butovskii, *Istoriia leib-gvardii Pavlovskago polka* (St. Petersburg, 1875), pp. 302 and 305.
20. Moltke, II, 253.

Deum on the Tsar's saint's day and fired cannon. All joined in sincere, devout prayer, "for only with God's help can we hope to overcome the elements and the enemy; we feel that if our prayer is not now heard, we shall be lost."[21]

In like manner, numerous examples appeared during the Crimean War to indicate the continuing importance of religion in the Russian army. As the Pavlovskii regiment prepared for the campaign in 1854, Maj. Gen. Gol'tgoier ordered little crosses for all the soldiers, which he had consecrated and distributed to them. "Wear these crosses on your necks," he said, with his blessing. "Grenadiers!" he continued, "We are preparing for a campaign; the Cross of our Lord, may it be a protection, fortress, and the strength of God against foes of Tsar and Fatherland. . . . Grenadiers, if God is with us, who is against us?"[22] At Sevastopol, Admiral Kornilov began the formal defense of the fortress with a religious procession, as the troops stood expectantly at their battle stations. "Clergy with images, banners, and crosses performed the procession of the Cross, slowly moving along the whole defense line. At almost every fortification the *cortège* stopped to perform a *Te Deum*, sprinkle the troops with holy water, and bless them with the sign of the cross."[23] Even within the Kornilov bastion, in the Malakhov tower—the key position—at the height of the siege there was religious observance. ". . . opposite the entrance hang several ikons; before them lamps are quietly burning, and with bright little flames tapers glitter. It is just like a little shrine."[24]

These examples from Russian army life, which could easily be matched with many others, indicate that religion was deeply interwoven with the life of the populace and had great influence upon the people, so that the military authorities could easily employ it to induce the enlisted men to be submissive to their officers and loyal to the divinely sanctioned monarch, whose enemies they should smite, in the name of the fatherland and the holy faith. Probably most of the commanders used religion in this way because to them it seemed the proper way to achieve what was vitally necessary, as there is reason to think that most of the respected generals were sincerely religious

---

21. "Pis'ma grafa V. A. Perovskago k A. Ia. Bulakovu," *Russkii Arkhiv*, XVI (1878), Pt. II, 38-39.

22. Voronov and Butovskii, p. 382.

23. Dubrovin, *Vostochnaia voina*, pp. 192-93.

24. V. Kolchak, *Voina i plen. 1853-1855 gg. Iz vospominanii o davno perezhitom* (St. Petersburg, 1904), p. 22.

and believed that support for the Tsar and war against his foes and those of the fatherland was work to which God and the Holy Church gave their blessing. Nicholas himself was apparently free from doubts about the sacredness of his task of ruling Russia, for to him the alternative to the existing state order was too dreadful to contemplate. Of course there were some military men who were not devout and who were cynical in their use of religious appeals to the soldiers. Prince A. S. Menshikov, commander in the Crimea in 1854, does not seem to have been religious, and no doubt there were others. But probably the vast majority of Russian officers and generals of this period were more or less sincere believers.

Even those commanders who were good Christians were not averse to using religion as an instrument for swaying the masses. As has already been seen, Nicholas set the precedent by attempting to use divine authority to calm the rebellious soldiers in December, 1825, when he instructed the Metropolitan of St. Petersburg and his clergy to admonish them. On a smaller scale, when peasants rioted against the authorities, the commander of the troop detachment sent against them had the task of trying to secure their submission through the exhortations of a local priest before he used force. Hence, when the military colonists of the settlements around Novgorod, crazed by an epidemic of cholera, in July, 1831, rose to slaughter their officers, it was only natural for the military authorities, who for the moment had no reliable forces at their disposal, to attempt to calm them by using religious ceremonies and the words of priests to remind them of their duty to submit to their superiors.

The colonists, who believed that their deaths resulted from poison administered by their officers instead of from cholera, were thoroughly out of hand. Since all troops of the area had gone off to fight the Poles, Lt. Col. Panaev, who had the task of pacifying one battalion of the colonists, decided to use religion and the name of the sovereign to restore order. He arranged for the performance of a mass on July 19, followed by a *Te Deum* and a prayer for salvation from cholera, while a procession from the neighboring convent would bring their miraculous ikon to the settlements. But before the mass could take place, the colonists again became hostile, and only the arrival of the religious procession with the ikon prevented a fresh outbreak. Four days later Panaev arranged that the local bishop should say a requiem for the slain officers. But when the bishop repeatedly spoke of the deceased as "innocent slain servants of God," the colonists became angry and threatened the bishop, who had to leave in haste.

As the Tsar had expressed a hope that the colonists might be brought to a state of repentance, Panaev planned to achieve this by means of religion. As his scheme called for performing service in each of the four churches every day during the summer fast period and to prepare the people for confession and communion, he arranged with the bishop to send five intelligent monks to the district, "who could counsel the erring at confession and bring the killers to repentance. The monks performed their work zealously." On August 1 there was a parade, a *Te Deum* of thanksgiving on the birth of the Tsar's son, and consecration of the waters of the river Volkhov. For two weeks after this the ritual of repentance was performed in all the churches. Finally, on August 18, the colonists attended a mass at which their priest, whom they had earlier sought to kill, told them that he could not leave them in doubt as to their fatal error, which had impelled them to raise their hands against their commanders, shedding the blood of innocent men. Later he added that they had "killed and outraged innocent men . . . ." There was no further trouble.[25]

In another district the battalion commander, in order to restrain the colonists from outbreaks, arranged with Father Voinov, the priest, to hold service on July 19 and to exhort the people against disorder. But before this could be done, the revolt began. The pastor, crucifix in hand, met the mob, but although they kissed his cross, they went on, and when he tried to reason with them, they called him a poisoner in league with the officers. On the 19th, however, the church was filled with colonists, who did not protest when the priest urged them to come to their senses. They were by no means submissive, however. But before the vesper service some of the colonists requested of Father Voinov that on the next day, a Sunday and the day of the Prophet Elias, there should be a solemn mass in the main church, with both priests present, to be followed by a religious procession to a nearby cloister, much revered by the populace. So on the following day the priests performed a liturgy, with a long sermon, before a large and reverent congregation, which lit an unusual number of tapers before the ikons. Then the religious procession set out to the cloister. After

25. *Bunt voennykh poselian v 1831 g. Razskazy i vospominaniia ochevidtsev* (St. Petersburg, 1870), pp. 104-5, 118-20, 124-27.

this the colonists dispersed and went back to work, and there was no more trouble.[26]

According to the Code of Military Regulations it was proper to use religious influence against subversion in still another fashion. If at confession any person should "declare to his spiritual father about intent against the honor and health of the Sovereign, or of intent to provoke rebellion and treason" and in so doing did not show repentance or readiness to abandon such a course, "then the spiritual father should at once report this, as such a confession is not a proper one, for the one who confesses does not repent of all his illegal acts." In making such a report the confessor should not reveal all the details of the disclosures, but should only say that the person, whom he should clearly identify, had evil intent toward the sovereign or the state. When the malefactor was under arrest, however, and the criminal investigation had begun, "the confessor is obliged to reveal what he heard, without any concealment, in all the details."[27]

Religion, as the incidents cited show, exerted great influence on the minds of the enlisted men and at times could bring them to submission, especially after the rebellious fervor had lost some of its strength. Its traditions and thinking had, over the centuries, gained considerable power over the peasants and hence over the soldiers who were drawn from them. Moreover, since the religious appeal was closely connected with the strong nationalist and patriotic sentiments of the Russians, it proved to be a highly effective means of indoctrinating the army. Undoubtedly, a part of the success of this indoctrination came from the fact that few of the soldiers could see any alternative to the establishment—to the existing system. After the failure of the Decembrists in 1825 there was no organized revolutionary movement until 1848, when poorly conceived efforts to change the system appeared. There were, of course, sporadic outbreaks and mutinies in individual troop units, but these were usually the result of desperation among the soldiers, who had no hope of success nor plans for converting their isolated risings into a nationwide movement. Thus the official indoctrination, which had as its allies inertia on the part of many as well as regimental traditions and *esprit de corps*, was able to induce a spirit of resignation and acceptance on the part of the soldiers which proved sufficient for the needs of the government.

26. *Ibid.*, pp. 149-53.
27. SVP, Pt. V, Bk. II, *O voennom sude*, arts. 57-58.

It is practically impossible to determine the prevailing attitude of the enlisted men of the army, because they almost never gave expression to it orally and never in writing or in print. What has been published on this topic has come from officers, whose testimony is not entirely convincing, as they rarely were close enough to the privates to know how they really thought and felt, and the judgment of the officers probably was colored by their social and hierarchical background. Moreover, the accounts and memoirs of the officers almost always dealt with campaigns and battles and only rarely told about the men in times of peace. Nonetheless, even this fragmentary evidence is worth considering.

One consistent theme of these accounts is the gayety of the enlisted men, whether on campaign or actually in battle. For example, in 1831 the Kiev Grenadiers, moving to storm the wall of the city of Warsaw, thundered out a peasant song that seemed to mock the Polish Revolution:

"Akh, why did they fence the garden?
Akh, why did they plant the cabbages?"[28]

In 1839 Col. R. K. Freitag, ordered to break the center of the enemy position in the Caucasus, advanced with two battalions of infantry. "With singers and dancers in front the detachment made a bayonet charge."[29]

P. Alabin, in his notes on the Russian campaign of 1853 on the Danube, describes the advance in the same terms: "We go joyfully, boldly, with loud songs and music. At the head of each company, as near as possible to the singers, gathers a crowd of jesters and men eager to hear the happy chatter and to laugh to their hearts' content. What is not talked over . . . ? What sort of commander is not picked apart into little bones?" This noisy chatter was replete with coarse but accurate and often malicious sayings, along with puns, bywords, and tales, frequently interrupted by bursts of loud laughter or jovial songs. What was really remarkable about this was that this cheerfulness continued in spite of fierce summer heat, the heavy knapsacks and the winter clothing of the soldiers, and marches of nearly twenty miles. ". . . the Russian soldier is submissive, patient, and capable of bearing great privations, if only his food is pretty good, his father the com-

28. Smitt, *Istoriia*, III, 547.
29. Glinoetskii, *Istoriia*, II, 217.

mander is with him, not estranged to them [the soldiers], and, finally, knows how to make himself loved."[30]

The author analyzed the soldier's attitude toward war in realistic terms. Enthusiasm over the issue at stake was not noticeable among them; but they went ahead gaily, "because the Russian soldier always goes joyfully in a campaign, because on the campaign there is no tiresome drill, and at times there flows an extra drink of vodka; change of place and lodging cheers the glance; finally, because, where you are going always seems better than it was where you came from." Above all, it was a welcome relief from summer camp in peace time, "which the soldier does not like, because of the difficulties of camp service."[31]

In encampment also the soldiers enjoyed themselves. While building huts they sang sad Russian songs; but at leisure they had simple amusements. They played tag and other traditional Russian games and presented crude pantomimes.[32] In the Transcaucasus army also the soldiers showed a spirit of gayety. After the unsuccessful and bloody repulse of their assault on the Turkish fortress of Kars they gradually returned to normal, and again began to play their games, did acrobatic tricks, and enjoyed other diversions.[33]

Other observers mentioned the bravery and endurance of the soldiers, which often brought success in battle, in spite of the mistakes of their commanders. In the campaign of 1829 against the Turks these failings were redeemed by the spirit of the troops, "their brilliant moral qualities, which never left them and served as guarantees of success in the grave minutes of trial." Moltke, who observed the Russian troops in this war, was of this opinion.[34] An officer of the Caucasus army in 1854 marvelled at the endurance of the soldiers, who often were quartered for the winter in a dark buffalo-shed with rotting manure. "But our soldier will sing a song even in that sad molehill." The officer saw in this the reason for Russian success over the Turks. "The Russian soldier is an astonishing person: he goes to sleep with a cobblestone under his head, he is well fed with black biscuits and water, and he sings a song in a buffalo-shed—that is his superiority."[35] Tolstoi in his "Sevastopol Stories" has given repeated testimony to the quiet, matter-of-fact bravery of the soldiers in the besieged fortress, who went

30. Alabin, *Pokhodnyia zapiski*, I, 25-26.
31. *Ibid.*, I, 2-3.
32. *Ibid.*, pp. 76-77.
33. I. Pisarskii, "Pod Karsom," *Voennyi Sbornik*, II (1895), 140.
34. Epanchin, I, 116.
35. Esaul, *Voennyi Sbornik*, III (1860), 187-98.

without a murmur to assignments that they knew meant almost certain death. Here was the true greatness of Russia.

And yet they were very human, and even pitiful at times. An officer writes of seeing a veteran cavalryman weeping because, on the morning before they attacked at Balaklava, his horse refused to eat. The soldiers firmly believed that the horses knew when they would be killed in battle, which they showed by refusing food. The man was heartbroken at the prospect. He told his officer that for seven years they had been together and had become so devoted to each other that the horse would not permit anyone else to take care of it. "Tomorrow I'll be an orphan, and there will be no one to love."[36]

Another characteristic of the Russian soldiers that observers reported was an innate friendliness and kindness to captured enemy soldiers. After the fall of Varna in 1828, the Turkish defenders, who were permitted to go back to Turkey, were too weak to endure the cold and hunger on the march and many of them died soon after setting out. Prince Madatov sent out Russian patrols to collect the sick, and at night set pickets on the roads, with fires burning and warm food. Many soldiers individually took Turks to their huts and shared their food with them.[37] In 1831, when one of the defeated Polish armies retreated into Austria, it left many stragglers without boots, in rags, and exhausted with hunger and weariness. Many of them were mere striplings. At this sight the Russian soldiers expressed strong sympathy, forgetting all hostility to their former foes.[38]

In 1854 a Turkish deserter came over to the Russian forces besieging Kars. The dragoons who captured him fed him heartily and then asked him to do the Turkish manual of arms. The deserter, who entered readily into the spirit of things, proved to be a fine mimic and greatly amused the dragoons, who sent him away with a pocket jingling with copper coins.[39]

Even during the bloody fighting at Sevastopol, the Russians were not personally antagonistic to their opponents. There was a curious little episode in 1854, when men in rifle pits before the British lines noticed a rabbit in the open. After killing it with a lucky shot, a

36. "Vospominaniia o Balaklavskom dele 13-go Oktiabria 1854 goda," in Dubrovin, ed., *Materialy*, IV, 43.

37. *Zhizn' Madatova*, p. 162.

38. "Izvlechenie iz zhurnala Gen. Golovina 1831 goda," *Voennyi Sbornik*, III (1860), 46.

39. Esaul, *Voennyi Sbornik*, III (1860), 375-76.

Russian dashed out of his hole to recover it. The English, seeing this, withheld their fire and even cheered the daring hunter. He thereupon took off his cap and bowed to them, and then made his way back to safety.[40] Some months later, after a bloody night sortie, the warring forces arranged a brief truce to collect bodies. Both armies came out of the trenches and went in crowds to and beyond the demarcation line. Paying no attention to the lines of guards, they gestured and exchanged tobacco in full amity, until their commanders enforced mutual isolation.[41]

Another attitude of the soldiers upon which observers commented was that they appeared to admire Nicholas I and his family. In October, 1854, two of his sons came to Sevastopol and greeted the troops in their father's name, to the apparent delight of the men.[42] Likewise, when, after the disastrous Battle of Inkerman, the Grand Dukes rode into the bivouacs, the soldiers crowded round, feeling that the youngsters, who had heard bullets whistle during the battle, were kindred souls. They talked freely with the visitors and told them details of the combat. The youths gave gold to wounded men and had their adjutants write down each man's story of the battle. They also visited the hospitals, requested the Cross of St. George for many of the men, gave them all sorts of aid, and looked after the families of those killed. The soldiers regarded them as guardian angels and cheered and blessed them.[43]

When, in February, 1855, some two hundred men of the Semenov-skii regiment learned of the death of Nicholas I, they groaned and there were dismayed cries: "It can't be! It can't be!" After leaving the church where they had taken the oath to Alexander II, many men wept, and some asked: "What will happen now?" Others said gloomily: "The father of the soldier is no more."[44] On March 1, an assembled body of troops at Sevastopol learned of the Tsar's demise, whereupon the men "crossed themselves; many muttered prayers; others fell to their knees and bowed to the ground, praying for the repose of the soul of the departed! When I began to read the manifesto, the soldiers, officers, generals—all wept."[45]

40. Alabin, *Pokhodnyia zapiski*, II, 246.
41. *Ibid.*, p. 192-94.
42. *Ibid.*, III, 64.
43. *Ibid.*, II, 96-97.
44. Kartsov, I, 100-1.
45. Alabin, *Pokhodnyia zapiski*, II, 178-79.

While the evidence presented is far from definitive, it is possible to draw from it a few tentative conclusions. First of all, in spite of the harsh treatment that they had received, the soldiers proved themselves effective in time of war and often redeemed by their courage and determination the mistakes of their commanders. They knew little about the causes of war, but they felt that it was their duty as Russians and as Christians to fight for Tsar and fatherland. In addition, they often welcomed war as a blessed relief from the brutalities and ennui of the paradeground. The informality of the campaign permitted a display of high spirits that rarely appeared in peacetime. When, as often happened, disease and battle took heavy toll, the soldiers displayed remarkable patience and endurance in the face of hardships that would have daunted many others. These resolute warriors, however, could feel sorrow and on occasion were able to display kindness and even friendship for the foe. Finally, they still seem to have believed that Nicholas I was the friend of the soldiers and they regretted his passing.

How much of this result was achieved by sheer brute force, which left the soldier no alternative to submission, cannot be determined, although it appears probable that this was an important factor. But to this one must add indoctrination of the enlisted men by their superiors, by the clergy, and also by the old soldiers, who kept alive the traditions of the regiment. As there was no rival propaganda effectively competing for the allegiance of the soldiers, the official indoctrination was sufficient to make out of the conscripts generally resigned and submissive soldiers in time of peace and devoted and effective warriors in war.

CHAPTER XIV. THE ARMY AND REPRESSION

Any doubt as to the ability of the authorities to keep the armed services under firm control must vanish before the evidence that the military leaders found it possible to use the army for a variety of repressive measures against the people of Russia and above all against the peasant millions. When one bears in mind that the vast majority of the soldiers were themselves of peasant origin and might be expected to feel sympathy for the tillers of the soil, the importance of this fact becomes evident. In part, of course, the government could take a leaf from the book of the Romans: soldiers of Polish origin were sent to the Ural area or to the Caucasus, while Orthodox soldiers of the Russian provinces were stationed near Catholic Warsaw. Probably almost never were soldiers stationed in the region from which they had come. As a result, they rarely established close bonds with the populace of the regions where they were on duty and hence were not likely to refuse to act against them. Whether it resulted from the use of this device or from compulsion, the influence of military tradition, or active indoctrination, the fact is that the former conscripts no longer had close bonds with the people from whom they had sprung and were, for the most part, submissive instruments in the hands of the authorities.

One duty that the government imposed on the troops in the first part of the reign of Nicholas was quarantine service against the plague, which had appeared in the Danubian Principalities. A cordon line was established late in 1824, with eight infantry regiments spread out over a distance of eighteen hundred *versts*. Just before the accession of Nicholas I, Gen. Kiselev, chief of staff of the Second Army, wrote to Count Diebitsch, chief of the Emperor's staff, that, while they were winning against the plague, their losses from scurvy and from desertions were greater than from the pest. The men, without shelter, were subjected to extremes of heat and cold, all of which "wears the soldier out, and ends with the most complete collapse of morale.

Only our soldiers can endure this service with patience and obedience, with which nothing can be compared. But, finally, there is a limit to all this."[1] During this period the troops had 7,368 men sick, 440 dead, and 147 desertions. Fortunately, by early 1827 the plague had almost ended, so that the cordon could be removed.[2] In 1830, with the cholera raging, the government used a division of uhlans to maintain a cordon between Moscow and Tver, with three-man pickets and mounted patrols behind the picketline.[3] According to Schiemann, dragoons, who were also used in the quarantine cordons near Moscow, for heavy bribes let peasants through their lines, which saved the city from starvation.[4] This seems to have been the last use of troops in quarantine lines, as no further references to this practice have come to light.

Guard duty in cities and towns was another service of the troops. The four corps of the Active Army on the western frontier, which changed locations every three years so that they would not establish ties with the people, did a great deal of guard duty in the cities,[5] and usually during the winter period one company or squadron of each regiment was on guard in the headquarters town.[6] Where local officials were unable to catch thieves and robbers or to cope with contrabandists, they had the authority to call on the nearest army units, if the Internal Defense forces were unable to handle the problem. Moreover, it was the duty of the military authorities to detail sufficient forces of men to deal with plagues of locusts.[7]

In St. Petersburg, guard duty, along with the incessant parades and reviews, was an important part of the work of the regiments of the Guard. In turn they sent out detachments to various posts in the city, where they posted a sentry, while the officer and the rest of the guard retired to the guard room, having stacked their muskets. When a general came by, the sentry rang a bell, and the men seized their muskets and formed to present arms at the command of their officer. Often at dusk the Grand Duke Michael, wrapped in his cloak, would drive by in his sleigh, to see if they would notice him properly.

1. A. P. Zablotskii-Desiatovskii, *Graf P. D. Kiselev i ego vremia. Materialy dlia istorii Imperatorov Aleksandra I, Nikolaia I, i Aleksandra II* (4 vols.; St. Petersburg, 1882), I, 235-36.
2. Epanchin, I, 178.
3. Krestovskii, pp. 391-93.
4. Schiemann, III, 33.
5. Sakovich, *Russkaia Starina*, XXII (1878), 381.
6. Anichkov, p. 470.
7. Vladislavlev, p. 459.

If they failed, on the next day they would all sit in the guardhouse.[8] While the detachments had the obligation of preserving order and arresting wrongdoers in their vicinity, this function actually seems to have been secondary to their ceremonial role.

A more clearly repressive role of the troops was that of helping to collect arrears of taxes from delinquent state peasants. In 1835 Count Kankrin, minister of finance, secured permission from Nicholas I to apply a system of "military execution" to them. This consisted of quartering detachments of troops in the villages, which had to feed the troops—from ten to fifty of them, under the command of sergeants —"with improved food without compensation." Sometimes the drag-onnades achieved their purpose in less than a week, while in other cases they lasted from nine to eleven days. In some instances they lasted over a month. The cost of feeding the soldiers and the atmosphere of terror that the latter created spurred the peasants to frantic efforts to rid themselves of the unwelcome guests, chiefly by "selling their extra cattle and other property." Twelve villages of Ekaterinoslav Province, containing twenty-one thousand male peasants, managed in this fashion to pay off more than one hundred and fifty thousand rubles, albeit they almost bankrupted themselves in the process. This practice apparently ceased in 1837.[9]

Troops also served to put down mutinous workers. In 1841 workers at a foundry in the Urals rose in desperation. As their defiance of the authorities was stubborn, the troops that marched against them opened fire, killing 33 men and wounding 114. A military court then dealt summarily with the survivors; out of 270 workers who came before it, they flogged every tenth man. They drafted twenty-five workers into the army, and the four leaders of the movement were exiled to penal labor.[10] While similar developments may have taken place elsewhere, they were probably not numerous, as there were not many industrial workers at this time.

Peasant outbreaks, however, were frequent and the government regarded the use of troops to subdue them as almost a routine matter. The military regulations provided that in most cases the provincial authorities should use the troops of the Internal Defense Corps to restore order. It was the duty of all government forces to assist the

8. "Vospominaniia Evgeniia Petrovicha Samsonova," *Russkii Arkhiv*, XXXII (1884), Pt. II, 134.
9. Druzhinin, I, 202-4.
10. Fedorov, *Russkaia armiia*, p. 17.

authorities, and if asked, the commander of the nearest military command had the obligation to send a force of sufficient strength to handle the matter.[11] A manifesto of May 12, 1826, provided that if a military force had been brought to an estate, the rebellious peasants were to be subject to court-martial.[12] According to V. I. Semevskii, noted historian of peasant affairs, in the whole period of Nicholas there were 556 peasant uprisings (although he believed these figures to be too low). The number increased rather steadily until 1850, when a slight decline took place. Out of the 261 outbreaks for which information was available, in 132 instances the authorities used armed force for suppression, followed by punishment. In many cases, however, the disorders were quelled by mere exhortation of the peasants or by flogging of some of their number.[13] I. I. Ignatovich, writing in 1902, listed 712 peasant outbreaks from 1826 to 1854; almost half of these were in the last decade. While the number increased fairly steadily, the Tsar, he found, was most severe in his early years: in the 1830's troops were sent to estates in 259 cases. The number of cases of court-martial dealing with the peasants was eighty for the whole period, with only three in the last four years. The troops fired on the peasants only four times in twenty-nine years, while cold steel came into play only twice. The largest disturbances came in 1855 and 1856, over the rights of men who joined the militia.[14]

While in most cases the peasants submitted in the face of overwhelming force, there were a few armed conflicts between peasants and the military. In 1826 peasants in the province of Pskov, seeking to rescue some comrades confined by troops, had a real clash with the soldiers in which eight peasants were wounded, two of them fatally. After this they became submissive and permitted the flogging of many of their number.[15] In 1830 peasants of Penza, already rebellious against increasing exactions, rose in revolt when a levy of recruits was proclaimed and hid in the woods. Officers sent to gather the fugitives met armed opposition and were wounded and driven out. When a force of troops marched in, the peasants at first took to the woods, and then actually attacked the soldiers, who had to fire three volleys of

11. SVP, Pt. III, Bk. I, *O vnutrennem upravlenii voisk*, arts. 457-58, 466-67, 473.
12. II PSZ, 1826, No. 515.
13. V. I. Semevskii, *Krest'ianskii vopros v Rossii vo vtoroi polovine XVIII i pervoi polovine XIX veka* (2 vols.; St. Petersburg, 1888), II, 595-97.
14. I. I. Ignatovich, *Bor'ba krest'ian za osvobozhdenie* (St. Petersburg, 1902), pp. 195-206.
15. *Ibid.*, pp. 80-88.

ball cartridges to make them submit. The officers of the detachment then set up a military court, which sentenced two ringleaders to run the gantlet, followed by assignment to a fortress penal battalion. Ten others were beaten with rods and then drafted into the army. In the province of Perm fear of a change in status that would result in new exactions led state peasants and Bashkirs in 1834 to fight outright battles against troops sent against them. Although the soldiers won these encounters, the outbreaks continued into 1835 and spread over much of two provinces. To suppress them the Minister of War ordered out an infantry division, four Don Cossack regiments, three sections of artillery, and troops of the Internal Defense. When Count Perovskii put down the insurrection, the Tsar thanked him personally. The sequel was punitive expeditions to the villages, which made participants run the gantlet, beat them with rods, or sentenced them to penal labor, exile, or drafting into the army.[16]

Another large-scale uprising came in the province of Vitebsk in 1847. The peasants, already unruly, suffered three bad harvests in a row, which brought them to desperation. Their landowners, who should have aided them in their distress, were in debt and could not help them. Many of the peasants became convinced that they would be resettled elsewhere with state aid and would receive their freedom. Strong in this belief, they moved, in bands of from two to five hundred each, with their wives, children, and belongings, to Pskov and St. Petersburg. Although the authorities told them to go home, many refused, and four infantry battalions and other troops moved against them and finally forced them to go back. The authorities then tried ninety-five leaders of the movement and punished them severely, and flogged over four thousand others with birches.[17]

Bad as these incidents were, they were surpassed by the revolt of the military colonists in 1831. From the first, as has been stated, the peasants compelled to accept the status of colonists had been highly dissatisfied, but under Alexander I their protests produced no improvement. Under Nicholas the opposition increased. Early in 1826 the first company of Arakcheev's regiment mutinied, demanding to be freed from their status. The sole result of this was to bring down ferocious punishment upon them.[18] In 1829 the peasants of a number

16. Druzhinin, I, 224-41.
17. Semevskii, *Krest'ianskii vopros*, II, 600-4; Ignatovich, p. 202.
18. P. P. Evstaf'ev, *Vosstanie voennykh poselian Novgorodskoi gubernii v 1831 godu* (Moscow, 1934), p. 92.

of villages rose in revolt when they were converted into colonists, fighting pitched battles with uhlans who came to subdue them. After the uhlans had killed several of them with their pikes, the peasants barricaded themselves in their village and continued their defiance. Finally the troops surrounded the settlement and bombarded it with shells and grapeshot, after which infantry stormed it with much carnage. Fifty-two rebels were killed and over sixty were gravely wounded, of whom many died later. Some fifty soldiers were wounded. The resistance collapsed, a court-martial began its work, and the usual harsh punishment followed.[19]

Although Nicholas had doubts as to the value of the military colonies, in his accession manifesto he declared that their "fortunate condition" was the result of the labors of Alexander I and his "fatherly care."[20] In the spring of 1826 Gen. Adj. Demidov reported that in his inspection of part of the Novgorod settlement their condition was excellent: the posture and marching of the men, the training battalions, and the schools of the cantonists. He mentioned "the majestic buildings of the staffs," the "astonishing order" of the drillfields, the "incomparable" hospitals, the "elegant cleanliness" of the homes of the colonists, and the excellent state of the farm work.[21] Following this, the Tsar issued orders that put the military colonies directly under his personal Staff.[22] Arakcheev, who thus lost his control over them, retired to his estate.

In 1828, the Tsar and his favorite, Count A. Kh. Benckendorff, visited part of the military colonies at Staraia Russa. They were struck by the magnificent buildings, the fine roads and sidewalks, and other signs of success. Hence, although Nicholas realized that the flood of complaints to Alexander indicated that this system required fundamental changes, "one should . . . put to use, as far as possible, these results of the unswerving will of the Emperor Alexander, which have swallowed so many millions and the labor of so many hands."[23] The foreign problems of 1828-31, however, diverted the Tsar from this project until an explosion forced him to act. Indeed, he even added

19. Ibid., pp. 93-94.
20. Schilder, Nikolai I, I, 310, cited in Evstaf'ev, p. 79.
21. SVM, II, Istoriia Gosudarevoi svity, Prilozhenie, 129-30.
22. II PSV, 1826, No. 644, cited in Alan Douglas Ferguson, Russian Military Settlements, 1810-1866 (unpublished dissertation, Yale University, 1953), p. 214.
23. N. K. Schilder, "Imperator Nikolai I v 1828-1829 gg. (iz zapisok grafa A. X. Benkendorfa)," Russkaia Starina, LXXXVII (1896), 21-22.

thousands of additional men to the military colonies in the first years of his reign, both near Novgorod and in the Ukraine.[24]

Although the immediate cause of the outbreaks at the military colonies in the region of Novgorod and Staraia Russa was the cholera epidemic that swept over Russia in 1831 and the stringent quarantine measures that the government imposed, there were many underlying causes that induced a rebellious attitude on the part of the colonists. The "householders"—the peasants whose farming formed the basis of the colonies—had to feed the soldiers quartered on them, on what proved to be insufficient resources. The land was poor and the meadows and pastures were too far from the barns. Although fine foreign cattle were brought in, many of them died, as there was not enough fodder for them.[25] According to one of the Tsar's aides, the economic situation of the Novgorod military colonies was hopeless, as the land was not sufficiently productive, and there was too little of it. Whereas one household in the fruitful steppe region required five *desiatinas* of plowland and three of meadows, the Novgorod householder had only four and one-half *desiatinas* of relatively infertile arable land and one and one-half of meadow and pasture on which to feed his family and two lodgers. Hence the peasants could barely feed their families, to say nothing of the troops quartered upon them. But actually, he asserted, the military colonies were only for show and the authorities had completely forgotten about agriculture. To make matters worse, the villages were built in single rows of houses, from two to three *versts* long, so that many fields were four *versts* or more from the houses. This made it impossible for the peasant, with his poorly fed horses, to haul enough manure from his barn to fertilize his field properly, as three round trips would mean thirty *versts* for the horse. During the harvesting season the same difficulties would appear. Moreover, the pasture was often far from the barn, provided poor grass, and often lacked water.[26]

In the light of this testimony, it is not surprising that the colonists and their lodgers complained that their food was never enough to last more than twenty-three or twenty-five days a month. They ascribed this to the demands of their superiors that the cattle should

24. II PSZ, 1826, No. 644; 1828, No. 1837; 1829, Nos. 2495, 2496, 2498, 2739, cited in Ferguson, pp. 214-17; Evstaf'ev, pp. 80-81.
25. Grishinskii, V, 142-43.
26. M. Semevskii, ed., *Graf Arakcheev i voennyia poselenyia, 1809-1831* (St. Petersburg, 1871), pp. 199-200.

be fat and sleek, which put before them the choice of feeding the animals on flour and going hungry themselves, or of facing severe punishment.[27]

The observer also remarked on the bad living arrangements of the peasants, with four householders and four lodgers in each house, along with the cattle and poultry. As the yards were small and shelter for the animals was insufficient, bitter quarrels among the householders were inevitable. He added that the condition of the peasants had deteriorated badly under the regime of the military colonies, so that "they are ruined."[28]

In addition to all this, the peasants were under stern military discipline and had to spend long hours at drill. Moreover, their sons were now enrolled in cantonist schools, where they were subject to the brutal treatment for which these schools were notorious. It is no wonder that the visitor wrote that the officials in command of the military colonies "have finally succeeded in turning the hearts of the peasants against the Sovereign, their benefactor."[29]

As for the regular soldiers who were quartered on the colonists, their lot also was unenviable, as they complained of the impossible demands that their superiors imposed on them. They spent three days each week in drill, from six to eleven o'clock in the morning, and from two to ten in the evening. On alternate days they dug ditches, cleared land of stones and stumps, or drained swamps. They told the investigator that the tasks set for them were "beyond their powers," so that they had to finish them on holidays, which left them no time for relaxation. They asserted that all the colonists were so worn out that they were more like shadows than men.[30]

In his memoirs I. I. Evropeus told of his service as district physician in the military colonies, during which he became familiar with the labor duty of the soldiers. He stated that it was very hard on the troops, who lived in dugouts until late fall, so that there was much illness among them and many died. ". . . at night all over the camp groans and moans were heard, for, because of the lack of stoves in the dugouts, the soldiers had no way to warm themselves, much less to dry their boots and clothing."[31]

27. *Ibid.*, p. 204.
28. *Ibid.*, pp. 200-2.
29. *Ibid.*, p. 196.
30. *Ibid.*, pp. 201, 203-6.
31. "Vospominaniia Evropeusa. Bunt voennykh poselian korolia prusskago polka," *Russkaia Starina*, VI (1872), 225-26.

Finally, Lt. Col. N. I. Panaev, who served in the military colonies, testified that the regime there was impossible, as they had to attempt tasks that were beyond all reason. As a result, the men were terribly overworked, with as many as one-eighth of them dying of exhaustion. The officers became demoralized and sought to shift the blame for failures to others, even telling the soldiers that they mistreated them only because their superiors required it. The superiors, in turn, while imposing bigger tasks on the men and sending them to work on holidays, were not above using trickery to persuade the soldiers not to complain against them at inspections. The soldiers thus became completely alienated from their commanders.[32] It is thus no wonder that in 1826 his aide warned Nicholas I that the military colonies posed a grave danger, as they were filled with dissatisfied armed men. He concluded his remarks by warning the Tsar that the dream of Alexander I had been forgotten, and there remained one thing—the imminent danger. He asked Nicholas to consider this carefully, as, if the catastrophe did not come in his reign, it would come under his successor.[33]

The explosion prophesied in 1826 came in 1831, when the regular troops of the military colonies were fighting in Poland. The onset of a frightful cholera epidemic and drastic measures of the authorities to check it, including the use of strange chemicals (chiefly chloride of lime), quickly convinced great numbers of the colonists that their officers were trying to poison them. Beginning on July 9, there were mass attacks on the officers of the military colonies, and in some cases on priests and sergeants. Most of the officers were killed, some of them dying slowly and in agony. The mobs even tortured some of their victims to compel them to sign statements that they had intended to poison the colonists.[34] The colonists did not attack the wives and families of the officers, however, although they abused them verbally and sometimes slapped them.

The authorities made several efforts to suppress the outbreaks, but lacking reliable troops, could do little. Lt. Gen. Eiler, whom Nicholas ordered to use drastic means, led some battalions to Staraia Russa, but did nothing against the mutineers there, and later fled in haste. Gen. Leontiev occupied Staraia Russa with two battalions and four

32. *Bunt voennykh poselian*, pp. 66-69.
33. Semevskii, *Arakcheev*, pp. 195 and 202-3.
34. *Ibid.*, pp. 9-84, *passim*; Gribbe, *Russkaia Starina*, XVII (1876), 514-30.

guns, but could do nothing. Eventually, when huge mobs approached the city, his gunners refused to fire on them and the rebels captured and killed all the officers. Gen. Tomashevskii led a considerable force against a mob, but his troops refused to fire and he had to retire.[35]

Apparently the colonists firmly believed that there had been an attempt to poison them, for one group of them, after killing their officers, drew up a petition to Nicholas I, in which they accused their commanders of trying to kill them and asked the Tsar to aid them against these enemies. They then sent this message to the Tsar by four deputies whom they chose from their number.[36] Lt. Col. Panaev, however, relates that when he urged one of the more intelligent of the military colonists to persuade the others that the stories of poisoning were absurd, the peasant said: "For fools, poison and cholera; but for us it is necessary that your noblemen's goat-tribe should not exist." This answer breathed class hatred, which probably was a considerable factor in the insurrection.[37]

Nicholas I apparently regarded this uprising as more than a temporary aberration, for he was greatly perturbed when a reserve battalion of regular soldiers joined it. He wrote: "The mutiny in Novgorod is more important than the revolt in Lithuania, for the consequences can be more frightening."[38] The Tsar went to Novgorod on July 25 to subdue the rebels, but found the situation completely out of hand. His manifesto to the rebels had little effect, and only one regiment of uhlans was reliable. He visited three of the mutinous regiments, but being unable to get them to submit, returned to St. Petersburg. On July 29, however, strong forces of fresh troops arrived in the area and the suppression of the insurrection could then begin.[39]

Not all of the colonists revolted. Several of the settlement battalions in the rural areas, thanks to the energy and authority of popular commanders, remained obedient and kept their areas under control. Col. Tolmachev, in command of a battalion of the 3rd Carabineer regiment, marched his force with loaded muskets and full military precautions to their headquarters, where he began to restore order.[40]

35. Evstaf'ev, pp. 124-57.
36. Gribbe, *Russkaia Starina*, XVII (1876), 530-31.
37. *Bunt voennykh poselian*, p. 105.
38. Evstaf'ev, p. 185.
39. *Ibid.*, pp. 158-65; *Bunt voennykh poselian*, pp. 121-23, 161-63. The text of the Tsar's manifesto is given in Adamovich, *Sbornik voenno-istoricheskikh materialov leib-gvardii Keksgol'mskago polka* (3 vols. in 2; St. Petersburg, 1910), III, 527-28.
40. Kartsov, I, 19-20.

Another officer, under special order from the Tsar, led two companies into Staraia Russa, where they occupied the guardhouse for five days, until fifty uhlans arrived and ended the danger of fresh outbreaks.[41]

By the end of July most of the rebellious colonists were close to submission, after exhortations from the Tsar, various generals, and the clergy. The 10th Military Workers' battalion, however, which had been actively in revolt, was subdued by a trick. On July 29 Gen. Mikulin, sent by the monarch, persuaded the men to march to Oranienbaum, outside St. Petersburg, where the Tsar would meet them and hear their grievances. After the first day's march, however, they were surrounded by large forces of cavalry and artillery. At Oranienbaum they marched onto barges as the cannon frowned on them, and landed on the grim fortress-island of Kronstadt, where imprisonment and punishment awaited them.[42]

By the end of July, large forces of troops occupied the area and with them, several regiments of Ural Cossacks, who were strongly resentful at having to leave their homes for this special duty and vented their wrath on the colonists with their whips.[43] Late in August Count Orlov, a favorite of the Tsar, arrived and set up investigating commissions to examine and try the colonists. Nicholas had written Orlov to "seize the instigators and murderers," and ordered him: ". . . do not hesitate to punish severely and without mercy."[44] This order was carried out. Kartsov, an officer of the military colonies, wrote that the punishment was "harsh to the point of ferocity." While he felt that the evil deeds of the colonists required penalties, it would be better to execute the guilty at once "rather than apply punishments which almost no one could stand, but died under the blows [sic]." He added that the mere finding of an officer's cup or handkerchief in a man's home was enough to bring him a terrible flogging, followed by penal labor.[45]

The courts-martial sentenced 235 ringleaders and instigators to beating with the murderous *knut*, from ten to forty blows; 1,926 received sentences to run the gantlet, which meant from 500 to 2,000

41. A. F. Ushakov, "Kholernyi bunt v Staroi Ruse. 1831 g. (Razskaz ochevidtsa)," *Russkaia Starina*, IX (1874), 157-58.
42. Evstaf'ev, pp. 202-23; Ushakov, p. 158.
43. Kartsov, I, 21.
44. Schiemann, III, 151.
45. Kartsov, I, 21.

blows with rods. The penalty for lesser offenders was the birch. In addition, many of the prisoners were transferred to disciplinary units, usually in the Urals or the Caucasus. Over four thousand persons were punished. Probably over two hundred died.[46]

For the running of the gantlet, two battalions, totalling fifteen hundred men, formed two concentric circles, facing each other. Each man held his musket in his left hand, a rod in his right. Fifteen men, each with bared back, were led between the circles by sergeants. Each sergeant held the butt of a bayonetted musket pointing at the breast of the victim, whose hands were bound to the musket. As the sufferer passed the soldiers, each man struck him with his rod. As the beating progressed, the voices of the victims were audible: "Brothers, be merciful! Brothers, be merciful!" If the prisoners fell and could not continue, they were laid upon sleds which soldiers pulled, and the flogging continued, often until they died. The officers watched the soldiers closely, to make sure that they did not strike lightly out of pity.

Many of the victims died either during or after the punishment. There was insufficient medical care for them, and as the punishment dragged on into the fall months, cold weather probably worsened the condition of the sufferers.[47]

For beating with the *knut*, they bound the victim to a shaped plank implanted at an angle in the ground. The executioner walked slowly up to the man and then brought the lash down with full force on his back. This always drew a groan, as the four-cornered rawhide thong lacerated the flesh and drew blood. After a score or more of blows, the executioner poured himself a glass of vodka and then went on with his work. "All this was done very, very slowly." When the victim fainted, the doctor revived him with aromatic spirits, and the torment continued. After striking the final blow, the executioner branded the man on the brow and both cheeks with a set of small spikes set to form a letter, which he forced into the flesh of the victim. He then rubbed gunpowder into the bleeding flesh, so that the mark would be permanent.[48]

Lt. Gen. P. F. Danilov, a humane man, who had to carry out and witness these punishments, suffered so from hearing the screams that

46. Evstaf'ev, pp. 210-23, 228-35.
47. Seriakov, *Russkaia Starina*, XIV (1875), 161-69. The author witnessed the punishment.
48. *Ibid.*, pp. 169-71.

his health was ruined and he died a broken man at fifty. He was succeeded by Gen. Skobelev, who gloated over the victims. When he thought that one of the executioners was too lenient with the *knut*, the general had Cossacks spur him on with their whips, and the punishment went on all day, to the loud shouts of Skobelev.[49]

A priest whose duty it was to minister to the prisoners, reported that the scenes were harrowing. "The blows of the *knut* and the flogging by willow rods, with the shrieks and moans of those flogged, resounded through the staff buildings, but the cries of the cantonists and the shrieks of the women under the rods drowned out and covered everything." Afterward, he had to go into the hospital wards to administer to the victims, where the sight of the torn flesh of the sufferers was terrible beyond description.[50]

These events, horrible as they were, did produce one beneficial result: Nicholas introduced fundamental changes in the military colonies. By a law in March, 1832, the colonists of the Novgorod area were now to become "plowing soldiers," who had much better conditions as to land and living conditions and were free from general military duty. They now paid rent to the state, provided recruits for the army by means of the usual conscription system, and bore the same obligation to quarter soldiers as the ordinary peasantry. The plowing soldiers were still subject to supervision from the authorities as to health and cleanliness, but in general their lot was greatly eased by this change.[51] In the military colonies of cavalry in the south of Russia, the colonists were also freed from general military duty and devoted themselves to farming. They worked three days a week to support the regular troops, in addition to doing their own farm work. Their children were no longer cantonists, but were subject to conscription like ordinary peasants.[52]

Far from dissolving the military colonies, however, Nicholas expanded them considerably. In 1837 a small settlement was set up in the Caucasus, composed mostly of Cossacks of the Caucasus Corps, who were farmers, but under military jurisdiction.[53] In the same year he ordered the creation of large military colonies in the provinces of Kiev and Podolia on estates confiscated from Polish insurgents of

49. Gribbe, *Russkaia Starina*, XVII (1876), 534-35.
50. *Bunt voennykh poselian*, p. 166.
51. II PSZ, 1832, No. 5251; Petrov, p. 427.
52. "Istoricheskoe obozrenie," *Sbornik IRIO*, XCVIII, 419.
53. II PSZ, 1837, No. 10576, cited in Ferguson, p. 237.

1831. The farming colonists here also did compulsory labor three days a week, supporting twenty cavalry regiments and two brigades of horse artillery.[54] By 1826 the area of the military colonies had increased by forty per cent, while the population had doubled.[55]

The position of the plowing soldiers improved greatly as a result of these changes, but, as they were under rigid military control, their lot was not good.[56] One observer reported that at haying time all the colonists had to wait two or three days for inspection, in spite of the urgency of the task ahead of them.[57] Reports by various officers that investigated the colonies in the 1840's stated that the peasants were terribly overworked and their farming was in poor condition, while the authorities robbed them and punished them freely. As a result, many of them fled into Turkey or the Caucasus. Neighboring peasants asserted that the colonists were so bitter that they would kill at the slightest pretext and that men drafted into the army rejoiced that they were no longer military colonists.[58] But, although there was considerable dissatisfaction, no further outbreaks occurred, and the military colonies remained in existence until the reign of Alexander II.

After 1831 the tempo of insurrectionary movements declined sharply, although there were occasional manifestations of dissatisfaction. During the Russian occupation of Warsaw in 1831, after the Polish Revolution, Nicholas expressed much concern over the fact that Russian officers eagerly bought forbidden documents such as the projected constitution that Novosil'tsev had drafted for Alexander I in 1819. In September, 1831, Nicholas wrote to Field Marshal Paskevich: "Of one hundred young Russians ninety will read it and not understand it, but ten will comprehend it, criticize it, and not forget it. That disturbs me above all." He ordered that because of this the Guard should leave Warsaw as soon as possible and the authorities should seize and destroy the forbidden documents.[59]

There also were isolated instances of mutinous conduct in the troops. In September, 1836, the commander of a company of the Pavlovskii Guards regiment, dissatisfied by their performance at a

54. II PSZ, 1837, No. 10775a, cited in *ibid.*, pp. 238-39.
55. "Istoricheskoe obozrenie," *Sbornik IRIO*, XCVIII, 419-20.
56. SVM, I, Danilov, *Istoricheskii ocherk*, 398-99.
57. Men'kov, II, 38-39.
58. Evstaf'ev, pp. 101-4.
59. Schiemann, III, 141.

review, kept them standing in formation for two hours without their dinner. When he returned, the men openly expressed their anger, and a sergeant addressed the soldiers: "We have endured enough; now what will come will come." The soldiers refused to obey their captain's orders to return to their barracks, and some even refused to surrender their weapons. The Tsar treated this as a serious mutiny and confirmed the sentence of the court imposing drastic penalties of flogging and penal labor. The rest of the company was sent to serve in action in the Caucasus Corps.[60] In April, 1837, during drill a *fel'd-febel* of the Tomsk Jaeger regiment attacked and wounded his captain with his bayonet, as the latter had already beaten him twice and had ordered men to bring sticks to beat him a third time. The sentence imposed was that the culprit was to run the gantlet through one thousand men six times, followed by penal labor in Siberia for life.[61] During this period there were fairly frequent cases of defiance of the authorities by the enlisted men, but they were isolated instances. In his report for 1840 Count Benckendorff, the chief of Gendarmes, wrote that complaints were not heard in the army and that for some time "there reigns a sort of quiet." He added, however, that this was not a result of satisfaction, but in general there was a sort of stifled feeling that compelled the personnel to use restraint and care in their expressions.[62]

The year 1849 brought more serious evidence of dissatisfaction, as many of the Russian officers disliked the intervention in the Hungarian Revolution. This feeling chiefly took the form of sympathy for the Magyars, but in a few cases it amounted to more. An Ensign Vasil'ev, captured by the Magyars, volunteered to enter their army, only to fall into Russian hands when the insurgents laid down their arms. Nicholas commuted the sentence of death decreed by the court to twenty years of penal labor in Siberia.[63] Even more serious was the case of Capt. Alexei Gusev, who told the enlisted men of his unit that the case of Hungary was a just one and that the Russian government was fighting, not to liberate the Slavs of Austria, but to put down the revolution. He actually called on his men to go over to the side of the Hungarian revolutionaries. The authorities, however, learning of his

60. Fedorov, *Russkaia armiia*, pp. 56-57.
61. *Ibid.*, p. 57.
62. Zaionchkovskii, *Voennye reformy*, p. 13.
63. Sokolovskii, *Russkaia Starina*, CXXIV (1905), 415.

efforts, arrested and shot him and several of his sympathizers.[64] Cornet Rulikovskii, of a hussar regiment, even went so far as to betray the outpost under his command to the Magyars. The hussars, however, refused to surrender, and some of them fought their way out of captivity; others were killed or gravely wounded. Eventually Rulikovskii, popular with everyone, was captured and sentenced to death. For some reason, Paskevich tried to find a pretext for softening the sentence, but, after some delay, the execution took place.[65]

Some of the enlisted men in the forces in Hungary also showed their dissatisfaction. Usually their reasons seem to have been to escape from brutal treatment at the hands of their superiors rather than sympathy with the Magyars. The records of the Auditor Department of the Ministry of War show that they deserted to Austria, Prussia, and to the Magyars. A Private Absamikov fled to the latter, and later was captured, weapon in hand, in their ranks. He, of course, was executed. Another private, who was left in hospital in one of the Hungarian towns when his regiment marched back to Russia, tried desperately to stay in Hungary forever.[66]

Another development in 1849 that perturbed the autocratic Tsar was the disclosure by an official of the Ministry of Interior of the widespread revolutionary movement headed by M. V. Petrashevskii, with branches in many cities. Although many of its members were followers of Fourier, others hoped for real revolution, including overthrow of the Tsar. Petrashevskii himself believed in the need for revolution, but felt that it was impossible at that time. The movement included N. P. Grigor'ev, a lieutenant in the Horse Guards, who wrote *Soldatskaia Beseda*, in which he expressed the views of the movement; Lt. N. A. Mombelli, an active member; and Capt. P. A. Kuz'min of the General Staff, in whose rooms several of the meetings of the circle in St. Petersburg took place.[67] In 1849 Nicholas received the report of the Third Section on the Petrashevtsy movement and at once ordered the arrest of all involved, with a minimum of publicity. In his letter to Count Orlov he wrote: "I shall demand Kropotov from you,

64. R. A. Averbukh, "Tsarskaia interventsiia v Vengrii. Razgrom vengerskoi revoliutsiei (Mai-sentiabr' 1849 g.)," *Revoliutsiia 1848-1849* (2 vols.; Moscow, 1952), II, 118-25.

65. Alabin, *Chetyre voiny*, I, 148.

66. R. A. Averbukh, *Tsarskaia interventsiia v bor'be s Vengerskoi revoliutsii 1848-1849 gg.* (Moscow, 1935), p. 142.

67. *Revoliutsiia 1848-1849*, II, 257-62.

when all have been firmly seized."[68] Kropotov was an officer on duty with the First Cadet Corps, who had been attending Petrashevskii's meetings for some time.

These manifestations, like the Society of Sts. Cyril and Methodius, which was crushed in 1847, caused considerable discomfort to the Tsar, as they indicated that something was stirring in Russia. The movement, however, was only beginning, and the imperial regime would survive for decades. Probably more important than these few idealistic army officers who dared to oppose the Tsar was the substantial number of enlisted men who showed their disaffection by deserting, in some cases to the enemy.

The most striking example of this was in the Persian army, where Russian deserters formed a whole battalion. Under the command of Samson Ia. Makintsev, former first sergeant of a dragoon regiment, who had risen rapidly in the Persian service, this battalion became an elite corps, and many of them married Persian women. Samson selected recruits from Russian deserters, many of whom had listened to the promises of the Persians. As some of the Russian regiments suffered from bad food, brutal discipline, and failure to receive their pay, life in Persia seemed very attractive, especially when Russian prisoners returning from Persia painted it in glowing colors.[69] During 1826 two companies of the Carabineer regiment stationed along the Armenian frontier suffered twenty-seven desertions into Persia. When in 1828 the Russian troops in Persia were ordered to return home, it became the signal for desertions from the Kabardinian regiment, which drove the colonel to despair. He finally was able to reduce the flow of deserters by paying the Persians as much as ten gold pieces for each man brought back. Even so, many stayed in Persia, including a young and able *fel'dfebel*. "Indeed, how could a soldier of those times avoid being seduced by the ... Persians? Here a grievous torment for long years, and there precious freedom and wives as you wish."[70]

Several of the Russian viceroys in the Caucasus tried to get the deserters to return to Russia, and after peace with Persia in 1828 strong diplomatic pressure was used to persuade the Persians to return them. During the Tsar's visit to the Caucasus in 1837 he promised

68. A. S. Nifontov, *Russland im Jahre 1848* (Berlin, ca. 1953), p. 315.
69. Ad. P. Berzhe, "Samson Iakovlev [*sic*] Makintsev i Russkie begletsy v Persii," *Russkaia Starina*, XV (1876), 771-75.
70. Ganglebov, *Russkii Arkhiv*, XXIV (1886), Pt. II, 248.

full amnesty if the fugitives would return. Finally, with much difficulty in 1839 the Russian government secured the return of 597 deserters, some with their families. The single men were assigned to battalions in Finland, while the married men joined the Cossacks of the Caucasus Line. Samson Makintsev-Khan, however, remained in Persia until his death.[71]

Apparently few Russian soldiers deserted to the Turks. Nonetheless, when the Kamchatka regiment was stationed along the Pruth, the advent of Gen. Rot, a martinet, as corps commander, was the signal for such an oppressive regime in his troops that an unusual number of desertions occurred, many of them by old soldiers. In a short time fifty men deserted from one battalion and crossed the Pruth to hide out among colonies of Russian Old Believers who had settled in Turkey in earlier periods.[72] One possible reason why few Russians deserted to Turkey was suggested by Nicholas in 1837, when he told a Persian prince that the Turks always returned deserters.[73] There is no evidence, however, to show whether this was indeed the case or whether this statement was merely a means of influencing the Persians.

Probably the most striking examples of desertion by Russian soldiers were in the Caucasus. In 1835 Lt. F. Tornov, a prisoner of the Kabardinians, conferred with them through the renegade Cossack Bragunov as translator.[74] In 1840 the Cherkasy, hard hit by famine, decided to attack the Russian forts on the Black Sea coast to gain food. They knew of the weaknesses of the positions, as "they always obtained the most reliable information about the position of our garrisons from Polish deserters." They easily overran several of the forts.[75]

The number of Russian deserters, whom the tribesmen welcomed and sheltered, increased in the 1840's. An officer of the General Staff ascribed this increase to the large number of recruits from Poland and the western provinces that the authorities sent to the Caucasus forces. "Worn out by uninterrupted and most exhausting campaigns, the enlisted men had neither the necessary relaxation nor the conveniences for life" and hence fled where life would be somewhat easier.[76]

71. Berzhe, "Makintsev," *Russkaia Starina*, XV (1876), 778-92.
72. I. L. Varun-Sekret, "Vospominaniia I. L. Varun-Sekreta o sluzhbe v armii, 1823-1860 gg.," *Russkaia Starina*, XXV (1879), 160.
73. Berzhe, "Imperator Nikolai," *Russkaia Starina*, XLIII (1884), 386-88.
74. Tornov, II, 85.
75. Ad. P. Berzhe, "Zashchita Mikhailovskago ukrepleniia 22-go marta 1840 g.," *Russkaia Starina*, XIX (1877), 277.
76. S. K. Bushuev, *Bor'ba gortsev za nezavisimost' pod rukovodstvom Shamilia* (Moscow, 1939), p. 104.

Poles and Lithuanians, however, were not the only ones who went over to the enemy. During the great offensive mounted by Shamil's forces in 1843, an Ensign Zaletov of the Tiflis Jaeger regiment, a recently promoted sergeant from the Borodino Jaegers, surrendered the hopelessly weak fortification that he commanded, upon summons from Khadji Murad. Shortly thereafter, Zaletov rode up to the fort at Gotsatl' and urged the garrison to surrender. When the Tsar read the report of this incident, he wrote on the margin the proverb, "There is no family without an idiot."[77]

By 1845 Shamil, the chieftain of the mountaineers, had received enough deserters to form small forces of them, some of whom manned a unit of artillery. After the Russian forces had occupied Shamil's fortress of Dargo, the latter, on the opposite side of the river, had "several companies of our deserters, who had been living at a suburb built at Dargo, march past" in a sort of parade, to the sound of trumpets and drums.[78]

In the 1840's Prince Vorontsov, the new viceroy of the Caucasus, disturbed by the flow of deserters to the mountaineers, secured permission to announce that those who would return would be spared trial and punishment and would be assigned to regiments far from the frontiers. Shortly thereafter, many of the deserters began to turn up at frontier posts. Few Poles came out of the mountains, however.[79] This measure did not fully eliminate the problem. In 1848 Shamil's cannon fired on the camp of Russian forces in the Chechen country. Russian patrols could hear the commands, "correctly pronounced in Russian—evidently, there were our deserters, who formed a whole settlement around the residence of the *Imam* [Shamil]."[80] At the siege of Akhty in the same year, the mountaineers built a two-gun battery overlooking the fort. Nikitin, a deserter from the Russian artillery, who commanded the battery, shouted that he did not miss his target, and, indeed, after half a dozen shots, a shell pierced a Russian powder-magazine and blew up one of the fort's bastions.[81]

In 1850 some scouts captured four armed bandits, all of whom proved to be Russian deserters, of the rash and energetic breed "who literally hasten to extinguish in streams of blood the last sparks of

77. Zisserman, *Istoriia Kabardinskago polka*, II, 277-78.
78. *Ibid.*, II, 425.
79. Tolstoi, *Russkii Arkhiv*, XV (1877), Pt. III, 296.
80. Potto, V, 141-42.
81. Schilder, *Totleben*, I, 49.

conscience."[82] In the same year a dragoon deserted openly while watering horses. Warmly welcomed by the tribesmen, he led raids against the Russians with great success and daring, until one of the mountaineers, bribed by the Russians, killed him.[83] Finally, in 1854 a Russian officer was a captive among the foe, where he encountered ten or twelve Russian renegades, several of whom hated the Russian army with ferocity, while a few yearned to return to their people.[84]

While most desertions were from troops in frontier regions, there always were some from units in the interior. The Iamburg Uhlans had 116 cases in ten years during the 1830's. These were usually recruits who became homesick in the fall and went off for about a week. Most of them returned voluntarily.[85] During the first twenty-five years of the reign of Nicholas there were 155,857 desertions from all the regular troops, or an average of 6,235 per year. The maximum desertions, 17,896, came in 1831, the year of the Polish War, while in 1847 a minimum of 2,692 occurred.[86] These figures suggest that there may have been a decline in the number of desertions in the latter part of the reign. They give no information as to the number of deserters who returned to duty voluntarily or through capture.

Throughout this study numerous examples have showed that the military authorities placed strong reliance on punishment, often severe, and sometimes terrible, as a form of repression. Nicholas himself shared this opinion, especially in the early years of his reign. In 1828 a private of the Grenadier Guards regiment killed his *fel'dfebel* and tried to take his own life. At his trial the General Auditoriat proposed to punish him with the *knut*, followed by penal labor. Gen. Adj. Demidov proposed to have him run the gantlet, through one thousand men, twelve times, followed by penal labor. (This sentence was almost equivalent to death). Count Diebitsch agreed with Demidov's proposal. The Tsar's resolution called for sending him through the gantlet "in accordance with the opinion of Gen. Adj. Diebitsch."[87]

In 1830, however, Nicholas approved a new provision that in time of peace the death penalty, except under exceptional circumstances, would not apply. Instead, the punishment for enlisted men should

82. Potto, VI, 18.
83. *Ibid.*, VI, 120-29.
84. I. N. Rumiantsev, *V plenu u Shamilia. Zapiski Russkago* (St. Petersburg, 1877), *passim.*
85. Krestovskii, p. 534.
86. "Istoricheskoe obozrenie," *Sbornik IRIO*, XCVIII (1896), 328-29
87. Sokolovskii, *Russkaia Starina*, CXXIV (1905), 408.

consist of running the gantlet, followed by penal labor. The law now forbade punishment with the *knut* and branding of convicts, except for Cossacks. It also set a limit of six times through one thousand men for those sentenced to run the gantlet, although courts might set more extreme penalties, subject, however, to the approval of the Tsar.[88] In addition, the law gave considerable latitude to the commanders in relatively minor offenses, in which they might determine the punishment, up to punishment with rods or running the gantlet once through five hundred men.[89] Desertion of enlisted men brought sentences to run the gantlet, from once through five hundred men for the first flight, and for the second, up to six times through five hundred men. Continued flights brought even higher punishments.[90]

These provisions represented definite moderation of the earlier extremes of cruelty that fell to the lot of the enlisted men, and form part of the trend during this reign to improve the position of the soldiers. They were, however, not fundamental changes, but merely alleviations. Severe repression remained one of the basic means for dealing with enlisted men.

Here, too, Nicholas sought to prevent obvious excesses. In 1827 three officers punished a Private Evseev for his third attempt at desertion by making him run the gantlet through one thousand men four times. During the carrying out of the sentence he fell on his second time through. The officers had him put on a cart and the punishment continued to the end, without the presence of a surgeon to determine whether he could endure the full sentence. The result was that Private Evseev died several hours after the flogging. This led to a court-martial which tried the three officers. The Tsar's resolution on the report of the case was: "Reduce all to privates until they serve out their terms."[91]

The monarch also was furious at the use of torture to extract confessions. Two officers in the Caucasus tried to compel two Cossacks to admit the theft of a considerable sum by starving them, and then they fed one of the victims on caviar without water to make him thirsty. They also had him placed in a cell with some decaying corpses of typhus victims. This resulted in a court-martial, which decreed that the culprits be reduced to the ranks. Nicholas added a stern resolution ordering to deprive them of ranks, orders, and nobility, and to "de-

88. SVP, Pt. II, Bk. I, *O prestupleniiakh i nakazaniiakh*, arts. 19-22, 29, 74, 69.
89. *Ibid.*, arts. 229-30.
90. *Ibid.*, arts. 248-54.
91. Sokolovskii, *Russkaia Starina*, CXXIV (1905), 404.

liver them for ten years as fortress prisoners." In a similar case in 1853 four men were made to confess theft through beating and thirst. The Tsar underlined the evidence regarding torture and issued a strong decree that torture was forbidden in investigations and calling for the trial of those guilty of using it.[92]

Thus Nicholas I sought to alleviate and moderate the worst features of the repression used in the army, without changing the fundamental nature of the system itself.

92. *Ibid.*, pp. 399-400.

CHAPTER XV. PASKEVICH AND THE AUNGARIAN CAMPAIGN OF 1849

In view of the fact that the Russian army served as an instrument of repression in Poland and in the Caucasus, as well as in European Russia, it is not surprising that Nicholas I also used it to crush the Hungarian Revolution in 1849. Thus for the first time since 1831 the army marched forth to war.

During this period of peace Paskevich had remained supreme in the army, thanks to the Tsar's complete trust in the Field Marshal after his victories in three wars. In spite of the imperial favor, however, he continued to display many of the characteristics of his earlier years. P. K. Men'kov, a clever officer who served in his headquarters in the 1840's, approvingly cited the comments of an official close to the Field Marshal. The latter was distinguished by "unusual vanity, distrust, suspiciousness, and a sort of strange fear that people did not fully appreciate him, that they esteem him only out of fear of his power and that each man close to him, if not openly, then inwardly is laughing at him. This thought constantly tormented him, . . ." so that anyone who had dealings with him had to act with extreme care, weighing the possible effect of each action and word so as not to give offence. Men'kov added that when Paskevich asked for comments on his proposals he wanted only approval and would not permit any objection or criticism.[1] On one occasion, Men'kov, while riding in the Field Marshal's carriage, had his ears filled with a long tale of the Persian War, full of his superior's boasting of his prowess and sneers at Ermolov, Diebitsch, and other rivals. Suddenly, seeing in a mirror that Men'kov was smiling, he flew into a rage, accusing the young officer of intellectual snobbishness, doubt, and criticism of him, and ended by forcing Men'kov out of his carriage.[2]

Mention has already been made (Chapter X) of Paskevich's

1. Men'kov, II, 194-95.
2. *Ibid.*, p. 195.

unwillingness to permit his subordinates, including the corps commanders, to have any initiative or independence and his insistence on blind obedience. This domineering attitude reached its peak in his treatment of Gen. M. D. Gorchakov, his chief of staff—a post that many able men avoided like the plague. Although the general was extraordinarily fussy, indecisive, and scatterbrained, the choice fell on him apparently because Paskevich knew that he was quiet, patient, and uncomplaining and would display no initiative at all. These were the qualities that counted with the commander in chief. For twenty-one years Gorchakov held this post, during which he became more and more fussy and timid, while Paskevich broke and fettered all that was alive in him. Gorchakov grew accustomed to seeing his subordinates browbeaten and tormented and degraded. Count P. E. Kotsebu, quartermaster-general of the Active Army, declared that when the Field Marshal learned in 1845 that the Tsar planned to make Gorchakov assistant viceroy, he said: "What sort of assistant would he be to me! He's a pawn! A cipher! Here's what!" and he made a sneering grimace. "Like all officers of the General Staff, he thought he would make a big splash, but I broke him! I break everyone, and I'll break you!" he said to Kotsebu and others in his office. Nicholas did not make Gorchakov assistant viceroy. On the other hand, Paskevich did not mistreat him, for "the frightful, unrestrained despot" was fully pleased with his chief of staff.[3]

As previously mentioned (Chapter XII), when Paskevich took command of troops of the Caucasus Corps during the Persian War he complained bitterly of their unmilitary appearance and lack of knowledge of formation drill and the manual of arms. The same sort of emphasis on external matters and lack of interest in musketry and other vital aspects of military training characterized him in his exalted post in Warsaw. He always had two officers assigned to check on the correctness of the detachments doing guard duty in the city. Invariably they found some trifles to report: an officer with his uniform not properly buttoned; a word omitted in a command to the guard; the failure of a sentry to hang up his sheepskin coat properly; a drummer who was slow in taking his sticks out of their case; the corporal leading the sentries with his musket in the wrong position; an officer who was slow in putting on his gloves when turning out; or a

3. N. B., "Kniaz' Mikhail D. Gorchakov," *Russkaia Starina*, XXIX (1880), 113-15 and 116n.

sentry who rang the warning bell three times instead of two. For such petty matters officers sat for days in the guardhouse.[4]

In 1849 this existence of petty routine was interrupted. Although Nicholas had been greatly concerned by the events of 1848, he did little but move an army corps into the Principalities, by agreement with the Turks, to quell the "dangerous disorders" produced there by foreign revolutionaries, chiefly Polish *émigrés*. Late in 1848 small detachments of Russian troops moved into southern Transylvania, after repeated requests from the Austrian commanders and the inhabitants of two of the cities.[5] In March, 1849, however, these measures appeared to be gravely insufficient, as a large and confident Hungarian army threatened to destroy the weakened and disheartened Austrian troops. In addition, many Poles were hoping that their day, too, would come, and Bem and Dembínski were actually leading Magyar forces. Consequently, when in March the Austrians asked help, Nicholas was ready to give it in substantial measure, with a large force to push through Galicia into Hungary, while a small force would enter Transylvania from the Principalities. Moreover, to give immediate aid to the main Austrian army under Gen. Haynau, which was in serious danger, late in April Paskevich sent one division of infantry, with forty-eight guns. On June 6, the main Russian column of 70,890 men, with 240 guns, under the personal leadership of the Field Marshal, entered Hungary from the Dukla Pass. Another column, further west, under Gen. Count Rüdiger, consisted of 31,600 men and 120 guns. The two forces, after uniting south of the Carpathians, would then march on Pesth on the Danube and also bar the valley of the Tisza to the Magyar forces. Osten-Sacken, with 9,200 men, remained behind to protect Galicia. At the same time, Gen. A. N. Lüders had the task of pushing into Transylvania from the Principalities in order to occupy the chief cities, pacify the area, and then move into Hungary proper. His Fifth Corps of twenty-six thousand men would have the support of Gen. Grotenholm, with eighty-five hundred men, who would enter Transylvania from Bukovina.[6]

The problem of provisions proved difficult, for although the Austrians made lavish promises of aid, there was little food available in Hungary and few wagons were on hand to haul supplies. Paskevich

4. "Dve sluzhby," *Russkii Arkhiv*, XXVII (1889), Pt. I, 435-38.
5. I. Oreus, *Opisanie vengerskoi voiny 1849 g.* (St. Petersburg, 1880), pp. 94-95.
6. *Ibid.*, pp. 105-15.

arranged to have abundant supplies from Russia and Poland made available in Galicia, thereby securing ample provisions for the troops while they were north of the Carpathians. When they moved into Hungary they had a twenty-day reserve supply of food.[7]

The main problem proved to be hauling the provisions, for in Hungary the Austrian officials had been driven out by the Magyars and the Russians could obtain little food and forage from the inhabitants, even though they paid in cash. Huge amounts of provisions from Russia and Poland piled up at the passes, but wagons were not to be had in any quantity. On June 14 Paskevich found it necessary to reduce the bread ration, while adding more meat, to be obtained locally. For eight days he held his army motionless, while he made efforts to buy food from the people and, if necessary, to requisition it. However, transportation was the great problem, which became worse as a result of a sudden outbreak of cholera in June and July, since thousands of sufferers had to be carried to hospitals. Paskevich now ordered the corps commanders to purchase large quantities of oxen, many of which should have harness and wagons, while others were to serve as pack animals, until they could be spared for meat. By these devices the army obtained supplies for one month, which enabled it to move to the Danube.[8] On the whole, Paskevich handled the supply problem well, with "his characteristic carefulness and foresight." He made one grave mistake, however. Apparently because of exaggerated fear of the enemy, he insisted on moving his entire army, with its wagon trains, along a single road, which made the problem almost insoluble.[9]

The cholera epidemic was one of the worst trials that the army experienced during this campaign. The men, worn out by the heavy exertions in crossing the Carpathians, had to march in frequent heavy rain and to bivouac on the wet ground, and also suffered from lack of pure water for drinking. These factors, along with eating of unripe grapes, made them easy prey for the infection, which hit about June 12. Suddenly in each company of the marching troops from thirty to forty men died in a space of six or eight days. The sufferers, groaning and vomiting in their agony, were piled in jolting peasant wagons and sent back through the advancing troops. In Kaschau (Košice) ten

7. Zatler, *Zapiski*, I, 162-72.
8. *Ibid.*, pp. 173-80; Aratovskii, pp. 226-37; Oreus, p. 161.
9. Oreus, p. 542.

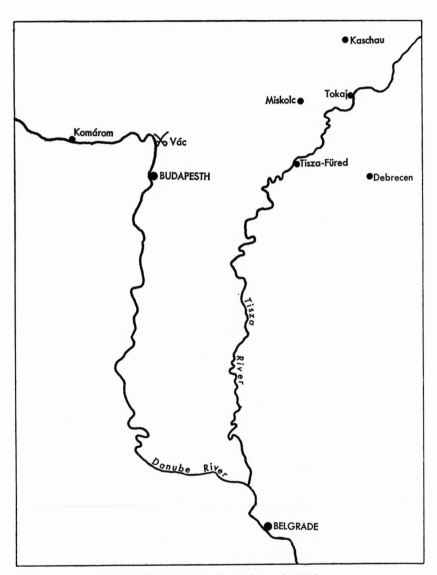

The Hungarian Campaign of 1849

thousand of them collected in hospitals with facilities for only twenty-five hundred, causing a crisis that was met only by requisitioning public buildings and private residences. By the middle of July, however, the incidence of the cholera declined.[10]

In spite of these obstacles, however, late in June Paskevich began to move toward Pesth, to threaten the rear of Görgey's army at Komárom (Komorn), some distance northwest of Budapesth. The latter now decided to strike the Austrians under Haynau, and at the same time on June 20 Haynau moved to attack Görgey, rashly dispersing his forces. This permitted the Magyar commander to inflict a defeat that threatened the destruction of the Austrian force. At this juncture Paniutin led his Russian troops to the rescue, driving back Görgey and saving the day for the Austrians. On June 29, Görgey, by a surprise attack, again threatened the Austrians with disaster, and once more Paniutin's division came up to turn the tide and, with the Austrian reserves, repulsed the Magyars. In recognition of these services to his troops, the Emperor Franz Joseph issued a letter to Paniutin, expressing his gratitude and admiration for the Russian achievements in these two battles.[11] Görgey, increasingly worried about Paskevich's threat to his rear, now decided to leave Komárom by the left bank of the Danube, hoping to get to Pesth before Paskevich could arrive, which would give him the possibility of joining Hungarian forces in the south.

Thus both the main Magyar army and the Russian army were moving toward Pesth. Paskevich, however, moved slowly, concentrating his troops at Hatvan on the northeast and sending only a small force of cavalry to scout the enemy, as he feared that the latter might be heading to the northeast, against the Russian line of communications. On July 3 Russian cavalry discovered the Magyars on the march toward Vác (Waitzen), on the Danube north of Pesth. Gen. Zass, who had made a dashing record in the Caucasus, on taking command of the advance guard, at once attacked. When the enemy cavalry retired, Zass eagerly pursued, only to run into the fire of massed enemy artillery, which severely punished his force. As this development disrupted the Field Marshal's plans for an attack to be made only after having carefully massed his whole army, he now felt it

10. Vernikovskii, *Russkii Arkhiv*, XXIII (1885), Pt. III, 515-18; A. O. Streng, "Voina protiv Vengertsev 1849 goda," *Russkaia Starina*, LXI (1889), 469-70; Zatler, *O gospitaliakh*, pp. 156-59.
11. Oreus, pp. 245-57.

necessary to bring up two army corps to rescue Zass from annihilation. Galloping from Hatvan, he urged on the troops, which marched all night, arriving before Vác early in the morning of July 4. Paskevich himself was feverishly active, driving on the troops, even pushing them hurriedly over hilly or swampy terrain. During an eighteen-hour period he rode twenty miles on his horse and thirty-five more in his carriage, without resting. Before the troops arrived, however, Zass' advance guard had retired out of danger and the crisis, real or imaginary, had passed.[12]

Paskevich now had the foe at bay, for his army barred the way to the south. Instead of attacking at once, however, he insisted, on the grounds that his men were completely exhausted, on waiting for the Fourth Corps, which did not come up until the afternoon of July 4. As he himself was worn out by his exertions, he put off the attack until the fifth, retiring to his tent with instructions not to begin action without orders. He failed, however, to say when to awaken him, so that it was midmorning before he arose and began to move. Although Görgey realized the danger of his position, he made no move until dusk on the fourth, when he ordered a retreat through Vác to the northeast. As it turned out, the numerous political refugees with his forces also tried to escape at the same time, producing terrible confusion at the bridge and in the narrow streets of the town, so that the last Magyar troops did not leave Vác until the middle of the morning on the fifth. Finally, a small force of Russian cavalry and horse artillery tried to cut off the retreat of the rear guard, only to be driven back by artillery fire. By dusk on July 5 Görgey's army was safe.[13] Thus for a brief period Paskevich had had a superb opportunity to destroy the main Magyar army, only to let it escape. The campaign was to drag on for another month, with the continued heavy losses from disease that that month would bring. Probably if he had forced a decisive battle on July 4, with all the bloodshed that would have resulted, more men of both armies would have survived the campaign than lived through the longer, indecisive period.

Not only did the Russian army let its opponents escape unscathed, but it actually lost touch with them for several days and was completely ignorant of their whereabouts. Baron Nikolai of Paskevich's staff relates how they pursued the Magyars for some distance, only to

12. Men'kov, III, 255-56.
13. Likhutin, *Zapiski*, pp. 153-54; Oreus, pp. 275-87.

lose track of them at Miskolc. "One cannot but regret and blush a little that, possessing such a numerous cavalry, we all the same clumsily lost the trail of the enemy." The reason was that Paskevich would not send out a real advance guard, under an energetic commander, to clear the path for the main army. This, Nikolai felt, was because Paskevich misapplied the Napoleonic principle of concentration of forces. The Corsican rightly took care to have his forces close enough so that they could support each other in time of need, "but not at all in the form of careful refusal to let even one detachment get out from under his wing."[14]

This was not a unique instance under the Field Marshal. Later in the campaign Maj. Gen. Blagovut, who had served in the Caucasus, led a small force of cavalry against a Magyar rear guard, beat it badly, and made it flee. Instead of praise for this he received a reprimand, as the regulations did not permit the attack of a small force upon a larger one. His contemporaries explained this result as an outgrowth of the current practice of controlling every step of a subordinate, thus destroying the latter's initiative and making them extra cautious—not out of fear of the enemy, but of their superiors.[15] The case of Gen. Freitag also illustrates this attitude. Although he was one of the most brilliant generals in the Caucasus Corps, he managed to incur the ill will of Prince Vorontsov, who had him transferred to the Active Army. Paskevich, instead of giving him a command of troops, with the independence and freedom of action that his talents merited, made him quartermaster-general, a routine post where his ability was completely wasted.[16]

In contrast to the indecisive campaign in Hungary proper, that of Gen. Lüders in Transylvania was a striking example of energetic action and readiness to force the enemy into large-scale battle. Although he was fighting an enemy approximately equal in numbers, well equipped and well led, Lüders inflicted two decisive defeats and also subdued an active partisan movement. Perhaps his chief advantage was the fact that, although he was nominally subject to Paskevich, the latter made no attempt to dominate his actions.

Early in June Lüders' forces pushed through the "impregnable" Temes Pass and quickly gained control of Kronstadt (Brazov) and

14. L. P. Nikolai, "Dnevnik Barona L. P. Nikolai vedennyi im po vremia Venger-skoi kampanii 1849 g.," *Russkaia Starina*, XX (1877), 119-20.
15. Likhutin, *Zapiski*, pp. 65-66.
16. *Ibid.*, pp. 69-70.

Hermanstadt (Sibiu). Finally Gen. Bem risked a pitched battle, at Semesvar, only to have his army routed with the loss of almost all its cannon. Bem sought to redeem himself by a skilful stroke against the small force of Gen. Gasford at Hermanstadt, with the aid of fresh troops in that area. When, several days later, Lüders learned of Bem's intention, after sending a hasty warning to Gasford, he ordered his men to go to the rescue by forced marches. Gasford made a skilful fighting retreat, keeping his disciplined troops intact in spite of the pressure of far superior numbers, while Lüders' forces were rushing to his aid. After marching almost sixty miles in thirty-six hours—a performance worthy of Suvorov—on July 25 Lüders massed his troops for an attack on Bem's forces. As Bem had refused to believe that Lüders was near, the latter was able to win an impressive victory, destroying the Magyar army and driving the remnants into Turkey. This was the last significant fighting in Transylvania, as the rest of the enemy forces soon laid down their arms.[17] In this campaign of only two months, the Russians in Transylvania had fought twenty-five battles and fourteen skirmishes, with two days of action for every inactive day. These successes were not a result of superior armaments, as their weapons were outmoded and the marksmanship of the troops was very poor. Probably it was a combination of strong discipline, experience in battle in the Caucasus, confidence in their general, and skilled leadership that produced these successes.[18]

While the campaign in Transylvania was in progress, Paskevich failed to destroy Görgey's army, which successfully eluded him to the end. When Nicholas I in his letter of July 16 expressed his annoyance that the Magyar chief had made good his escape, his "Father-Commander" answered: "Of course it is bitter that Görgey got away; but he had to get away, as he did not wish to give me battle anywhere." But while the Magyar army had successfully fled, Paskevich, with far superior forces, had abundant opportunity to cut him off and annihilate his army. This, however, was not his intention. In his memorandum to the Tsar on the course of the campaign, he stated that after Vác the war would be won not by battles, but by maneuvering—which is what he did, and to little purpose.[19]

17. Daragan, *Zapiski o voine v Transil'vanii, v 1849 g.* (St. Petersburg, 1859), pp. 45-230, *passim.*
18. *Ibid.,* pp. 243-49.
19. Oreus, p. 327.

At first, after Görgey's escape, Paskevich was uncertain what his opponent would do next, feeling that he might again head for Komárom or march against the Russian base at Miskolc, or perhaps turn and rend Rüdiger's Third Corps, which was nearest to him. It soon became evident, however, that the Magyar leader would seek to cross the upper Tisza and then slip southward to join the Hungarian troops there. So the Field Marshal, although fearful for his communications at Miskolc, decided to march to the upper Tisza, to bar Görgey's path to the south. In spite of the insistence of the careful Count Rüdiger that the Magyars were weak and dispirited, Paskevich still ascribed to them great strength and, having no desire to join battle, sent only weak forces against them. At the same time, the Fourth Corps had the task of protecting the Russian bases at Tokaj and Miskolc and threatening the enemy's flank, while fresh troops under Osten-Sacken would push south from Galicia. Thus, once he was sure that Görgey was definitely heading east, Paskevich moved with the Second and Third Corps to Tisza-Füred, where Gorchakov forced a crossing under fire and built a bridge across the river. As the Russian troops closed in on Görgey's army his position grew increasingly perilous and it needed only a vigorous push by Paskevich from his bridgehead over the Tisza to cut off his retreat. This, however, he did not do, and the Magyar commander was thus able to avoid the jaws of the trap.[20]

During this period, Görgey remained inactive further to the north, sure that Paskevich would not cross the Tisza. Cheodaev was following him with considerable caution. Gen. Grabbe, however, with rather weak forces, pushed ahead and ran into Görgey's main forces, which mauled him badly and forced him to retire in haste. Shortly thereafter the Magyar commander, learning that Paskevich was seriously threatening his line of retreat, hastily retired east of the Tisza to begin his march to the south. Paskevich again became gravely concerned that Grabbe's setback indicated that Görgey was about to strike at the Russian communications. This caused him to move his bridge at Tisza thirteen miles to the north, from which point he could strike at either Miskolc or Debrecen.[21] Thus, just when the Magyars were hastily moving to the southeast, Paskevich retreated to the north. He

20. *Ibid.*, pp. 288-316.
21. Shcherbatov, VI, 143-45.

also showered Count Grabbe with all sorts of incoherent and un-suitable orders, which almost reduced that general to a frenzy.[22] Gen. Cheodaev also received numerous orders enjoining "caution carried to extremes," on occasion even having to withdraw before threats of enemy action that never materialized.[23]

By about July 20, Paskevich decided to push to Debrecen to cut off Görgey's retreat, not knowing the latter was already east of the Tisza and had moved southeast of Debrecen en route to Gross Wardein. Nagy Sandor, with his First Corps, held Debrecen as flank guard for the main forces. As he made the mistake of staying on longer than his function required, the Russians learned of the presence of his forces there as they approached. The Russian advance guard came under the heavy fire of Sandor's guns, which led Paskevich to believe that he was facing all of Görgey's troops. Instead of sending reinforcements at once to the advance guard, he formed his whole army in battle order fourteen miles from the foe and then marched them ahead in formation. As the terrain soon made this impossible, more time had to be spent forming them into columns so that, once more, they could march forward. Even when they had come close to Debrecen and again deployed. Paskevich refused to permit the Second Corps to advance until six o'clock. A cavalry division was sent ahead on the right, where they halted under the concealment of a tall field of corn, with strict instructions not to move until ordered. Finally the whole Russian army rolled ponderously ahead, with the Magyar troops already in full retreat. Some of the Russian cavalry attacked their baggage, capturing four guns, but no orders came to the cavalry division lurking in the corn field, although if it had attacked it would have completed the destruction of Sandor's corps. The latter, although badly disorganized, escaped, and eventually joined Görgey's forces.[24]

In his report to the Tsar, the Field Marshal explained his slow-ness in attacking by the need to win even if all the enemy troops were there. "We had to be especially careful, because we were obliged definitely to beat the enemy on this day and to take the town, for we had no water." After winning the victory, with the foe in full retreat, "It was impossible to pursue farther, for we might expect the corps

22. Grabbe, "Iz dnevnika," *Russkii Arkhiv*, XXVI (1888), Pt. I, Supplement, 428-31.
23. Alabin, *Chetyre voiny*, I, 144-45; Oreus, p. 544.
24. Oreus, pp. 444-52; Streng, *Russkaia Starina*, LXI (1889), 475-77.

of Görgey."[25] In his letter of July 29 congratulating Paskevich on his victory Nicholas wrote: "I very much regret that Görgey got away with his army and I shall be able to understand it completely only when you can explain to me in person what here can scarcely be understood."[26]

After the battle Paskevich remained in Debrecen for about ten days, collecting provisions for twenty days, while Görgey again escaped.[27] The campaign was virtually at an end, however, for Baron Haynau had led the Austrian army southward from Komárom and, after beating Dembínski's army, attacked the Magyars, who now were under Bem, near Temesvar (Timişoara) and won a decisive victory, taking fifteen thousand prisoners, and the Magyar army collapsed.[28]

Gen. Haynau, however, was not to have full satisfaction from his victory, for Görgey, who had already been negotiating with Paskevich, now offered to surrender to Gen. Rüdiger rather than to the Austrians. Paskevich at once wrote to the Tsar: "Hungary lies at the feet of Your Imperial Majesty." With the permission of the Field Marshal the surrender was made in considerable haste, as Rüdiger was afraid that many of the Magyars would refuse to lay down their arms. They still were eager to fight the Austrians, if only the Russians would let them alone.[29] Görgey was well pleased with his treatment by the Russians, for after his surrender he received word that the Tsar had pardoned him and was sending his oldest son to intercede with Franz Joseph for him. The latter shortly pardoned the Magyar chief, who, with eleven hundred gold pieces given him by Paskevich, went to live in Klagenfurt.[30]

Görgey also urged the commandant of the fortress of Arad to surrender to the Russians, saying in his letter of August 2: ". . . they are treating us in such a fashion that we marvel at it and are almost ashamed, for if we were in the reverse position I could not, it seems, guarantee such kind and magnanimous treatment on the part of our officers toward enemy prisoners of war."[31] The commandant readily

25. Letter of Paskevich to the Tsar, July 23, 1849, cited in Oreus, Prilozheniia, pp. 107-8.

26. Shcherbatov, VI, 150-51.

27. Streng, *Russkaia Starina*, LXI (1889), 478.

28. Oreus, pp. 462-86.

29. Message of Gen. Rüdiger to Prince Paskevich, Aug. 4, 1849, cited in Averbukh, *Interventsiia*, pp. 317-18; Alabin, *Chetyre voiny*, I, Prilozheniia, p. xxix.

30. Artur Görgei, *Mein Leben und Wirken in Ungarn in den Jahren 1848 und 1849* (2 vols.; Leipzig, 1852), II, 429-32.

31. Men'kov, III, 275.

agreed to surrender, as his position was desperate, but he, too, would surrender only to Gen. Buturlin of Rüdiger's corps, instead of to the Austrian Gen. Schlik, who had been besieging the fortress. Buturlin, who had only two squadrons of cavalry, accepted the surrender, agreeing to protect the Magyars from the Austrians. Field Marshal Haynau, however, was furious at this and, according to Görgey, ordered Schlik to obtain the prisoners by force if need be. Rüdiger, however, sent word to Haynau that this would mean war between Russia and Austria, at which Haynau backed down.[32] Whether matters actually had gone so far is hard to tell, but there certainly was severe friction between Gen. Rüdiger and the Austrian authorities. On August 8, Rüdiger wrote to Paskevich of Gen. Schlik's "feeling of vengeance" toward the Magyar officers, and that the Russians had the duty to support the Magyars against Austrian revenge.[33]

In similar fashion, the Russians took the surrender of the fortress of Munkach, compelling the Austrian troops to withdraw. The Russians permitted Magyar officers on parole to wear their swords, and officers of the two armies enthusiastically caroused together. A Russian there present wrote: "One cannot but admit that at the time of the Hungarian campaign between us and our enemies there always appeared the most cordial relations, which one cannot say about the relations with our allies the Austrians. . . ."[34]

Both Rüdiger and Paskevich favored intervention by the Tsar to secure leniency to the captured Hungarian officers, and on August 8, the Field Marshal wrote Rüdiger that he had asked both Nicholas I and Franz Joseph for moderation in punishing them.[35] In spite of this feeling, however, reasons of state decided the issue. Some days later Paskevich sent out the following order to his commanders:

> This measure [the promise to protect Görgey and other Magyars], by which I withheld for several days the surrender of the prisoners to the Austrians, now has become unnecessary, for matters are approaching the end, and the last Seckler troops are surrendering or in flight, and the corps of Vechei, numbering about 10,000, are also surrendering to our troops. Hence I issue orders for the immediate handing over of the prisoners to the Austrians.[36]

32. Görgei, II, 435-36; Alabin, *Chetyre voiny*, I, Prilozheniia, XLI.
33. Men'kov, III, 286-89.
34. P. Bogdanovskii, "Iz vospominaniia o Vengerskoi i Krymskoi kampaniiakh," *Russkaia Starina*, LXXVII (1893), 244.
35. Men'kov, III, 286-89.
36. Averbukh, *Interventsiia*, pp. 174-75.

Paskevich, perhaps to justify this action, wrote to Rüdiger on August 8 that the Austrians talked much more fiercely than they acted, for they never shot anyone or carried out their threats.[37] Unfortunately, Paskevich's appraisal of the Austrians was far from accurate, for, shortly after he wrote this, under the guidance of Baron Haynau, Austrian military courts shot or hanged numbers of Magyar officers.

The friction between the Austrians and the Russians had made its appearance almost as soon as the Russian troops crossed the Carpathians. As early as June 15, Gen. Adj. Berg, Russian representative at Austrian headquarters, wrote Nicholas that the Austrians were complaining of ignorance of Paskevich's whereabouts and intentions, all of which prevented them from functioning properly. Three weeks later Paskevich sent a bitter letter to Berg complaining of lack of co-operation on the part of Haynau. Later in July he wrote that the latter had no understanding of the campaign. It was the Russian army, not the Austrian, that was crushing the enemy. In a letter to Berg on August 11, he belittled the Austrian victory at Temesvar, claiming that the *Russians* really had won the war.[38]

There was constant friction over provisions and wagon trains. In mid-July Paskevich sent Col. Zatler and Count Zicci, an Austrian commissar, to Pesth, to prepare and send provisions to the Russian forces. Baron Haynau, learning of this, commandeered all the provisions and the wagons, in spite of Zatler's strong protests.[39] When the Austrians complained of the slowness of the Russian movements, Paskevich was quick to complain to Prince Schwarzenberg, on July 25, that Austrian failure to help him obtain supplies had prevented him from moving against the Magyars.[40] In his report to the Tsar on July 28, the Field Marshal, in addition to voicing sharp complaints against his own generals, charged that Baron Haynau had been discourteous in his messages, and, more significantly, had hampered his efforts at provisioning his army. When the Russians were pursuing Görgey's army, Paskevich's messages asking the co-operation of the Austrians had no result except messages from Haynau lecturing him on strategy. The wrath of the Field Marshal against the Austrian commander was almost boundless, and his anger against Gen. Berg, for

37. Men'kov, III, 289.
38. I. I. Oreus, ed., "Russko-Vengerskaia voina 1849 goda," *Russkaia Starina*, LVIII (1888), 584-92.
39. Shcherbatov, VI, 115-17.
40. Men'kov, III, 265.

siding with the Austrians, was almost as great. In other words, *he* had been right and all others wrong.[41]

For their part, the Austrians had ample reason to be angry with their allies. Paskevich was tactless, as shown by his famous "Hungary is at the feet of Your Majesty" and his unwillingness to credit the Austrians with any real part in the victory. Count Otto von Bray-Steinberg, a Bavarian diplomat, wrote of "the complaints of the Viennese court about the haughtiness and arrogance of the elderly Field Marshal Paskevich, the soundness of which were recognized by the fairminded monarch [Nicholas I?]."[42]

The Austrians had other reasons to express displeasure, for, according to Görgey, Russian officers "went so far in their anger against the Austrians as to honor the Hungarian prisoners of war in striking fashion right in the presence of Austrian officers, and even to meet the latter in the presence of the former with unconcealed disregard." There were duels between individual Russians and Austrians, and rumors began to circulate regarding the inevitability of war between Russia and Austria, with Hungary on the side of the Russians.[43] In the 1920's, Lajos Steier, a Magyar historian, published four large volumes on the revolution of 1848-49, based on material in the Staatsarchiv in Vienna. In Vol. II, entitled *Haynau and Paskevich*, he related that after the Magyar surrender Haynau sent the Prince of Liechtenstein and Lt. Gen. Parro to Paskevich to express to him extreme displeasure regarding cordial Russian relations with captured Hungarian officers. Haynau, referring in an especially sharp tone to the "relations of the staff of the Russian army with the Hungarians who laid down their arms" with Görgey, stated that this kindness went far beyond that dictated by human feelings toward defeated foes. "They received the attentiveness of officers. . . of all ranks, who receive them warmly as comrade warriors; moreover, on the part of Count Rüdiger, entertainment was provided. The rebel military leaders wore their weapons and revolutionary decorations." Haynau ordered his officers to make a formal protest to Paskevich in the name of the Austrian commander in chief. In his report to Franz Joseph on August 18 Haynau charged that Rüdiger had allegedly openly condemned the Austrian policy and that as a result of careless guarding by the

41. *Ibid.*, pp. 266-71.
42. Otton de Bray, "Imperator Nikolai I-i i ego spodvizhniki," *Russkaia Starina*, CIX (1902), 121.
43. Görgey, II, 437.

Russians, only half of the prisoners remained. The number of captured officers had considerably increased, however, as those who surrendered counted on protection by the Russians.

Gen. Parro, in his report on the attitude of the Russian military toward the Magyars, stated to Haynau that the Hungarians had probably surrendered to the Russians because of the threats of the Austrians and the friendly attitude of the Russians toward them. "Not only the [Hungarian] soldiers, but even the people are more favorably inclined toward the Russians," so that they would probably regard leniency by the Austrian authorities "not as grace on the part of the Sovereign, but as a result of the mediation of the Russians."[44]

That the Austrians had good reason to be angry with the Russians is shown by P. Alabin's account of his stay in Debrecen at the end of the war, where he spent most of three days in a large saloon, packed tight with the officers of three armies, with the Austrians usually by themselves in a corner. There was much gayety, with dashing gypsy music, quantities of Hungarian wine, and attractive women. At times, the Magyars would dance the czardas, with drunken Russians joining in.

The Austrian officers, understandably, always tried to leave when the carousing grew boisterous. "At each step they were convinced of the evident mutual sympathy of our men with the Hungarians and our general open antipathy to them." The Russians offered a multitude of trifling insults to the Austrians, irritating them over each insignificant incident, every tiny matter. The Russians kept stressing the superiority of their own troops, reproaching the Austrians for the defeats they had suffered and reminding them that without Russian aid they would long ago have lost. The Russians with pleasure recounted everything unfavorable to the Austrians. They even took women away from them. In one saloon a clash ended with the Russians throwing several Austrians out the window because one of them said that the Russians had intentionally dragged out the war, as it was profitable for hirelings to stretch out their task! In another place the Russians simply gave an Austrian a sound beating with *nagaikas* (Cossack whips) for an incautious word. At Russian headquarters there was a duel between a Russian lieutenant of hussars and Count Makezi, an Austrian hussar, which ended in the death of the latter, although the cause was some

44. A. V. Fedorov, *Obshchestvenno-politicheskoe dvizhenie v russkoi armii 40-70 gg. XIX v.* (Moscow, 1958), pp. 53-56.

trifling matter. It was rumored that Prince Paskevich had the cause of his death listed as cholera. Many variants of this story circulated. One stated that when the Russian paid his bill in gold, the Austrian, who had only dubious paper, remarked that only hirelings paid in gold —hence the duel. Another version had it that when Nicholas I heard of the incident, he ordered: "To give a stern rebuke to the Russian officer for putting his life in danger in time of war. He should have killed the Austrian on the spot!"

While the conduct of many of the Russians must have been insufferable, they in turn charged the Austrian officers with much boasting, swaggering, and extravagant talk. This the Russians could not tolerate, especially as the Austrian armies had been badly beaten until the very last. The Austrians, however, refused to admit their defeats, but presented them as victories. "It is even laughable to hear their stories about their deeds."[45]

In contrast to their hostility toward the Austrians, "with the Hungarian officers ours drew close, in spite of the instructions of the Field Marshal . . . forbidding such friendship." The Russians scoffed at this order, believing it to be a result of fear that they might be infected by the same revolutionary ideas as the Magyars. So they continued to fraternize with the Hungarian officers, whom they admired for their courage, their picturesque uniforms, their unrestrained gaiety, and the obvious friendliness that they showed toward the Russians. Hence at every drinking party at which Magyars were present, after the toasts to the Tsar, one could hear: "to the Hungarian people," "to the alliance of Russia and Hungary." If they became still more drunk, the next toast would be: "To the ruin of Austria!" All this had no real significance, as there was no political basis for it, but merely a feeling of good fellowship with the Magyars, the novelty of being among former enemies, and, finally, an unexpressed readiness to make friends with the opponent in an open, honorable struggle.[46]

But while the Russians so confidently gloried in their victories and sneered at the Austrians, their allies had considerable reason to criticize them. Except for the actions of Lüders in Transylvania, the Russian strategy was sadly deficient, for, even with superior morale and numbers, the Russians were unable to bring about a decisive battle. Moreover, in other ways, the Russian army also displayed

45. Alabin, *Chetyre voiny*, I, 124-26.
46. *Ibid.*, I, 128-29.

weaknesses, both trivial and grave. One of these was a severe loss from disease, which, in a campaign that lasted only eight weeks, totalled about eighty-five thousand, of whom almost eleven thousand died. As the Russians sent approximately three hundred and sixty thousand men to Hungary, this means that almost one out of four became sick.[47]

Another failing was looting. Alabin reported: "It is a sad fact that our men looted wherever they could." Usually the regular troops were not involved, for they rarely occupied towns and villages and hence did not have the opportunity; "but none the less the Cossacks, the Moslems [irregular troops], the convoys with the baggage, whole hordes of orderlies and foragers, were not fools! These marauders roamed through the villages left in the rear or on the flanks of our forces and looted all that they could lay their hands on."[48] A more severe case of looting occurred when Cheodaev's forces attacked Tokaj on June 16. During the fighting civilians allegedly fired on some of the troops from houses. After the enemy had been driven off, troops— apparently Cossacks—broke into the buildings, killed citizens taken "gun in hand," and ravaged the whole western part of the city.[49] There also was considerable looting in Vác after the battle there early in July.[50]

The tactics of the Russian forces were especially faulty. The cavalry had no knowledge of scouting and pursuit, so that all too often the commanders lacked information as to the whereabouts of the enemy, to say nothing of their numbers.[51] The infantry, as usual, had firm discipline and great endurance, but as their muskets were highly inaccurate and their firepower was ineffective, their chief value was in massed attack with the bayonet. In battle they fired almost without aiming. Most of the cannon used were light guns, which five years later proved too light for effective fire.[52] Moreover, on occasion the troops failed to take even elementary military precautions. When Görgey's army was on the march after the battle of Vác, Paskevich, fearing that it might strike at Russian bases at Eperies and Kaschau, ordered them to retire in great haste to the north. Alabin organized the retirement from Kaschau, finally catching up with the other troops

47. Oreus, *Opisanie*, p. 539; Zatler, *O gospitaliakh*, p. 147.
48. Alabin, *Chetyre voiny*, I, 142-43.
49. *Ibid.*, I, 116-17.
50. Streng, *Russkaia Starina*, LXI (1889), 473.
51. Alabin, *Chetyre voiny*, I, 140.
52. Daragan, pp. 245-46.

at Samos. Here he found them all sleeping soundly at night, with no patrols or guards—infantry, cavalry, artillery, Austrians, Cossacks, all massed in the town, completely at the mercy of a surprise attack. Alabin felt that some day they would receive a fine lesson from the enemy "for the unceasing ignoring of military rules."[53]

While many of the weaknesses of the army were a result of outmoded concepts and antiquated weapons, it still had considerable power and, handled by a skilful commander, could have accomplished much more than it did, especially in view of its numbers and discipline. The successes of Lüders in Transylvania indicate that, with effective leadership, it was worthy of respect. In the main theater of war, however, its achievements were in no way proportionate to its strength. Large numbers of its officers ascribed this poor result to the commander in chief.

According to Alabin, criticism of Paskevich was extremely widespread in the army. While the main accusation was that he failed to destroy Görgey's army when it was in a trap at Vác, they also blamed him for a slow and ineffective pursuit after the action there, when the movement of Rüdiger, Cheodaev, and other forces could have compelled the Magyars to fight under ruinous circumstances. They condemned him for the useless movements of Cheodaev's corps back and forth between Miskolsc and Debrecen, which exhausted the troops and achieved nothing. Someone even made up a humorous soldier's song, one verse of which termed Cheodaev a hero for having captured Meso-Kevedz five times. They also accused the Field Marshal of the feeble movements of Cheodaev to Tokaj and the ludicrous battle at Debrecen, in which the whole Russian army struck a blow that hit little but air.[54]

The substance of this analysis of the Field Marshal's failures is contained in an article in *Jahrbücher für die deutsche Armee und Marine* (1874, no. 35-36). In the author's view, the Hungarian War was most inconvenient for him, and "his fearful caution here reached its highest degree of development, although the numerical superiority ... of Austria and Russia in comparison with Hungary could hardly leave room for cares and perils. Even in Poland the army had wished to have another commander—Ermolov. From this time forth the number of voices raised in the troops against Paskevich constantly

53. Alabin, *Chetyre voiny*, I, 101.
54. Alabin, *Chetyre voiny*, I, 144-45.

increased and grew louder. This was known to the Emperor. . . ." The only result of this was the order of the Tsar that the Field Marshal should everywhere receive the same honors as the Emperor himself— an action that silenced the critical voices.[55]

Nicholas continued to show his admiration for his "Father-Commander," for before the celebration of the twenty-fifth year of his reign, he visited Paskevich. To him he declared that all the glory of his reign was because of him. When the December revolt had shaken the regime, he had helped the Tsar; he had taken hold during the crisis in the East; he had won the Polish War and gained the loyalty of the Poles (!). Then in six weeks he had subdued the Magyars. The Tsar closed with the words: "Ivan Feodorovich! Thou art the glory of my twenty-five-year reign—thou art the history of the reign of Nicholas!"

With tears in his eyes, Paskevich told this to P. K. Men'kov of his staff.[56]

It seems impossible to escape the conclusion that the dominance of Paskevich over the Russian army throughout this period was not a blessing, but a grave misfortune for the army and the men who composed it. As yet the results of this misfortune had not made themselves felt to any degree, for Russia's opponents up to this time had been so weak that their defeat always came, even with Paskevich in command of the Russian army. The time was rapidly approaching, however, when the effects of this system would result in defeat at the hands of enemies much more powerful than any that the Field Marshal had encountered.

55. Translation in N. K. Schilder, "Fel'dmarshal Paskevich," *Russkaia Starina*, XIII, 606-7; Shcherbatov, IV, 193.
56. Men'kov, II, 168-70.

CHAPTER XVI. THE CRIMEAN WAR: THE FIRST PHASE

In letting the Crimean War get started, Nicholas I made his greatest mistake. It was essentially a diplomatic blunder, for in seeking to check the growth of French influence at Constantinople and to restore the dominant position that Russia had had there in 1833, he failed to comprehend the obstacles in his way. France, of course, would be hostile; but the Tsar counted on the support of Prussia, the friendship of Austria, and the neutrality of Britain—all of which failed to materialize. Thus, instead of an easy war against Turkey, he had to fight Britain and France as well, with Sardinia thrown in for good measure. Austria repeatedly threatened to join the coalition, and Prussia, while opposed to war, was against Russian domination of the Straits. Even Sweden appeared ready to join a general alliance, hoping to recover Finland and the eastern Baltic coast. Thus Nicholas, fearful of an Austrian attack on Russian Poland, never dared devote more than a fraction of his army to the struggle against the French, the British, and the Turks. In spite of this and other crippling handicaps, however, the Russians fought with great bravery and determination and almost won a resounding victory in the Crimea. While the innate weaknesses of the military machine of Nicholas I made this impossible, nevertheless the Russians were able to deny to the allied powers a complete triumph and to accept a compromise peace that, although painful to Russian vanity, did little harm to vital Russian interests.

At first Nicholas planned to capture Constantinople by a sudden blow by his Black Sea fleet, which would transport several divisions to the Bosporus. After warnings from Paskevich, however, that this might lead to general war,[1] by April 8, 1853, the Tsar reluctantly dropped the idea of seizing Constantinople and, worried about the increasing activities of the British and French in the Near East, began to favor

1. Zaionchkovskii, *Vostochnaia voina*, I, Prilozheniia, 599-600.

occupation of the Principalities as the first step.[2] On May 16-17 Nicholas, in consultation with Paskevich, drew up his plans for three phases of activity. The first was to be occupation of the Principalities, without fighting, if possible, as a means of compelling the Turks to accept the Russian demands. The second phase called for blockading the Bosporus and a threat to declare the independence of the Principalities and Serbia. The third move would be to recognize their independence and thus "to make a start to the destruction of the Ottoman Empire." He added that even then he did not intend to proceed to far-reaching actions.[3]

Following up this scheme, in the summer of 1853 he moved Russian troops under Prince M. D. Gorchakov into the Principalities, where they stayed largely on the defensive. The Turks demanded that the Russians evacuate the area, declaring war when the Tsar refused to leave. When the Turks crossed the Danube at Oltenitsa, south of Bucharest, on Oct. 23, 1853, a Russian force under Gen. Dannenberg attacked their fortifications under highly disadvantageous conditions. The Russians, although losing very heavily, were on the point of driving out the Turks when Dannenberg halted the attack and withdrew his forces. Although the general bungled badly, the stubbornness of the Russian troops prevented a worse outcome.[4] On December 25, a force of eighteen thousand Turks attacked Col. Baumgarten, with twenty-five hundred men and six guns at Chetati. These troops, while isolated, made a terrific fight and repeatedly beat off the attackers with heavy losses. Nonetheless, they were on the point of collapse when another small force of Russians attacked the Turks in the rear, suffering heavy losses as it did so. Finally, when the main Russian force approached, the Turks withdrew to safety. Once more, the Russian commanders had mishandled their troops, for they had exposed small units to strong Turkish attack.[5] On the other hand, Gen. Soimonov skilfully repulsed the Turks on the lower Danube when they attempted to cross. (See map facing page 56.)

In the meantime, the war also spread to the Caucasus, where the Russian troops were weak, as the struggle against Shamil demanded very large forces. Prince Vorontsov, gravely concerned, informed Nicholas that he could spare only six battalions to protect the frontier,

2. *Ibid.*, I, 601-3.
3. *Ibid.*, I, 603.
4. Bogdanovich, *Vostochnaia voina*, I, 131-38.
5. *Ibid.*, I, 167-83.

menaced by large Turkish armies and numerous bands of Kurds and other warlike residents of the area. The Tsar, "with great unwillingness," sent one division by sea to strengthen the defenses south of the Caucasus. On November 1, Prince Bebutov, who had been ill, took command of the army in Armenia. In November he permitted Prince Orbeliani to move with a small force to protect the Armenian population against the Kurds, in spite of the contrary advice of his other commanders. Orbeliani, proceeding without patrols or flank guards, blundered into a force of twenty thousand Turks at Baiandur, where for two hours his troops were exposed to punishing Turkish artillery fire, while irregulars attacked his flanks and rear. Finally Bebutov came to the rescue, at which point the Turks withdrew. As the Russian forces had lost heavily, for no good reason, it was a poor beginning.[6]

The situation soon improved, however. Late in October, when a Turkish army of eighteen thousand moved against Akhaltsykh, the key to Georgia, Prince Andronikov, whose troops had been reinforced, attacked them with two columns, from the front and the flank. The Turks, thoroughly beaten, lost about thirty-five hundred men, with their camp, provisions, and thirteen guns. The Russians lost only 361 men. Following this, Prince Bebutov, with a small force of inspired troops, moved to save the Armenians from the depredations of the Kurds. At Bash-Kadyk-Lar they met a vastly larger Turkish army which expected to capture them all. For a time Bebutov hesitated to attack, but finally the Russian center and right charged the Turks and with the help of effective artillery fire routed them. In the center there was a fierce combat, until finally the Turks gave way and fled, only to be looted by the Kurds as they ran. The Russians took twenty-six guns and two Turkish camps, although there were few prisoners. While the Russian losses were fairly heavy, they had thoroughly beaten and demoralized the main Turkish army, which lost eight thousand men, and the Transcaucasus was safe until spring.[7]

In the meantime, the position of the Russian forts on the Black Sea coast was increasingly desperate. On September 11, 1853, Paskevich urged the Tsar to evacuate them, as it would be impossible to hold them against a naval attack.[8] While Nicholas at first refused, Admiral Serebriakov reported that, as it was impossible to provision

6. M. Ia. Ol'shevskii, "Russko-turetskaia voina za kavkazom v 1853 i 1854 gg.," *Russkaia Starina*, XLIV (1884), 179-82.

7. Ol'shevskii, "Russko-turetskaia voina," *Russkaia Starina*, XLIV (1884), 420-26.

8. Zaionchkovskii, *Vostochnaia voina*, II, Prilozheniia, 106.

the forts, they could not hold out against even the Turks. In addition, the tribesmen of the mountain regions were preparing to attack at the first appearance of foreign war vessels. So it was decided to evacuate all but those close to the Kuban. After the Tsar had compelled Admiral A. S. Menshikov to supply some vessels to Serebriakov, the evacuation took place. The navy was able to rescue 3,849 men, as well as most of the artillery, by March 5.[9]

In 1854 the Turks made great efforts to put powerful armies in the field in the Asian theater of war. British and French officers helped them reorganize and trained and equipped the troops. New forces came from Egypt and Tunisia. Thus the Turks, by May, had the largest and best armies that they had ever led in eastern Turkey. The Russian forces were also reinforced, but their numbers were much smaller than those of the enemy.[10] (See map facing page 22.)

The first fighting came in western Georgia, where Turkish forces came in from Batum. First Prince Eristov, with about one regiment, smashed a detachment of twelve thousand Turks, and then Prince Andronikov led a force of ten thousand men, with eighteen guns, against thirty-four thousand Turks and thirteen guns. In a fierce battle the Russians beat and dispersed the invaders, who lost all their baggage, all their artillery, and four thousand men. This ended all danger from Batum.[11] In June, Prince Bebutov permitted Gen. Wrangel to advance against a body of Turks based on Baiazet, southwest of Erivan. The troops had a difficult climb through the mountains, arriving at the crest of the pass so exhausted that the men lay down and slept for two or three hours, in spite of the fire of irregulars from the surrounding heights. Then they attacked through the narrow pass, scattering the irregulars, and at the bottom charged the Turkish infantry and artillery. Most of the Turks fled, while those who tried to stand were cut down. Thus the Russian forces had routed enemy troops almost seven times as numerous. By this sweeping victory the Russians had ended the threat to Erivan, while the capture of Baiazet after the battle put them astride an important caravan route from Tabriz to Erzerum and Trebizond (Trabzon).[12]

These successes, which doubtless disheartened the Turks and increased the confidence of the Russians, were minor actions, and the

9. Dubrovin, *Vostochnaia voina*, pp. 32-37.
10. Kazbek, p. 196.
11. Bogdanovich, *Vostochnaia voina*, II, 157-62.
12. Likhutin, *Russkie*, pp. 90-104.

area between Alexanderopol and Kars would again be the scene of the deciding battle. Both armies moved out to the frontier, where they occupied fortified camps facing each other. While the Russian troops were only about eighteen thousand men, with sixty-four guns, they were in excellent condition and full of confidence. The Turkish army, with sixty thousand men and at least seventy guns, was weakened by disease, poor food, and a shortage of forage for the horses. Both armies moved on July 23. The Turkish advance was made in great secrecy, taking the Russians by surprise, so that in the morning they discovered that the Turkish right wing held a ridge overlooking their position, a great mass of regular infantry and artillery threatened their center, and strong forces of Turkish and irregular cavalry were ready to attack the right flank and rear. In this dangerous situation, the Russian army attacked, driving the Turks off the ridge on the Russian left, and pushing relentlessly with infantry and artillery against the battalions in the center, who outnumbered them four to one. In spite of heavy losses, the massed forces in the center gained the upper hand over the Turks and drove them from the field, although they retreated in good order. The Russian right, meanwhile, had been hard pressed by the masses of Turkish horse, but as the tide of battle turned in the other sectors the latter broke and fled, hotly pursued by some of the Russian forces. The latter, with losses of about three thousand killed and wounded, captured fifteen Turkish cannon and two thousand prisoners. The total Turkish losses amounted to about ten thousand men, in addition to about twelve thousand irregulars who deserted. This Battle of Kürük-Dar, while far from decisive, established a stalemate for the rest of 1854. The Russians, although victorious and confident, were not strong enough to march against Kars, while the Turks had no more taste for offensive action.[13]

In the Caucasus also, the Russians managed to maintain their position, albeit with considerable difficulty. Actually, before war came the policy of subduing the Chechens by cutting the forests that sheltered their auls was well advanced. Large areas of their land were exposed and helpless and increasing numbers of families were evading Shamil's control and moving to safety under Russian protection. In January and February, 1853, Prince Bariatinskii won a big victory by crossing the hitherto impassable Michik River, destroying villages

13. Ol'shevskii, "Russko-turetskaia voina," *Russkaia Starina*, XLIV (1884), 500-10.

and building bridges and roads. The coming of war with Turkey, however, weakened the Russians, who had to withdraw several battalions from the mountains to bolster up the armies on the frontier, and also greatly encouraged the mountaineers. Prince Vorontsov, who did not favor the war, was in bad health and went to pieces when it came, and the elderly Prince Bebutov also was sick and dispirited. Most of the work of holding the Caucasus fell to Prince Bariatinskii.[14] In September, 1853, Shamil massed fifteen thousand men for an assault on the Russian defense line in the Lezgin country. Some three thousand Russians beat them back, however. Shamil now made a great detour, hoping to find a weak spot in the defenses. His bands attacked the unfinished fort at Mesel'deger, held by two companies without proper supplies, but the defenders beat them back with bayonet charges until relief came up, after five days of heavy fighting.[15]

This achievement, and the Russian victory at Sinop and the successes of Princes Andronikov and Bebutov against the Turks, quieted the tribesmen for a time and encouraged the Russians. Gen. Read, a dashing cavalryman, completely ignorant of the Caucasus, replaced the ailing Prince Vorontsov. The coming of war with Britain and France and the prospect that the Persians might attack caused some panic among the Caucasus commanders, who suggested evacuation of many of the Caucasus forts. Even Bariatinskii, who expected an Anglo-French landing in the Caucasus, supported this mistaken view. Nicholas, however, was violently opposed to this, telling Read to hang on and to harass Shamil as best he could.[16]

The entry of France and Britain into the war encouraged the mountaineers, as did the relative inactivity of the Russians over the winter of 1853-54. The latter continued to cut the forests of Chechnia and destroy food supplies, but there were no large-scale actions. In July Shamil, with fifteen thousand men, took the offensive over the Caucasus range to break through the Lezgin Line and take Tiflis, hoping later to join the Turks who would advance from the Black Sea. With most of their troops facing the Turks, the Russians, after holding Shamil's advance guard, retired under heavy pressure to a village only forty miles from Tiflis, and a breakthrough of the tribesmen appeared imminent. At this point, however, the peasants of Kakhetia rose up

14. Zisserman, "Bariatinskii," *Russkii Arkhiv*, XXVI (1888), Pt. II, 292-303.
15. Bestuzhev, p. 53.
16. Zisserman, "Bariatinskii," *Russkii Arkhiv*, XXVI (1888), Pt. III, 50-68.

and attacked Shamil's bands from the rear and held them off for three days, during which Russian reserves arrived. Shamil and his followers now fled back to the fortresses of Dagestan.[17]

In the meantime, the Russians were raiding the lands of the Chechens with some success, to the great misery of these unhappy people. Late in September, an attack on the Russian fortress of Andreeva failed when reserves came to the rescue. Shamil now decided on a new and powerful offensive to crush the tribesmen who had settled under Russian protection. Although no one knew the objective of the drive, Baron Nikolai in the Chechen region massed his small forces in readiness. Shamil struck at the position of Istisu, where the village and two small redoubts were under terrific pressure. Hearing the cannon fire, Baron Nikolai rushed his troops to the rescue, where they shook the attackers, and a flank attack of the cavalry threw them into panic. The Russians thus had won a decisive victory at little cost. Shamil's hopes were dashed and his supporters lost heart.[18]

This resounding success permitted the Russians to continue the offensive in the Chechen lands, where they burned vast quantities of corn, millet, and hay, as well as many villages. They also continued the cutting of the forest, in spite of the efforts of Shamil to prevent this. While many of the tribesmen retired deeper into the mountains to make new homes for themselves, faith in Shamil and their defenses was declining and larger numbers made their peace with the Russians, who settled them on protected lands.[19] Shamil still sought to encourage his followers by promises that in 1855 the French, British, and Turks would come to their rescue, but, while many of the mountaineers, especially in Dagestan, still believed this, the evidence of Russian power had shaken the faith of the Chechens, more and more of whom evaded Shamil's control and settled under Russian protection.

But while the Russian forces had some success in the Asian theater of operations, those along the Danube never could achieve anything of importance. The chief reason for the lack of accomplishment in the Balkan region was not Russian military weakness, however, but the rapidly changing political situation, which repeatedly upset their calculations and prevented them from formulating sound policies.

Early in 1854, Nicholas I asked Paskevich to come to St. Peters-

17. *Ibid.*, pp. 167-71; Bestuzhev, p. 73.
18. Zisserman, *Istoriia*, II, 170-98.
19. Zisserman, *Dvadtsat'piat' let*, II, 236 and 255.

burg to confer on plans for the war. When they met early in February, the Field Marshal argued that they should not mount a large offensive, but hold as best they could. He regarded Austria and Prussia as the chief dangers in sight, as they could field large armies, which the Russians would have difficulty in checking. As for allied landings in the Crimea or at Odessa, he believed that these would present no real danger and could be contained by thirty-five thousand men in each place, along with reserves. He felt it desirable to push on against the Turks and to capture Silistria and Turtukai, as this would compel the allies to rescue the Turks. The Russian army could then crush the allied contingents. His main point, however, was the urgent necessity to form a large reserve army in the center to deal with the Austrians and the Prussians.[20] The Tsar's views differed considerably from those of his general. In a letter to Prince Gorchakov on February 1, he took the view that Austria and Prussia had not committed themselves to either side, although the former was sending "extremely friendly assurances" to Russia. Adding that "*I regard it now necessary* to begin the siege of Silistria," Nicholas hoped that by capturing it and Rushchuk, his forces would be protected against an allied landing at Varna and would be able to support an uprising of the Serbs.[21]

The Germanic powers showed their increasing opposition to Russian domination of the Balkans by signing a Protocol at the Vienna Conference of April 9 calling for the preservation of the Turkish Empire and for evacuation of the Principalities. They also called for an offensive and defensive alliance (April 20, at Berlin) to protect their territories against attack.[22] Paskevich's concern grew. In a memorandum of April 15, he expressed dismay at the possibility of an Anglo-French landing at Varna, backed by a Turkish force of seventy thousand men, which could compel the Russian forces to evacuate Bucharest. If, in addition, Austria declared war, they would be taken in the rear and would have to try to fight their way out, with a possible loss of half of their strength. He advised that it would now be sensible to leave the Danube and the Principalities and retire behind the Sereth or the Pruth.[23] This opinion, which in various forms Paskevich continued to express for several months, was characterized by his grave fear of attack by Austria, which was the leitmotiv of his

20. Shcherbatov, VII, 97-102.
21. Zaionchkovskii, *Vostochnaia voina*, II, Prilozheniia, 313-14.
22. *Ibid.*, pp. 338-41.
23. *Ibid.*, pp. 396-98.

thinking until the end of the Crimean War. Probably at this particular moment this proposal would have been more sensible than to proceed with the siege of Silistria. If the Russians had evacuated the Principalities and at the same time had taken strong measures to defend the Crimea (something that Paskevich did not believe in), this might have eliminated all pretexts for war and would have made a landing in the Crimea a hazardous venture. But Nicholas did neither the one nor the other.

In the early months of 1854, the Russians had considerable success in gaining control of the Danube channel. Although the Turks had flotillas of gunboats on it, Gen. Schilder, an erratic but talented engineer, built batteries at strategic points that hemmed the Turkish vessels in and eventually burned or sank them. Gen. Khrulev had similar success along higher reaches of the river.[24] In mid-March the Russian forces, with heavy batteries dominating the chosen points, forced their way across the river at three places with a minimum of difficulty. Gorchakov's handling of the crossing was brilliant, with the leaders thoroughly prepared and instructed.[25]

But while Paskevich's realization of the rashness of the attack on Silistria is to his credit, he never dared express his opposition to the Tsar's wishes and instead on various pretexts delayed opening the siege, in spite of the sovereign's repeated urging. On April 29 he wrote to the Minister of War: "I lost three or four days, awaiting news from Austria." As, however, the danger from this source now seemed less, "the siege of Silistria will be opened in three or four days."[26] The delay of which he wrote, however, was much more than three or four days. He spent weeks inspecting the troops and the terrain, and when he heard of the signing of the Austro-Prussian convention for mutual support he wanted to withdraw all his troops behind the Sereth or the Pruth. He also worried about allied landings on the Black Sea coast. Even as late as April 27, he wrote Nicholas that the Austrians would attack on May 20 and by the 27th the Russian forces would be in danger. He actually took some of the preliminary steps for retirement, but when the Tsar wrote that the Austrians would not dare attack, he finally marched to Silistria on

24. Bogdanovich, *Vostochnaia voina*, I, 185-207.
25. *Ibid.*, I, 19-32; Men'kov, I, 127-28.
26. Schilder, *Totleben*, I, 18-19.

May 4.[27] Thus, after crossing the Danube, Paskevich took six weeks before beginning the siege.

Before the siege started, Gen. Schilder had promised to take Silistria in one week, basing this prediction on his plans for an attack from the east, along the river bank. The Field Marshal, however, refused to permit this, but insisted on attacking Arab-tabia, a stone outwork some distance from the city to the southeast, against the strenuous objections of Schilder. The first trench was dug out of range of the enemy, and the first parallel was over one mile from Arab-tabia. No attempt was made to blockade the fortress, although Schilder strongly urged it. Paskevich was more concerned with an attack from the Turks in Shumla or from the British and French than he was with the siege, to the extent that he diverted many men from the siege work to build a fortified camp on the heights south of the city, and at one time withdrew much of the siege artillery from the batteries and emplaced it in the fortified position, to beat off an expected attack which never came. Thus, although the Russians had ninety thousand men against eighteen thousand defenders, the siege went very slowly.[28] Prince Vasil'chikov expressed a widely held opinion when he asserted that the Field Marshal, lacking the moral courage to refuse the Tsar's demands for an attack on the fortress, merely went through the motions of besieging it, hoping that in some way he could lift the siege. Vasil'chikov held that while Paskevich had been correct in his opposition to the Tsar's policy, he should have resigned his command rather than pretend to carry it out.[29]

During this period Paskevich was busily making plans for withdrawal from Silistria and built a second bridge over the Danube for that purpose. Nicholas I, however, wrote him five letters during May, urging him on and belittling the danger from Austria. On May 23, for example, he wrote that the news from Vienna was favorable, as the Prussians and other Germans were restraining the Austrians, and the mobilization of the Russian reserves was very successful. He ended with the injunction: "Do not despair!"[30] Finally, however, on June 1 the Tsar sent Paskevich the word that he had been longing for. While he believed that the Austrians would not be ready to move for another month, he urged his "Father-Commander" to ship out of the Princi-

27. Shcherbatov, VII, 138-42, 151-55.
28. Bogdanovich, *Vostochnaia voina*, II, 60-68; Men'kov, *Zapiski*, I, 164-68.
29. Vasil'chikov, *Russkii Arkhiv*, XXIX (1891), Pt. II, 174-75.
30. Shcherbatov, VII, 159-69.

palities the wounded and sick and all unnecessary baggage. He also advised that if Silistria had not fallen by the time Paskevich received this letter, and the latter could not guarantee the date when it would fall, he should lift the siege and retire across the Danube.[31]

On May 29 an event occurred that is still shrouded in mystery. Paskevich with a considerable body of troops rode forth to reconnoiter the Turkish position. The enemy, seeing the concentration of troops and commanders, threw shot and shell at long range. One projectile landed not far from the Field Marshal, who apparently was not hit. Some reports say that at first there was no sign of injury, but later the Field Marshal complained of severe pain in his shoulder and rode off in his carriage back across the Danube. Prince Gorchakov took command of the troops.[32] It is perhaps worthy of remark that, at the assault on Warsaw in 1831, Paskevich had suffered a contusion, after which he turned his command over to Count Toll. While the parallel between the two incidents is interesting, the evidence is not conclusive.

Under Gorchakov the siege continued, although without rapid progress. On June 7 a large mine under Arab-tabia blew up much of its wall and gave the opportunity for an assault. On the night of June 9 the troops—six regiments, with twelve battalions in reserve—were eagerly awaiting the signal for the attack, when suddenly Gorchakov received a categoric order from Paskevich to lift the siege and retire across the Danube. To the great indignation of the troops, this powerful, confident army had to retire before a weak and almost helpless enemy.[33] The Tsar explained the cause of this action in a letter to Prince Gorchakov: "How sad and painful for me, dear Gorchakov, that I had to agree to the insistent arguments of Ivan Fedorovich [Paskevich] concerning the danger threatening the army from the faithlessness of Austria, whom we had saved."[34]

By June 11 the Russian forces were back across the Danube, untroubled by the Turks, who did, however, push across the river and occupied Zhurzha. The Russians withdrew slowly from the Principalities, which eventually were occupied by the Austrians, by agree-

31. *Ibid.*, VII, 170.
32. Bogdanovich, *Vostochnaia voina*, II, 90-93; Men'kov, I, 162-63; Shcherbatov, VII, 172-73. One author, who claims to have treated Paskevich after the incident, suggests that it was not a genuine injury. Pavlutskii, "Kontuziia Fel'dmarshala Paskevicha," *Russkaia Starina*, XII (1875), 634-36. The various accounts do not agree as to the date of the incident.
33. Shcherbatov, VII, 184-87.
34. *Ibid.*, p. 187n.

ment with the Turks. Late in August all the Russian forces were on their own soil.[35]

On the whole, this outcome of the campaign appears to have been wise, even though it might have been better never to have moved against Silistria. On the other hand, Russian military men have argued that if Paskevich had really made a determined effort to take it, it would have fallen in mid-May and the Russians would have had a firm foothold across the Danube from which to threaten the Turks. This, it is held, would have compelled the French and the British to commit their troops in the Balkans to rescue the Turks, and hence there would have been no landing in the Crimea in 1854. On the other hand, the danger from Austria probably was grave enough to warrant Paskevich's action.

As the Russian troops retired, French and British troops landed at Varna in Bulgaria. Here cholera and other diseases smote them sorely and, with the burning of much of their supplies, prevented them from striking at the Russians. With Austrian troops occupying the Principalities, by July the Danube campaign was at an end. Before the allied forces there could reorganize for a fresh venture, however, the Baltic Sea became the main theater of war.

In March, 1854, a British fleet under Admiral Sir Charles Napier entered the Baltic, hoping to strike a telling blow at the Russians. Some enthusiastic Britons even expected him to take St. Petersburg, or at least bombard it. Actually, he could accomplish little. The Russian fleet did not come out, and the British could not hope to attack Kronstadt. Beaten off at Åbo and Hangö in Finland, the most that Napier's force could do was raid small ports and burn Finnish and other small vessels. The moral effect of this expedition, however, was great. The Tsar and his officials could see hostile sails off Kronstadt, which created an impression of real danger. Heavy reinforcements poured into Finland, and other divisions strengthened the defenses of Estonia and Latvia.[36]

By mid-July Napier, realizing the hopelessness of an attack on the main Russian position, decided to strike at the small fort of Bomarsund in the Åland Islands. It proved impossible, however, to attack it by sea, and only with the arrival of a French fleet with ten thousand

---

35. Zaionchkovskii, "Vostochnaia voina," in Grishinskii, X, 42-44.
36. M. Borodkin, *Voina 1854-1855 gg. na finskom poberezh'e. Istoricheskii ocherk* (St. Petersburg, 1904), pp. 77-118.

troops could the siege begin. The Russian garrison defended the fortress strongly, but by August 4/16, with all its guns silenced, it surrendered. The French then blew up the defenses and sailed back to France.[37]

Admiral Napier stayed on in the Baltic for some weeks, seeking to induce Sweden to enter the war. The Swedes, however, although eager to recover Finland, feared the Russians too much to give up their neutrality. The government felt that only if Austria would take the offensive against Russia and if a large French army committed itself to a Baltic campaign would it be safe for Sweden to fight.[38] As neither Austria nor France would meet these terms, the Swedes remained neutral.

Thus Napier's expedition proved to be merely a large-scale raid. But in spite of strong British disappointment, the venture produced one important result. The Tsar and his advisers could not be sure that a powerful allied offensive in the Baltic was not imminent. Hence the best Russian troops massed in Finland and along the Baltic coast and powerful artillery and supplies stood ready for the attack that did not come. Thus when the allied offensive did finally come, in the Crimea and not in the Baltic, much of Russia's strength was concentrated over one thousand miles away.

The Russian authorities had long considered the possibility of an allied landing in the Crimea. In fact, as early as January, 1854, Admiral Menshikov, commander at Sevastopol, after the sighting of allied ships near the peninsula, asked for reinforcements. In February, the Ministry of War gained reliable information that the allies were planning to land in the Crimea near Sevastopol. There had been talk of this in both the French and the British parliaments; *The Times* had predicted it; and numerous other signs indicated the Crimea as the place for a landing. Late in February, 1854, the Russian Ministry of War actually ordered reinforcements for the Crimea to go in haste. At this point, however, Paskevich convinced St. Petersburg that the chief danger was to the western frontier, not to Sevastopol. The reinforcements were not sent. Nevertheless, the frequent sighting of allied vessels off the Crimea, some of which made soundings, and the calls in France and Britain for decisive action—all indicated that a move would be made, especially after Turkey was no longer in danger

37. *Ibid.*, pp. 118-77.
38. Tarlé, I, 491-503.

on the Danube. In June *The Times* actually named Sevastopol as the objective.[39]

In addition, the Russians had little difficulty in deciding on the probable landing point. In his memorandum on the defense of the Crimea, Menshikov on June 29 pointed to Evpatoria as the most suitable spot to land troops for an attack on Sevastopol. He reported that his troops consisted of twenty-six battalions, eight squadrons of hussars, and thirty-six light guns—somewhat less than twenty-five thousand men.[40] As he expected that the allies could land fifty to sixty thousand men, he wrote Prince Gorchakov an urgent letter on June 30 asking him to send to the Crimea the 16th Division from the troops released by the evacuation of the Principalities.[41] Gorchakov hastened to grant this request, thereby annoying Field Marshal Paskevich, who felt that Menshikov had enough troops to defend Sevastopol, whereas the front against Austria would require vastly more troops.[42] Nicholas, however, wrote Paskevich that the sending of the 16th Division was necessary "for the defense of the Crimea and Sevastopol."[43]

One of the chief reasons for Menshikov's concern was that Sevastopol was not in good condition for defense. Against a naval attack its fortifications were powerful, but the landward defenses were in part non-existent, with several of the most important bastions only on paper, and no wall connecting what defense works there were. On the northern side, where the foe would probably attack, the bastion was not completed and the defense walls were very weak. While Menshikov tried to speed up the construction, as a local commander he lacked authority and had to refer all problems to St. Petersburg. In a letter to Gorchakov in March he wrote: "You cannot imagine how much I have to struggle against the stupidity of the engineers here, who build breastworks no higher than a twelve-year-old child."[44]

Little improvement occurred during the summer, in part because of Paskevich's clamor about the Austrian danger and his underestimation of the threat to the Crimea. On July 31, Menshikov complained

39. Dubrovin, *Vostochnaia voina*, pp. 42-57.
40. A. D. Krylov, "Kniaz' A. S. Menshikov, 1853-1854," *Russkaia Starina*, VII (1873), 851-54.
41. "Oborona Sevastopolia. Pis'ma Kniazia A. S. Menshikova k Kn. M. D. Gorchakovu," *Russkaia Starina*, XII (1875), 304-5.
42. Schilder, *Totleben*, I, Prilozheniia, 36-37.
43. Shcherbatov, VII, 200.
44. "Oborona Sevastopolia," *Russkaia Starina*, XV (1875), 302.

to Prince Dolgoruki, minister of war, about the weakness of the fortifications. The city was not walled in and had little shelter for supplies and munitions, except a few powder magazines. The engineers were not co-operative and were absorbed in paperwork. They continued to cut stone for defensive barracks when they should have been meeting more immediate needs, justifying this action by complaints about the lack of picks and mattocks and the absence of proper timber.[45] Nicholas responded by giving Menshikov a free hand in rushing the defense works and ordered the engineers to carry out his orders at once.[46] He especially emphasized the completion of the 3rd and 4th bastions and the connecting wall—"to make all efforts to complete them by April, without sparing labor." Menshikov's answer was that this would take years, even in normal times. Moreover, the whole fortification plan required technical study. He especially stressed the weakness of the northern side, where the walls built of shale crumbled badly.[47] By the time this message arrived, the allied landing at Evpatoria was about three weeks away.

It is interesting to note that Nicholas set the completion date for the work in April, 1855. This was a result of the widespread belief that the allies would not try to land in 1854, because of the lateness of the season and the nearness of the equinoctial storms. In several messages to the Ministry of War, Menshikov declared his belief that the landing would not come until 1855,[48] and in a letter of August 26 he expressed surprise that Gorchakov still expected one in 1854.[49]

One of the chief reasons for Menshikov's failings as an administrator was his lack of a staff capable of handling the necessary routine work, which led to general disorder. One officer who was in Sevastopol reported: "His whole staff consisted of Col. Wunsch, chief of staff, and several clerks: the army had no Quartermaster General, no intendant, no director of hospitals. In the clerical section . . . there was such chaos that sometimes they did not know where a certain regiment was. . . ."[50] According to a Col. Batezatul who served in the Crimea, Col. Wunsch "concentrated in his person all

45. Schilder, *Totleben*, I, 39-41.
46. *Ibid.*, pp. 45-46.
47. V. D. Krenke, *Oborona Baltiiskago priberezh'ia 1853-1856 gg.* (St. Petersburg, 1887), pp. 12-16.
48. On July 28, Aug. 2 and 5. Schilder, *Totleben*, I, 41-42.
49. N. K. Schilder, "Priezd E. I. Totlebena v Sevastopol' v Avguste 1854 g.," *Russkaia Starina*, XVIII (1877), 510n.
50. Shcherbachev, *Russkii Arkhiv*, XXVIII (1890), Pt. I, 267.

the functions: chief of staff, general on duty, Quartermaster General, intendant, director of the chancellery, hospitals and posts, general police master, and so on." Thus from the beginning of operations in the Crimea, great disorder existed in the administration of the army.[51]

When the allied landings occurred on September 1, after the fleet had sailed, fully visible, past Sevastopol, the Russian forces permitted them to capture Evpatoria and land unopposed. During the four days of the landings the Russians did not trouble them. While the latter could not have stood up to the naval artillery, they could easily have annoyed the enemy by using horse artillery, cavalry, and sharpshooters against them, especially in night attacks. Nothing of the kind was tried, however,[52] and the Russian troops camped quietly on the river Alma, awaiting the allied advance.

Menshikov, who thoroughly distrusted his subordinates, held no formal conferences with his generals, most of whom he kept ignorant of his intentions. His plan was to fight a delaying action on the steep banks of the Alma and then to retire to a rear position. As the allied forces, with sixty thousand men, far outnumbered his thirty-five thousand, he had no hope of victory. Many Russian writers have held that a better strategy would have been to occupy a position some distance from the sea, where allied naval superiority would have been useless and Russian superiority in cavalry would have counted heavily. The allies, with few horses and scanty transport, could not have pushed far inland, so they probably would not have dared to attack him. If they tried a march on Sevastopol, Menshikov could easily have hit them in the flank and rear with devastating effect. Thus if he had followed this strategy, the allies would probably have been in a highly difficult situation.[53]

Apparently, in his dismay at the unexpected allied landing, the Russian commander did not think of this stratagem, but rather chose the more obvious measure of occupying a strong defensive position on the Alma. Here, too, he made mistakes. Although the Russian force were encamped on the Alma for a week, little was done to strengthen the position. They did not destroy the vineyards and stone walls in the valley that later gave valuable cover to allied sharpshooters and they built almost no field fortifications, especially on the crest of the

51. Dubrovin, *Vostochnaia voina*, pp. 173-74.
52. *Ibid.*, pp. 88-89.
53. Bogdanovich, *Vostochnaia voina*, III, 32.

ridge overlooking the valley. Menshikov made no general reconnaissance of the position, entrusting this important function to a young and inexperienced aide.[54]

The worst error was on the Russian left, near the shore of the sea. The Russian commanders apparently felt that the steep bluffs along the river were impregnable and merely stationed two battalions to watch this sector. Even the most casual reconnaissance, however, would have revealed a roadway up which the local Tatars had hauled wagonloads of hay and melons. The troops could easily have made this impassable by digging out the road, constructing entrenchments and rifle pits to guard it, and putting artillery, behind parapets, to sweep it. Thus the left flank would have been fully secure, in spite of the fire of distant naval vessels. The French historian Bazancourt stated that Menshikov committed "an irreparable error" in failing to take these measures.[55]

In other respects as well, Menshikov failed to prepare properly for the conflict. He did not issue an order of battle to the troops, so that even the two leading field commanders had no instructions, no information as to ammunition supplies, reserves, field hospitals, or other essential matters. As Menshikov furnished no effective leadership or advice, the commanders had to fight in haphazard fashion, as if in a fog.[56]

The battle itself, on September 8, which was delayed by the slowness of the British to advance, was stubborn on the right, where the redcoats attacked, and in the center. In spite of the superiority of the British rifles and the French Minié balls over the Russian weapons, the Russian infantry repeatedly drove back the British by bayonet charges and artillery fire and kept the French center at bay. Finally, however, the allied forces drove the Russians back from the river to the hills beyond, but it was a hard fight to the end. The masses of Russian cavalry, however, failed to take any part in the action, although they might have harassed the British flank and rear.[57]

It was on the left flank, however, that the Russian forces lost the battle. The troops of Gen. Bosquet's division quickly discovered the road and the paths to the high left bank of the Alma and even brought

54. *Ibid.*, pp. 32-33.
55. César Lecat Bazancourt, *L'expédition de Crimée jusqu'à la prise de Sébastopol* (2 vols. in 1; Paris, 1856), I, 212n.
56. Dubrovin, *Vostochnaia voina*, pp. 90-91.
57. *Ibid.*, pp. 96-97.

up artillery. The weak Russian forces on this flank tried to drive back the French forces, who were constantly reinforced and whose musketry fire inflicted heavy losses on the defenders, armed with inferior weapons. Menshikov sent up reinforcements of infantry and light artillery, but the zouaves cut down the gunners and the horses with their fire. After a fierce contest the French gained the upper hand and the Russians retreated. This permitted the French artillery to fire on the flank of the Russian center, which also had to retreat. The failure of the Russians to hold on the left clearly decided the issue of the day.[58]

By mid-afternoon the Russians were in full retreat, although covered by several regiments and a heavy concentration of artillery. The allies made little effort to pursue, as they were tired and also lacked the cavalry for effective pursuit. The Russians had 5,709 men out of action, while the allies lost 3,353 men.[59] At first the retreat was orderly, but as they proceeded to their new position on the Kacha River, without guidance or instructions, they became more and more confused. At the bridge over the river, troops, artillery, and wagons became jammed in a disorderly mass. Eventually they all made their way back to Sevastopol.[60]

The plight of the wounded was another scandal. Little was done about caring for them and evacuating them, so that most of them had to shift for themselves. Many returned to their units three or four days after the battle. As late as September 14—six days after the battle—Cossack scouts reported that there still were wounded on the Alma. The authorities at once sent out wagons, which brought back 120 of them. The allies picked up some of the Russian wounded, but most were neglected, and probably most of the severely wounded died where they fell.[61]

After the troops had returned to Sevastopol after the Alma, their commanders reorganized them and restored discipline. Menshikov, who had blamed the defeat on the lack of bravery of the troops,[62] had gone into retirement. He conceived a plan for a flank march with his army in the direction of Bakhchisarai, where he could maintain

58. D. V. Il'inskii, "Iz vospominanii i zametok Sevastopol'tsa," *Russkii Arkhiv*, XXX (1892), Pt. III, 460-62; A. P. Khrushchov, *Istoriia oborony Sevastopolia* (2d ed.; St. Petersburg, 1889), pp. 10-14.
59. Bogdanovich, *Vostochnaia Voina*, III, 27-30.
60. Dubrovin, *Vostochnaia voina*, pp. 98-100.
61. *Ibid.*, pp. 102-3.
62. *Ibid.*, p. 101.

his communications with Russia and threaten the rear of the allies if they tried to attack Sevastopol. Characteristically, he said little about his plans, although he did tell Admiral Kornilov of his intentions. Consequently, when he marched off with all his army, Kornilov and the naval personnel and the few troops left behind believed that Menshikov had abandoned them to the enemy.[63]

It was characteristic of Menshikov that the flank march, which began on September 11, was poorly organized and that Gen. Kiriakov, in command of one of the columns, lost the road and delayed the movement. During this risky venture, the Russians, who had large forces of cavalry, were completely out of touch with the enemy and had no knowledge of their movements.[64] Strangely enough, the allied troops also were making a flank march at the same time, as they had decided to move to the south of Sevastopol. Thus, when Menshikov's army was marching to the northeast, the French and British were marching southward. As neither army had flank patrols or scouts around it, each was ignorant of the movement of the other. On September 13, to the great surprise of both sides, some of Lord Raglan's cavalry blundered into the end of the Russian wagon train and captured twenty-five wagons. This was inexcusable carelessness on both sides. If Menshikov had known of the allied movement, he could have inflicted a painful defeat on them, while if the allies had known of the Russian moves they probably could have destroyed the Russian army.[65]

In Sevastopol, meanwhile, the forlorn defenders, inspired by Admirals Kornilov and Nakhimov, decided to fight to the last and, in order to make a better defense, undertook to build earthworks as quickly as possible, with the aid of Col. E. I. Totleben, an excellent engineer trained under Schilder, whom Gorchakov had sent to Menshikov. On August 15, Totleben had entered in his notebook favorable comments on the seaward forts, but he found the landward defenses "very exposed," for they consisted only of earthworks armed "with guns of very small caliber, which could only give some opposition to Tatars."[66] From September 14 on the building of defenses went ahead at a furious pace, guided by Totleben. Instead of the fine masonry favored by the regular engineers, multitudes of soldiers, sailors from

63. Bogdanovich, *Vostochnaia voina*, III, 43-44.
64. Khrushchov, *Istoria oborony*, pp. 21-24.
65. *Ibid.*; Panaev, *Russkaia Starina*, XVIII (1877), 487-90.
66. Schilder, *Totleben*, I, Prilozheniia, 43-44.

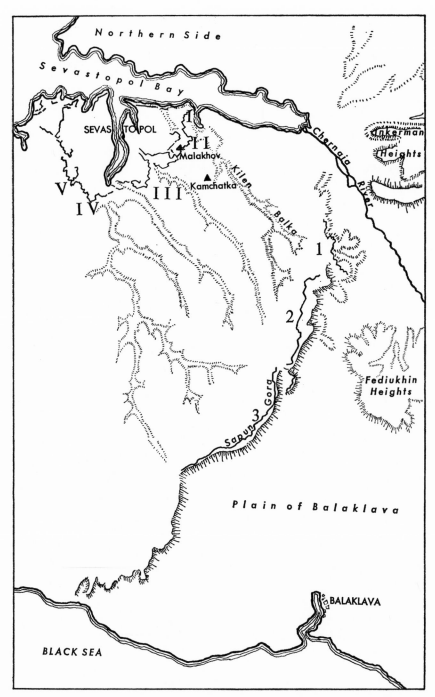

The Siege of Sevastopol. The roman numerals indicate the landward
bastions of the Russian position. The arabic figures mark fortifications protecting the Allied flank.

the fleet, volunteers, and prisoners from the guardhouse dug, carried dirt in baskets, hauled up timbers, fascines and gabions, and cannon to cover the city with earthworks. At first they concentrated on the northern side, but after the allied armies had moved to the south, they worked on the southeastern sector, on the 3rd, 4th, and 5th bastions, and the Malakhov Kurgan (hill), all of which were very weak. While hampered by a shortage of entrenching tools, they threw up walls, dug ditches, built powder magazines and batteries as best they could, although the shale made digging hard and walls made of it crumbled easily. By the time that the main army returned on September 18, the constant work of five or six thousand men had greatly strengthened the position. Morale increased greatly, as the garrison now had real strength. The allies, amazed at this sudden appearance of formidable works, did not dare risk an assault, and on September 27 the French opened the first trench almost twelve hundred yards from the fortress. This indicated that the allies would besiege Sevastopol instead of trying to carry it by storm. The Russian forces thus had gained time to make further preparations.[67]

Unfortunately, the Crimean army never received the reinforcements that it needed to win a decisive victory, in large part because Prince Paskevich kept insisting that the real danger was from Austria, which might attack in Poland. The Crimea, he held, could hold out indefinitely. On October 7 he wrote to Gorchakov: "It is incontestable that he [Menshikov] . . . could easily get along without reinforcements." The army on the Danube, however, was threatened by two hundred thousand Austrians and perhaps eighty thousand Turks.[68] The fact that the aged Baron Jomini also stressed the Austrian danger while disregarding the Crimean problem[69] helps to explain why reinforcements reached the Crimea only in driblets. After the Alma, Menshikov received two uhlan divisions, which he did not need, the 12th Infantry Division, and a few weeks later two more infantry divisions and the Dragoon Corps. Later one more division came in, a brigade at a time, while the allied armies were receiving heavy reinforcements.[70]

Another grave difficulty was provisions, of which only small

67. E. I. Totleben, *Opisanie oborony g. Sevastopolia* (2 vols. in 3; St. Petersburg, 1863-1878), I, 245-74.
68. Shcherbatov, VII, 210.
69. *Ibid.*, pp. 212-22.
70. Vasil'chikov, *Russkii Arkhiv*, XXIX (1891), Pt. II, 254.

amounts were on hand in September, 1854. With the Crimea producing little except hay and firewood, everything had to be hauled in. As the cavalry and the Cossacks quickly stripped the countryside, hay soon became scarce, which made it difficult for wagon trains and hired wagons to make the journey of 270 miles from Perekop to Sevastopol and back. As long as the roads were dry the situation was not grave, but in the fall the hauling of provisions became an almost insoluble problem.[71] Corruption also appeared. On November 21 Menshikov wrote to Prince Gorchakov that while a large part of the biscuits that he had sent to the Crimea were "positively worthless," the connivance of various responsible officials made it impossible to find those to blame.[72] In addition, the opening of the allied bombardment of Sevastopol quickly produced a shortage of powder among the defenders, which led to frantic efforts to haul in more of this essential commodity.

The allies, who had built numerous batteries for heavy artillery, opened their bombardment on October 5 by land and sea. The Russian forts easily scored on the allied fleets and drove them off, but the land contest was more dangerous. By the afternoon of the first day, the British, who had concentrated their fire on the 3rd bastion, silenced most of its guns and blew up the powder magazine with terrible effect. Only two guns continued to fire. Against the French, however, the Russians gained the upper hand, blowing up several magazines and silencing their guns by the end of the day. Nevertheless, the allies could have stormed and held the 3rd bastion, which would have made the Russian position in the city untenable.[73]

As the bombardment continued, the supply of powder ran low. In large part this was caused by the naval gunners manning many of the batteries, who fired furiously and with little regard for aim.[74] By October 11, Col. Popov, who had joined Menshikov's staff, reported that there was only enough powder for two or three days of heavy firing, which caused Menshikov to insist on action to divert the enemy from the siege.[75]

The result of this concern was the Battle of Balaklava on October

71. Bogdanovich, *Vostochnaia voina*, III, 193-99.
72. "Oborona Sevastopolia," *Russkaia Starina*, XII (1875), 315.
73. Il'inskii, *Russkii Arkhiv*, XXXI (1893), Pt. I, 274-83.
74. Vasil'chikov, *Russkii Arkhiv*, XXIX (1891), Pt. II, 194.
75. A. E. Popov, "Zapiski o prebyvanii ego pod Sevastopolem s 1-go oktiabria po 1-e dekabria 1854 g.," *Russkaia Starina*, XXI (1878), 308-19.

12. Gen. P. P. Liprandi with the 12th Division moved against the British flank in front of their base at Balaklava, easily seizing four redoubts manned by Turks. Russian cavalry sent to attack a British park, however, ran into considerable opposition, including artillery fire, and had to retire. After the Russian attacks had ceased, the British Light Brigade made its famous charge into the heart of the Russian position, only to be severely punished as they rode back. The Russians kept control of the redoubts that they had captured and also were much encouraged by having inflicted greater losses on the enemy than they had received.[76]

On the other hand, this incident had the effect of indicating to the allies the weakness of their flank from their position before Sevastopol down to Balaklava. They hastened to fortify the Sapun-gora (the high ground southeast of Sevastopol), and the French stationed an observation corps under Gen. Bosquet to protect this sector. Many Russians have held that Menshikov should have waited for the arrival of the 10th and 11th divisions, when he could have attacked with all three, which almost certainly would have led to the capture of Balaklava and destruction of the British communications.

By October 21 these two divisions had arrived, along with considerable cavalry. Menshikov massed these troops near Balaklava, to threaten the British position there, but on the 22nd he moved them at night to Sevastopol, for an attack on the next day. At a conference of the generals he explained his plans, although he felt that they understood so little of what he intended that he thought of putting off the action. Nevertheless, as the Grand Dukes (the Tsar's two sons) had come from St. Petersburg, he felt impelled to go ahead with the battle.[77]

The Battle of Inkerman on October 24 was poorly managed. No one had made a reconnaissance of the terrain,[78] and there was no good map of the area. An excellent map in St. Petersburg was kept in such secrecy that a copy of it did not arrive at headquarters in Sevastopol until the day after the battle.[79] The plan of attack was extremely complicated and the chain of command was not at all clear. Soimonov's division was to go up a ravine (Kilen-balka) from the eastern

---

76. Adolphe Niel, *Siège de Sébastopol. Journal des opérations du génie* (Paris, 1858), pp. 76-77; Dubrovin, *Vostochnaia voina*, pp. 254-65.
77. Panaev, *Russkaia Starina*, XIX (1877), 63-65.
78. Men'kov, I, 227-28.
79. Vasil'chikov, *Russkii Arkhiv*, XXIX (1891), Pt. II, 206.

part of the town to strike at the British position on the heights, while Gen. Pavlov would lead his division north of the bay, cross the Chernaia River on a special bridge, and climb the steep road to the heights, where the two forces would join in driving back the British. Liprandi's division had the task of demonstrating toward Balaklava to keep Bosquet's force from aiding the British. Finally, after the major attack had achieved some measure of success, Gen. Timofeev was to lead a large sortie from the fortress to capture and destroy as much of the enemy position as he could. Gen. Dannenberg, who had done badly in the Danube campaign, was to take command of the main attack after Pavlov and Soimonov had joined forces, while Menshikov would remain with the rear guard and supervise the whole action. To add to the confusion, Gen. Dannenberg issued some orders of his own at the last minute, so that it was not clear just on which side of the ravine Soimonov should attack.[80]

Things went wrong from the beginning. Pavlov's march was held up by delay in building the bridge over the river, while part of Soimonov's troops were slow in reaching the battlefield. In spite of this, however, the Russians achieved almost complete surprise and, overcoming the first British resistance, took one of their batteries. As the British rallied, Soimonov was killed and British rifle fire drove the Russians back. The rest of Soimonov's forces arrived and once more forced the British to retire under destructive Russian artillery fire. The British again rallied, only to meet the first troops of Pavlov to reach the heights. A confused and fierce hand-to-hand combat developed, with the British getting the worst of it. Some French troops also arrived, only to be driven back. The Russians were on the verge of a real triumph.[81]

In the meantime, Liprandi's division, under the elderly Prince P. D. Gorchakov, had demonstrated against the allied flank by opening long-range artillery fire, without making any sign of attacking the heavily fortified positions in front of them. While Liprandi was not strong enough to make a determined attack on the foe, his gestures against them were not convincing and Bosquet, realizing that this was an empty threat, sent much of his force off to rescue the helpless British. The French reserves decided the battle. The

80. Bogdanovich, *Vostochnaia voina*, III, 130-35.
81. *Ibid.*, pp. 136-46.

Russian forces by this time were badly disorganized, with almost all officers above the rank of captain out of action. Under heavy pressure from the French they retired slowly, bringing off all their artillery.[82]

For the Russians this was an extremely costly battle, as they lost almost twelve thousand men, including six generals. The allies lost much less, although they perhaps minimized their losses, which they reported as 4,338.[83] While the allies had escaped disaster, the victory that they had won "was costly and soberly impressed them with the strength of the enemy and the enormity of the task which lay ahead." Some of the British generals felt that the siege was hopeless, with De Lacy Evans urging evacuation of the Crimea.[84] The French historian Guérin wrote, "What is certain is that on the evening of the battle of Inkerman the allied generals were not sure of having gained a victory and that they strongly suspected that they [the Russians] would recommence the attack on the next day."[85]

For the Russians, Inkerman was a terrible blow, especially as it proved impossible to care properly for the thousands of wounded. By October 25 all barracks, magazines, and batteries of the northern side were filled with them, which led Menshikov to delegate several men to find space for them.[86] He had lost all hope of winning, unless the weather would co-operate by depriving the enemy of supplies. "All this brings me to despair."[87] Certainly from this time forward he had no thought of a fresh offensive, even though favorable opportunities appeared. Prince Vasil'chikov, who became chief of staff shortly after Inkerman, complained bitterly of the inertia and timidity in Sevastopol.[88] Menshikov became more and more aloof from the soldiers and officers, giving no sign that he cared about their well-being. Dr. N. I. Pirogov, the great surgeon, complained that the commander came to the hospitals only once, to see a general, "and did not come to see how the huddled, befouled, half-rotting legions that had been sent out to death lay on benches." He added: "The soldiers

82. Charles Auger, *Guerre d'Orient. Siège de Sébastopol* (2 vols.; Paris, 1859), I, 124-25.
83. Bogdanovich, *Vostochnaia voina*, III, 150-52.
84. Brison D. Gooch, *The New Bonapartist Generals in the Crimean War. Distrust and Decision-making in the Anglo-French Alliance* (The Hague, 1959), pp. 148-50.
85. Leon Guérin, *Histoire de la dernière guerre de Russia (1853-1856), écrite au point de vue politique, strategique et critique, sur les documents comparés français, anglais, russes, allemands et italiens.* (2 vols.; Paris, 1858), I, 404.
86. Dubrovin, *Vostochnaia voina*, p. 312.
87. "Obrona Sevastopolia," *Russkaia Starina*, XII (1875), 313.
88. Men'kov, I, 244.

do not know their leader and the leader does not show care for the soldiers."[89]

The great storm of November 1-2 did much to improve the Russian position, for it destroyed a number of the enemy's supply ships, as well as hitting their camps very hard. The British, who had been living in tents, were at once deprived of all shelter and exposed to drenching rains, followed by bitter cold. The French suffered somewhat less, for they had wooden barracks. The British also had to move their supplies for long distances up heavy grades, over roads that were ruined by the storms. As they had almost no horses to haul their necessities, they put their cavalry horses to work, killing most of them in short order. Then the men had to move their provisions to the front lines on their backs. All this resulted in much illness and death among the British forces, whose numbers declined drastically. For a period in November and December the British army in the Crimea was almost incapable of fighting.

The Russian forces also suffered in the cold, although they had much better means of protecting themselves. As the bombardment came to an end during the winter months, they could repair and improve their defenses and accumulate gunpowder. They also engaged in numerous sorties against the enemy, which often proved costly, but at times achieved some success. But in spite of the urging of Nicholas I and officers like Prince Vasil'chikov, there was no attempt to make a large-scale attack on the enemy during the months when the allied position was most desperate. While this inertia was in part a result of the lack of strong reinforcements, it chiefly proceeded from the absence of effective and energetic leadership. It is impossible to say whether the Russians could have won a victory over the besiegers at this time, although many intelligent men firmly believed so. But whether or not the opportunity existed, the fact is that the defenders failed to make the attempt during what was probably their last chance for success.

89. N. I. Pirogov, *Sevastopol'skie pis'ma i vospominaniia* (Moscow, 1950), pp. 21-22.

CHAPTER XVII. THE LAST STAGES OF THE CRIMEAN WAR

Although during the winter of 1854-55 the Russian army did not try a major offensive, it was not idle. Mine warfare was in progress from late 1854 until the end of the siege operations, mostly before the 4th bastion. The French, with their attack on this key position halted by Russian fire, began mine operations, apparently in hopes of advancing by creating and occupying mine craters. Learning of this from French deserters and from a map in a French periodical that indicated their mines beneath the 4th bastion, the Russians, under Col. Totleben, at once started extensive countermining. On January 21, after they had detected French miners some distance from the bastion, they set off a large blast that wrecked the French mine corridors. The French then blew up their own mine system and retired to their trenches some distance to the rear. Totleben then had the craters seized and from them dug further toward the French, making new craters which he formed into a strong trench system that kept the enemy at bay for months. He also dug another tier of mines below the first, whereby all of the French approaches were endangered.[1]

While Totleben, as chief engineer, received much of the credit for this, the actual work of conducting the operations was in the hands of Capt. A. V. Mel'nikov, who even slept in the mines. He successfully trained infantry soldiers as miners and greatly inspired his men, who termed him "Chief mole." His determination cost him his health and the enmity of Totleben.[2]

French accounts minimize the success of the Russian miners, claiming that their efforts to blow up works of the attackers were foiled by the French.[3] Weigelt, a Prussian military writer, believes

---

1. Frolov, pp. 5-45; Schilder, *Totleben*, II, 12.
2. N. S. Miloshevich, *Iz zapisok Sevastopol'tsa* (St. Petersburg, 1904), pp. 33-34; A. Detengof, "Zabytyi geroi. Iz vospominanii starago sapëra," *Russkii Arkhiv*, XLIII (1905), Pt. II, 546-51.
3. Auger, I, 406.

that the Russians were highly successful, as they kept the French from advancing before the 4th bastion, although the latter continued to approach the 5th and 6th bastions. "It seems that this siege again presents an illustration of with what success a good and strongly defended mine system can hold up the attack on a fortress."[4]

Frequent night sorties by the Russians—usually in detachments of two or three hundred men, although sometimes in much greater force—were another form of activity, especially against the British, whose trench guards were less effective than those of the French. The attacking parties usually had little difficulty in penetrating the enemy trenches, seizing prisoners and driving back working groups. At such times they often levelled the trenches, spiked captured cannon, and sometimes carried off small mortars.[5] These exploits delighted many young daredevils, who rejoiced in the exciting adventures and on occasion made sorties without orders, although this was quickly forbidden. Some of these hardy spirits became adepts at taking prisoners, using short pikes, with the points bent into hooks, to catch unwary sentries.[6] Much annoyed at this, the French Gen. Canrobert sent a note of protest to Gen. Adj. Sacken, commander of the Russian garrison, saying that the Russians were using hooks and ropes to capture men and "que ce ne sont point là des armes courtoises."[7]

On the whole, these sorties were of dubious value. Although they troubled the foe and raised Russian morale, the results obtained were rarely effective. The enemy could easily restore his trenches, and it was not difficult to unspike cannon. Moreover, the attackers could rarely inflict heavy losses on the enemy, and sometimes suffered severely themselves when they encountered large forces of the foe.[8]

The Russians derived more benefit from their practice of sending sharpshooters out in front of their lines, where from skilfully constructed rifle pits they troubled working parties, trench guards, and artillerymen. The allied forces could easily capture the pits, but unless they occupied them permanently, the Russians were sure to come back, and often the rifle pits were extended and connected into a regular trench system, backed up by the cannon of the fortress. Only well-

4. Weigelt, pp. 245-46.
5. Calthorpe, II, *passim*; Khrushchov, p. 59.
6. Bogdanovich, *Vostochnaia voina*, III, 169.
7. *Ibid.*, p. 170.
8. Men'kov, I, 246 and 342; Weigelt, pp. 158-59.

placed artillery and small mortars in the trenches gave good results against these advanced positions.[9]

But while sorties and sharpshooters proved troublesome to the besiegers, they gave no promise of the decisive success that the Tsar longed for. He was completely committed to achieving victory. According to D. A. Miliutin, who was in the center of the military administration in the capital, Nicholas trusted no one but himself and undertook to handle all the assignments of troops. Every night from his study he sent whole packets of handwritten memoranda to the Ministry of War, where they were hastily copied and sent to the proper quarters.

> These notes in the Emperor's own handwriting consisted of the most detailed instructions concerning the formation of troops, their supply needs, their distribution, and so on. The Sovereign with unusual watchfulness followed the orders of the local commanders, the movement of each battalion, and frequently in his notes went into such detail that they only bound the hands of the commanders and hampered them. . . .[10]

In December, 1854, he repeatedly wrote to Prince Menshikov at Sevastopol, urging him to attack the weakened and demoralized enemy at once, as before long the foe would be reinforced and would then seize the initiative. "For God's sake lose no time, it is precious, from the information forwarded to you you will see everything that we have suffered from the sending of reinforcements to the Crimea. . . ."[11]

In January of 1855, the Tsar continued to demand offensive action. On the 21st, Menshikov wrote to Gorchakov that he had just received two letters from Nicholas, demanding an attempt against Evpatoria and an attack on the British positions. Although Menshikov felt that the latter operation was impossible, he believed that the Evpatoria operation was both possible and useful.[12]

This port, in itself unimportant, was held by Turkish forces and a few French troops, backed by the guns of the allied fleet. The Russian command was always troubled by the possibility that the

9. Auger, I, 230-31; Adolphe Niel, *Siège de Sébastopol. Journal des opérations du génie, publié avec l'autorisation du Ministère de la Guerre* (Paris, 1858), pp. 108-9; Delafield, pp. 50-51.

10. "Zapiski D. A. Miliutina," cited in Tarle, II, 268-69.

11. Schiemann, IV, 344.

12. "Oborona Sevastopolia," *Russkaia Starina*, XII (1875), 326-27.

allies might strike inland to cut the communications of Sevastopol with the mainland. Actually, as it turned out later, this danger was never great.

In response to the urging of Nicholas, Menshikov had Gen. K. E. Wrangel, commander of the Russian forces near Evpatoria, and Col. N. Batezatul, reconnoiter the town. These two experienced officers decided that it would be impossible to take this fortified position without heavy losses and even if they did, they could not hope to hold it. But as the dashing Lt. Gen. S. A. Khrulev declared that he would promise success if put in command, Menshikov, without inspecting the position, gave him carte blanche.[13] Khrulev made skilful plans for the attack, but when he attempted it on February 5, 1855, his forces met a heavy resistance and found the ditch filled with water to be impassable. After three units had failed in storming the defense wall, Khrulev halted all attacks and retired from his positions, but not before his forces had lost 769 officers and men. The allies lost substantially less.[14]

Thus by mid-February, Nicholas I perceived that the Russian forces in the Crimea had not been able to take advantage of the disorganization of the British and French during the winter months and that with the warmer weather the balance would be against the defenders. In a letter of February 2, accompanied by a long memorandum, he told Gorchakov of the danger from Austria that would require maintaining a strong army in Poland, as he expected Austria to invade with an army of one hundred and fifty thousand men. He did not believe that the Prussians would fight beside the Austrians, but there was a possibility that French troops would join in the invasion of central Russia.[15] It was with this gloomy prospect before him that the Tsar removed Menshikov, whose health was bad and whose mental outlook was extremely somber, replacing him with Prince Gorchakov. This was the last important act of Nicholas I, for before Gorchakov could take command the Tsar had died. He had been bitterly disappointed at the failure of his diplomacy and the inability of his beloved army to defeat his foes in the war that he himself had brought about. Shattered in spirit, he fell prey to a severe

13. Panaev, *Russkaia Starina*, XIX (1877), 300-5; Vasil'chikov, *Russkii Arkhiv*, XXIX (1891), Pt. II, 219-20.

14. Totleben, I, 646-50.

15. Nikolai I, "Predsmertnoe pis'mo Imperatora Nikolaia—Kniaz'iu M. D. Gorchakovu," *Russkaia Starina*, XXXII (1881), 895-99.

cold that, because he neglected to take proper care of himself, developed into pneumonia, which quickly proved fatal. On February 18, 1855, he breathed his last.

On the whole, the death of the Tsar had little effect on the course of the war, which continued without moderation. One account indicates that there was much grief among some of the troops at Sevastopol, where, when the manifesto was read to them, "the soldiers, officers, generals—all wept."[16] There is, however, no way of knowing how typical this attitude was.

Before his death Nicholas had sought to end the war by accepting the demands of the allies for renouncing his protectorate over the Principalities, Serbia, and the Orthodox subjects of the Sultan. On the remaining point, however—revision of the Treaty of 1841 regarding the Straits—the talks broke down. A peace conference which met in Vienna in March to clarify this point split over the allied position that it meant that Russia should give up the right to a fleet on the Black Sea. Prince A. M. Gorchakov strongly opposed this demand for the new Emperor Alexander II. To break the deadlock, Count K. F. von Buol, the Austrian foreign minister, who now leaned toward the Russians, proposed that the Russian Black Sea fleet be limited to its prewar strength. Russia did not reject this, but the British and the French military leaders demanded full victory over the Russians, including the fall of Sevastopol. Louis Napoleon accepted the demands of his generals, and so the war went on.[17]

The attitude of Austria was extremely troublesome to the Russians during much of the war. In the first weeks of the Crimean campaign, Austria, with the support of many of the German states, had proposed mobilization of the forces of the Germanic Confederation, and when this had suffered rejection, had mobilized its own forces. The allied setback at Inkerman sobered the Austrians, however, and they demobilized part of their army.[18] Early in 1855 the Austrians again proposed general mobilization, which again was rejected, in large part through the efforts of Bismarck and Frederick William IV of Prussia.[19] Nevertheless, Austria on the whole sided with the allies

16. Alabin, *Pokhodnyia zapiski*, II, 178-79.
17. Hans Delbrück, *Istoriia voennogo iskusstva v ramkakh politicheskoi istorii* (5 vols.; Moscow, 1937), V, 81-82. This is a translation of his *Geschichte der Kriegskunst* (7 vols.; Berlin, 1900-1936).
18. *Ibid.*, pp. 46-60.
19. Schiemann, IV, 349-50.

against the Russians, and in spite of the promises of Franz Joseph, Gorchakov found it impossible to obtain audience with him. "From all this one could conclude that any day we might receive news *that Austria also had declared war on us*."[20] Because of the danger that an Austrian attack would draw all Germany, to say nothing of the Swedes, against the Russians, the latter felt compelled, as before, to keep most of their army in the Baltic region and in Poland. As before, the Crimea received insufficient reinforcements.

In beleaguered Sevastopol the defenders continued to show determination and skill. In the early months of 1855, Gen. Adolphe Niel, a skilled engineer who enjoyed the full trust of Napoleon III, decided to center the attack on the Kornilov bastion on the Malakhov Kurgan, as the fortifications and intricate defenses of the Russians before the 4th and 5th bastions made success there look too costly.[21] Hence the French moved a large part of their army to take over from the British the sector on the allied right, against the 1st and 2nd bastions and the Malakhov. The much smaller British forces continued to attack the 3rd bastion (the Great Redan), where they made little progress.

As the French began to build approaches and batteries in their new sector, the Russians soon realized what this meant and acted to counter the new attack. On February 9, Totleben laid out a redoubt on the extreme left, near the Chernaia River, which was built by the Selenginsk regiment and guarded by the Volhynia regiment under Gen. Khrushchov. The French, quickly realizing that this new work would outflank their approaches to the Malakhov, sought to capture it, but the Russians beat them back with considerable losses. As soon as this Selenginsk redoubt was armed with cannon, Totleben laid out another fortification four hundred paces ahead, which became known as the Volhynia redoubt. These two (known to the allies as the White redoubts, from the color of the soil) enfiladed the French trenches and batteries and thus halted the advance toward the Malakhov. The attackers had to construct many new batteries to overpower them before they could resume their advance toward their objective. But as the French painfully built new batteries against the White redoubts and dragged up cannon,[22] the Russians again seized the initiative.

20. Dubrovin, *Vostochnaia voina*, p. 416.
21. Niel, pp. 135-40.
22. *Ibid.*, pp. 155-57; Auger, I, 198-200.

During the night of February 28, the besieged began to build a lunette on the Green Hill (Mamelon Vert), which overlooked the Malakhov, as the latter dominated the harbor and the city. The French had planned to occupy this hill, but now by a bold stroke the Russians had taken it. About eighteen hundred feet from the Malakhov and some twelve hundred feet from the first French lines, they erected the Kamchatka lunette, which troubled the flanks of the attackers. Once more the latter had to defer their advance until they could cope with this new obstacle. Moreover, the Russians built rifle pits and trenches in front of it, from which sharpshooters harassed French workers in the trenches. As the lunette was protected by the fire of the two redoubts and the 3rd bastion, the French did not try to storm it, but made numerous attacks on the Russian trenches, whereby both sides lost heavily.[23]

By these bold strokes the defenders had turned the tables on the allies, who now had to build batteries and approaches against the new defenses before they could hope to attack the Malakhov.[24] Sir John Burgoyne, chief engineer with the British forces, held that the Green Hill was of great importance and that the French would have to take it. "I think that the Russian engineers have displayed great cleverness and ability in the manner in which they have up to the present time conducted the defense of Sebastopol."[25] The French, whose plans had been so ably countered by Totleben's efforts, began to think that he was learning their intentions through spies. Gen. Bosquet said: "It seems really that the Russian engineers respond day by day to all our ideas, all our projects as if they had been present at our conferences. . . . I think today especially about spies."[26] Col. Guérin wrote on March 16 (N.S.): "We are attacking an enemy who envelopes us and who, by his right, rests on a formidable entrenchment. . . . We came here to deliver a major defeat to the Russians, and for the moment we do not seem to be on the road to this."[27]

Nevertheless, although the Russians had achieved a brilliant success, it was to prove very costly. Because the redoubts and the lunette were built when the French were already massing their strength in this sector, the works were hastily constructed and the builders could not

23. Khrushchov, pp. 74-79; Auger, I, 211-14.
24. Niel, pp. 167-70.
25. Calthorpe, II, 146.
26. Schilder, *Totleben*, I, 419.
27. Guérin, II, 129-30.

properly supply them with secure dugouts for the troops, powder magazines safe against enemy bombs, and traverses to protect the flanks of the guns. Also the terrain consisted largely of shale, which was hard to dig and did not hold its shape well, so that walls crumbled under bombardment. It was impossible to dig an effective ditch at the Kamchatka lunette.[28]

It is noteworthy that after Inkerman, Admiral Istomin had urged the building of a redoubt on the Green Hill,[29] while Nicholas I and Paskevich had both called for occupation of the forward positions. On March 20, 1855, Alexander II wrote to Prince Gorchakov, the new commander at Sevastopol, rejoicing over the successful construction of the three works. He added: "I am only sorry that their conclusion was not accomplished three months before, as our unforgettable benefactor [Nicholas I] *repeatedly pointed out to Prince Menshikov*. At that time the loss would probably not be so considerable as now."[30] Paskevich also proposed something of the sort in his letter of Nov. 13, 1854. On November 17, Nicholas replied: "Thy plan of defense is word for word what I repeatedly asked Menshikov to adopt, but up to now without success, and why I do not know."[31] Undoubtedly it would have been of immense advantage to have built these fortifications earlier. It must not be forgotten, however, that in 1854 the pressure was still on the 4th bastion and not on the Malakhov. Much had to be done to strengthen the existing works, and during the bad weather of the winter it would have been difficult to undertake this formidable new construction. Probably a really effective commander would have seen the need for this and would have found the means. This was impossible for a broken man like Menshikov.

On March 8, 1855, Prince M. D. Gorchakov arrived to take command of the Crimean army, bringing with him his able staff. Full of confidence that the war would be over in little more than six weeks, in his order of the day to the troops he assured them that the most difficult period had passed, as abundant supplies and reinforcements were coming. "Taking command over you, I am in full trust that soon, with the help of God, final success will crown your efforts and that

28. Vasil'chikov, *Russkii Arkhiv*, XIX (1891), Pt. II, 222-24.
29. M. G. Cherniaev, "Vo vremia Russko-Turetskoi voiny v 1853-1856 godakh," *Russkii Arkhiv*, XLIV (1906), Pt. I, 457.
30. M. I. Bogdanovich, ed., "Imperator Aleksandr II v epokhu voiny 1855 g.," *Russkaia Starina*, XXXVII (1883), 118
31. *Ibid.*, p. 118n.

we shall justify the expectations of our Sovereign and of Russia."[32] The army, however, which realized its desperate position, "received his assurances of speedy expulsion of the enemy from the Crimea with icy indifference."[33] And in truth, the commander himself soon decided that all was lost. In his letter of March 9 to the Minister of War, he stated that Menshikov's blunders, especially at Inkerman, had made victory impossible. On March 18 he wrote: "It is a deadly heritage that I have received. . . . I am exposed to being turned, cut off, and perhaps broken, if the enemy has a little good sense and decision." And he continued to send letters of the same dismal content.[34]

After the Russians had constructed the Kamchatka lunette, they built an elaborate series of trenches in front of it, which the French vainly tried to take. The besiegers also pushed their approaches toward the lunette, using two saps and many workers, until in the middle of March, Khrulev led a sortie of five thousand men against them and captured and destroyed their saps. The Russians even penetrated the main French parallels and drove off the guards, and it was with difficulty that Khrulev recalled them. Although the Russian losses were almost one thousand men, they were exultant at having halted the enemy advance.[35] But on March 28, the French and the British, after having constructed many new batteries, opened a heavy bombardment of the lunette and the two redoubts, which lasted until April 10. As the besieged were desperately short of gunpowder they had to curtail their fire and could hardly reply except with small arms. Eventually, however, when the allied powder was exhausted, the advance defenses were still in Russian hands.[36]

The Russians also pushed their counterapproaches on their right, but with poor results. The French succeeded in storming their trenches in front of the 5th bastion and Schwartz battery, using ten thousand men at the latter point. The defenders lost 833 men, while the French admitted losses of 791 men killed and wounded. Nothing daunted, Totleben, over the objections of many Russian leaders, insisted on building a trench system on Cemetery Hill on the far right, from which he hoped eventually to strike the flank of the whole allied attack. On May 9 Khrulev led a large force to build lodgements there, which

32. Khrushchov, pp. 76-77.
33. Bogdanovich, *Vostochnaia voina*, III, 259.
34. Schilder, *Totleben*, I, 409-11.
35. Vasil'chikov, *Russkii Arkhiv*, XXIX (1891), Pt. II, 226-27.
36. *Ibid.*, p. 228; S. K. Gershel'man, *Nravstvennyi element pod Sevastopolem* (St. Petersburg, 1897), pp. 236-37.

resulted in a massive French attack on the night of the 10th. Although the latter had committed sixteen battalions to this effort, which at first took the Russian trenches, Khrulev led a counterattack which regained and held them. At this point, however, Gorchakov, deciding that it would be too costly to hold these defenses, ordered that they be lightly held and that his men should withdraw if the French attacked in force. Thus when the next French attack came, the Russians retired. In these two nights they had lost 3,400 men, to no good purpose.[37] The French lost 2,303 men, which Napoleon III termed greater than the loss at Austerlitz. ". . . to see the bravest soldiers perish in such indecisive combats was terrible."[38]

Early in May, Gen. Pélissier, who had succeeded Canrobert in command of the French, pushed the attack on the Russian left, with the Malakhov the main objective. He constructed new batteries in this sector and advanced the trenches close to the two redoubts and the Kamchatka lunette. On May 25 they opened a heavy cannonade which continued until dusk on the 26th. Then five divisions of fine troops rushed to the assault, while the British stormed Russian positions in stone quarries and trenches near the 3rd bastion. Because Gorchakov, fearing a heavy loss from gunfire, had reduced the garrisons of the three works, the French easily took the two redoubts on the left, and a Russian counterattack merely retook a mortar battery. The French also stormed the Kamchatka lunette and pursued the retiring garrison to the very Malakhov itself. Here the guns of the Kornilov bastion inflicted heavy losses on them, and Russian reserves attacked and retook the lunette. French reserves rushed to the spot and drove the Russians out, occupying the lunette firmly. In all this desperate fighting, the Russians reported their losses as twenty-five hundred men, while the French lost almost three thousand. The British lost approximately five hundred.[39]

Gen. Daniel Lysons described the British part of the action as follows: "We advanced; took the quarries and parallels in front of our right attack. The Russians fought desperately; drove us out of the works three times. Each time we retook it and ultimately kept it. . . . Our loss has been very great."[40] As for Gen. Pélissier, who had

37. Khrushchov, pp. 96-100.
38. Gooch, pp. 213-14.
39. Vasil'chikov, *Russkii Arkhiv*, XXIX (1891), Pt. II, 231-32; Khrushchov, pp. 108-9.
40. Lysons, p. 188.

made the attack contrary to orders, he waited several days before reporting to the Emperor. When Napoleon failed to reply, the General demanded if the Emperor was going to congratulate the troops. Napoleon's reply by telegraph was:

> I wished before sending congratulations on the brilliant success to learn how great the losses were. I am informed of the figure by St. Petersburg. I admire the courage of the troops, but I would observe to you that a battle fought to decide the fate of the entire Crimea would not have cost you more. I persist then in the order . . . to make all your efforts to enter resolutely into a field campaign.[41]

The Emperor's remarks illustrate a divergence in plans that troubled the allied armies. He strongly held the opinion that it would be much less costly to defeat the Russians by a new landing at Alushta on the south coast of the Crimea, from which a strong drive would strike at the vital Russian communication center of Simferopol. As its loss would quickly starve out the forces in Sevastopol, Gorchakov would have to move his army to protect his base, which in turn would permit the allies to strike at the remnants at Sevastopol. According to Col. Guérin, by May the allies far outnumbered the Russians, as the invaders had more than two hundred thousand men in the Crimea, of whom one hundred and ten thousand were French. But as Gen. Pélissier insisted on capturing Sevastopol, "in spite of the contrary opinion of General Niel, they were rivetted to the siege without investiture and without strategy."[42] Except for a raid into the Sea of Azov, which troubled the Russians but accomplished little, the allies continued to attack Sevastopol. According to Guérin, after winning the redoubts the French were exposed to heavy fire, which inflicted such losses that the soldiers demanded an immediate assault. "It required great strength of character in Gen. Pélissier . . . not to give in to this poorly reasoned striving of the troops. . . ."[43]

After the allied successes, Gorchakov was more pessimistic than ever. He wrote the Tsar that superior numbers had caused the defeat, although the Russians had fought extremely well. The allies now would build new batteries and push the siege unrelentingly. He emphasized his shortage of powder, of which he had less than ten days' supply, if they made moderate answer to the allied fire. "Now I think only

41. Gooch, p. 217.
42. Guérin, II, 274.
43. Ibid., II, 266.

of how to leave Sevastopol without suffering undue loss, perhaps over twenty thousand. One cannot think of saving the ships and the artillery. It is frightful to think of it."[44]

After the capture of the Russian redoubts and the Kamchatka lunette, Pélissier, confident of success, determined to storm the Malakhov and end the war. New batteries were built and the bombardment continued. By agreement with Lord Raglan the assault on the positions on the Russian left was set for three A.M. on June 6. A general bombardment opened on the 5th, followed by mortar fire all night. The defenders, however, managed to repair their works, so that their fire remained effective.[45] The Russians heavily reinforced the threatened sector, which they entrusted to Gen. Khrulev, who inspired the men and aroused their desire for battle.[46]

Although the attack had been planned for three A.M., Gen. Maillerand on the extreme right of the French through an error opened the battle half an hour ahead of schedule. When his forces drew near to the 1st and 2nd bastions, they were driven back by terrible fire from the works and from steamers in the bay. After two attempts to take their objectives, they had to retire in disorder. At the appointed time the main French attack on the Malakhov developed, only to be halted by heavy fire, which inflicted severe losses. The troops of Gen. d'Hautemar, however, carried the neighboring Gervais battery and penetrated the buildings at the foot of the Malakhov Kurgan, which they threatened to cut off. But at this point Khrulev with powerful reserves forced them out of the buildings and compelled them to make a disordered flight. The French made three more efforts to mount a successful attack, but the defenders crushed them all.[47] As for the British, after some delay they attacked the 3rd bastion with dismal results. Gen. Lysons reported: "We have had a dreadful day." He led a storming party for eight hundred yards under "a perfect storm of grapeshot," through which only handfuls reached the abbatis before the bastion, where they had to lie down. "At last I was left with about five or six men, and then thought it high time to be off; we were the last to go in. They fired at us all the way back." As a result of their heavy losses, which some put as high as three thousand, "I don't think

44. Bogdanovich, *Vostochnaia voina*, III, 356-57.
45. V. M. Anichkov, *Voenno-istoricheskie ocherki Krymskoi ekspeditsii* (2 vols.; St. Petersburg, 1856), II, 142-44.
46. Khrushchov, pp. 110-11.
47. Anichkov, *Ocherki*, II, 145-51.

they can call upon us again to storm. Some of our regiments have only two officers left; somebody else must take a turn."[48]

In the bombardment and the fighting the Russians lost almost 5,000 men, while the British losses were 1,570. The French reported 3,338 casualties, of whom almost half were killed. As the usual proportion of killed to wounded, however, was one to five, it seems probable that the French losses must have been almost six thousand.[49]

Understandably, Napoleon III was dismayed by the bloodshed, although he realized that Pélissier believed he could take Sevastopol. The failure of the assault made a deep impression on Gen. Simpson, the new British commander in chief, who by late July was saying that the allied position would be untenable over another winter. Gens. Niel and Harry Jones, the chief engineers of the allied armies, drew up a memorandum stating that if the fortress held out until winter, the allies should raise the siege. Pélissier, however, objected vehemently to this view.[50]

Like most of the army at Sevastopol, St. Petersburg was delighted with the victory. Alexander II wrote an exultant letter to Gorchakov praising the "heroic repulse" of the attack, adding: "I hope that with the help of God there will be no more talk of leaving Sevastopol." But Gorchakov's letter of the day after the battle still spoke of having to evacuate the city at a cost of ten or fifteen thousand men and complained of the lack of gunpowder. A week later, however, he was more cheerful. Two new divisions had joined his forces, and the slackening of the allied fire had permitted him to be sparing in the use of powder. But he still believed that his position was very grave, although he felt that if he received enough reserves he could try an offensive. Moreover, the allies could not stay through another winter.[51]

Nevertheless, Gorchakov soon showed his usual pessimism, and with good reason. Not long after the unsuccessful allied attack, Prince Vasil'chikov, chief of staff of the garrison, conferred with two other courageous and experienced staff officers, who unanimously decided that the superiority of the enemy fire and the terrible losses of the defenders would make defeat inevitable. As for an offensive against the foe, they felt that the position of the latter was so impregnable that to attack would be ruinous. For these reasons their conclusion was

48. Lysons, pp. 192-95.
49. Anichkov, *Ocherki*, II, 154-55.
50. Gooch, pp. 224 and 234-35.
51. Bogdanovich, *Vostochnaia voina*, III, 390-92.

that the best course would be a voluntary evacuation of the army to the northern side of the Sevastopol position, thereby preserving the strength of the army and saving the lives of thousands of men. Gorchakov and his staff rejected this proposal, although in reality it corresponded with the commander's views.[52]

Among the reasons for the hopelessness of the Russian outlook was the attitude of Prince Paskevich. Fearful of attack by the Austrians, he strenuously opposed the dispatch of troops from his forces to the Crimea and, when the Tsar categorically ordered them to go, according to Vasil'chikov, he marched and countermarched them to delay their departure. Finally, after the Austrians moderated their tone in the spring of 1855 he released some of his men, but when they arrived in the Crimea they were worn out and prone to disease. "Such diseases appeared in the Grenadier Corps that it definitely overflowed all the hospitals. This, in my opinion, is the real cause of our lack of success."[53]

Another reason for the failure to reinforce the southern city was that in the summer of 1855 a strong allied fleet entered the Gulf of Finland. Although its efforts to strike an effective blow, at Vyborg, at St. Petersburg, and at the forts at Helsingfors, failed, they had the effect of tying down large numbers of the best Russian troops, whose presence in the Crimea might have turned the tide.[54] In his memoirs P. K. Men'kov in Sevastopol wrote bitterly that while the capital constantly "grieved" about the Crimea, they kept it badly supplied with powder, modern weapons, and projectiles. At the same time three hundred thousand of the best troops, with many rifles, marked time on the swampy Baltic shore behind fortresses and never fired a shot.[55]

But in spite of these and other grave handicaps, such as a most difficult supply problem, corruption, and a catastrophic medical situation, many of the defenders did not lose heart. Totleben proposed to make the Malakhov and the 2nd and 3rd bastions secure by adding sixty heavy guns to their armament, which would be supported by an equal number of large-caliber guns in two new batteries to be constructed on the rear flanks of the Malakhov. He also urged the immediate digging of a mine system from this bastion to halt the French

52. Men'kov, I, 385-87.
53. Vasil'chikov, *Russkii Arkhiv*, XXIX (1891), Pt. II, 255.
54. M. Borodkin, *Voina 1854-1855 gg. na Finskom poberzh'e. Istoricheskii ocherk* (St. Petersburg, 1904), pp. 251-320.
55. Men'kov, I, 390-91.

approaches, as had been done at the 4th bastion. Unfortunately for the success of his plans, on June 8 he suffered a bad leg wound which put him out of action for several crucial months. Although the allies were inactive for some weeks after their disaster, no one did much to carry out his program.[56]

For a time the situation appeared to favor the defenders, as four divisions and thirteen thousand of the newly formed Kursk militia arrived to swell their numbers. While this probably did not give the Russians superiority in numbers, they felt strong and as many of the troops held that it would be better to have one big battle than to waste away under the increasing fire of the enemy, strong voices began to demand an attack. In mid-June, Baron Vrevskii, an adjutant general and a high figure in the Ministry of War, arrived as the envoy of Alexander II. Making light of the difficulties, he held that the daily losses from enemy fire were intolerable and that an attack might achieve real success.[57] Although in a memorandum of July 11, Gorchakov opposed an offensive as "an extremely dangerous matter," he admitted that it was highly probable that the allies, who were drawing very close to the Malakhov and to the 2nd bastion, and were also endangering the 4th and 5th bastions, might soon silence the Russian cannon and then storm the works. Thus an attack might be the lesser of two evils. Vrevskii continued to urge offensive action, with the result that the Minister of War, with the Tsar's approval, instructed Gorchakov to call a council of war to decide what to do.[58]

When the council of war met on July 28, the majority approved an attack along the Chernaia River, although Osten-Sacken, Khrulev, and Totleben opposed. Gorchakov decided to order the attack for early August, although he wrote to the Minister of War that he expected to fail, as the situation had been hopeless ever since he had arrived in the Crimea.[59]

In spite of Russian efforts at secrecy, the allies had ample warning of the Russian attack. Gen Lysons wrote home that "Four days' warning was given that the Russians intended to attack in force."[60] As the attack did not come as soon as expected, however, they de-

56. Schilder, *Totleben*, I, 439-45.
57. Bogdanovich, *Vostochnaia voina*, IV, 2-4.
58. Totleben, II, Pt. II, 56-62.
59. Bogdanovich, *Vostochnaia voina*, IV, 7-14.
60. Lysons, p. 208.

cided that it had been postponed. Thus the Russians achieved some slight surprise, although not enough to help them.[61]

The allied position along the Chernaia River was immensely strong by nature and had been well fortified. From the river the slope rose steeply to the Fediukhin Heights, on which the French were entrenched, with numerous artillery, and behind it was the escarpment of the Sapun-gora, all but impregnable. Further up the river was the Telegraph Hill, north of the river, which was weakly held by Sardinian troops. Gasfort Hill, on the southern side, was entrenched and strongly held with the Sapun-gora behind it. Gorchakov's orders for the attack on August 4 called for Gen. Liprandi, with sixteen thousand men, to capture the Telegraph Hill and then to push into artillery range of Gasfort Hill, while Gen. Read, with almost fifteen thousand, was to fire on the Fediukhin Heights. Gorchakov, who perhaps had no desire to attack either point, commanded the two generals to do nothing further without orders from him. At the outset Liprandi easily captured his first objective. Gorchakov, however, noticing that Read had not yet opened fire, sent an aide to tell him to begin. When the aide arrived, Read was already firing at the heights, so that the order "to begin" seemed to mean an infantry attack. The troops crossed the river and a canal and clambered up the heights, but under deadly enemy fire faltered and had to retreat. Reinforcements arrived, only to suffer the same fate. Read was killed and several other generals were hit. Gorchakov, with Liprandi's force, now had to throw it into the fray to support Read. The Russians climbed Gasfort Hill and pierced the French line, but were thrown back across the river. At 8 A.M. Gorchakov halted the battle, although he did not at once withdraw.[62]

This battle was a real disaster for the Russians, for they lost eight thousand men, including eleven generals; while the Sardinian and French losses were perhaps eighteen hundred. The allies captured most of the Russian wounded. Naturally the victors were jubilant. They now no longer had to fear a Russian attack, but could push the siege with renewed vigor.[63] Thus, because of the confusion caused by the inexact orders of Gorchakov, much of his army was destroyed. It was a battle that never should have been fought, for even if the Russians

61. Kolchak, p. 68.
62. Totleben, II, Pt. II, 101-25; Krasovskii, "Delo na Chernoi," *Russkii Arkhiv*, XII (1874), Pt. II, 210-11; D. A. Stolypin, "Iz lichnykh vospominanii o Krymskoi voine," *Russkii Arkhiv*, XII (1874), Pt. I, 1362-66.
63. Totleben, II, Pt. II, 126-27.

had taken the Fediukhin Heights they never could have held them, but would have been driven off by the allied reserves. This conflict probably made the fall of Sevastopol certain.

As early as June, Gorchakov had prepared plans for evacuating the city, which were worked out in detail by Vasil'chikov. The commander also sought to build a bridge across the bay to facilitate the retreat of the troops, although most of the engineers opposed. Lt. Gen. Bukhmeier, however, agreed to build it. Vast quantities of timber, bought in southern Russia and hauled by enormous lines of wagons, supplied the floats on which the roadway rested, extending some eighteen hundred feet across the bay.[64] This remarkable feat, which probably saved much of the army from capture or annihilation, was not complete until the Battle of the Chernaia.

On August 6 the French and the British opened a general bombardment of the Russian defenses, especially against the Malakhov. At first the defenders returned a vigorous fire, but the allies gradually gained superiority. Night gave the besieged the opportunity to repair the damage so that they could resume fire the next day, but as more and more guns were silenced their reply became weaker. The French engineers could push their saps onward with little difficulty. The Russians used mortar fire against the attackers and made frequent sorties to destroy their work, which sometimes resulted in stubborn and bloody battles. But the advance continued relentlessly.[65]

The Russians were gravely hampered by shortages of both powder and projectiles. By the last week in August their reserves of powder were so low that they practically had to cease replying to the enemy. They also were woefully lacking in bombs and shells, especially for mortars, which were the most effective way of hitting the foe. The government stripped the fortresses of southern Russia of bombs, which they rushed to the Crimea, but this supplied only a fraction of the need.[66] Thus at a time when the garrisons of the bastions were losing heavily from the fire of huge allied mortars and cannon, they had to slacken their fire. They bore up bravely under it, however. When Gen. Gorchakov asked an artilleryman of one of the most dangerous bastions how many men were there, the answer was: "Enough for

64. Vasil'chikov, *Russkii Arkhiv*, XXIX (1891), Pt. II, 236-37.
65. Auger, I, 397-401.
66. A. Orda, "Ob"iasneniia vyzvannyia stat'eiu G. Artillerista," *Voennyi Sbornik*, II (1859), 62-67.

three days."[67] The soldiers had a proverb that reflected their stoic courage: "There cannot be two deaths, but you cannot escape one."[68]

Under such conditions the soldiers, worn out by endless exertions and incessant alarms, were far too few to hold their positions. On August 25 an officer reported to headquarters that if the Malakhov were not reinforced it would be taken by storm the next day, but no reinforcements arrived. On the morning of the assault, the bastion was in worse shape than before, as the men had been unable to repair the damage during the night. Out of its sixty-three cannon and mortars, only eight could fire on the enemy.[69] During the last weeks, the Russians "fought under the knee of the besiegers." They built new trenches in front of their parapets, from which their small-arms fire was effective, and they continued to make sorties, although with little success.[70] During the last days before the allied assault, the Russian losses averaged twenty-five hundred men per day.[71]

By the eve of the assault on August 26, the Russians in the Malakhov and the 2nd bastion were helpless, with most of the men forced to take refuge in dugouts to escape the deadly mortar shells that the French rained on them. The French would fire heavily for a time and then halt the bombardment for a brief period before resuming in full force. Rockets were sent up as false signals for attack, so that the defenders became confused and ceased to pay much attention to such tricks.[72] On the day of the assault, the allies opened a heavy bombardment in the morning, which then ceased for two hours. Shortly before noon they opened fire again. Promptly at twelve the cannon lengthened their fire and ten thousand French under Gen. MacMahon dashed the forty paces to the Kornilov bastion on the Malakhov. Thousands of others stormed the 2nd bastion, the connecting wall, and the batteries.[73]

In the Kornilov bastion, many of the defenders were eating, others were asleep in dugouts. The guards on duty barely had time to give the warning when the French were upon them. The Russians at once dashed to arms, but, unorganized and leaderless, they were overpowered by the masses of French soldiers and, fighting furiously,

67. Bestuzhev, p. 143.
68. Dubrovin, *Materialy*, V, 341.
69. N. V. Berg, *Zapiski ob osade Sevastopolia* (2 vols.; Moscow, 1858), II, 32-33.
70. Guérin, II, 381-82.
71. Bogdanovich, *Vostochnaia voina*, II, 125.
72. Auger, I, 409-17.
73. *Ibid.*, I, 423-34; Bogdanovich, *Vostochnaia voina*, IV, 93-96.

were pushed to the rear of the redoubt. Several companies of infantry rallied and drove back the French with the bayonet, but fresh forces poured in and once more drove the Russians to the last corner of the bastion.[74]

Elsewhere along the defense line the French also had success, storming the 2nd bastion, the curtain wall, and several of the batteries, and pushed the Russians to the second line. Russian reserves quickly came up, however, and, aided by the fire of steamers, drove them out. The French again attacked and forced the Russians back, but Khrulev with strong reserves appeared and with the regrouped defenders forced the French to retire. They made one more attack, but the Russians beat them off and finally held the 2nd bastion and the nearby batteries. Khrulev then rushed with his troops to the Malakhov to retake the Kornilov bastion, but too late. The attackers by this time had consolidated their position and held it in strength. In the attempt to regain it, Khrulev was wounded and his men thrown back, but as more Russians came up and penetrated the bastion, twenty thousand men were locked in close combat. Other Russian generals came up, with fresh regiments, and the tide of battle ebbed and flowed. Finally, in midafternoon a tall general led a column of Russians, with drums beating, into the bastion, only to be decimated by the French fire. The French charged and drove the survivors out, never to return.[75] It is almost certain that the efforts of the Russians to retake this bastion were severely hampered by the fact that Totleben had insisted on closing the rear part (the gorge) of the fortification, so that the Russian reserves had great difficulty in penetrating its walls.[76]

There was heavy fighting on other parts of the defenses as well. The British, with fourteen thousand men, made a belated attack on the 3rd bastion, only to have their troops mowed down during their long advance toward it. Some of them managed to penetrate the salient, but the Russians rallied and drove them out. British reserves charged again, but were beaten back by superior Russian forces and had to give up the attempt.[77] On the Russian right, the French attacked the 5th bastion and adjacent batteries with eighty-four hundred men, but were completely repulsed.[78]

74. Guérin, II, 399-400.
75. Guérin, II, 415-17, 434-35; Totleben, II, Pt. II, 200-10.
76. Men'kov, I, 412n.; Vasil'chikov, *Russkii Arkhiv*, XXIX (1891), Pt. II, 216-17; Guérin, II, 378.
77. Bogdanovich, *Vostochnaia voina*, IV, 108-12; Lysons, pp. 213-14.
78. Totleben, II, Pt. II, 228.

In this day's fighting the Russians lost 12,913 men, while the allies had losses of at least 10,000, and probably considerably more. In all the allies made twelve charges, of which only the one against the Malakhov had success. All the others were repelled. Hence, except for the loss of the Malakhov, "the honors of this day completely belong to the Russian arms. . . ."[79] The Russian soldiers were convinced that they had won a victory even greater than that in June. After the assault "soldiers of all ages, when they were getting them ready to amputate a leg or an arm, said with enthusiasm how gladly they agreed to endure this, knowing that they had succeeded in beating off the enemy."[80] As for the allies, they expected that a long and costly effort would be necessary to complete the capture of the city. Gen. Pélissier even ordered his subordinates to make careful preparations to beat off the renewed attacks that he believed the Russians would make to regain the Malakhov.[81]

Prince Gorchakov, however, realized that it would be almost impossible to recapture the Kornilov bastion and an effort to hold out in the shattered defenses would be impossibly costly. Consequently, at five o'clock on the day of the assault, he issued orders for the complete evacuation of the fortress and the city. By seven the troops began to retire across the bay to the northern side, as volunteers who had stayed in the works kept up fire against the enemy to mislead them, while a rear guard manned barricades in the city to hold off the enemy if they pursued. The troops took all night to get across by the floating bridge or by steamers and other boats. All the wounded, except a few hopeless cases, who were left behind, were taken to safety on the northern side. Some confusion developed during the night, which led to the throwing of numerous cannon into the bay. Late at night the rear guard withdrew and volunteers lighted fuses laid to powder magazines, which blew up at various times. Much of the city burned. The remaining ships were burned or sunk.[82] Maj. Delafield, U.S.A., termed it "a masterly retreat that does great credit to Russian military genius and discipline."[83]

The allies detected heavy movements of Russian troops during the

79. *Ibid.*, pp. 229-31.
80. Anton Christian von Hübbenet, *Ocherk meditsinskoi i gospital'noi chasti v Krymu v 1854-1856 g.* (St. Petersburg, 1870), p. 150. The author was a surgeon who served in the hospitals in Sevastopol.
81. Guérin, II, 437-38.
82. Bogdanovich, *Vostochnaia voina*, II, 127-31.
83. Delafield, pp. 52-53.

night, but, not dreaming that the evacuation was in progress, they contented themselves with desultory firing at the bridge. Still licking their wounds, the French and the British made no effort to pursue and, indeed, the fires and explosions kept them from occupying the city for some time.[84]

The end of the siege ended the major fighting of the Crimean War, for the new position of the Russians was too strong for the allies to attack and, after some skirmishing on the flanks of the armies, the war came to an end in 1856.

The magnitude of the campaign in the Crimea is indicated by the losses of the armies. The Russian figure of killed, wounded, and missing, was 104,000. The French reported losses of 82,133 men. While no figures for those of the British, Turks, and Sardinians are at hand, it seems probable that they were large enough to raise the total to at least that of the Russians.[85] These losses, while impressive, do not tell the whole story, for they do not include the enormous numbers of men who fell sick during the conflict.

One of the chief reasons why Russia lost Sevastopol was the abominable logistical problem. Whereas the French and the British could move their supplies by sea, and the British even had a cable-railway from Balaklava to their siege operations,[86] Russia had no railroad south of Moscow. Thus all provisions had to be hauled in wagons, often for hundreds of miles. While the mud in fall and spring made the roads almost impossible, the problem of hay was an even worse nightmare. By March, 1855, the Russian forces in the Crimea numbered about three hundred thousand, with one hundred thousand animals that had to be fed. Most of them were in the farthest corner of the peninsula, some 140 miles from the mainland. Special measures to secure hay to feed these horses and oxen of the wagon trains included drafting or hiring peasants to cut it in the northern Crimea, but red tape and delay hampered this work. It proved possible to obtain less than one-tenth of the total needed (almost two hundred thousand tons) in the Crimea. Hence most of this had to be imported. At times the shortage of hay was so great that the cavalry fed their horses brush or chopped oak leaves mixed with flour. Nevertheless, the Intendancy managed to cope with the problem, supplying vast

84. Guérin, II, 438-39.
85. Khrushchov, pp. 154-56.
86. Niel, p. 137.

numbers of wagons and the horses and oxen to pull them. The price of hay rose to fabulous heights, until finally great quantities of it were brought in by contractors. But in spite of the difficulties and the high prices, the army obtained its provisions and was not compelled to retire from the Crimea. This was a real miracle.[87]

This miracle was costly, for especially during the months of bad weather the toll of animals and humans was great. The wagoners had to take large supplies with them, as hay was difficult to obtain on the way. The road was a picture of desolation, with parties of convalescent soldiers, wagons whose horses had dropped with exhaustion, and everywhere dead animals. The postal stations were scenes of disorder, with horses unfed for as long as a week and the postriders worn out and often dying of typhus.[88] Inevitably corruption appeared, becoming a national scandal before the war ended. This was probably unavoidable, as during the war the government had to spend vast sums, often with no possibility of observing the proper safeguards against thievery. More significant than this, however, was the fact that for eighteen months Russia fought a major war under the most unfavorable circumstances and, by a supreme exertion of the nation's strength, managed to avoid a real disaster.

That the cost of the war in human terms was great becomes evident from the figures of the Medical Department of the Ministry of War. These data indicate that in the years 1853-1856 a total of 450,015 men of the army died of enemy action or disease. This total does not include the number of men wounded, many of whom fully recovered, while others were permanently disabled by amputation or other major surgery.[89]

Although the surgeons at Sevastopol used chloroform in almost all their serious operations,[90] the wounded suffered greatly from terrible crowding in the hospitals, lack of surgeons and orderlies, and other necessities. In the spring of 1855 at Sevastopol, it became necessary to put amputees into soldiers' tents, on straw mattresses on the ground. When heavy rains fell the doctors had to bandage them, "standing up to their knees in mud."[91] As the limited facilities in the southern Crimea became impossibly crowded, the authorities had to ship thou-

87. Zatler, *Zapiski*, I, 230-31; Dubrovin, *Vostochnaia voina*, pp. 332-34; Bogdanovich, *Vostochnaia voina*, IV, 147-59.
88. Men'kov, I, 257.
89. Bogdanovich, *Istoricheskii ocherk*, I, 171-74.
90. Pirogov, p. 183.
91. *Ibid.*, pp. 68-70.

sands of convalescents to hospitals in areas outside the peninsula, which doomed these unfortunates to hundreds of miles of travel in rude conveyances without springs over terrible roads. One observer termed the peasant carts and the army wagons instruments of torture for the wounded. They had narrow beds, on which only one man could lie, on his back. Two others were put in, lying on their sides on the sloping sides of the cart, often pressing on the man at the bottom. When the wagon moved, over rough, stony ground, "the wounded uttered such sounds that I cannot remember them without shuddering."[92] Often the wagons with their pitiful freight had to move hundreds of miles before they could find hospitals that could receive the men. "At times on the bare steppes bad weather seized these caravans of unfortunates; the horses or oxen, worn out by the bad road, stopped as if fettered, and there were no dwellings near by where the sick could be sheltered nor firewood to warm them, nor food to maintain their strength." As a result, far from the transfer point, they inevitably had to die. "We do not intend to enumerate here all the abuses with which the maintenance and transport of the sick were accompanied—society is already sufficiently acquainted with them."[93]

Thus the Crimean campaign presents a grim picture of suffering and death, relieved somewhat by the heroic deeds of the warriors and by the compassionate efforts of those who tried to care for the wounded and sick. But the Crimean conflict was not the whole war. It is necessary, then, to consider other areas where heavy and important fighting took place.

In the Caucasus almost all of the action took place in the land of the Chechens, with Shamil, who had received grave setbacks in 1853 and 1854, waiting to see what the Turks would do. As the latter accomplished nothing, the Imam remained inactive.[94] After a period of quiet in the Chechen area, in April, 1855 Gen. Wrangel, the Russian commander, made a sudden raid to destroy anew the huts that the inhabitants had begun to restore. At about the same time Baron Nikolai marched into their land, where he caused much damage, in spite of the fact that Shamil had stationed a force to protect the tribesmen. In May, Baron Vrevskii took command of the troops on the Left Flank. A very aggressive leader, he intensified the actions of his

92. Dehn, *Russkaia Starina*, LXV (1890), 679.
93. Obruchev, *Voennyi Sbornik*, I (1858), 438.
94. D. I. Romanovskii, "General-fel'dmarshal Kniaz' Aleksandr Ivanovich Bariatinskii i Kavkazskaia voina, 1815-1879," *Russkaia Starina*, XXX (1881), 286.

troops, destroying villages, trampling great fields of corn, and persuading some of the Chechens to settle in areas under Russian protection. Wrangel and Baron Nikolai pursued the same course and
also continued cutting the forests and clearing sections that they had
cut several years before. All of these actions made a strong impression
on the Chechens, as they proved that the Russians were still powerful
and that Shamil could not prevent their punitive efforts. The Caucasus was a region in which the Russian position was secure.[95]

But while the Russians were not in danger in the Caucasus, in
1855 the Turks, aided by British officers, made a great effort to re-
establish their power in Transcaucasia. As they no longer had to keep
an army on the Danube, where the Austrians occupied the Principalities, and with the French, British, and Sardinians pushing the war
in the Crimea, the Turks could concentrate their efforts in Asia Minor.
They built up a powerful army at Erzerum and fortified and pro-
visioned the fortress of Kars. Gen. N. N. Muraviev, who had taken
part in the campaigns of Paskevich against the Persians and the Turks,
was named viceroy in the Caucasus late in 1854. Although the situation in the Crimea and the conflict in Dagestan and Chechnia permitted few reinforcements for the troops facing the Turks, when he
took the field in May he had a veteran army, which was eager and
confident and had much better artillery than the foe.[96]

In spite of earlier experience with the Caucasus troops, the elderly
commander antagonized them by writing in a letter to Ermolov that
they had "sunk into laziness, dissipation, luxury," and by making this
letter public.[97] Although some of the officers in the Caucasus Corps
probably did not have clean hands, this blanket indictment understandably angered all of them. In addition, he assigned Gen. Bebutov,
his predecessor, to command the reserve troops in the rear, although
the latter was a fighting general who had won the admiration of the
troops the year before.[98] Several other proven warriors sought assignments elsewhere, as they were repelled by Muraviev's attitude, "especially his distrustfulness, his faultfinding, and that curt treatment to
which all . . ., with a few exceptions, were subjected."[99]

95. Zisserman, *Istoriia*, II, 213-34.
96. Dubrovin, *Vostochnaia voina*, pp. 499-500.
97. Zisserman, "Bariatinskii," *Russkii Arkhiv*, XXVI (1888), Pt. III, 234-35.
98. Ad. P. Berzhe, "N. N. Murav'ev vo vremia ego namestnichestva na Kavkaze,
1854-1856 g.," *Russkaia Starina*, VIII (1873), 608-9.
99. *Ibid.*, pp. 602-3.

In June, 1855, Muraviev with about twenty-five thousand fine troops moved toward Kars, while a small force under Gen. Suslov seized Baiazet, southwest of Erivan, and Gen. Kovalevski, with ten thousand, watched the Turks in the vicinity of Batum. The Turks had no thought of an offensive, but sought to hold Kars, while other Turkish forces gathered at Erzerum, to the south. In the middle of June Muraviev, urged by Alexander II "to win decisive results," appeared before Kars.[100]

On June 13 and 14, Muraviev, after reconnoitering Kars with a large force of infantry and cavalry, decided not to attack it, but to blockade it. This was contrary to the desires of many of the troops, and Gen. Brimmer, commander of the Caucasus Corps, favored an immediate attack. Gen. Ia. I. Baklanov, a dashing Cossack officer, especially advised an immediate assault, as the fortifications south of the city were extremely weak, being still under construction and not connected. Hence an immediate attack from the south would have every chance of success.[101] That his views were well founded is indicated by the account of Col. Atwell Lake, a British engineer who served in Kars. The British had found the fortress very short of ammunition and poorly supplied with food. Moreover, many of the fortifications did not exist or were in extremely weak condition, so that a determined Russian attack would surely have taken the position.[102] Muraviev, however, while admitting that an attempt might succeed, reasoned that failure of an attack would compel the Russians to retire across the frontier and stand on the defensive. As this in turn would greatly encourage Shamil, the Turkish population of Transcaucasia, and the Persians to make incursions, the risk was too great. Hence the cautious general contented himself with blocking Kars in hope of starving it out.[103]

The blockade was not complete, as Muraviev did not have enough troops to bar all approaches. In June, however, he led half of his army toward Erzerum to capture supplies destined for the city, in which he had great success. During the seven days that they were gone, the Turks made no effort to attack the small observation force

100. Dubrovin, *Vostochnaia voina*, pp. 500-1.
101. Ia. I. Baklanov, "Blokada i shturm Karsa," *Russkaia Starina*, II (1870), 572.
102. Sir Henry Atwell Lake, *Narrative of the Defence of Kars. Historical and Military* (London, 1857), pp. 95 and 103.
103. Baklanov, *Russkaia Starina*, II (1870), 572-73.

before Kars.[104] Muraviev also had Gen. Suslov move with his small army from Baiazet toward Erzerum, passing south of Kars. Although his superior's caution let slip several opportunities to capture Erzerum, which would have had immense moral effect on the Turks, these expeditions did intercept many provisions intended for Kars and helped to tighten the cordon around it.[105]

By August there appeared strong indications that the defenders of Kars were close to starvation. Rejoicing on this score, however, was soon stemmed by the news that Omer Pasha had landed with forty thousand men at Batum and had promised to relieve Kars in twenty days. On September 12 Muraviev also learned of the fall of Sevastopol, which, of course, greatly encouraged the Turks. He at once called a council of war and, although Baklanov and Brimmer raised objections, decided to storm Kars before the Turks could arrive. Actually Omer Pasha had turned back to Batum after marching two days, but as Muraviev did not know this, he ordered the assault.[106]

When the Russians attacked the Turkish fortifications on September 17, the defenders discovered them before they could achieve a surprise. Hence the Turks made a courageous defense of their main redoubts and, although the Russians broke into their rear, poured a heavy fire into them. After repeated costly attacks on the redoubts, which lasted much of the day, the Russians retired to their camp, having suffered losses of 7,478 men. The Turkish losses were much smaller.[107] Several of the defenders bear testimony to the great courage of the Russians in the face of a withering fire. Col. Lake mentioned "the firmness of the enemy, who. . . stood for more than seven hours, exposed to such a heavy fire of musketry. . . ." In his official report on the battle to the Earl of Clarendon, Brig. Gen. Williams, who commanded at Kars, stated: ". . .as long as there was a chance of success he [the enemy] persevered with undaunted courage, and the Russian officers displayed the greatest gallantry. Their loss was immense. . . ."[108] György Kmety, a Magyar officer in Turkish service, wrote of the Russians' "wonderful contempt of death" as they advanced through a murderous crossfire for nearly half an hour. "The

104. N. N. Murav'ev, *Voina za Kavkazom v 1855 godu* (3 vols. in 2; St. Petersburg, 1876), I, Pt. I, 226.

105. Likhutin, *Russkie*, pp. 306-414.

106. Murav'ev, II, 4-5; Baklanov, *Russkaia Starina*, II (1870), 585-91; Bogdanovich, *Vostochnaia voina*, IV, 302-5.

107. Bogdanovich, *Vostochnaia voina*, IV, 314-38; Murav'ev, II, 81-82.

108. Lake, pp. 220-21, 232-33.

bearing of the Russian infantry. . . was most gallant from the beginning to the end of this engagement. . . ."[109]

Edified by this severe lesson, Gen. Muraviev abandoned hopes of taking Kars by a *coup de main*, although he surprised many of his officers by refusing to retire to Russian territory. Instead, he tightened the blockade of the fortress, and, after arranging provisions for several months, had the men construct comfortable earth huts for the cold weather that speedily followed. Already the Turks were beginning to die of hunger and cold, so that the end appeared near.[110]

Before the city could fall, however, the Russians won a modest success in another sector. In October, Omer Pasha, with twenty thousand regular troops, pushed inland from Batum, hoping to capture Tiflis. Much smaller Russian forces under Prince Mukhranskii tried to hold a river line, but eventually the Turks outflanked and drove them back with much loss. Fortunately for them, Omer delayed his advance against the new Russian position until heavy rains came, flooding the rivers and making an attack impossible. When the news of the fall of Kars came late in November, Omer Pasha retreated to safety.[111]

By November the Russian forces before Kars were reinforced and reorganized, while the defenders were dying. Gen. Williams, feeling it was hopeless, with the permission of the Turks sent out a flag of truce. Terms were easily arranged, and the surrender took place on November 16. The Russians permitted the irregulars to go, while the eight thousand regulars were fed and made prisoners. Dr. Sandwith, who was with Gen. Williams in Kars, remarked on "the most delicate attentions" that the Russians gave to the captured officers and "the most chivalrous bearing to their prisoners of war." Col. Lake also commented on the "kindness and good feeling" toward the prisoners throughout their captivity.[112]

By this victory the Russians redeemed a little of their tarnished glory and improved their bargaining power at the peace conference. Nevertheless, many army officers felt that with more effective leadership they might have achieved much more at lower cost. If Muraviev

---

109. György Kmety, *A Narrative of the Defence of Kars on the 29th of September, 1855* (London, 1856), pp. 26 and 36.
110. Bogdanovich, *Vostochnaia voina*, IV, 372-80.
111. *Ibid.*, IV, 346-66; Murav'ev, II, 268-325.
112. Humphrey Sandwith, *A Narrative of the Siege of Kars* (London, 1856), p. 305; Lake, pp. 304-5.

had taken Kars in June, Erzerum would probably have fallen soon after and the whole position of the Turks in eastern Anatolia would have crumbled. Hence, in spite of the victory in November, in army circles the belief persisted that the Russian record during the Crimean War presented a series of opportunities that had not been grasped: Silistria, Inkerman, the defense of Sevastopol, and Kars. In spite of superior allied weapons and technical ability, men felt, the Russians could have won the war if their leaders had known how to make proper use of their resources. And yet some, however, drew different conclusions from the results. Prince Vasil'chikov, one of the more enlightened officers of the period, wrote: "From on high it was decided otherwise; probably in order that we Russians should not become completely conceited, should look seriously at our internal disorders, and should take thought about curing our failings."[113] The failings were those of the regime of Nicholas I.

113. Vasil'chikov, *Russkii Arkhiv*, XXIX (1891), Pt. II, 255

CHAPTER XVIII. CONCLUSION

The army of Nicholas I, which in 1825 experienced a crisis, in 1855 suffered a limited but resounding defeat. This result was a logical outcome of his reign, for to the end his military establishment remained one based on the old servile system and unprepared for combat with the armies of the mid-nineteenth century. The Tsar, to be sure, had made earnest efforts to eliminate some of its failings, and with some success. His achievements, however, had not gone far enough.

Thanks to Nicholas I, the term of service with the colors had been cut by ten years, so that men with good conduct records returned to civilian life after fifteen years in the army. In addition, the military colonies, after 1831, lost many of their worst features. Changes in the central administration of the army and in its accounting system reduced (but did not eliminate) the corruption that bore so heavily on the enlisted men. The feeding of the soldiers became better. This fact, along with an extended and improved system of army hospitals, brought about a noticeable decline in the sickness and the mortality of the troops. The Emperor sponsored a revision of the military legislation that reduced some of the most brutal punishments and urged more humane treatment of the enlisted men, which bore fruit in a decline in the number of desertions.

This period saw relatively little improvement in Russian military technique, although the infantry received percussion muskets in the 1840's, and the number of riflemen increased slightly. The Emperor and his generals gave much attention to the training of the troops, with the result that Russian reviews and parades were famed for their magnificence and elegance. Training for combat showed little change for the better. Only the artillery and the field engineers maintained a high level of military competence.

Under Nicholas I military education expanded, with the number of cadet corps increasing from five to twenty-three, so that a larger number of officers than ever before now received formal training in the art of war. A Military Academy, whose function was to train officers of the General Staff, began its activities in 1832. Its students received instruction from some of the most brilliant theorists in Russia.

Understandably, the Tsar took great pride in his military establishment, to which he devoted so much attention and effort. It was the largest and most imposing army in the world and, as its admirers were never tired of stressing, after its victorious role in the Napoleonic Wars it had won a series of victories over Persians, Turks, Poles, and Magyars, and by 1853 it was making steady progress against the Caucasian mountaineers under Shamil. Nevertheless, the failure of the Russian forces to repulse the invaders of the Crimea in 1854 and 1855 indicated that it still suffered from grave failings, which Russian military men were not slow to point out.

The fundamental cause of Russia's defeat was the system of serfdom, which prevented the adoption of an effective military establishment. The government of Pre-Reform Russia served the interests of the nobility, who brought to naught the repeated efforts of the autocrat to abolish bondage. This compelled the retention of a long period of service for a limited number of serfs and made it impossible to create a citizen army, which would provide large reserves of trained men. The imperatives of Russia's repressive policy, both at home and abroad, required large numbers of soldiers available at all times. Hence Nicholas I had to rely on a large standing army of peasants, beaten into unquestioning obedience under a system of brutal discipline, little alleviated by his reforming efforts. Educating these gray-coated masses seemed dangerous, as literacy might make them question the justice of their lot and induce protest against the harshness and the corruption of their officers.

The officers of this army of peasant automatons were almost all nobles. Only a fraction of them had been trained in cadet corps, so that the great majority had had no formal military education, but had learned soldiering by serving as sergeants, with little or no schooling. Few of them studied after receiving their commissions, for their superiors did not encourage it. Unquestioning obedience was what their superiors required, and those who refused to conform found their way hard. Field Marshal Paskevich handled his generals in the same fashion. They needed little mental baggage other than knowledge of the field regulations and ability to bring their units to the perfection needed at reviews and parades. Little attention was given to realistic preparation for battle, for the army relied on bayonet charges by masses of men in close columns and regarded musketry as a non-essential. Skirmishers in open order did little to provide firepower, which, in large part, was supplied by the artillery rather than by the infantry. Russian field regulations did not envisage use of extended order, in which small units of soldiers led by able junior commanders would supply effective small arms fire against the enemy. Instead, all officers, from ensigns to generals, concentrated on skill on the parade ground and on dense columns on the field of battle. They compelled unthinking obedience from their soldiers by fist and stick and, not infrequently, stole funds allotted for the feeding and care of their men.

This system rarely produced able generals, as intelligent, energetic men found themselves stifled by the demands for unquestioning obedience and the denial of all scope for initiative, while uninspired timeservers could thrive. The General Staff, which in earlier periods had often supplied brilliant generals, could no longer do so, as the Decembrist uprising had brought suspicion upon its members, and staff officers had little opportunity to attain high command. Hence by the end of the reign the army lacked effective generals, especially at the top. Most of the men who had won glory in the Napoleonic Wars had gone, through death or retirement, or, like Ermolov, had been forced out. A few able men had somehow risen to command—such as Rüdiger, Bariatinskii, Lüders, and Khrulev—but the key positions during the Crimean War were held by elderly commanders of little or no ability—Paskevich, Gorchakov, and Menshikov.

Thus, in spite of victories in four wars—over weak and poorly organized opponents—the Russian army had innate weaknesses, which came into view in the Crimean War. Lack of strong small-arm fire was a glaring defect, while the absence of trained reserves prevented the necessary expansion of the army. Above all, it was poor technique and inefficient leadership, more than the absence of railroads south of Moscow, that brought Russian defeat. This defeat, of course, was far from decisive, and the Russian army still was a strong fighting force, much of which had not been engaged. It is significant that none of the opposing powers but Great Britain had any desire for a third campaign against the Russians. But the fact is that the once mighty Russian army had suffered defeat on its own soil. It is safe to say that it was not so much the strength of the allies, but the failings of the Russian military system, that produced that defeat. The Crimean War was thus a fitting climax for the army of Nicholas I, whose monument was the burned-out ruins of Sevastopol, which it had bravely but vainly defended.

BIBLIOGRAPHY

I. BOOKS

Adamovich, B. *Sbornik voenno-istoricheskikh materialov leibgvardii Keksgol'mskago imperatora Avstrii polka.* 3 vols. in 2. St. Petersburg, 1910.

Alabin, P. V. *Chetyre voiny. Pokhodnyia zapiski v 1849-53-54-55 gg. i 1877-78 gg.* Vol. I only. Samara, 1888.

———. *Pokhodnyia zapiski v voinu 1853, 1854, 1855, i 1856 godov.* 2 vols. in 1. Viatka, 1861.

Andreevskii, I. E. (ed.). *Entsiklopedicheskii slovar'.* 41 vols. in 82. St. Petersburg, 1903.

Andrianov, A. *Inkermanskii boi i oborona Sevastopolia. Nabroski uchastnika.* St. Petersburg, 1903.

Anichkov, V. M. *Voennoe khoziaistvo. Sravnitel'noe izsledovanie polozhitel'nykh zakonodatel'stv Rossii, Frantsii, Prussii, Avstrii, Sardinii, Bel'gii, i Bavarii.* St. Petersburg, 1860.

———. *Voenno-istoricheskie ocherki Krymskoi ekspeditsii. 2-ia chast'. Opisanie osady i oborony Sevastopolia.* 2 vols. St. Petersburg, 1856.

Aratovskii, Vladimir. *Obzor rasporiazhenii po prodovol'stviiu deistvuiushchei armii, v 1831, 1848, 1849, i 1853-55 gg.* St. Petersburg, 1874.

Auger, Charles. *Guerre d'Orient. Siège de Sébastopol. Historique du service de l'artillerie. 1854-1856.* 2 vols. Paris, 1859.

Averbukh, Rebekka A. *Tsarskaia interventsiia v bor'be s Vengerskoi revoliutsiei 1848-1849 gg.* Moscow, 1935.

Barsukov, Ivan P. *Graf Nikolai Nikolaevich Murav'ev-Amurskii po ego pis'mam, ofitsial'nym dokumentam, razskazam sovremennikov i pechatnym istochnikam.* 2 vols. Moscow, 1891.

Bazancourt, César Lecat. *L'expédition de Crimée jusqu'à la prise de Sébastopol. Chronique de la guerre d'Orient.* 2 vols. in 1. Paris, 1856.

Berg, Nikolai V. *Zapiski ob osade Sevastopolia.* 2 vols. Moscow, 1858.

Bestuzhev, I. V. *Krymskaia voina 1853-1856.* Moscow, 1956.

Bliokh, I. S. *Finansy Rossii XIX stoletiia.* 4 vols. St. Petersburg, 1882.

Bobrovskii, P. O. *Istoriia 13-go leib-grenaderskago Erivanskago Ego Velichestva polka za 250 let.* 5 pts. St. Petersburg, 1892-1898.

Bogdanovich, M. I. *Istoricheskii ocherk deiatel'nosti voennago upravleniia v Rossii v pervoe dvadtsatipiatiletie blagopoluchnago tsarstvovaniia gosudaria imperatora Aleksandra Nikolaevicha (1855-1880).* 6 vols. St. Petersburg, 1879-1881.

————. *Vostochnaia voina 1853-56 gg.* 4 vols. in 2. St. Petersburg, 1876.

Borodkin, M. *Voina 1854-1855 gg. na finskom poberezh'e. Istoricheskii ocherk.* St. Petersburg, 1904.

Bunt voennykh poselian v 1831 g. Razskazy i vospominaniia ochevidtsev. St. Petersburg, 1870.

Bushuev, Semen K. *Bor'ba gortsev za nezavisimost' pod rukovodstvom Shamilia.* Moscow, 1939.

[Calthorpe, S. J. G.]. *Letters from Headquarters; or, the Realities of the War in the Crimea. By an Officer on the Staff.* 2 vols. London, 1856.

Daragan. *Zapiski o voine v Transil'vanii, v 1849 g.* St. Petersburg, 1859.

Delafield, Richard. *Report on the Art of War in Europe in 1854, 1855, and 1856. From his Notes and Observations Made as a Member of a "Military Commission to the Theater of War in Europe."* Senate Executive Document No. 59, 36th Cong., 1st Sess. Washington, 1860.

Delbrück, Hans. *Istoriia voennogo iskusstva v ramkakh politicheskoi istorii.* (Translation of his *Geschichte der Kriegskunst.* 7 vols. Berlin, 1900-36.) 5 vols. Moscow, 1937.

Dirin, Petr P. *Istoriia leib-gvardii Semenovskago polka.* 2 vols. St. Petersburg, 1883.

Doblestnye podvigi russkikh voinov v voinu s Anglo-Frantsuzami i Turkami. Moscow, 1855.

Dobrovol'skii (comp.). *Rukovodstvo zakonovedeniia. Polnoe rukovodstvo dlia voenno-uchebnykh zavedenii.* 2 vols. St. Petersburg, 1853-54.

Druzhinin, Nikolai M. *Gosudarstvennye krest'iane i reforma P. D. Kiseleva.* 2 vols. Moscow, 1946-58.

Dubnow, S. M. *History of the Jews in Russia and Poland, from the Earliest Times until the Present Day.* 3 vols. Philadelphia, ca. 1918-20.

Dubrovin, Nikolai F. *Istoriia voiny i vladychestva Russkikh na Kavkaze.* 2 vols. in 5. St. Petersburg, 1871-88.

———— (ed.). *Materialy dlia istorii krymskoi voiny i oborony Sevastopolia.* 5 vols. in 16. St. Petersburg, 1871-74.

————. *Vostochnaia voina 1853-1856 godov; obzor sobytii po povodu sochineniia M. I. Bogdanovicha.* St. Petersburg, 1878.

Epanchin, N. *Ocherk pokhoda 1829 g. v Evropeiskoi Turtsii.* 3 pts. St. Petersburg, 1905-07.

Evstaf'ev, P. P. *Vosstanie voennykh poselian Novgorodskoi gubernii v 1831 godu.* (Vol. 98 of *Istoriko-revoliutsionnaia biblioteka.*) Moscow, 1934.

Fadeev, Rostislav A. *Shest'desiat let Kavkazskoi voiny. Pis'ma s Kavkaza.* St. Petersburg, 1899.

————. *Vooruzhennye sily Rossii.* Moscow, 1868.

Fedorov, A. V. *Obshchestvenno-politicheskoe dvizhenie v russkoi armii 40-70 gg. XIX v.* Moscow, 1958.

————. *Russkaia armiia v 50-70 godakh XIX v.* Leningrad, 1959.

Fedorov, Vladimir G. *Vooruzhenie russkoi armii v krymskuiu kampaniiu.* St. Petersburg, 1904.

Ferguson, Alan Douglas. *The Russian Military Settlements, 1810-1866.* Unpublished Ph.D. Dissertation, Yale University, 1953.

Fonton, F. *Vospominaniia. Iumoristicheskiia, politicheskiia i voennyia pis'ma iz glavnoi kvartiry Dunaiskoi armii, v 1828 i 1829 gg.* 3rd ed. 2 vols. Leipzig, 1866.

Frolov. *Minnaia voina v Sevastopolia v 1854-1855 g. pod rukovodstvom Totlebena.* St. Petersburg, 1868.

Gersevanov, N. *O prichinakh tekhnicheskago prevoskhodstva Frantsuzov v kampanii 1855-56 gg.* St. Petersburg, 1858.

Gershel'man, Sergei K. *Nravstvennyi element pod Sevastopolem.* St. Petersburg, 1897.

Gershenzon, M. O. (ed.). *Epokha Nikolaia I.* Moscow, 1911.

Glinoetskii, N. P. *Istoricheskii ocherk Nikolaevskoi akademii General'nago shtaba.* St. Petersburg, 1882.

—————. *Istoriia russkago General'nago shtaba.* 2 vols. St. Petersburg, 1888-94.

Görgei, Artur. *Mein Leben und Wirken in Ungarn in den Jahren 1848 und 1849.* 2 vols. Leipzig, 1852.

Gooch, Brison D. *The New Bonapartist Generals in the Crimean War. Distrust and Decision-making in the Anglo-French Alliance.* The Hague, 1959.

Goremykin, F. *Rukovodstvo k izucheniiu taktiki v nachal'nykh eia osnovaniiakh i v prakticheskom primenenii.* 3 pts. in 1. St. Petersburg, 1849.

Grekov, V. *Istoricheskii ocherk voenno-uchebnykh zavedenii 1700-1910.* Moscow, 1910.

Grishinskii, A. (ed). *Istoriia russkoi armii i flota.* 15 vols. Moscow, 1911-13.

Guérin, Léon. *Histoire de la dernière guerre de Russie (1853-1856), écrite au point de vue politique, stratégique et critique, sur les documents comparés français, anglais, russes, allemands et italiens.* 2 vols. Paris, 1858.

Hübbenet, Anton Christian von. *Ocherk meditsinskoi i gospital'noi chasti v Krymu v 1854-1856 g.* St. Petersburg, 1870.

Ignatovich, I. I. *Bor'ba krest'ian za osvobozhdenie.* Leningrad, 1924.

Istoriia leib-gvardii Egerskago polka za sto let, 1796-1896. 3 pts. St. Petersburg, 1896.

Ivanov, P. A. *Obozrenie sostava i ustroistva reguliarnoi russkoi kavalerii ot Petra Velikago do nashikh dnei.* St. Petersburg, 1864.

Karnovich, E. P. *Tsesarevich Konstantin Pavlovich.* St. Petersburg, 1899.

Kartsov, Pavel P. *Iz proshlago. Lichnyia i sluzhebnyia vospominaniia, 1831-1878.* 2 vols., St. Petersburg, 1888.

Kazbek, G. (comp.). *Voennaia istoriia gruzinskago grenaderskago E. I. V. Velikago Kniazia Konstantina Nikolaevicha polka, v sviazi s istoriei Kavkazskoi voiny.* Tiflis, 1865.

Khrushchov, A. P. *Istoriia oborony Sevastopolia.* 3rd ed. St. Petersburg, 1889.

Kmety, György. *A Narrative of the Defence of Kars, on the 29th September, 1855.* London, 1856.

Kolchak, V. *Voina i plen. 1853-1855 gg. Iz vospominanii o davno perezhitom.* St. Petersburg, 1904.

Kovalevskii, M. A. *Piat'desiat let sushchestvovaniia leib-gvardii Dragunskago polka.* Novgorod, 1870.

Krenke, V. D. *Oborona baltiiskago priberezh'ia 1853-1856 gg.* St. Petersburg, 1887.

Krestovskii, V. *Istoriia 14-go ulanskago Iamburgskago Eia Imperatorskago Velichestva, Velikoi Kniazhny Marii Aleksandrovny polka.* St. Petersburg, 1873.

Lalaev, M. *Istoricheskii ocherk voenno-uchebnykh zavedenii podvedomstvennykh Glavnomu ikh upravleniiu. . . . 1700-1880.* 2 vols. St. Petersburg, 1880-1882.

Lebedev, Viktor. *Pravda russkago voina.* St. Petersburg, 1835.

Leslie, R. F. *Polish Politics and the Revolution of November, 1830.* London, 1956.

Likhutin, M. D. *Russkie v Aziatskoi Turtsii v 1854 i 1855 godakh,* (iz zapisok o voennykh deistviiakh erivanskago otriada). St. Petersburg, 1863.

———. *Zapiski o pokhode v Vengriiu v 1849 g.* Moscow, 1875.

Lysons, Daniel. *The Crimean War from First to Last. Letters from the Crimea.* London, 1895.

Mazour, Anatole. *The First Russian Revolution, 1825. The Decembrist Movement.* Stanford, 1937.

Medem, N. V. *Taktika. Uchebnoe rukovodstvo dlia voenno-uchebnykh zavedenii.* 2 pts. St. Petersburg, 1837.

Men'kov, P. K. *Zapiski.* 3 vols. St. Petersburg, 1898.

Miliutin, D. A. (comp.). *Opisanie voennykh deistvii 1839 goda v severnom Dagestane.* St. Petersburg, 1850.

———. *Statistika. Pervye opyty voennoi statistiki.* 2 vols. St. Petersburg, 1847-48.

Miloshevich, N. S. *Iz zapisok sevastopol'tsa.* St. Petersburg, 1904.

Moltke, Graf Helmuth Karl Bernhard. *Der russisch-türkische Feldzug in der europäischen Türkei 1828 und 1829, dargestellt durch Freiherr von Moltke, Major im königlich-preussischen General-stabe.* Berlin, 1845.

Monteith, William. *Kars and Erzeroum; with the Campaigns of Prince Paskiewitch, in 1828 and 1829.* London, 1856.

Mordecai, Maj. Alfred. *Military Commission to Europe, in 1855 and 1856. Report of Major Alfred Mordecai of the Ordnance Department.* Senate Executive Document No. 60, 36th Cong., 1st Session. Washington, 1860.

Murav'ev, N. N. *Voina za Kavkazom v 1855 godu.* 3 vols. in 2. St. Petersburg, 1876.

Nechkina, M. V. *Vosstanie 14-go dekabria 1825 g.* Moscow, 1951.

Neelov, N. *Ocherk sovremennago sostoianiia strategii.* 3 pts. St. Petersburg, 1849.

Niel, Adolphe. *Siège de Sébastopol. Journal des opérations du génie, publié avec l'autorisation du Ministère de la Guerre.* Paris, 1858.

Nifontov, A. S. *Russland im Jahre 1848.* Berlin, ca. 1953.

O., I. *Vospominaniia ofitsera zakavkazskoi armii. (1853-1856).* St. Petersburg, 1857.

Okun', S. B. *Ocherki istorii SSSR.* Leningrad, 1956.

Oreus, I. [Konevskii, Ivan]. *Opisanie vengerskoi voiny 1849 g.* St. Petersburg, 1880.

Osten-Saken, Dmitrii I. *Deistviia otdel'nago otriada general-maiora, potom general-leitenanta Barona Osten-Sakena v voinu 1831 g.* St. Petersburg, 1865.

Petrov, A. N. (ed.). *Russkaia voennaia sila. Istoriia razvitiia voennago dela ot nachala Rusi do nashego vremia.* 2 vols. Moscow, 1897.

Pirogov, Nikolai I. *Sevastopol'skie pis'ma i vospominaniia.* Moscow, 1950.

Polievktov, Mikhail A. *Nikolai I. Biografiia i obzor tsarstvovaniia.* St. Petersburg, 1914.

Potto, Vasilii A. *Istoriia Novorossiiskago Dragunskago polka, 1803-1865.* St. Petersburg, 1866.

Presniakov, A. E. *14 dekabria 1825 goda.* S prilozheniem voenno-istoricheskoi spravki G. S. Gabaeva, "Gvardiia v dekabr'skie dni 1825 goda." Moscow, 1926.

Prokof'ev, E. A. *Voennye vzgliady Dekabristov.* Moscow, 1953.

Puzanov. *Istoriia leib-gvardii grenaderskago polka.* St. Petersburg, 1845.

Puzyrevskii, Aleksandr K. *Pol'sko-russkaia voina 1831 goda.* St. Petersburg, 1886.

Revoliutsiia 1848-49 gg. 2 vols. Moscow, 1952.

Romanovskii, Dmitrii I. *Kavkaz i Kavkazskaia voina. Publichnyia lektsii, chitannyia v zale passazha, v 1860 godu.* St. Petersburg, 1860.

Rostovtsev [I. I.?]. *Nastavlenie dlia obrazovaniia vospitannikov voenno-uchebnykh zavedenii. Vysochaishe utverzhdeno 24 dekabria 1848 goda.* St. Petersburg, 1849.

Rumiantsev, I. N. *V plenu u Shamilia. Zapiski Russkago.* St. Petersburg, 1877.

Russia. *Polnoe sobranie zakonov rossiiskoi imperii. Vtoroe polnoe sobranie.* 53 vols. St. Petersburg, 1830-1884.

————. *Svod voennykh postanovlenii.* 1838 ed. 5 pts. in 12 vols. St. Petersburg, 1839.

————. *Svod Zakonov Rossiiskoi Imperii.* 1832 ed. 15 vols. St. Petersburg, 1832.

————. Voennoe Ministerstvo. *Stoletie Voennago Ministerstva 1802-1902.* 13 pts., summary, and 2 indices in 56? vols. St. Petersburg, 1902.

————. Voennoe Ministerstvo. Voenno-uchebnyi komitet. *Rukovodstvo dlia artilleriiskoi sluzhby.* St. Petersburg, 1853.

Russkii biograficheskii slovar'. 25 vols. St. Petersburg, 1896-1918.

Sandwith, Humphrey. *A Narrative of the Siege of Kars, and of the Six Months' Resistance by the Turkish Garrison, under General Williams, to the Russian Army.* London, 1856.

Sbornik sochinenii ofitserov Nikolaevskoi Akademii General'nago Shtaba. 2 vols. St. Petersburg, 1863.

Schiemann, Theodor. *Geschichte Russlands unter Kaiser Nikolaus I.* 4 vols. Berlin, 1904-19.

Schilder, Nikolai K. *Graf Eduard Ivanovich Totleben; ego zhizn' i deiatel'-nost'.* 2 vols. St. Petersburg, 1885-86.

————. *Imperator Nikolai I. Ego zhizn' i tsarstvovanie.* 2 vols. St. Petersburg, 1903.

Semevskii, M. (ed.). *Graf Arakcheev i voennye poseleniia. 1809-1831.* St. Petersburg, 1871.

Semevskii, V. I. *Krest'ianskii vopros v Rossii vo vtoroi polovine XVIII i pervoi polovine XIX veka.* 2 vols. St. Petersburg, 1888.

————. *Politicheskie i obshchestvennye idei Dekabristov.* St. Petersburg, 1909.

Shabanov, Capt. *Istoriia 13-go leib-grenaderskago Erivanskago Ego Velichestva polka.* 3 pts. Tiflis, 1871.

Shcherbatov, A. P. *General-fel'dmarshal kniaz' Paskevich, ego zhizn' i deiatel'nost'. Po neizdannym istochnikam.* 7 vols. in 8. St. Petersburg, 1888-1904.

Shcherbinin, M. P. *Biografiia General-fel'dmarshala kniazia Mikhaila Semenovicha Vorontsova.* St. Petersburg, 1858.

Skobelev, I. *Podarok tovarishcham, ili perepiska russkikh soldat v 1812 godu.* St. Petersburg, 1833.

Smitt, Friedrich von. *Feldherren-Stimmen aus und über den polnischen Krieg vom Jahr 1831.* Leipzig, 1856.

————. *Istoriia pol'skago vozstaniia i voiny 1830 i 1831 godov.* 3 vols. St. Petersburg, 1863.

Tarle, Evgenii V. *Krymskaia voina.* 2nd, rev. and enl. ed. 2 vols. Moscow, 1950.

Timchenko-Ruban, G. *Ocherki deiatel'nosti Velikago Kniazia i Imperatora Nikolaia Pavlovicha kak rukovoditelia voenno-inzhenerskoiu chast'iu.* Vol. I. St. Petersburg, 1912.

Tornov, F. *Vospominaniia kavkazskago ofitsera.* 2 pts. Moscow, 1864.

Totleben, Eduard I. *Opisanie oborony g. Sevastopolia.* 2 vols. in 3. St. Petersburg, 1863.

Ushakov, Aleksandr K. *Istoriia voennykh deistvii v Aziatskoi Turtsii, v 1828 i 1829 godakh.* 2 vols. St. Petersburg, 1836.

Vladislavlev, Vladimir A. *Pamiatnaia knizhka voennykh uzakonenii dlia shtab- i ober-ofitserov.* St. Petersburg, 1851.

Voronov, P., and V. Butkovskii. *Istoriia leib-gvardii Pavlovskago polka.* St. Petersburg, 1875.

Weigelt. *Osada Sevastopolia, 1854-1856.* St. Petersburg, 1859.

Zablotskii-Desiatovskii, A. P. *Graf P. D. Kiselev i ego vremia. Materialy dlia istorii Imperatorov Aleksandra I, Nikolaia I, i Aleksandra II.* 4 vols. St. Petersburg, 1882.

Zaionchkovskii, Andrei M. *Vostochnaia voina 1853-1856 gg. v sviazi s sovremennoi ei politicheskoi obstanovki.* 2 vols. in 3. St. Petersburg, 1908-13.

Zaionchkovskii, P. A. (ed.). *Dnevnik D. A. Miliutina.* 4 vols. Moscow, 1947-50.

————. *Voennye reformy 1860-1870 godov v Rossii.* Moscow, 1952.

Zatler, Fedor K. *O gospitaliakh v voennoe vremia.* St. Petersburg, 1861.

————. *Zapiski o prodovol'stvii voisk v voennoe vremia.* 4 pts. St. Petersburg, 1860-65.

Zhizn' General-leitenanta kn. Madatova. 2d ed. St. Petersburg, 1863.

Zisserman, Arnol'd L. *Dvadtsat' piat' let na Kavkaze (1842-1867).* 2 pts. St. Petersburg, 1879.

————. *Fel'dmarshal kniaz' Aleksandr Ivanovich Bariatinskii, 1815-1879.* 3 vols. Moscow, 1889-91.

————. *Istoriia 80-go pekhotnago kabardinskago general-fel'dmarshala kniazia Bariatinskago polka (1726-1880).* 3 vols. St. Petersburg, 1881.

Zubov, P. *Podvigi Russkikh voinov v stranakh Kavkazskikh, s 1800 po 1834.* 2 vols. St. Petersburg, 1835-36.

————. *Kartina poslednei voiny s Persieiu 1826-1828.* St. Petersburg, 1834.

II. ARTICLES

B., N. "Kniaz' Mikhail Dmitrievich Gorchakov, 1792-1861 gg.," *Russkaia Starina*, XXIX (1880).

Baklanov, Ia. I. "Blokada i shturm Karsa," *Russkaia Starina*, II (1870).

B[artenov], P. "K biografii fel'dmarshala kniazia Paskevicha," *Russkii Arkhiv*, XXIX (1891), pt. 3.

Berzhe, Ad. P. "Imperator Nikolaia na Kavkaze v 1837 g.," *Russkaia Starina*, XLIV (1884).

————. "N. N. Murav'ev vo vremia ego namestnichestva na Kavkaze, 1854-1856 gg.," *Russkaia Starina*, VIII (1873).

————. "Samson Iakovlev [sic] Makintsev i russkie begletsy v Persii," *Russkaia Starina*, XV (1876).

————. "Smert' A. S. Griboedova," *Russkaia Starina*, VI (1872).

————. "Zashchita Mikhailovskago ukrepleniia 22-go marta 1840 g.," *Russkaia Starina*, XIX (1877).

Bogdanovich, M. I. (ed.). "Imperator Aleksandr II v epokhu voiny 1855 g.," *Russkaia Starina*, XXXVII (1883).

Bogdanovskii, P. "Iz vospominaniia o Vengerskoi i Krymskoi kampaniiakh," *Russkaia Starina*, LXXVIII (1893).

Brant, P. "Zhenatye nizhnie chiny," *Voennyi Sbornik*, III (1860).

Bray, Otto de. "Imperator Nikolai I i ego spodvizhniki," *Russkaia Starina*, CIX (1902).

Buturlin, M. D. "Zapiski grafa M. D. Buturlina," *Russkii Arkhiv*, XXXVI (1898), pt. 2.

Cherniaev, M. G. "Vo vremia russko-turetskoi voiny, 1853-1856 gg.," *Russkii Arkhiv*, XLIV (1906), pt. 1.

D., M. "N. O. Sukhozanet i Imperator Nikolai I," *Russkaia Starina*, LXV (1890).

Davydov, Denis V. "Zapiski partizana Denisa Davydova. Vospominaniia o pol'skoi voine 1831 goda," *Russkaia Starina*, VI (1872).

Dehn, Vladimir I. "Zapiski," *Russkaia Starina*, LXV and LXVI (1890).

"Desiat' mesiatsev na Dunae," *Voennyi Sbornik*, I (1858).

Detengof, A. "Zabytii geroi. Iz vospominanii starago sapëra," *Russkii Arkhiv*, XLIII (1905), pt. 2.

Detlov, K. "Neskol'ko slov o dragunakh," *Voennyi Sbornik*, II (1859).

Dragunskii Ofitser. "Vospominaniia o zakavkazskom pokhode 1853-1854 godov," *Voennyi Sbornik*, III (1860).

"Dve sluzhby," *Russkii Arkhiv*, XXVII (1889), pt. 1.

Esaul. "Pokhodnyi dnevnik (1854-1855 gg.)," *Voennyi Sbornik*, III (1860).

Eugene, Prince of Württemberg. "Turetskii pokhod 1828 goda i sobytiia, za nim sledovavshiia. Zapiski Printsa Virtembergskago," *Russkaia Starina*, XXVII and XXVIII (1880).

Evropeus, I. I. "Nikolai Nikolaevich Murav'ev," *Russkaia Starina*, XI (1874).

―――. "Vospominaniia I. I. Evropeusa. Bunt voennykh poselian korolia prusskago polka," *Russkaia Starina*, VI (1872).

Filipson, G. I. "Vospominaniia Grigoriia Ivanovicha Filipsona," *Russkii Arkhiv*, XXI (1883), pt. 3, and XXII (1884), pt. 1.

Gagern. "Rossiia i russkii dvor v 1839 g.," *Russkaia Starina*, LXV (1890).

Ganglebov, A. S. "Vospominaniia Aleksandra Semenovicha Ganglebova. Kak ia popal v Dekabristy, i chto za tem posledovalo," *Russkii Arkhiv*, XXIV (1886), pts. 2 and 3.

Golitsyn, N. S. "Imperatorskaia voennaia Akademiia v 1834-48 gg.," *Russkaia Starina*, XXXVII (1883).

"Golos iz armii," *Voennyi Sbornik*, I (1858).

Grabbe, P. Kh. "Iz dnevnika i zapisnoi knizhki grafa P. Kh. Grabbe," *Russkii Arkhiv*, XXVI (1888), pt. 1, Supplement.

―――. "Raport ko grafu Chernyshevu," *Akty Kavkazskoi Arkheograficheskoi Komissii*, IX, 251.

Gribbe, A. K. "Kholernyi bunt v novgorodskikh voennykh poseleniiakh, 1831 goda," *Russkaia Starina*, XVII (1876).

Grzhegorzhevskii, Isidor. "General-leitenant Kliuki-fon-Klugenau. Ocherk voennykh sobytii na Kavkaze, 1818-1850 gg.," *Russkaia Starina*, XI (1874).

Hessen, Sergei Ia. "Soldaty i matrosy v vosstanii Dekabristov," *Katorga i Ssylka*, 1930, No. 3.

Il'inskii, D. V. "Iz vospominanii i zametok sevastopol'tsa," *Russkii Arkhiv*, XXX (1892), pt. 3 and XXXI (1893), pt. 1.

"Instruktsiia dlia ispravnago soderzhanii v voiskakh ruchnago ognestrel'-nago oruzhiia," *Artilleriiskii Zhurnal*, 1852, no. 1.

"Istoricheskoe obozrenie voenno-sukhoputnago upravleniia s 1825 po 1850 god," *Sbornik Imperatorskago Russkago Istoricheskago Obshchestva*, XCVIII (1896).

"Ivan Nikitich Skobelev," *Russkaia Starina*, I (1870).

"Izvlechenie iz voennago zhurnala generala Golovina 1831 goda," *Voennyi Sbornik*, III (1860).

"Iz zapisok sevastopol'tsa," *Russkii Arkhiv*, V (1867).

"K istorii voenno-uchebnoi reformy Imperatora Aleksandra II-go, 1856-1870," *Russkaia Starina*, LIV (1887).

Kolokol'tsev, D. G. "Leib-gvardii Preobrazhenskii polk v vospominaniiakh ego starago ofitsera," *Russkaia Starina*, XXXVIII (1883).

Kozhukhov, Stepan. "Iz Krymskikh vospominanii o poslednei voine," *Russkii Arkhiv*, VII (1869).

Krasovskii, I. I. "Delo na Chernoi, iz vospominanii o voine 1853-1856 gg.," *Russkii Arkhiv*, XII (1874), pt. 2.

Kravtsov, I. S. "Kavkaz i ego Voenachal'niki: N. N. Murav'ev, kn. A. I. Bariatinskii i gr. N. I. Evdokimov, 1854-1864," *Russkaia Starina*, L (1886).

Krylov, A. D. "Kniaz' A. S. Menshikov, 1853-1854," *Russkaia Starina*, VII (1873).

Kutuzov, N. "Sostoianie gosudarstva v 1841 godu, (Zapiska N. Kutuzova, podannaia imperatoru Nikolaiu I)," *Russkaia Starina*, XCV (1898).

M—v, A. "Otryvki iz pokhodnykh zapisok o voine v Pol'she 1831 goda," *Voennyi Sbornik*, III (1860).

Madatova, Kniaginia S. A. "Kniaz' V. G. Madatov, leitenant-general," *Russkaia Starina*, VII (1873).

Murav'ev, N. N. "Iz zapisok," *Russkii Arkhiv*, XXVI (1888), pts. 2, 3, and XXVII (1889), pts. 1, 2, 3.

N——. "Neskol'ko zamechanii po povodu stat'i: 'Vzgliad na sostoianie Russkikh voisk v minuvshuiu voinu'," *Voennyi Sbornik*, I (1858).

Neizvestnyi. "Za mnogo let. Vospominaniia neizvestnago," *Russkaia Starina*, LXXXI and LXXXII (1884).

N. N. "Mysli o chastnoi i sluzhebnoi zhizni artilleriiskikh ofitserov," *Artilleriiskii Zhurnal*, 1857, no. 2.

Nikolai, Baron A. P. "Iz vospominanii moei zhizni. Darginskii pokhod 1845 goda," *Russkii Arkhiv*, XXVIII (1890), pt. 2.

Nikolai, Baron L. P. "Dnevnik barona L. P. Nikolaia vedennyi im po vremia Vengerskoi kampanii 1849 g.," *Russkaia Starina*, XX (1877).

Nikolai I. "Perepiska Nikolaia I s gr. Iv. Iv. Dibichem Zabalkanskim vo vremia russko-turetskoi voiny 1828-1829 g.," *Russkaia Starina*, XIX (1872). Title varies.

. "Predsmertnoe pis'mo Imperatora Nikolaia—kniaziu M. D. Gorchakovu," *Russkaia Starina*, XXXII (1881).

. "Zapiska Imperatora Nikolaia I o voennykh deistviiakh na Kavkaze," *Russkaia Starina*, XLVIII (1885).

"Ob ispytanii mednoi oblegchennoi pushki," *Artilleriiskii Zhurnal*, 1854, no. 6.

Obninskii, K. A. "Pokhodnyia zametki," *Russkii Arkhiv*, XXIX (1891), pt. 3.

"Oborona Sevastopolia. Pis'ma kniazia A. S. Menshikova k kn. M. D. Gorchakovu," *Russkaia Starina*, XII (1875).

Obruchev, N. "Iznanka krymskoi voiny," *Voennyi Sbornik*, I (1858).

"Ob upotreblenii boevykh raket pri Silistrii i pri gorode Babadage," *Artilleriiskii Zhurnal*, 1855, no. 2.

"O legkovesnykh orudiiakh," *Artilleriiskii Zhurnal*, 1860, no. 3.

Ol'shevskii, M. Ia. "Kavkaz s 1841 po 1866 god," *Russkaia Starina*, LXXIX (1893).

. "Pervyi kadetskii korpus, 1826-1833," *Russkaia Starina*, IL (1886).

. "Russko-turetskaia voina za Kavkazom v 1853 i 1854 gg.," *Russkaia Starina*, XLIV (1884) and XLV (1885).

Orda, A. "Ob"iasnenii vyzvannyia stat'eiu G. Artillerista," *Voennyi Sbornik*, II (1859).

Oreus, I. I. (ed.). "Russko-vengerskaia voina 1849 goda," *Russkaia Starina*, LVIII (1888).

Osten-Saken, Graf D. E. "Nikolai Nikolaevich Murav'ev v 1828-1856 gg.," *Russkaia Starina*, XI (1874).

"O zazhigatel'nykh raketakh (kongrevskikh)," *Voennyi Zhurnal*, 1828, no. 3.

Panaev, A. A. "Kniaz' A. S. Menshikov v razskazakh ego ad'iutanta A. A. Panaeva," *Russkaia Starina*, XVIII (1877).

Pavlutskii. "Kontuziia fel'dmarshala Paskevicha. 1854," *Russkaia Starina*, XII (1875).

Perovskii, V. A. "Pis'ma grafa V. A. Perovskago k A. Ia. Bulgakovu," *Russkii Arkhiv*, XVI (1878), pt. 2.

Pisarskii, I. "Pod Karsom s 2-go avgusta do 1-e dekabria 1855 g.," *Voennyi Sbornik*, II (1859).

Pokhvisnev, M. I. "Aleksei Petrovich Ermolov," *Russkaia Starina*, VI (1872).

Popov, Aleksandr E. "Zapiski o prebyvanii ego pod Sevastopolem s 1-go oktiabria po 1-e dekabria 1854 g.," *Russkaia Starina*, XXI (1878).

Romanovskii, D. I. "General-fel'dmarshal kniaz' Aleksandr Ivanovich Bariatinskii i kavkazskaia voina, 1815-1879," *Russkaia Starina*, XXX (1881).

Rozen, Baron A. E. "Dekabristy na Kavkaze v 1826-1850 gg. Zapiski Mikhaila Iv. Pushchina," *Russkaia Starina*, XLI (1884).

Rudakov, Pavel D. "Dva epizoda iz voiny v aziatskoi Turtsii. Iz zapisok ochevidtsa, gener.-leiten. Pavla Dmitrievicha Rudakova. 1853-1856," *Russkaia Starina*, XL (1883).

"Russians and Persia," *Literary Gazette*, nos. 583-86 (1828), April.

S., A. "Zametki o prodovol'stvii kavalerii furazhem," *Voennyi Sbornik*, II (1859).

Sakovich, P. M. "Georgii Vasil'evich Novitskii. Biograficheskii ocherk, 1800-1867," *Russkaia Starina*, XXII (1878).

Samsonov, E. P. "Vospominaniia Evgeniia Petrovicha Samsonova," *Russkii Arkhiv*, XXII (1884), pts. 1 and 2.

Schilder, N. K. "Fel'dmarshal Paskevich v Krymskuiu voinu, 1854-1855 g.," *Russkaia Starina*, XIII (1875).

———. "Imperator Nikolai I v 1828-1829 gg. (iz zapisok grafa A. Kh. Benkendorfa)," *Russkaia Starina*, LXXXVII (1896).

———. "Nemets i frantsuz v zapiskakh o Rossii 1839 g.," *Russkaia Starina*, LI (1886).

———. "Priezd E. I. Totlebena v Sevastopol' v avguste 1854 g.," *Russkaia Starina*, XVIII (1877).

———. "Voina Rossii s Turtsiei v 1829 godu," *Russkaia Starina*, XXX (1881).

———. "Voina s pol'skimi miatezhnikami 1831 goda v perepiske imperatora Nikolaia I-go s grafom Dibichem," *Russkaia Starina*, XLI and XLII (1884), and XLVI (1885).

Seriakov, L. A. "Moia trudovaia zhizn'," *Russkaia Starina*, XIV (1875).

Shcherbachev, G. D. "Dvenadtsat' let molodosti. Vospominaniia," *Russkii Arkhiv*, XXVIII (1890), pt. 1.

"Shkola gvardeiskikh podpraporshchikov i iunkerov v vospominaniiakh odnogo iz eia vospitannikov, 1845-1849 gg.," *Russkaia Starina*, XLI (1884).

Skorov. "Riadovoi Zinov'ev," *Voennyi Sbornik*, III (1860).

Sokolovskii, Mikhail. "Imperator Nikolai I v voenno-sudnykh konfirmatsiiakh," *Russkaia Starina*, CXXIV (1905).

Stepanov, P. A. "Pod Varnoiu, 10 sentiabria 1828 g. (iz vospominanii o leib-gvardii Egerskom polke)," *Russkaia Starina*, XV (1876).

Stolypin, D. A. "Iz lichnykh vospominanii o Krymskoi voine," *Russkii Arkhiv*, XII (1874), pt. 1.

Streng, A. O. "Voina protiv Vengertsev 1849 goda," *Russkaia Starina*, LXI (1889).

Tolstoi, Vladimir. "Kniaz' M. S. Vorontsov," *Russkii Arkhiv*, XV (1887), pt. 3.

Tornov, F. F. "Gergebil'. Iz vospominanii," *Russkii Arkhiv*, XIX (1881), pt. 2.

Ushakov, A. F. "Kholernyi bunt v Staroi-Ruse. 1831 g. (Razskaz ochevidtsa)," *Russkaia Starina*, IX (1874).

Varun-Sekret, I. L. "Vospominaniia I. L. Varun-Sekreta o sluzhbe v armii, 1823-1860 gg.," *Russkaia Starina*, XXV (1879).

Vasil'chikov, V. I. " 'Sevastopol'.' Zapiski nachal'nika shtaba sevastopol'-

skago garnizona kniazia Viktora Ilarionovicha Vasil'chikova," *Russkii Arkhiv*, XXIX (1891), pt. 2.

Verigin, A. "Shturm Varshavy v 1831 godu i nekotoryia zamechaniia o pol'skoi voine," *Voennyi Sbornik*, III (1860).

Vernikovskii, A. L. "Vengerskii pokhod 1849 goda. Vospominaniia armeiskago ofitsera," *Russkii Arkhiv*, XXIII (1885), pt. 3.

Vrioni, P. I. "Ermolov, Dibich i Paskevich; perepiska ikh i doneseniia imperatoru Nikolaiu Pavlovichu o sobytiiakh na Kavkaze i o voine s Persieiu 1826-1827 g.," *Russkaia Starina*, V and VI (1872).

V——skii, S. "Ob ofitserakh armeiskikh pekhotnykh polkov," *Voennyi Sbornik*, II (1859).

"Vzgliad imp. Nikolaia Pavlovicha o smertnoi kazni v rossii," *Russkaia Starina*, XL (1883).

"Vzgliad na sostoianie russkikh voisk v minuvshuiu voinu," *Voennyi Sbornik*, I (1858).

"Vzgliad na stepen' obrazovaniia Russkikh ofitserov v armii," *Voennyi Sbornik*, I (1858).

Zhukovskii, P. V. "V obraztsovom kavaleriiskom polku, 1844-1845," *Russkaia Starina*, LV (1887).

Zisserman, A. L. "Fel'dmarshal kniaz' A. I. Bariatinskii," *Russkii Arkhiv*, XXVI (1888), pts. 1, 2, 3.

———. "Zametki o krymskoi voine," *Russkii Arkhiv*, II (1859).

Zolotar'ev, M. "Zametki o sovremennom sostoianii nashei kavalerii," *Voennyi Sbornik*, I (1858).

INDEX

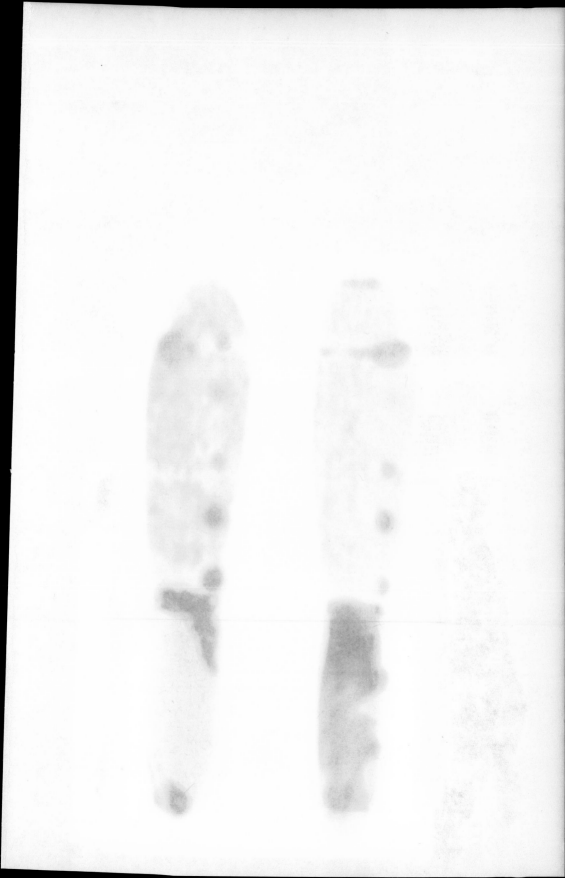